MUCH LOVE TO YOU RON.
CHRISTMAS 1999.
BABS
XX

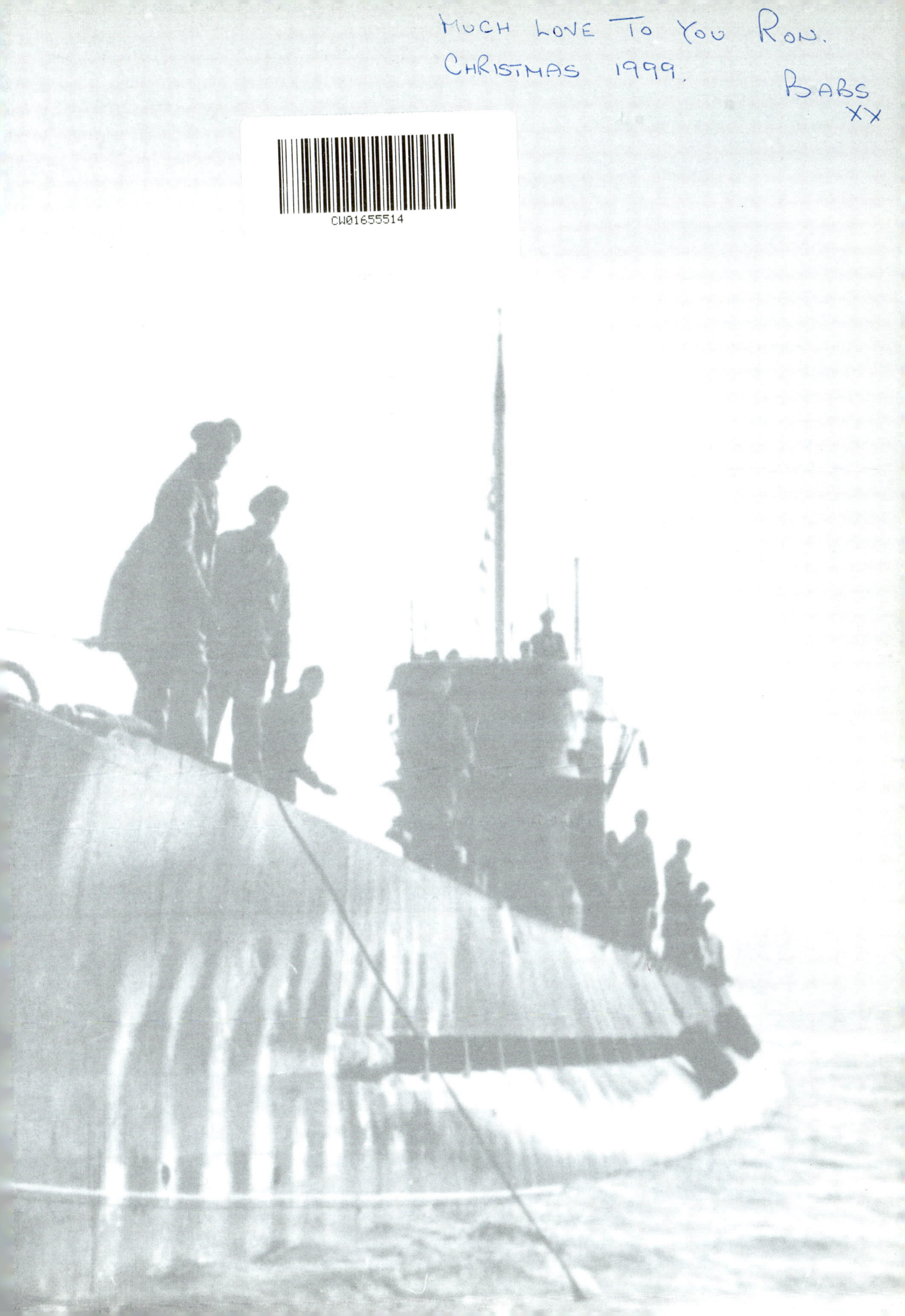

U-BOATS
IN CAMERA

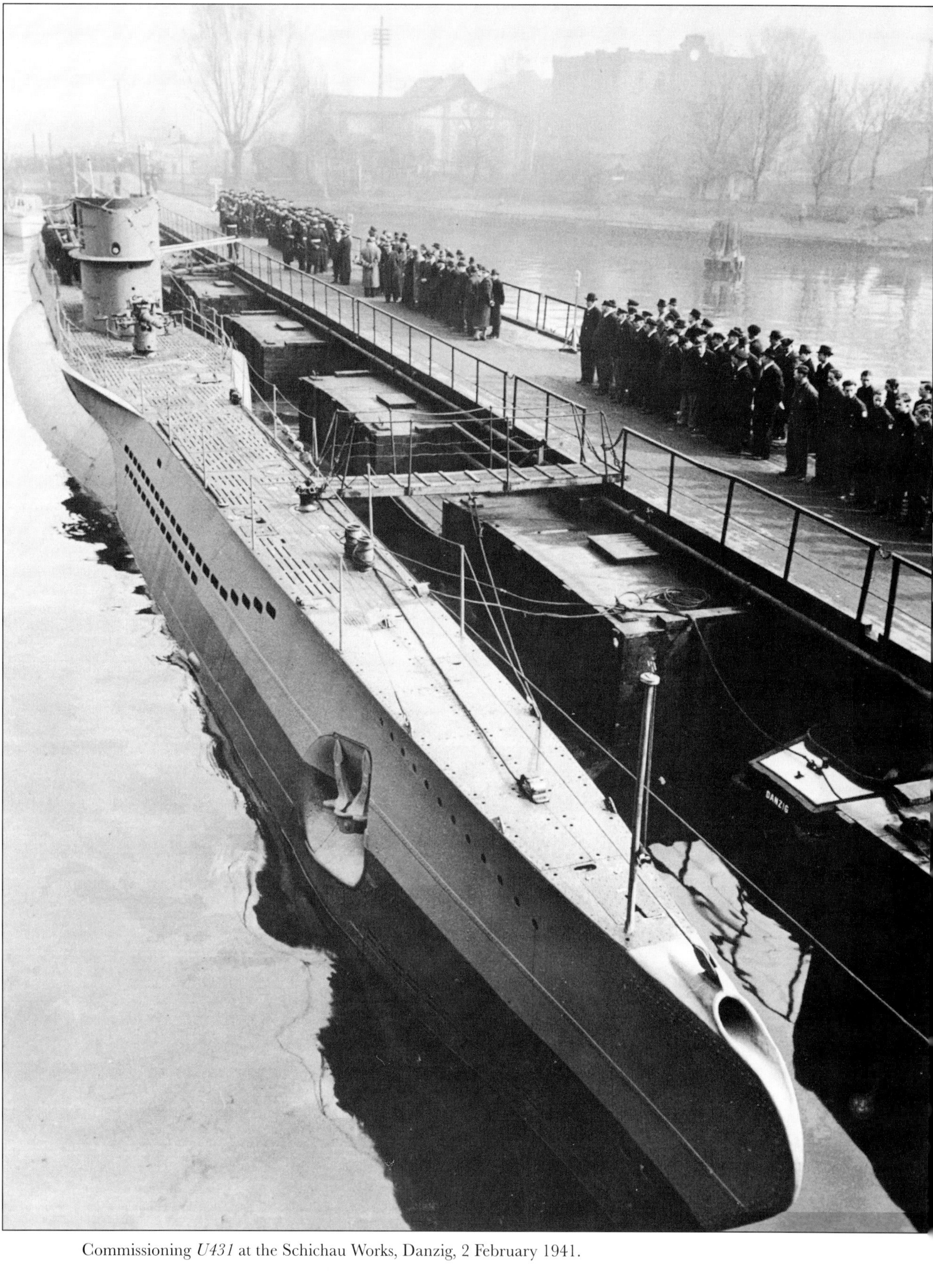

Commissioning *U431* at the Schichau Works, Danzig, 2 February 1941.

U-BOATS
IN CAMERA
1939–1945

JAK P. MALLMANN SHOWELL

in conjunction with
The International Submarine Archive
U-Boot-Archiv,
Germany

SUTTON PUBLISHING

First published in 1999 by
Sutton Publishing Limited · Phoenix Mill
Thrupp · Stroud · Gloucestershire · GL5 2BU

British Library Cataloguing in Publication Data
A catalogue record for this book is available from the British Library

ISBN 0 7509 1557 9

Endpapers: *Front, U178* or *U181*; *back, U441 manoeuvring in port.*

Typeset in 11/15 pt Baskerville.
Typesetting and origination by
Sutton Publishing Limited.
Printed in Great Britain by
Bath Press Ltd, Bath.

CONTENTS

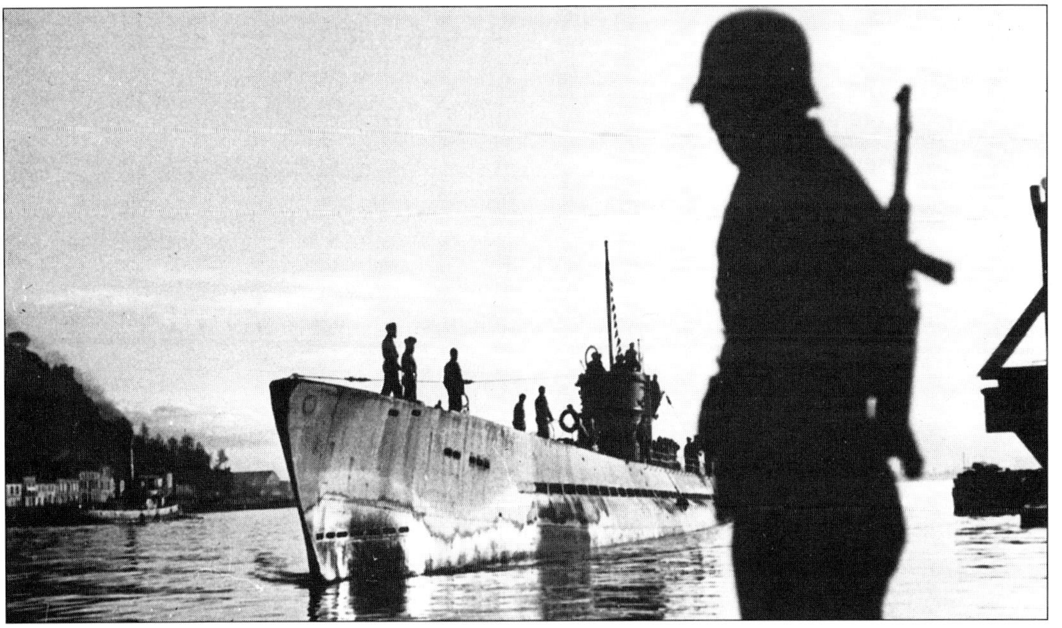

U178, one of the large, long-distance boats of Type IXB built by Deschimag AG Weser in Bremen returning to port after her first operational voyage. The pennants flying from the extended periscope indicate that it had been a successful undertaking.

Glossary and Abbreviations

Ausbildungsgruppe für Frontunterseeboote *or* Agru-Front	operational training for boats going to the front
FK *or* Fregattenkapitän	Captain (Junior)
flak	derived from Flugzeugabwehrkanone, an anti-aircraft gun
Holmwerft	name of a shipyard
IWO/IIWO/IIIWO	First/Second/Third Watch Officer
KK *or* Korvettenkapitän	Commander
KL *or* Kapitänleutnant	Lieutenant-Commander
KS *or* Kapitän zur See	Captain (Senior)
Lt *or* Leutnant zur See	Lieutenant (Junior)
Maschinengefreiter	Able Seamen (Engineer)
Maschinenobergefreiter	Leading Seamen (Engineer)
Maschininemaat	Petty Officer (Engineer)
Matrosengefreiter	Able Seaman
Nachrichtenmitteler-probungskommando Obermachinist	command for testing communications equipment
Obersteuermann	Navigator/Chief Boatswain
Oderworks	name of a shipyard
OL *or* Oberleutnant zur See	Lieutenant (Senior)
Seebeckwerft	name of a shipyard
UAK *or* Unterseebootsabnahmekommando	Submarine Acceptance Command
wintergarden	gun platform

INTRODUCTION

This book is dedicated to the memory of 'Professor' Gus Britton MBE whose loyalty, strength of character and intense determination helped bring together former adversaries to create a large family of friends dedicated to exposing the horrors and injustices of warfare.

Gus worked for many years at the Royal Navy's Submarine Museum (HMS *Dolphin* in Gosport, England) where he helped and inspired generations of historians. Many admired him for his immense knowledge and for making such a positive effort in wanting to leave the world in a more peaceful condition than it was when he first climbed into a submarine. He became one of the first British members of the German Submariners' Association (Verband Deutscher U-bootfahrer) and for many years supported the Munich branch. Gus was an ordinary seaman with a great personality, a true friend and supporter of submariners, historians, researchers and authors of all nationalities. He is sadly missed.

This glimpse into the domestic life of the German U-boat Arm focuses on the things ordinary men, the Gus Brittons of this world, would have seen and experienced during their first weeks aboard a brand new submarine during the Second World War. Much of their training took place in the Baltic because large parts of its waters were out of the reach of enemy forces. Training continued there more or less unabated until the advancing Russian forces pushed the establishments west. Then, while the main schools and training flotillas were being decimated, a tiny but profoundly determined remnant found shelter in a handful of isolated Norwegian fjords and remained there until the bitter end of the war.

The Baltic is slightly smaller than the North Sea but, being completely surrounded by land, is without any great oceanic influence and without a significant tide. The waters are salty, although in places they may be diluted by the many rivers pouring into them. The most dominant feature of life is the incredible annual temperature fluctuation from relatively hot summers to excruciatingly cold winters, when it is not uncommon for the sea to freeze over for a period of between three and five months. Towards the east and north this icy period is longer and more severe but despite these hard conditions the edges of the sea contain a good number of idyllic bays and sheltered lagoons, ideal for all types of boating activities. Indeed, these natural features have given rise to a long history of highly individualistic, small boat building industries and have helped to create massive centres of commerce. This was the home of the Vikings, who built magnificent boats before people had even thought of harbours. These ingenious constructions allowed cattle and horses to be loaded from shallow sandy beaches without cranes and allowed their builders to reach America long before Christopher Columbus.

Most Baltic waters are only about 55 m deep, just a little less than the average of 60 m for the North Sea. This means the majority of large city churches would not get the tops of their towers wet if they were placed on the seabed. However, glaciers from several ice ages have hollowed out a number of deep basins reaching down to 450 m and these make ideal locations for submarine diving trials.

* * *

A few of the photographs in this book were collected privately by Gus Britton, but the majority have come from the German U-Boot-Archiv. They show the kind of things that a new recruit would have seen and experienced during the period from joining his new boat while it was still on the builder's slipway until the day he set out for his first operational cruise.

The U-Boot-Archiv was founded and is directed by Horst Bredow who served as an officer in U-boats during the war. An injury incurred in action forced him into hospital while his boat sailed on a voyage from which it never returned. Everybody on board was killed. Horst made it his duty to find out what had happened in order to inform the next of kin of his dead comrades and the humble beginnings of his research grew into a massive collection which must now rank as the largest source of U-boat information in the world. By the end of 1998 he had amassed more than 100,000 photos and several volumes would be required to catalogue the rest of the material.

Anyone interested in further information about the archive is invited to send two international postal reply coupons to U-Boot-Archiv, D-27478 Cuxhaven – Altenbruch, Germany, for copies of its brochures.

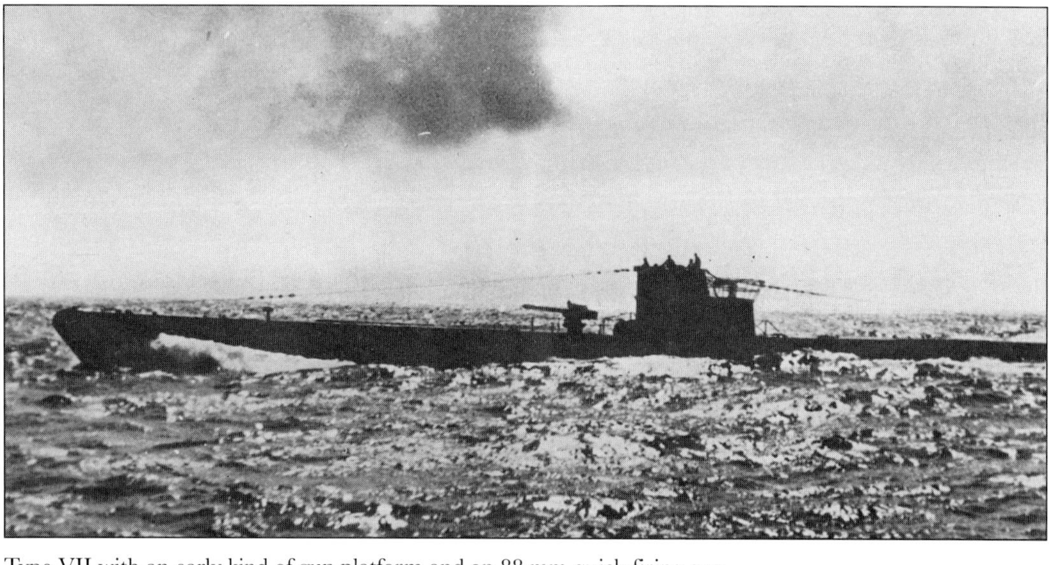

Type VII with an early kind of gun platform and an 88 mm quick-firing gun.

RECONSTRUCTION OF THE TRAINING LOG FROM *U1230*

This is a typical example of boat which passed quickly through the training and working-up process. This boat does not fit in with the photo sequence, but the log will add some explanation to the pictures. The layout used below is similar to that in German log books.

Date and Time	*Position*	*Occurrences*
26 January 1944	Finkenwerder (Hamburg)	*U1230* was commissioned at Deutsche Werft by KL Hans Hilbig. [Hilbig was born in 1917 and joined the navy in 1936, the year of the Olympic Games in Berlin and Garmisch-Partenkirchen. He served as a naval officer with the Luftwaffe until March 1943 when he went to U-boat school and continued in a variety of training positions until December 1943. Then he and some other members of *U1230*'s crew arrived at the dockyard in Hamburg. Although Hilbig is an unusual name in Germany, there was also a Kurt Hilbig who commanded *U993* and *U3526*.]
27 January		Stores loaded
28 January	backwards and forwards along the River Elbe	First trials with guns
29 January	left Hamburg for Brunsbüttel and on through the canal to Kiel	
30 January	arrived in Kiel	
31 January		The boat was tested by the U-boat Acceptance; its communications equipment was trialled by Nachrichtenmittelerprobungskommando; and it was also checked by the Naval Artillery Testing Centre and the Torpedo Trials Centre. [All new boats went through this acceptance procedure and the various commands had offices in several Baltic ports.]
8 February	On passage to Sonderburg in Denmark	
9 February	In Sonderburg	Trials with the U-boat Acceptance Command
10 February	On passage to Kiel	
11 February	In Kiel	Continuation of tests with the U-boat Acceptance Command
12 February	In Kiel	Continuation of tests
13 February	In Kiel	Continuation of tests
14 February	In Kiel	Continuation of tests
15 February	Departed for Swinemünde	

Date and Time	*Position*	*Occurrences*
16 February	Arrived Swinemünde	
17 February	Swinemünde	At the Naval Artillery School for training with anti-aircraft guns
18 February	Swinemünde	Anti-aircraft gun training
19 February	Swinemünde	Anti-aircraft gun training
20 February	Swinemünde	Anti-aircraft gun training
21 February	On passage to Danzig [now Polish and called Gdansk]	
22 February	Arrived in Danzig	
23 February	In the Bay of Danzig	Checked navigation instruments along the measured miles followed by deep diving trials
24 February	On passage to Pillau	
25 February	Arrived in Pillau	Trials and training as directed by the U-boat Acceptance Command
26 February	In Pillau	Continuation of training
27 February	In Pillau	Continuation of training
28 February	In Pillau	Training in port
29 February	In Pillau	Training in port
1 March	In Pillau	Training in port
2 March	In Pillau	Training in port
3 March	On passage to Hela	
4 to 8 March	In Hela	Boat with the Torpedo Trials Centre
9 March–6 April	Hela and in Danzig Bay	Continuous training with the Agru-Front. [This name was derived from Ausbildungsgruppe für Frontunterseeboote (Operational Training for boats going to the front).]
7 April	On passage to Pillau	
8–18 April	Pillau and eastern Baltic	Continuous tactical training with the 20th U-boat Flotilla [This flotilla specialised in training activities.]
19 April–3 May	Pillau and eastern Baltic	Torpedo shooting training by day and night with the 26th U-boat Flotilla. [This flotilla also specialised in training boats with new crews.]
4–15 May	Gotenhafen (now Gdynia in Poland)	Tactical training with the 27th U-boat Flotilla [also a specialist training flotilla]
16 May	On passage to Kiel	
17 May	On passage to Kiel	
18 May	Arrived in Kiel	
19 May	On passage to Wesermünde [now Bremerhaven]	
20 May–18 July	Wesermünde	Boat with the Seebeckwerft for finishing-off work
19–23 July	Wesermünde	Continuation of finishing-off work at the ship yard and loading stores
24 July	On passage to Kiel	
25–27 July	In Kiel	New 37 mm anti-aircraft gun fitted
28 July	In Kiel Förde	Tested the new gun
29 July	On passage to Gotenhafen (Gdynia)	
30 July	On passage to Gotenhafen	
31 July	On passage to Gotenhafen	
1– 7 August	Gotenhafen	Boat with the 27th U-boat Flotilla for tactical trials
8/9 August	In Danzig	Trials with the snorkel
10 August	On passage to Rönne	Cruising past the listening post on the island of Bornholm to check that machinery was running silently

Date and Time	*Position*	*Occurrences*
11 August	On passage to Swinemünde	
12–21 August	In Swinemünde	Training for the crew and practice with the anti-aircraft guns
22 August–15 September	To Stettin	Continuation of finishing-off work at the Oderworks.
16 September	To Swinemünde	Loading of stores for first operation.
17 September	On passage to Kiel	
18 September	Arrived in Kiel	
19–25 September	In Kiel	With the 5th U-boat Flotilla for fitting out. [This flotilla specialised in fitting out new boats, and so virtually every U-boat passed through it, and it can claim to have been the largest during the Second World War.]

U1230 was an ocean-going Type IXC boat. The boat was in Norway during the autumn of 1944 and at Heligoland when the war ended. From there *U1230* was moved to Wilhelmshaven before going over to Britain to be sunk during Operation Deadlight.

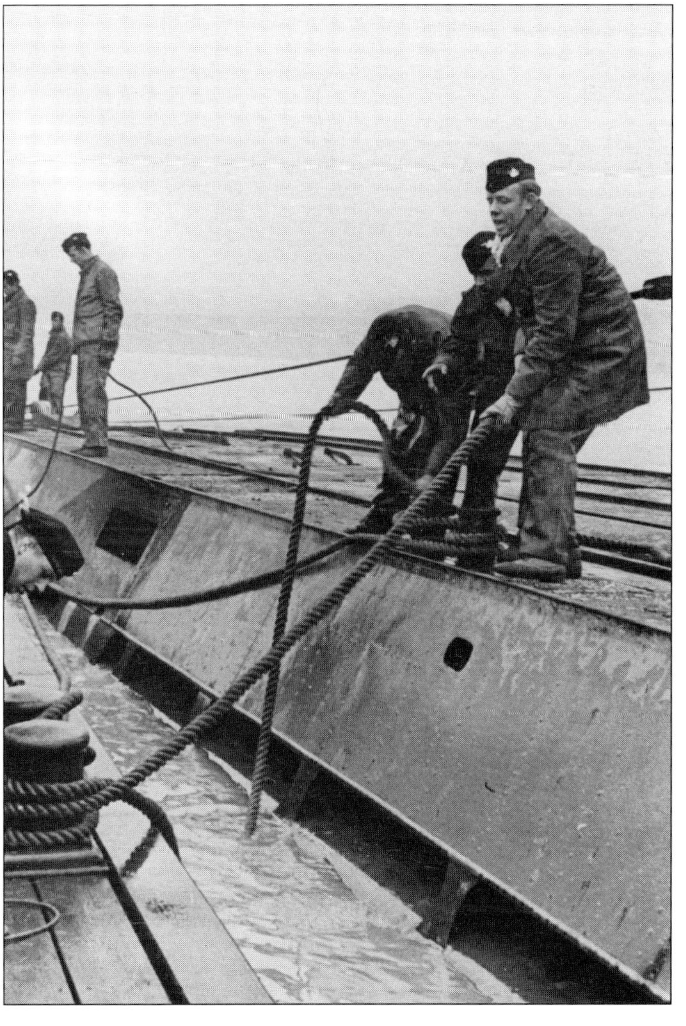

U178, a Type XI boat. Bootsmaat Klute is holding the howser as the boat makes fast. The rectangular hole is one of the diesel exhausts.

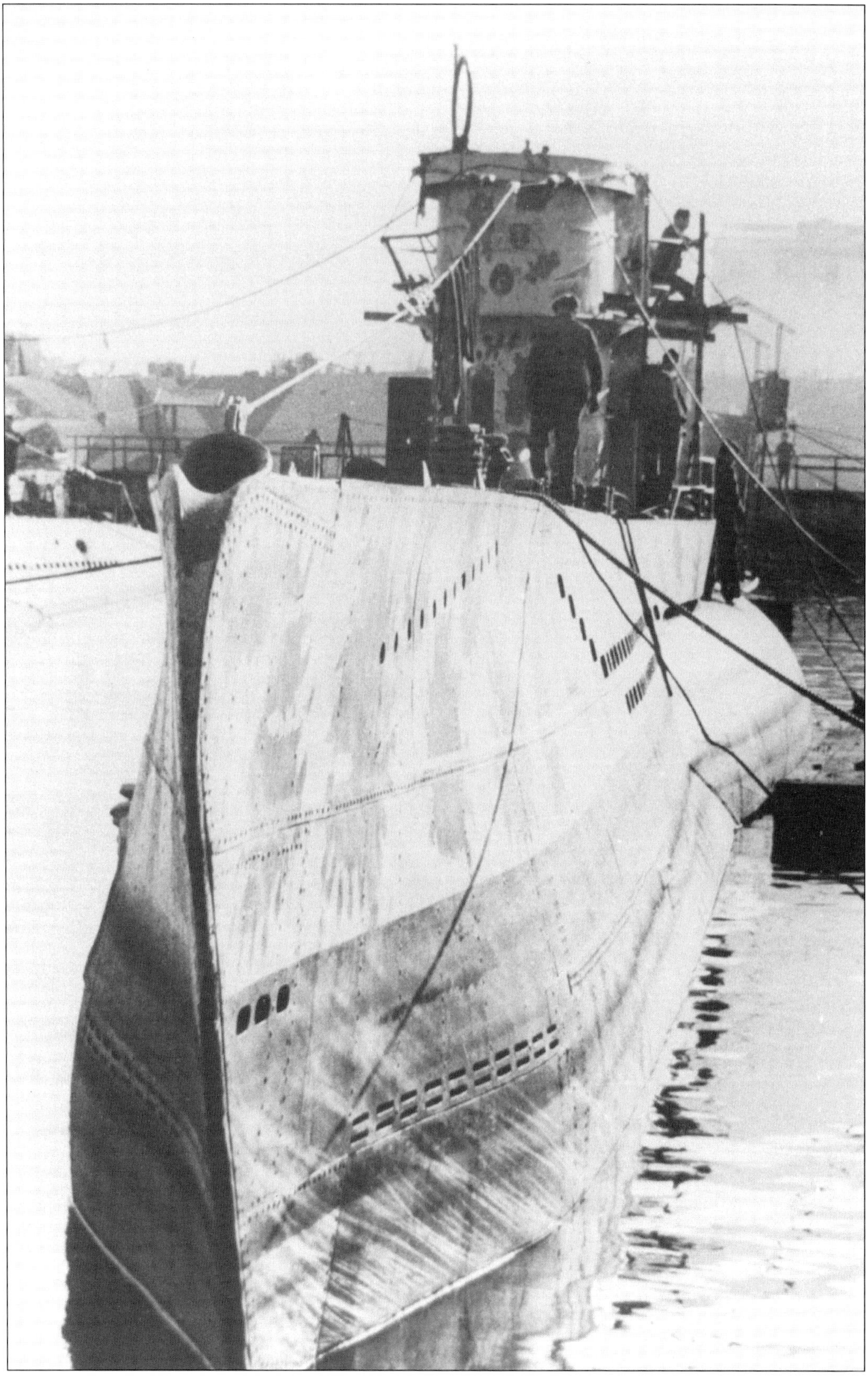

U407, a Type VIIC built at Danziger Werft.

RECONSTRUCTION OF THE TRAINING LOG FROM *U421*

Date and Time	*Position*	*Occurrences*
13 January 1943, 1130 hr	Danzig	OL Hans Kolbus took over the boat from the Danziger Werft and commissioned her as *U421*. [Kolbus was born in 1919 and joined the navy in 1938. He had served as naval officer with the Luftwaffe from September 1940 until he started his submarine training in January 1941. Following this he served for eleven months as IWO of *U409* under KL Hans-Ferdinand Massmann (experienced commander and former watch officer) before going on to U-boat Commanders' School. *U421* became his first command.]
1500hrs		Moved boat over to the U-boat Acceptance Command
14 January	Bay of Danzig	Trials with U-boat Acceptance Command. Finishing-off work while boat was frozen in
5 February	Bay of Danzig	Trials continued with U-boat Acceptance Command
6 February	On passage to Gotenhafen	With the Torpedo Trials Centre in Gotenhafen
10 February	Gotenhafen	With the Torpedo Trials Centre
11 February	Danzig	Continuation of U-boat Acceptance Command trials
12 February	On passage to Rönne	[There were underwater sound detectors near Rönne, on the island of Bornholm, for checking that machinery on U-boats was running silently.]
13 February	Near Rönne	A gale of force 6–7 tore the ice protection cap off the bows. Made fast in Rönne because the sound detection trials had to be postponed due to the bad weather.
14 February	On passage to Kiel	Left at 1300 hr
15 February	In Kiel	Made fast at the Blücher Pier at midday. Sound trials with the U-boat Acceptance Command, followed by degaussing and compass compensation
16 February	In Kiel	
17 February	In Kiel	At the Naval Repair Yard to have a new ice protection cap fitted over the bows and for the checking of net deflectors and radio aerials
1530 hr		Moved over to the Naval Dockyard on the other side of the water
1600 hr	Naval Dockyard in Kiel	Made fast at mooring no. 26
18 February 1430 hr		Departed for Danzig
19 February, 1930 hr		Made fast in Danzig.

Date and Time	*Position*	*Occurrences*
20 February		Moved to the Holmwerft for repairs to diesel engines and engine-room vents.
23 February	On passage to Hela	
24 February	At sea around Hela	Training and trials with the Agru-Front.
25 February		Trials and training continued.
3 March		Tactical training for commander, watch officers and radio operators
5 March	At sea near Hela	*U421* was employed as school boat for engineering officer trainees
0930 hr		The attack periscope was bent by a trawler's otter board
9 March, 1930 hr		Cast off in Hela for voyage to Danzig.
10 March	In Danzig	Made fast at the Holmwerft to have a new periscope fitted
11 March	Boat used for engineering officer training during the day and for tactical training with the Agru-Front at night.	
19 March	In Hela	Beginning of individual training
20 March up to 1200 hr	In Hela Trials and training	
1200 hr		Departed for Gotenhafen.
1300 hr	In Gotenhafen	Made fast by the oiling pier
1825 hr		Cast off
1910 hr	In Hela	Made fast in the Naval Dockyard
21 March		Individual training
22 March	North of Danzig Bay	Pre-tactical training started
28 March	In Hela	Individual training and then another training cruise
29 March	In Hela	Dismissed from the Agru-Front
30 March	Moved to Gotenhafen for loading stores	
31 March	On passage to Pillau	Boat with the Torpedo Shooting Training Flotilla
1 April	With 26th U-Flotilla	Torpedo shooting training started
14 April	On passage to Danzig	At the Holmwerft for minor repair to diesel engines
18 April	On passage to Gotenhafen	With the 27th U-boat Flotilla for tactical training in the central and eastern Baltic.
30 April	On passage to Danzig	Loading stores and then made fast at 8th U-boat Flotilla's pier [a training flotilla]
3 May	On passage to Rönne	Sound tests to check that machinery was running silently
4 May	Near Rönne	Sound detection tests completed
2200 hr	Left for Swinemünde	For anti-aircraft gun training
5 May		Passed picket ship *Arkona* and turned on a heading 153°. Mine detonation 50–100 m on starboard bow. Both engines stopped and crew ordered out on to the upper deck [on the outside]. Boat remained seaworthy and the only leaks were from a flooded torpedo tube. Crew ordered back to their stations. Continued on a heading of 153° while crew cleared up the mess inside the boat
0337 hr		Sent radio signal 'Damaged by mine at 54°35.8'N, 13°43.2E. Making for Swinemünde.'

Date and Time	*Position*	*Occurrences*
0450 hr		Summary of Damage Report: a large number of lights not working; various hatches have burst open; some vents cannot be closed; battery 2 is dead and battery 1 is badly damaged; both periscopes out of action; torpedo aimer not working; diving tank 5 damaged; a large number of pipes have been torn from the hull and dropped by 4 mm; auxiliary oil pump broken; clutches for the diesels making a grinding noise; torpedo adjustment system not working; wooden cladding in various compartments detached from the walls. [It is rather strange that there are no reports of injuries to the men: judging by the damage it must have been a considerable ordeal for the 'software' inside the boat.]
0750 hr	In Swinemünde	Made fast
2030 hr		Cast off and on passage to Stettin
6 May	At U-boat base in Stettin	Into dock at the Oderwerke for assessment of damage and initial repairs
14 May	Out of dock	Made fast in the naval dockyard
18 May	Arrived in Danzig	Four months have passed since the boat was commissioned here. At least it is now a little warmer. Made fast in the naval dockyard
24 May		Moved boat into dock at Holmwerft
10 August	In Danzig	The boat remained in dock for repairs and finishing-off work while the crew underwent further training and helped out with other tasks elsewhere
0800 hr		Cast off for sea trials and deep diving tests
2000 hr	Returned to Holmwerft.	
14 August		Running tests at the measured miles and radio tests. Returned to Holmwerft at the end of the day
16 August	On passage to Hela	Individual training and then a day with the Agru-Front. Afterwards back to Hela
18 August	On passage to Pillau	Trials with Torpedo Inspectorate and then degaussing the boat
19 August	Alongside *Frieda Horn*	
1750 hr		Cast off and made for Danzig
2200 hr		Arrived in naval dockyard. Tests during the previous days revealed that there were still several potential leaks and therefore the boat returned to Holmwerft
20 August	Holmwerft	Some of the crew travelled to Swinemünde for anti-aircraft gun training
21 September	By Danziger Werft	Trimming trials in shipyard's pit
23 September	In Pillau	Degaussing and then commenced voyage to Swinemünde
24 September	In Swinemünde	Made fast in the coaling station
25 September		Training with anti-aircraft guns
2 October	On passage to Sonderburg [Denmark]	
3 October	In Sonderburg	Excessive noise from the electric motors prevented the completion of sound detection and silent running tests
4 October	On passage to Kiel	Made fast in naval dockyard
5 October	In Kiel	At Deutsche Werke for repairs

Date and Time	*Position*	*Occurrences*
28 October		Boat remained in the dockyard for fitting of the new anti-aircraft guns and some other finishing-off work. This showed up a fault with the armour protection of the conning tower, which was also rectified
29 October	On passage to Sonderburg	
30 October		Sound detection trials and then commenced journey back to Kiel
1 November		Beginning of fitting out the boat for operational service
6 November		Left for first operational cruise

U421 was a Type VIIC and later sailed into the Mediterranean where it was sunk during an air raid on Toulon on 29 April 1944.

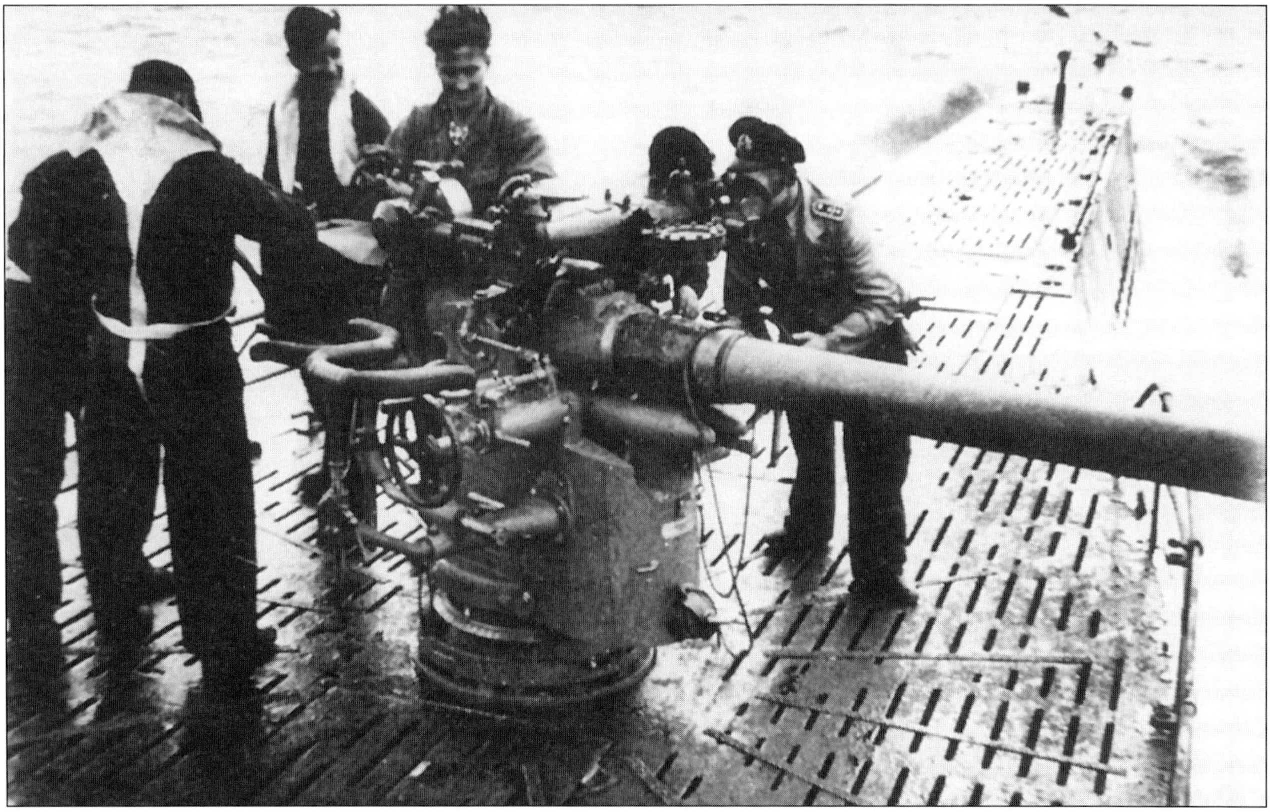

The 88 mm gun aboard *U552* with the head of a sound detector in the distance.

U-BOATS
IN CAMERA

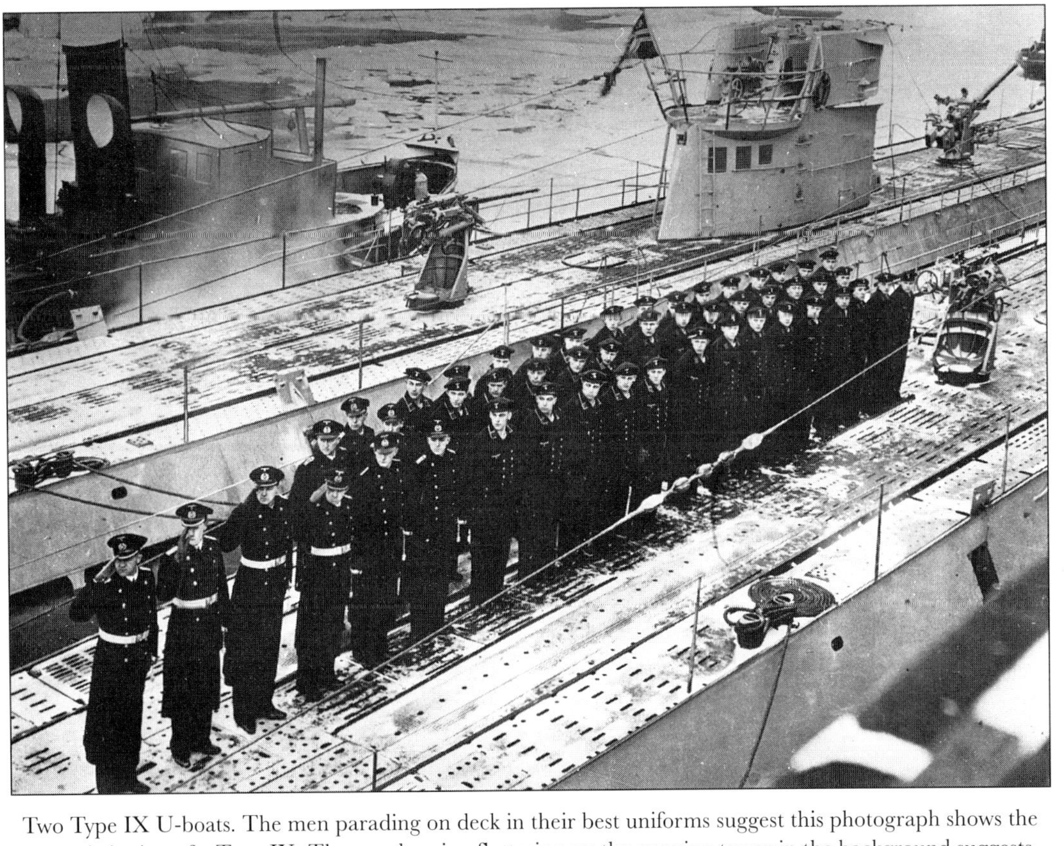

Two Type IX U-boats. The men parading on deck in their best uniforms suggest this photograph shows the commissioning of a Type IX. The naval ensign fluttering on the conning tower in the background suggests that the second boat had already been commissioned. There is a 105 mm quick-firing gun in front of the conning tower and another 37 mm deck gun behind it.

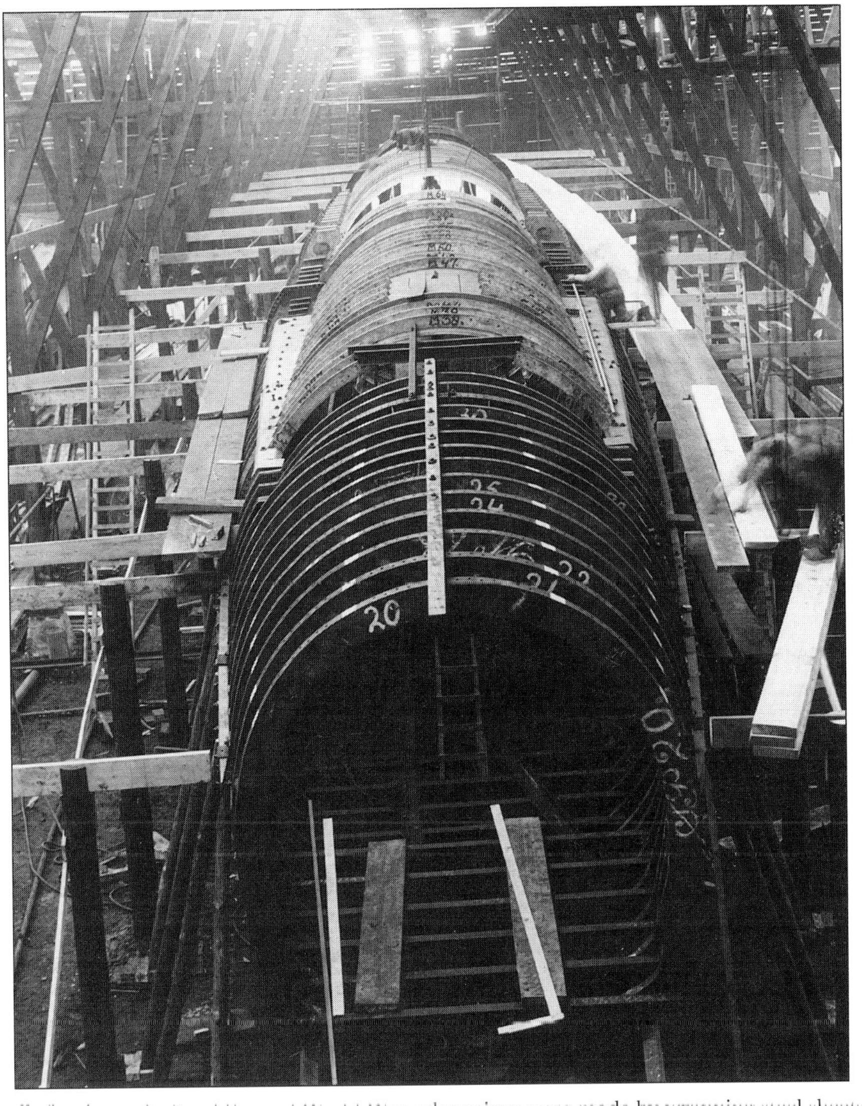

Pressure hulls for the majority of Second World War submarines were made by wrapping steel sheets around a mass of circular ribs. Much of this intricate work was carried out in the open, where welders were exposed to the elements, although portable sheds were provided to protect them from the worst weather. In this case it looks as though a wooden framework has also been added as a temporary measure. It is somewhat difficult to distinguish the nationality of the boat at this early stage of construction and it could well be that this is the beginning of a British submarine.

Only the Krupp Germania Works in Kiel produced their submarines under the protection of a glass roof. Plans for this steel-framed building were actually made some ten years before the first submarines were built inside it. In the 1890s, when the still small private yard approached the heavy industrial giant Krupp to construct the massive frame, it was intended to be a shelter for the construction of surface ships. The glass house was thought necessary because Germania Works' excellent reputation for high quality torpedo boats had generated a demand for bigger ships with increasingly complicated technology. The structure was much higher than it needed to be to accommodate the small submarines later built inside it. The cooperation between the two companies in building the massive, 36 m high, glass house coincided with a time of expansion, when the small shipyard purchased more land. This ambitious programme also led to Germania being taken over in 1902. The company name was consequently changed to Friedrich Krupp Germaniawerft. The huge lettering seen in the photograph on p. 4 did not appear until some years after the end of the First World War.

In its day, the construction shed was among the largest structures in north Germany – quite something – and inside was a further technical innovation of the time: a crane which could run over the entire system of slipways with loads of up to 6 tons. Today, just a short distance from this site, is a modern crane capable of carrying some 450 tons, an indication of how technology has moved on in the last eighty years.

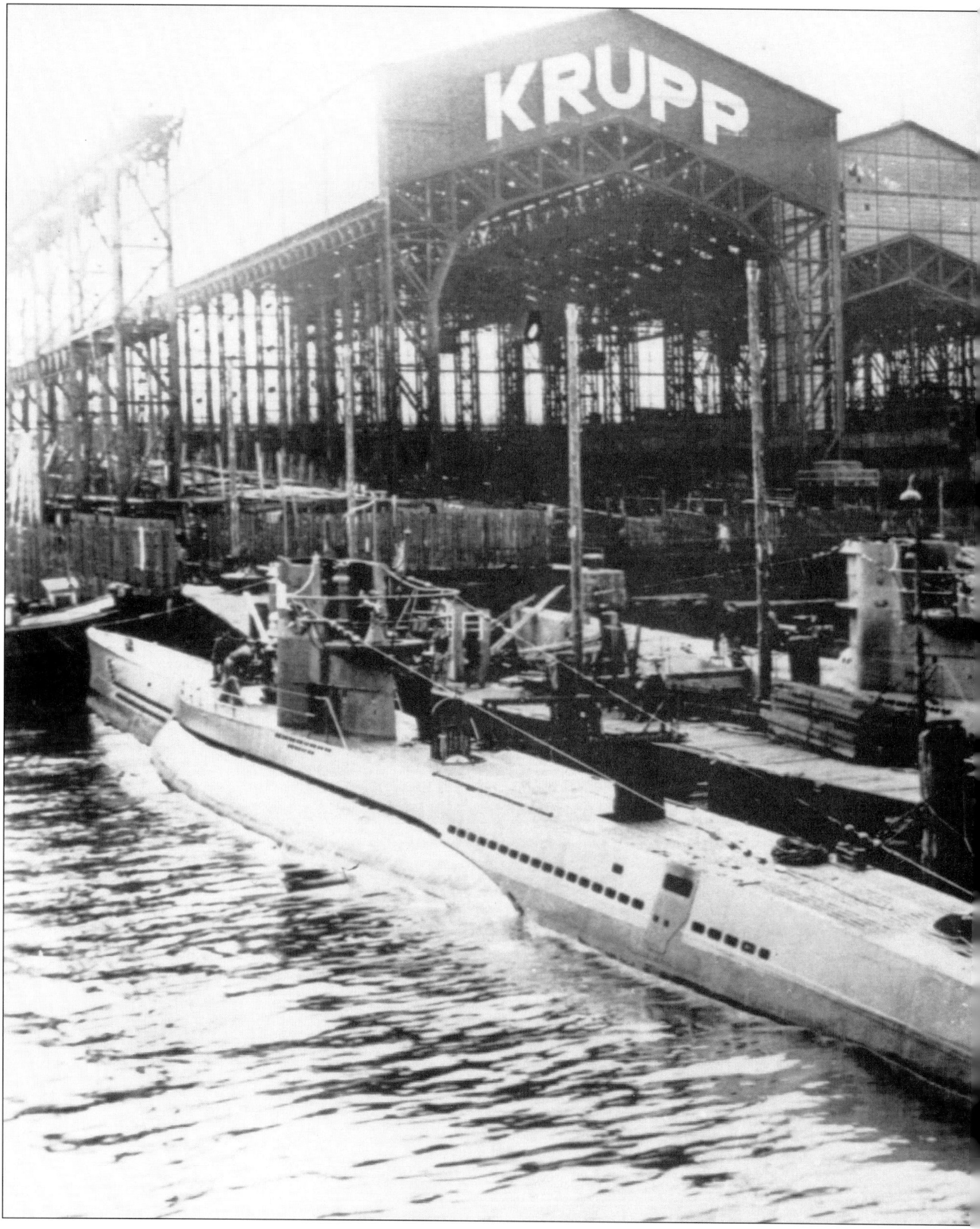

The massive glass-covered slipways at Germania Works in Kiel during the Second World War and before bombing raids had blown the glass out of the steel frame. The boat in the foreground is *U227*, which was commissioned by KL Jürgen Kuntze on 22 August 1942. It was sunk less than eight months later by a

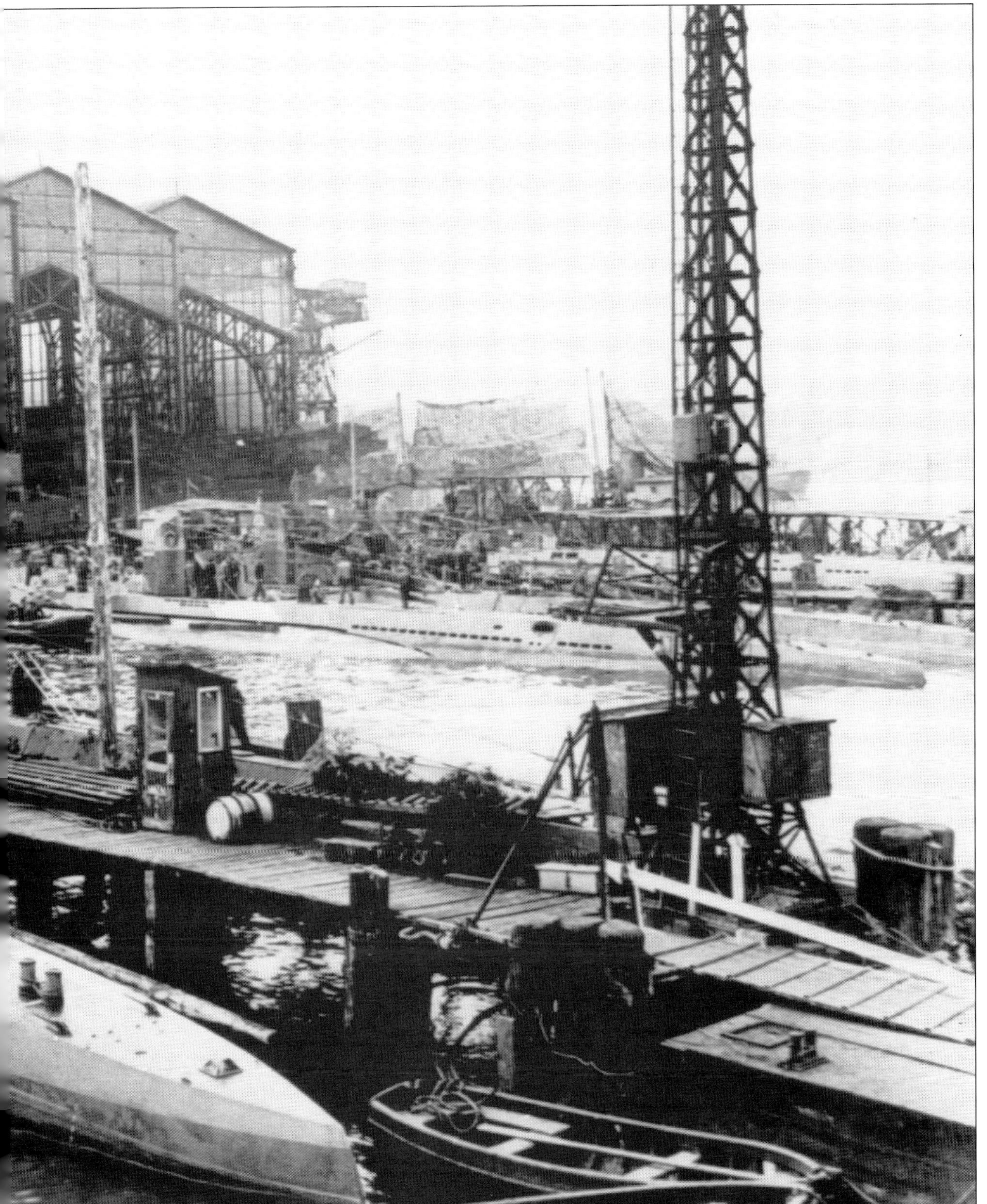

Hampden aircraft of 455 Squadron Royal Australian Air Force, piloted by Flt Sgt J.S. Freeth. Some thirty men climbed into life-rafts, but none of them ever reached land. Kuntze was twenty-six years old when he died and the majority of his men were several years younger.

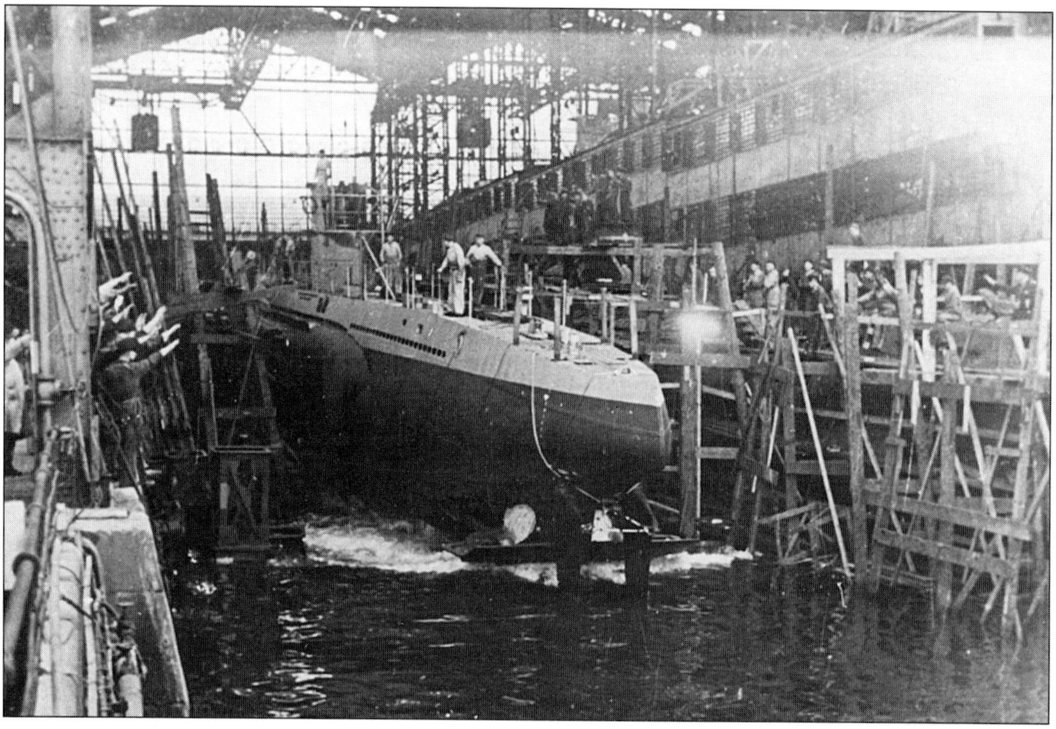

An example of modern high technology sliding past crude wooden supports inside the glass house at the Krupp Germania Works in Kiel. She is a Type VII boat, produced during the Second World War.

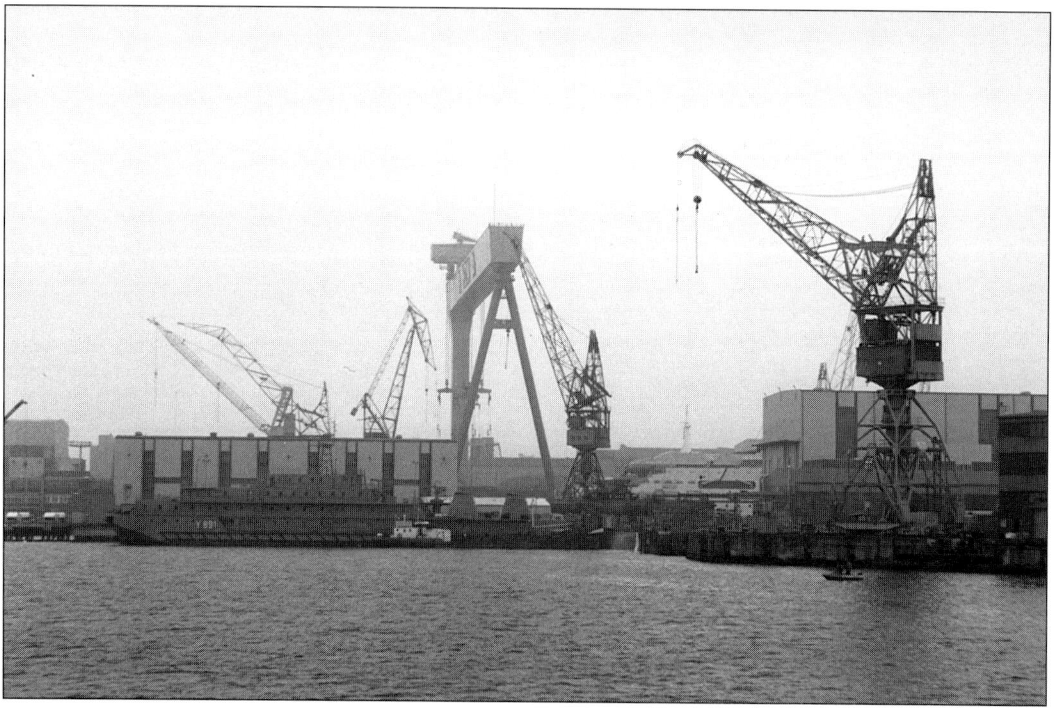

A view of the modern Howaldtswerke-Deutsche Werft shipyard in Kiel photographed in 1998 with the massive 450-ton crane (centre) over a dry construction dock. The box-like housing of the cable drum on the top, which runs from side to side, is about as high as a three-storey block of flats and bigger in floor area than an average family house. This picture was taken from roughly the same position as the previous one, but looking to the left, along the waterfront. The massive hangar-like sheds are the modern equivalent of Krupp's steel-framed glass hangar. They have been built over the top of dry docks, making the launching process obsolete because the finished product can be floated out.

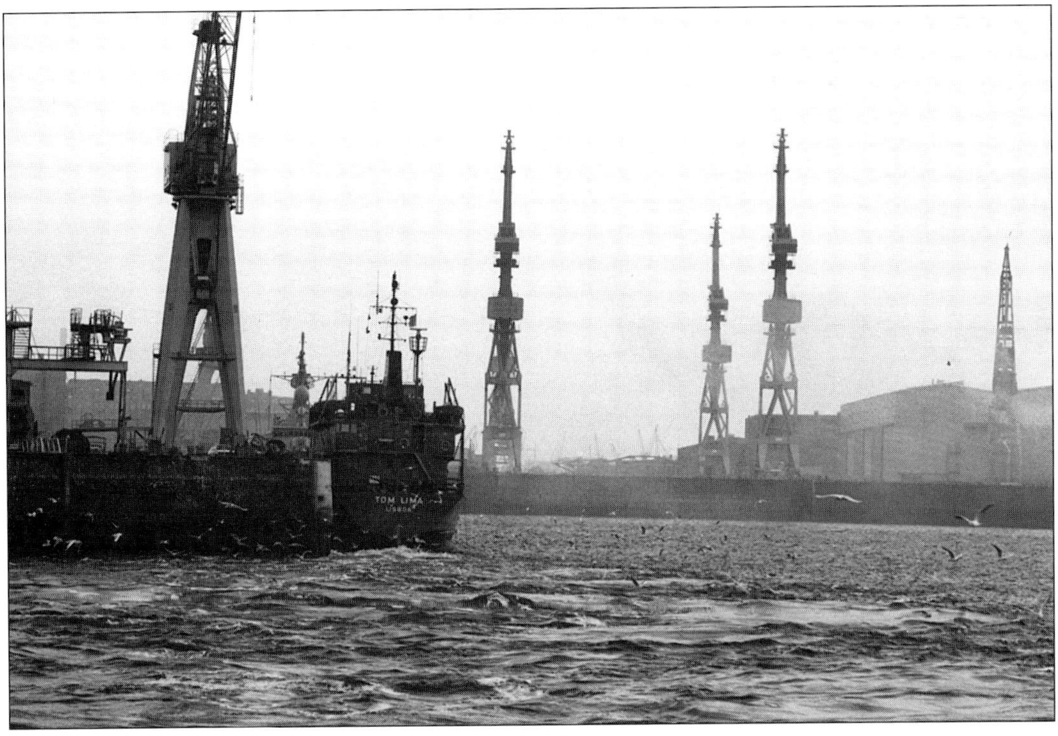

The U-boat fitting-out quay at Blohm und Voss in Hamburg towards the end of the 1980s, at a time when shipbuilding in Europe had already shrunk drastically. Although there were still an impressive number of high cranes dominating the skyline, many of them did not move for long periods, even during weekdays. In earlier years there were times when the noise and motion of the yards on the River Elbe never ceased, not even at night or at weekends. Blohm und Voss was not drawn into U-boat production until comparatively late in the war, but the firm very quickly produced the most efficient production line in terms of man-hours required for each job.

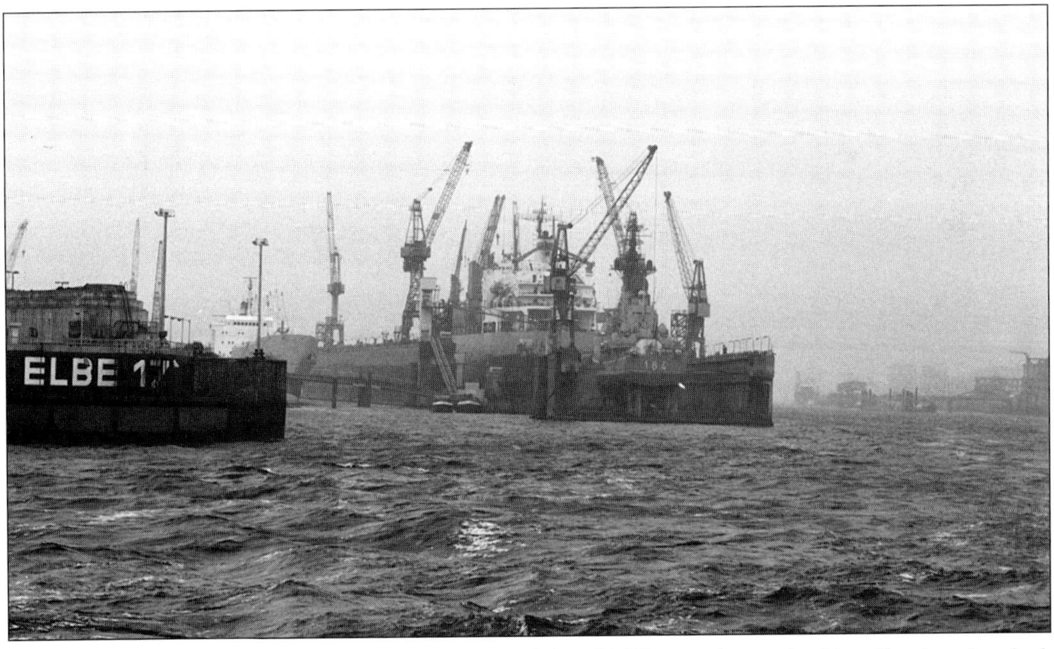

A view along the River Elbe from almost on top of the old Elbe road tunnel with a floating dry dock dominating the water's edge by Blohm und Voss where U-boats were built during the Second World War. These massive floating platforms are similar to submarines inasmuch as they have flooding tanks. These allow the submersion of the structure up to the tops of the high walls along both sides. An ocean-going giant can be nudged in by tugs and then the entire structure lifted up again, raising the ship's hull clear of the water.

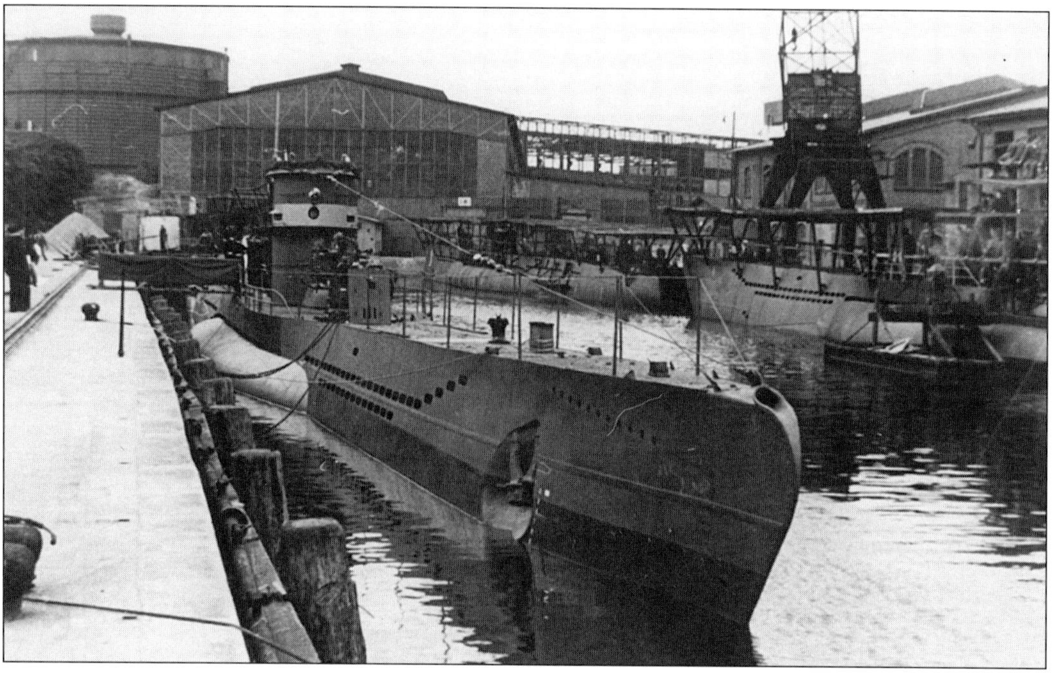

This picture brings us to an enigma – is this *U441* or *U442*? On this occasion it seems highly likely to be the former. The boat is made fast in a smallish rectangular fitting-out bay at Danziger Werft. The building with the pitched roof in the background belongs to the shipyard but the circular structure behind it is a gas tank belonging to the neighbouring gasworks. Of special interest are the two boats on the right, which have obviously been launched but not yet completed. Note that they have been covered with scaffolding and roofs.

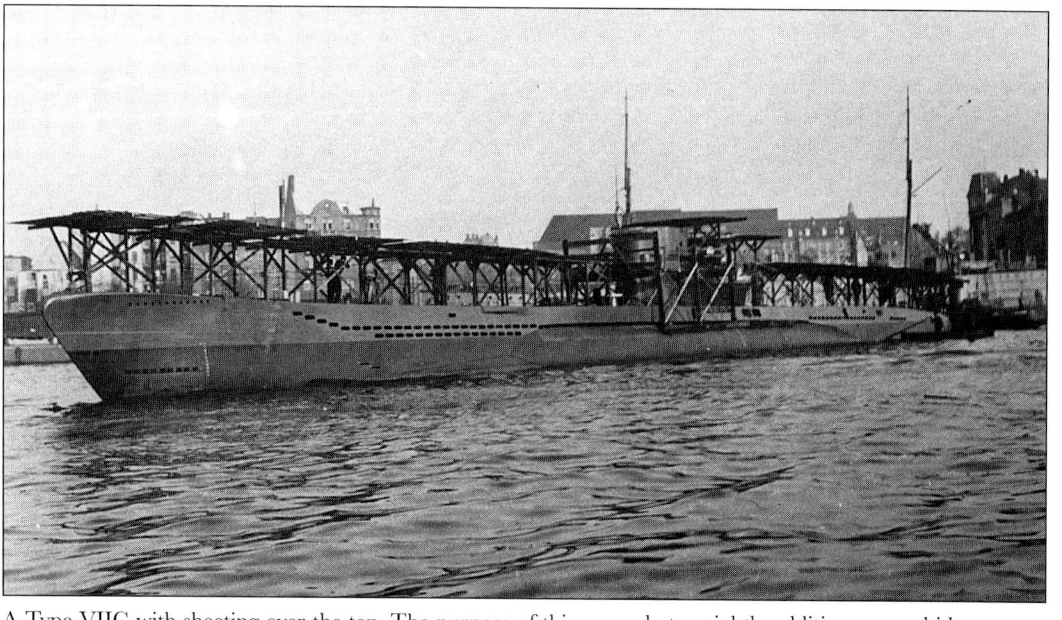

A Type VIIC with sheeting over the top. The purpose of this somewhat unsightly addition was to hide progress from the prying cameras of enemy reconnaissance planes. Unfortunately for the Germans it did not make much difference because David Brachi, a photographic interpreter with the Royal Air Force Photo Reconnaissance Unit, cracked the pattern of their methodical camouflage rules. He numbered newly laid keels and then followed their progress until the submarines had vanished from the shipyard, suggesting they had gone on trials. For example, boats were covered with a flat sheet until work started on the conning towers, when a raised section was added to the middle. Thus, by looking at the camouflage Brachi could produce a timetable of how long it was likely to be from each particular stage to completion, enabling him to accurately forecast the number of U-boats which were likely to appear in the Atlantic.

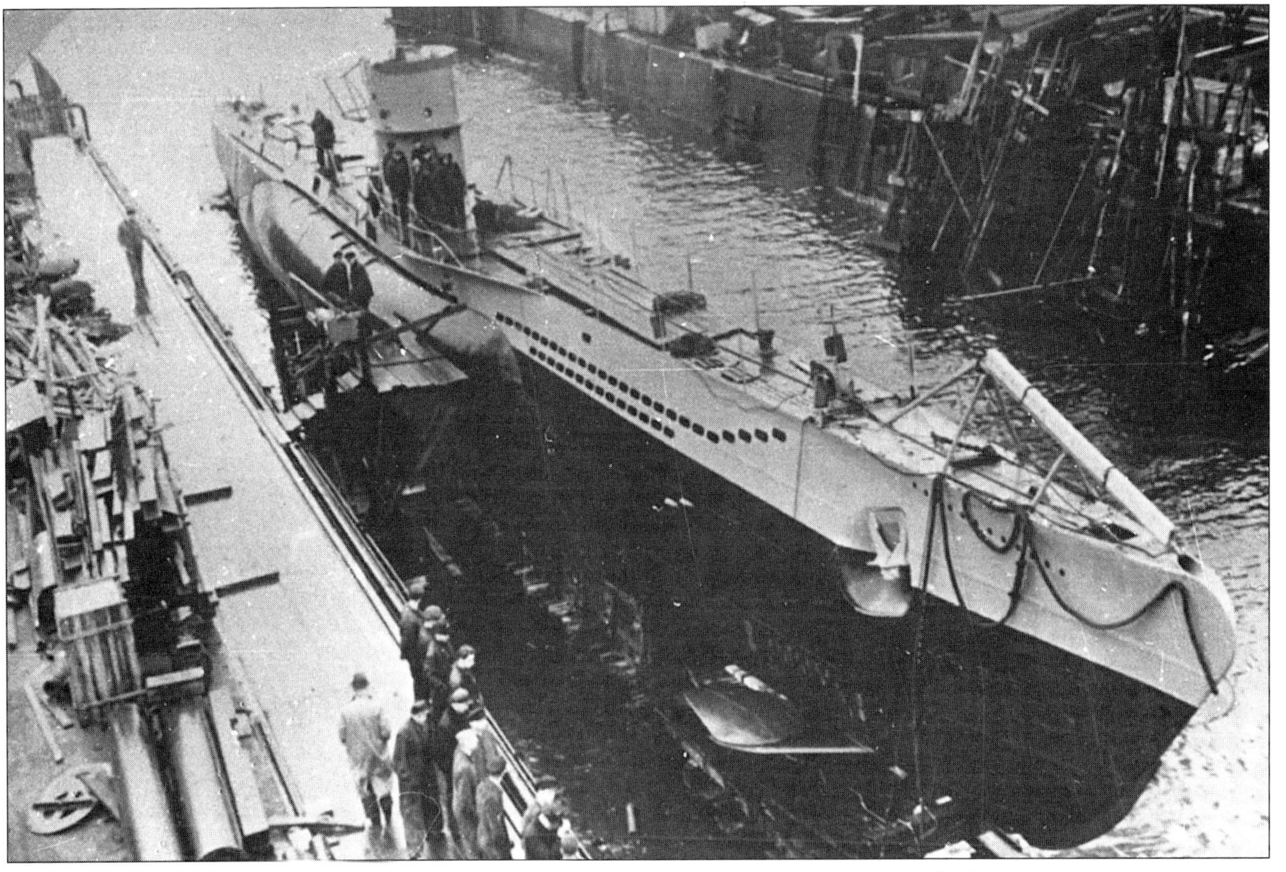

People who have not been in close contact with shipbuilding communities will probably never appreciate the euphoria created by a launch. Whether the vessel is a large ocean liner or a small boat, this is the day when someone's baby comes to life, when a temple of steel acquires a personality and relationships begin between flesh and iron which can become stronger, more loving and more infuriating than friendships between people.

This photograph was taken at the launch of *U70* by KL Joachim Matz at Germania Works in Kiel on 12 October 1940. This launch of the second Type VIIC boat took place less than a month after the first (*U69* by KL Jost Metzler). The image shows the boat had several of the Type's early features, the most obvious being the well-protected, serrated edge of the net-cutter on the bows. Although such structures had ceased to have a net-cutting function by the end of the First World War, they remained part of the design as an anchorage for the forward jumping wire running up to the top of the conning tower. (The latter had not yet been fitted to *U70* when this picture was taken.) The equipment had originally been conceived as a way to prevent the tower from fouling nets and possibly to add stability to it when it was battered by water. The wires remained *in situ* until the end of the Second World War because they also served as a radio aerial and as a safety harness anchorage for men working on the upper deck in foul weather. The other noticeable feature of early boats was the gun platform just forward of the conning tower. In this picture it can be seen to form a flat extension, protruding over the sides. In later boats the hull was curved to run around the outside edge, rather than underneath it, as can be seen here.

Matz and twenty-four of his men were lucky to survive a depth charge attack on *U70* near Rockall in March 1941, the month when U-boats commanded by the aces Günter Prien, Otto Kretschmer and Joachim Schepke were also sunk.

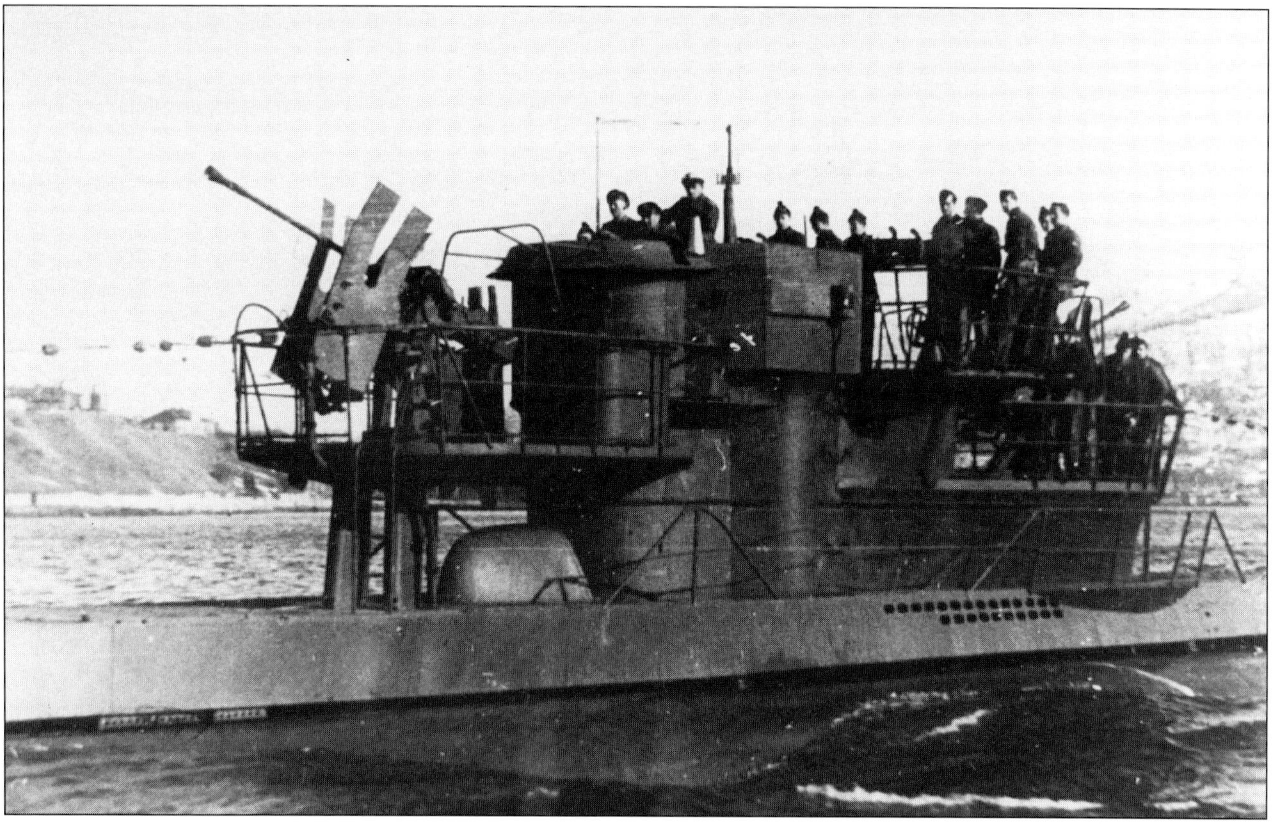

Probably *U673* refitted with additional anti-aircraft guns to act as a 'flak' or aircraft trap.

The following sequence of pictures shows the launching of *U441* by KL Klaus Hartmann on 13 December 1941 and *U442* by KK Hans-Joachim Hesse on 12 January 1942 at Schichau Works in Danzig.

Distinguishing between these two boats is not easy and while looking for clues in the U-Boot-Archiv, I stumbled upon the most unexpected document. On opening the *U441* file I was faced with a copy of a letter written by her second commander, KL Götz von Hartmann, some eleven years earlier. The astonishing point, which immediately caught my eye, was that the letter with information about his boat had been addressed to me – but this was the first time I had seen it. The original never arrived. Sadly, the sender had been dead for several years by the time I read it, and on following his suggestion of telephoning the boat's first Obersteuermann (Navigator), I discovered that the latter, Wilhelm Matheis, had died less than a week before my call.

U441 was one of the few boats converted to become a 'flak-trap' aircraft trap for a few months of 1943, but injuries were so severe that all six boats with modified conning towers were quickly reconverted back to the standard design. The story of *U441* also serves as a trap for the unwary historian: the boat was commissioned on 21 February 1942 by KL Klaus Hartmann. KL Götz von Hartmann took over in May 1943 until Klaus returned in August, to go down with the boat less than a year later.

The U-boat Arm was saturated with confusing names, many of them far worse than those of the two men commanding *U441*. For example, among the commanders were Schulte, Schultz, Schultze, Schulz and Schulze and photos showing many of these men have appeared in postwar books with the caption 'Herbert Schultze of *U48*'. Some commanders hit historians even harder! There was a Hermann Bauer and a Max-Hermann Bauer, a Heinz Wolff and a Karl-Heinz Wolff as well as a Günter Keller and a Günther Keller. Despite the vast choice of names, the navy even managed to appoint two U-boat commanders with the names Klaus Becker, two called Hans Falke and two called Eberhard Hoffmann. *U957* was commissioned by Franz Saar and commanded by Gerd Schaar when it was sunk. No doubt, anyone searching through the records will find even more potential confusion.

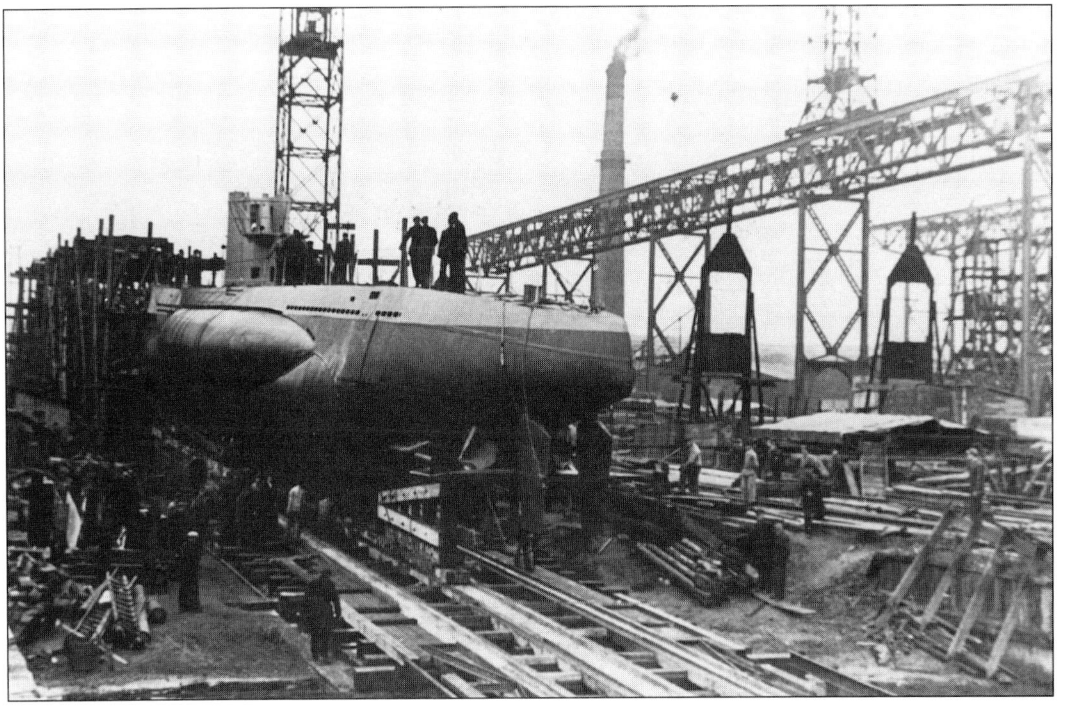

Because shipyard cranes ran on rails, it was easy to change the skyline around any slipway and considerable deliberations have gone into the identification of these two photographs. At first it was thought that both show the same U-boat with the chimney in the background of the picture above being hidden by the crane in the one below. However, it would appear that they do not show the same boat. Above is *U441* and below is *U442*. The horizontal gantry (above) was capable of moving along the entire shipyard and the tall crane mounted on its top ran from one end of the structure to the other. It may be surprising that such high-precision technology as a submarine was put together in such untidy surroundings and that timber played such an important role in the welding of steel.

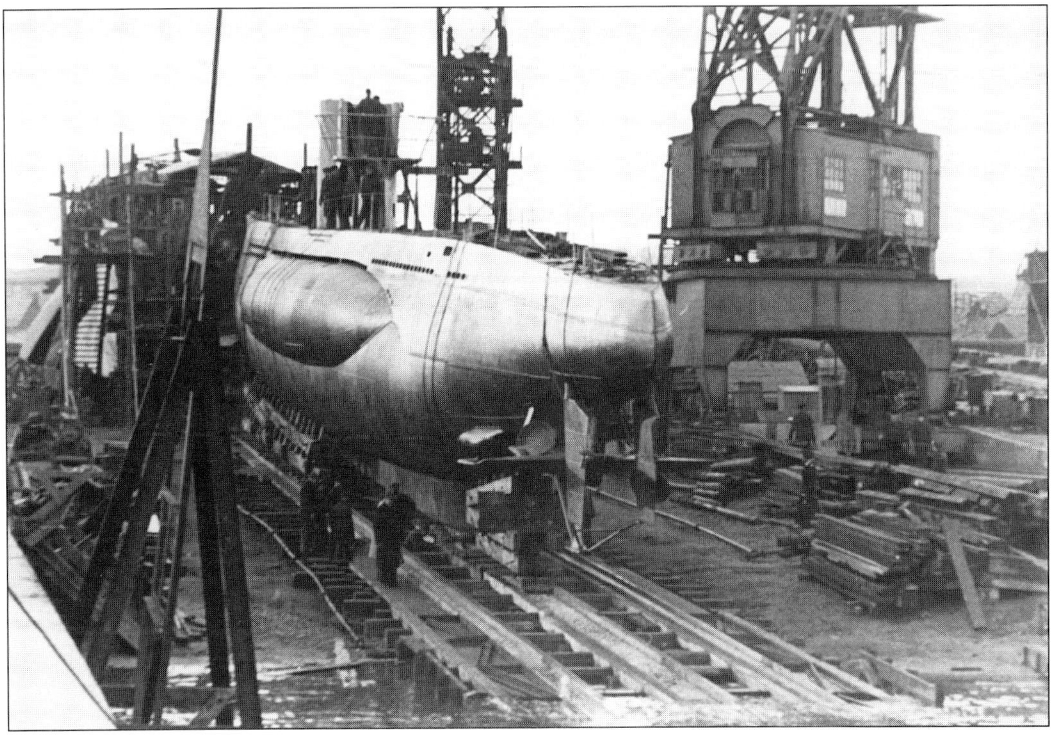

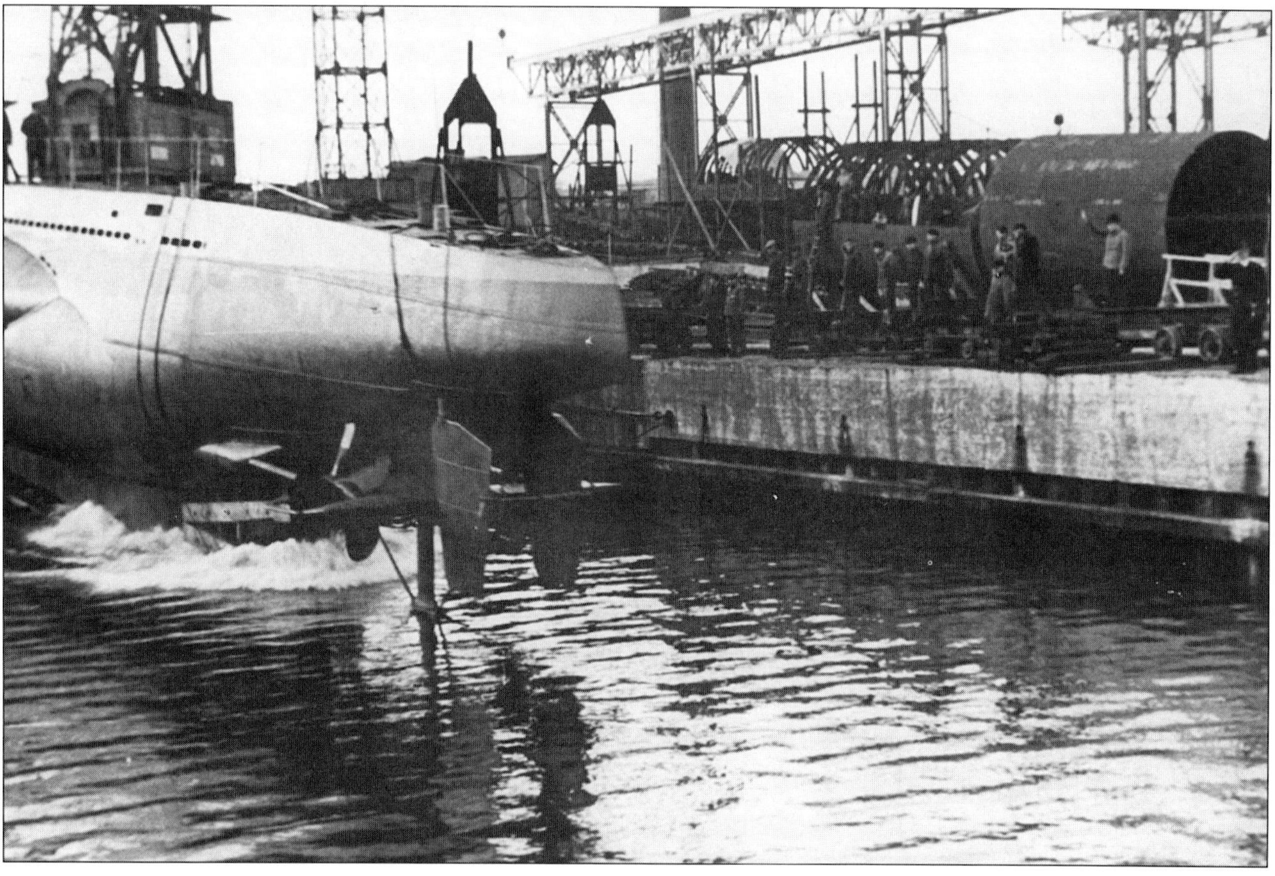

U442 with numerous submarine sections lying in the background, waiting for their turn to be laid on the slipway. There were always tense moments at the start of a launch. Engineers wondered how easily the massive weight would be induced to move. Sometimes considerable coaxing was required to persuade the mass of steel to take to the water. However, once in motion, there was very little anyone could do to stop the launch and often the dead-weight gathered sufficient momentum to continue gliding for a long distance through the water. Large, heavy anchors, often from old redundant ships, were carried on the vessel to arrest this wild action and to prevent the boat from grounding on the opposite shore.

The period between laying down the keel and launching the boat varied from yard to yard – bigger concerns could employ a larger number of men more efficiently along better production lines. Towards the beginning of the war, Blohm und Voss in Hamburg required about 11–12 months for building a sea-going boat of Type VIIC and another two months passed before it could be commissioned. Strangely enough, the Allied intensive bombing campaign did nothing to slow down this process. If anything, the construction period was shortened by the best part of a month. This is quite amazing when one considers that the terror-bombing created more damage in the city of Hamburg during a period of three weeks in 1943 than German action caused in all of Britain during the entire war. The building time for the more complicated and larger, ocean-going boats of Type IXC was slightly shorter. This could well have been due to the massive yard of Deschimag AG Weser having been geared to submarine construction since long before the war.

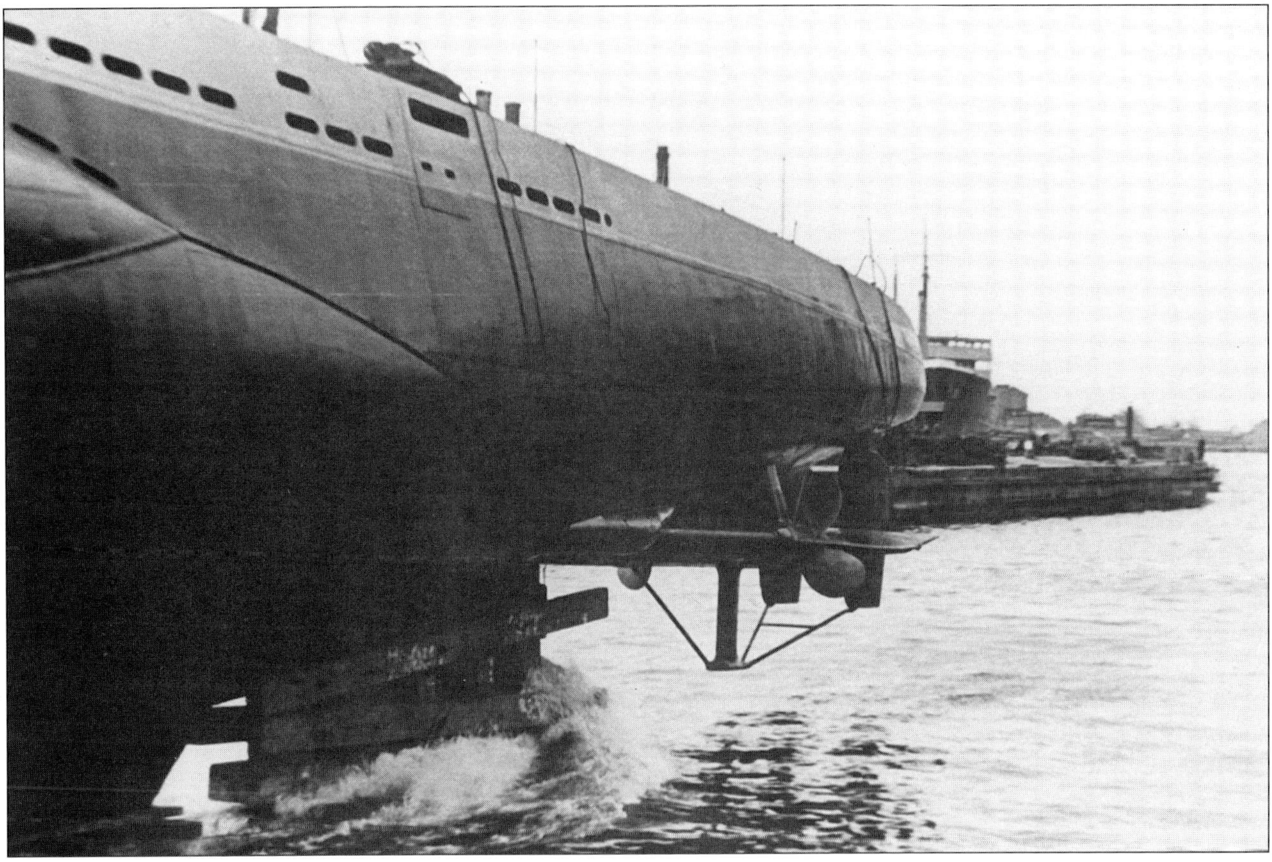

Launching *U442* at the Schichau Works in Danzig.

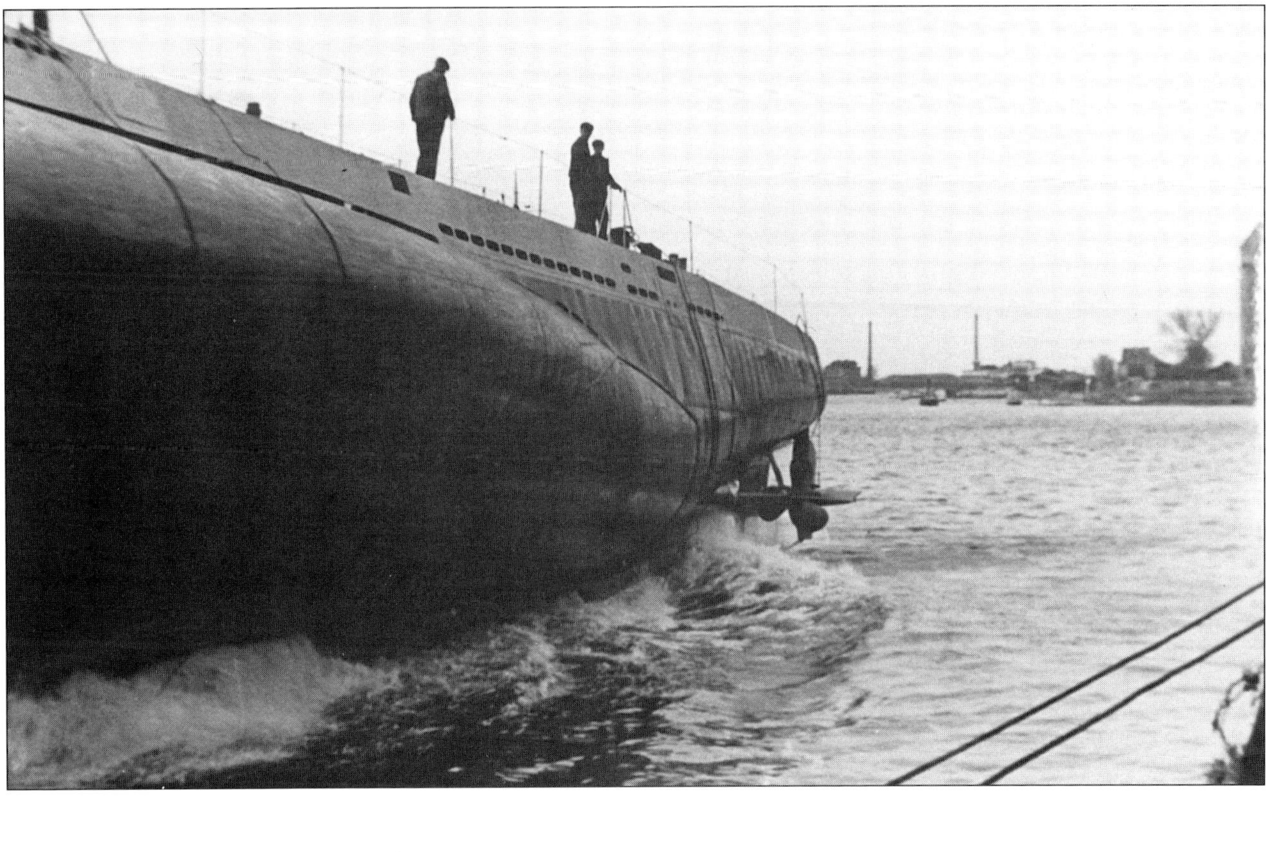

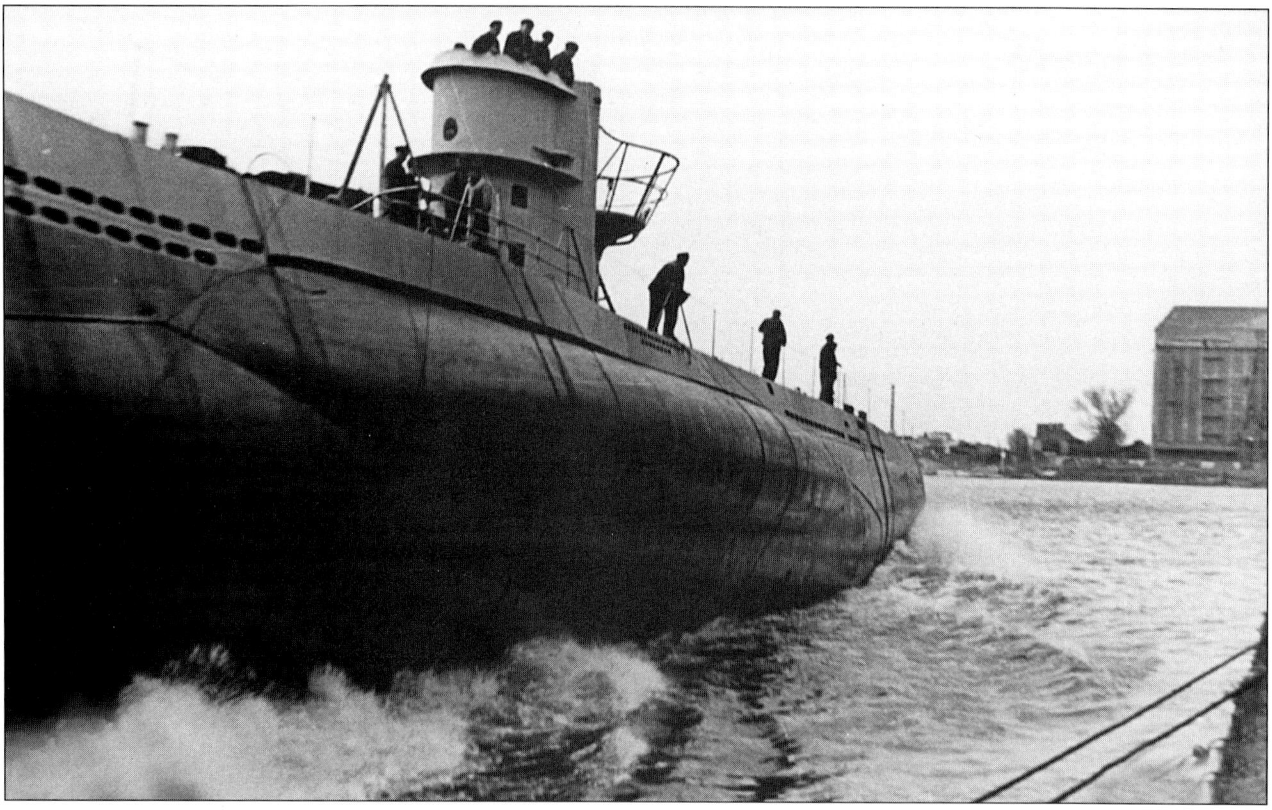

U442 settles on to the cold waters of the Baltic on 12 January 1942. The harsh preceding winter had made such launches impossible because the water was frozen to a depth of around 1 m.

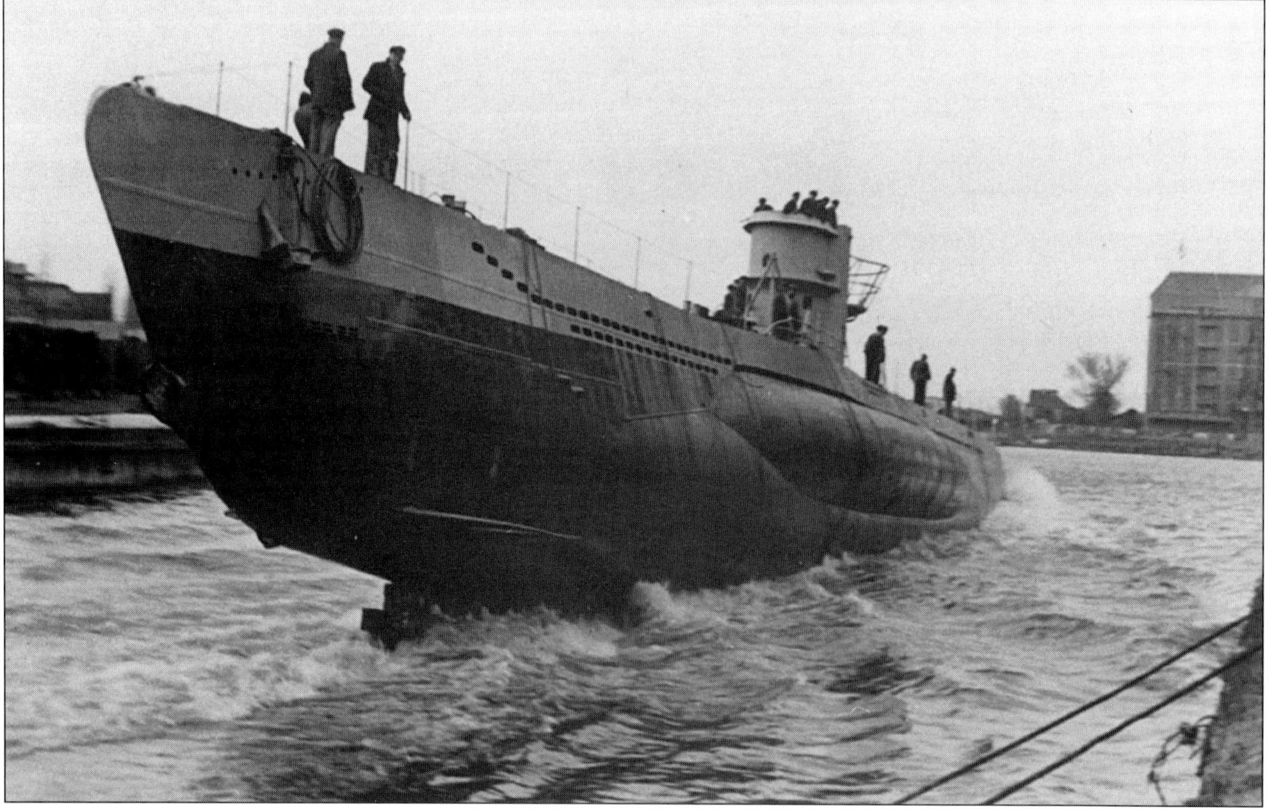

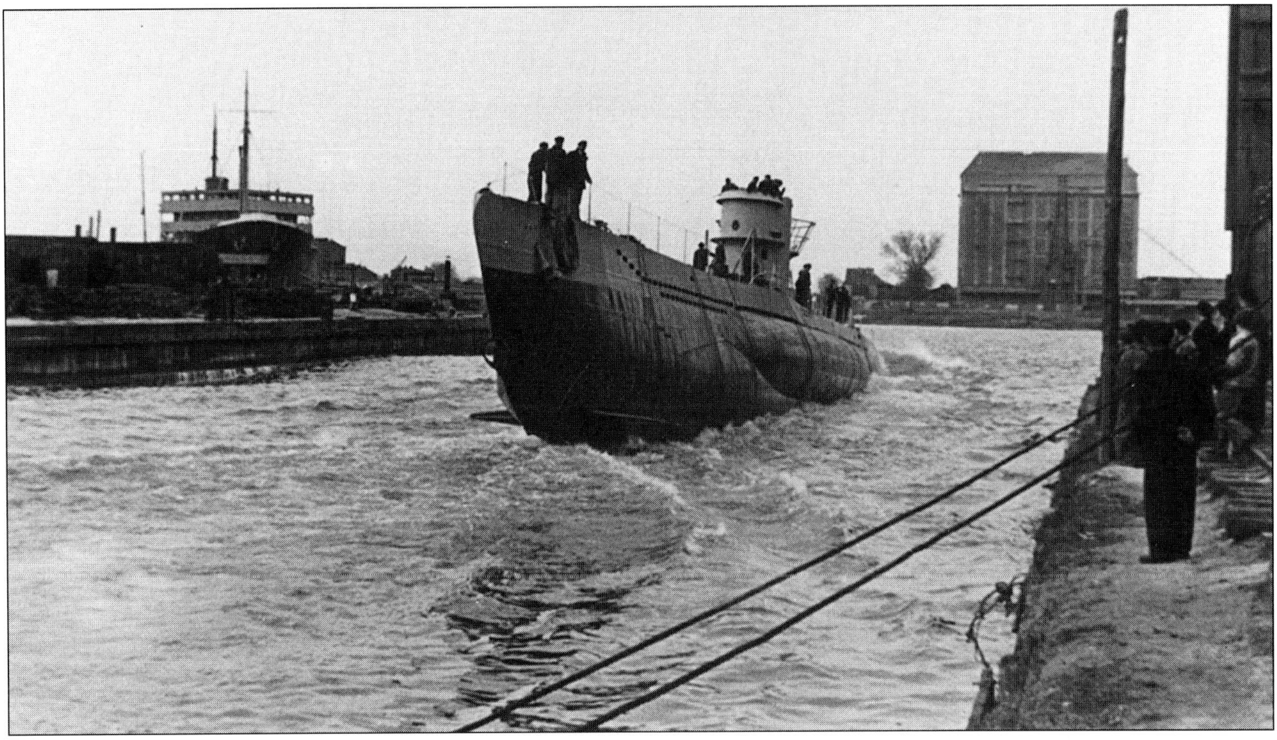

U442's launch is safely completed.

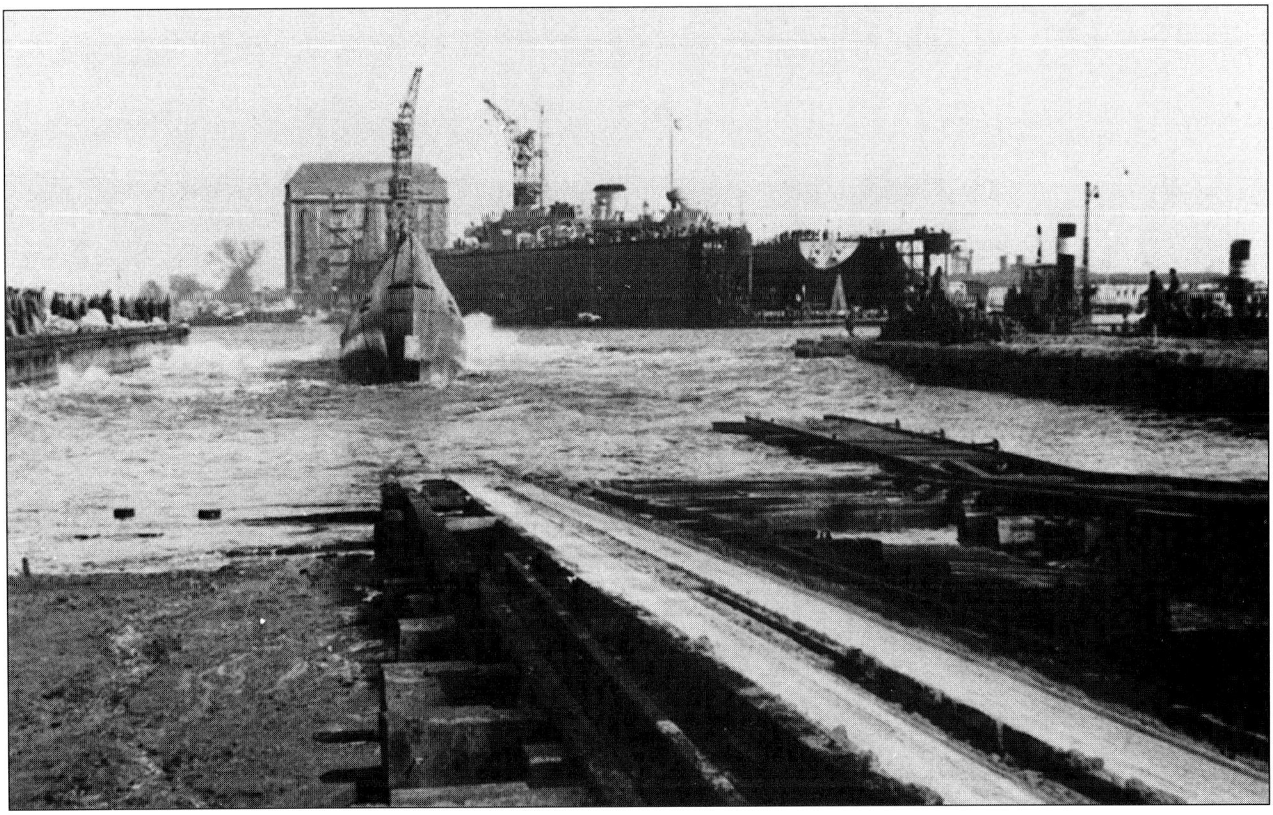

This photograph probably shows *U441*. Notice that although the building in the far distance appears to be identical to the one in the previous picture, the somewhat eroded quay seen in the earlier pictures seems to be further towards the right and there is a huge floating dry dock further out in the basin.

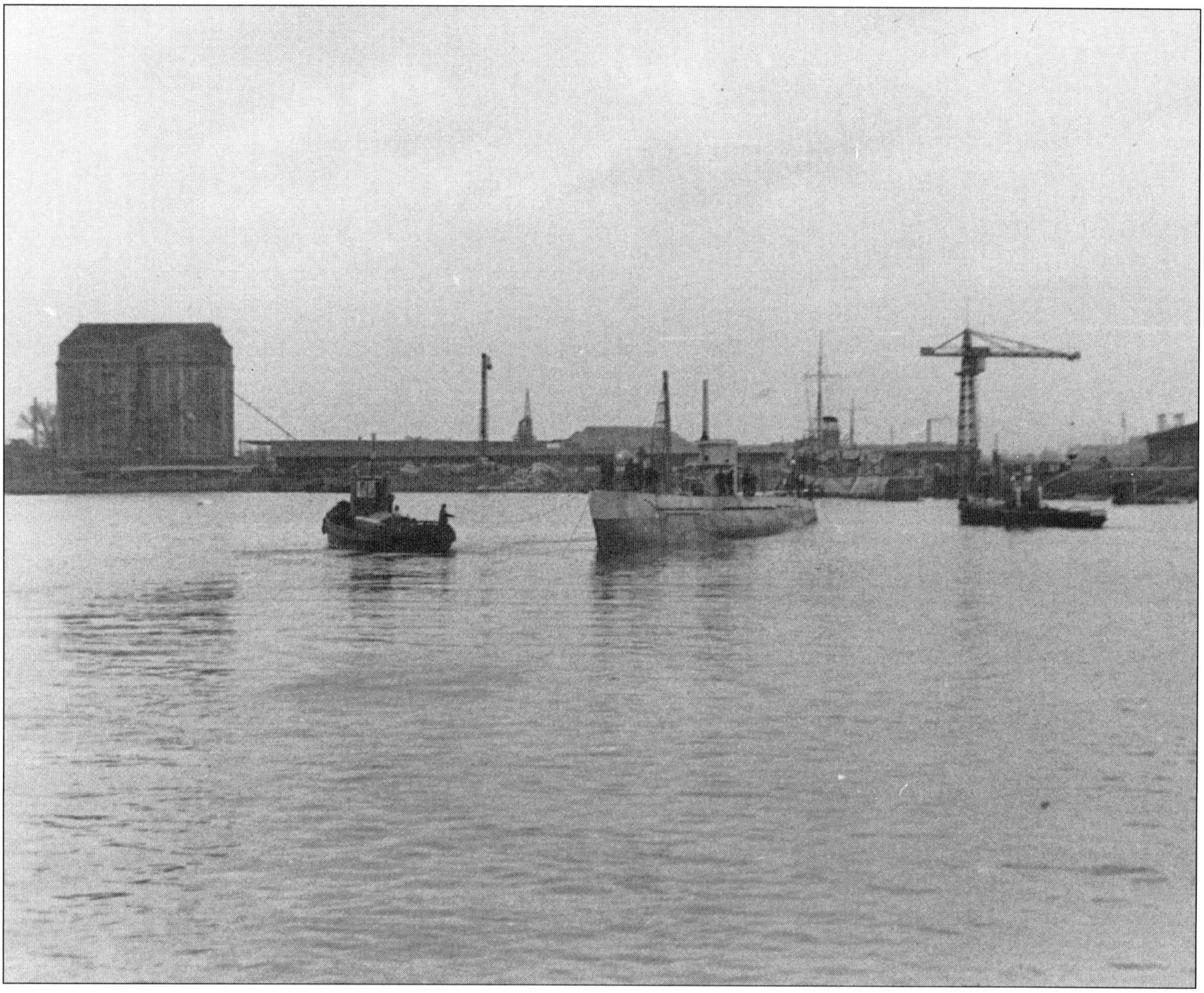

Having launched the boat, with everybody on board pleased that it did not sink, it was necessary for a tug to bring it back to the fitting-out quay. Some boats were launched without propellers and others without the conning tower fairing in place, but even those which were very nearly complete did not start their heavy machinery until some time after launching.

Most of the crew was assembled while the boat was still lying on the stocks so that they could get to know their machinery from the very beginning. Despite this technical training, many men had hardly any experience with submarines. They were acquainted with the main procedures of their trade at the U-boat School, but there it was very much a case of following lessons in classrooms for part of the day and then going to sea for a few hours to practise what had been learnt. Before the Second World War it was customary for warships from private yards to go through a thorough training and testing process before being handed over to the navy for commissioning. During the war, however, this practice had to be changed because the yards did not have the spare personnel for testing and the critical inspections were usually carried out by the still inexperienced crew.

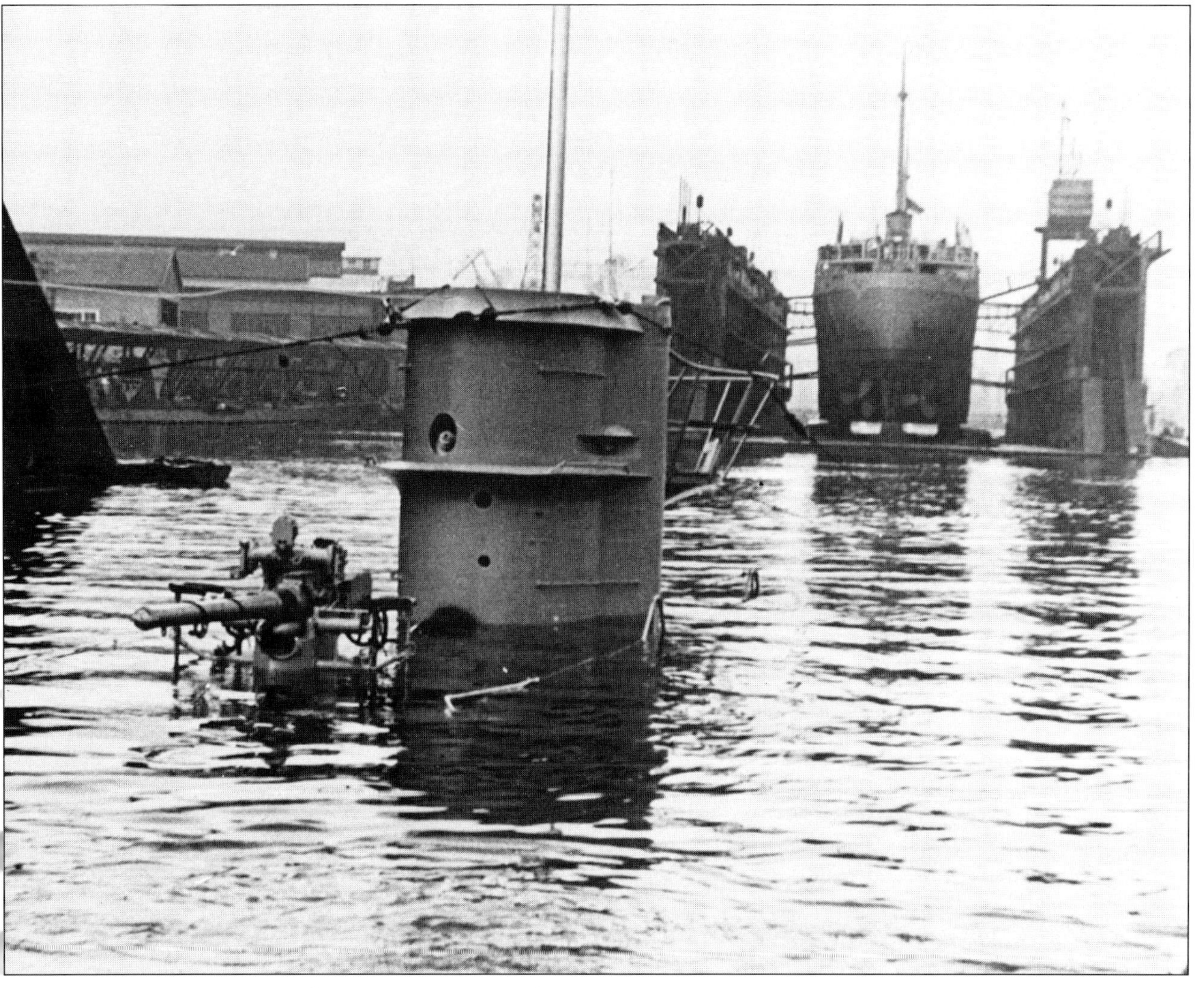

U441 conducting her first diving tests. The trick was to examine the entire diving and trimming systems in such shallow water that the crew could get out of a submerged boat if things did not go quite according to plan. The majority of Baltic shipyards had a deep pit excavated somewhere close to their shallow-water fitting-out bays for this purpose. Those in tidal waters, and that included Hamburg, waited for high tide.

In the background is a floating dry dock with a ship riding piggyback, well clear of the water. This entire contraption was anchored and could submerge the working platform, enabling ships to move in or out. Smaller vessels did this under their own steam, while bigger ones were assisted by tugs. The high-sided walls were necessary because not all ships had flat bottoms and would therefore have needed a good number of supports along both sides to prevent them toppling over once the hull was clear of the water.

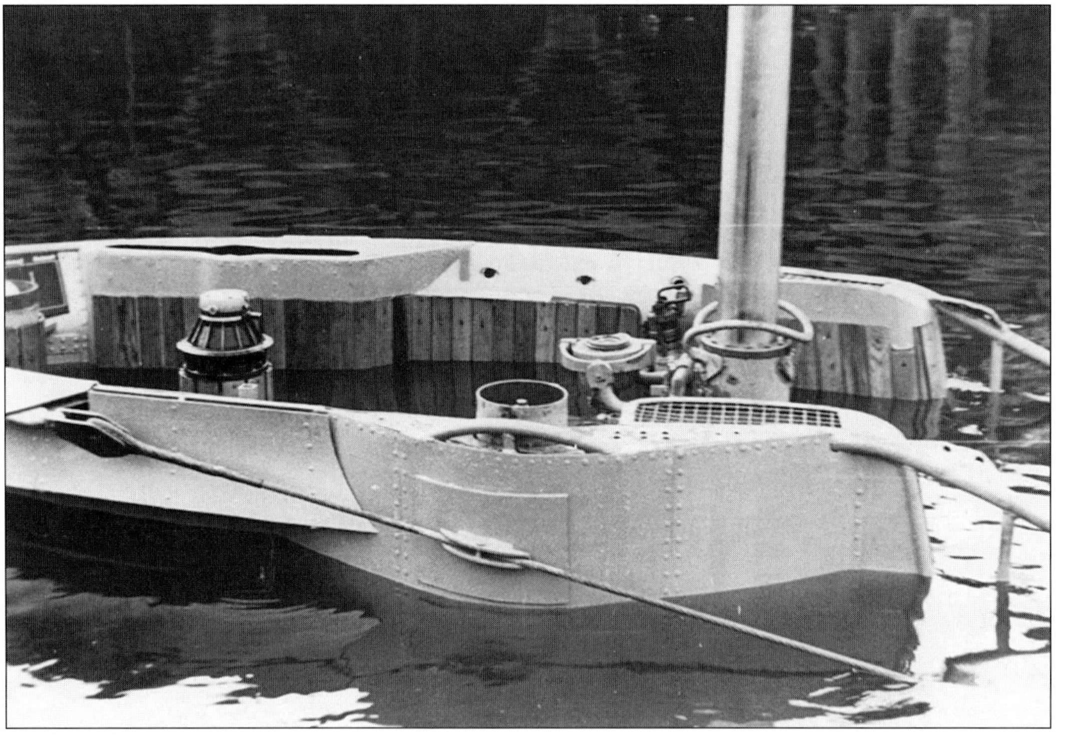

This close-up of the conning tower shows the long slot for the circular loop aerial of the radio direction finder in the far wall on the left. The support of the raised periscope has a magnetic sighting compass on its forward (left) edge. The low circular structure just forward of the air duct with a grid over the top is a periscopic rod aerial.

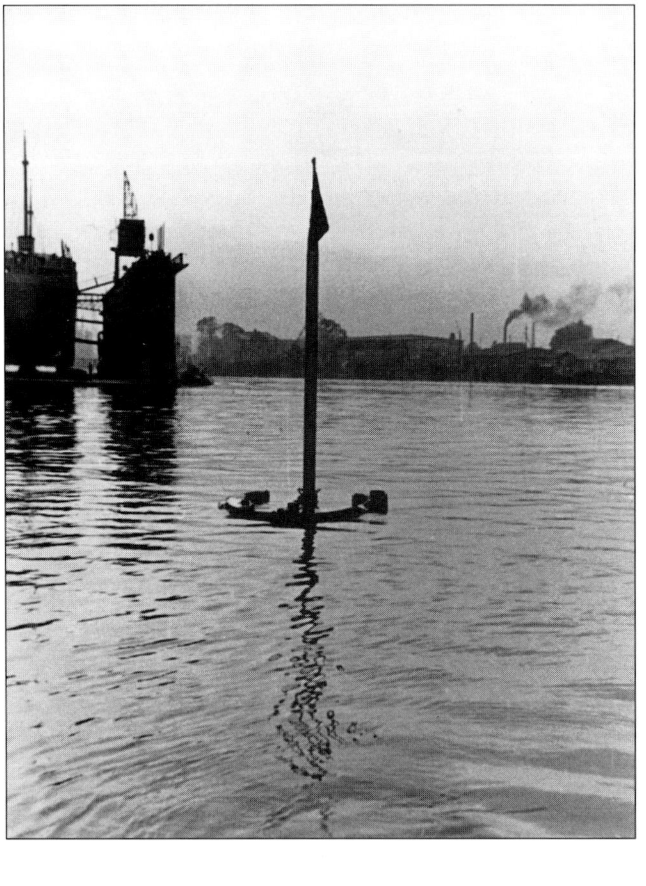

U441 with a red flag tied to the top of the periscope to mark the position of the submerged boat.

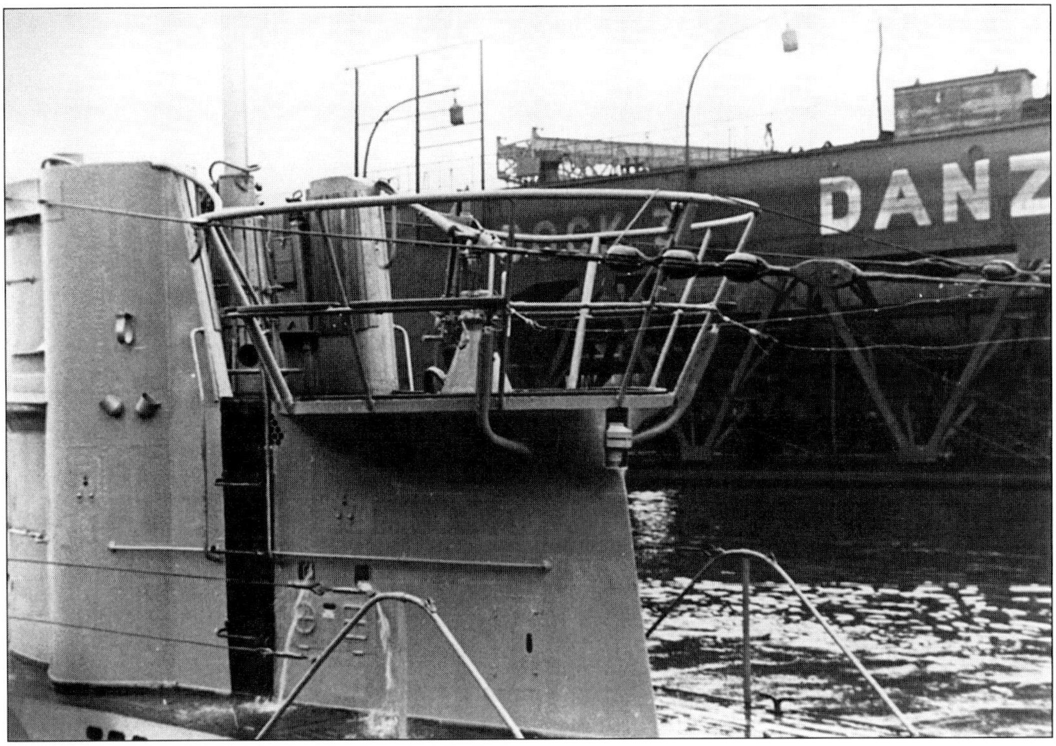

The inside core of the conning tower formed part of the pressure hull and accommodated the commander's control room for submerged attacks. This tiny compartment was covered with a streamlined fairing to also make it easier for men standing on the top. When diving, the space between the pressure hull and the outside fairing would fill with water – this can be seen flooding out of the just surfaced *U441*. Note that the anti-aircraft gun has not yet been fitted and in the background is the high wall of another floating dry dock. The circle and square with crosses welded on to the side are part of the boat's system for marking the locations of numerous filler caps for fuel, oil, water, etc.

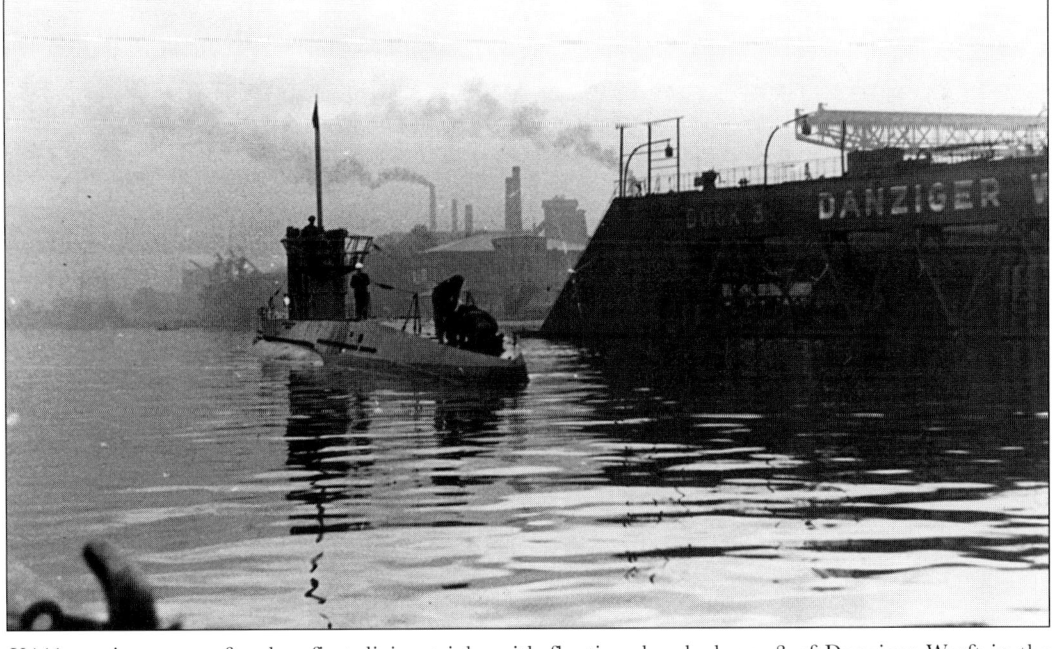

U441 moving away after her first diving trials, with floating dry dock no. 3 of Danziger Werft in the background. There were two major submarine yards in Danzig – Schichau Works and Danziger Werft – that shared some facilities for the building of U-boats.

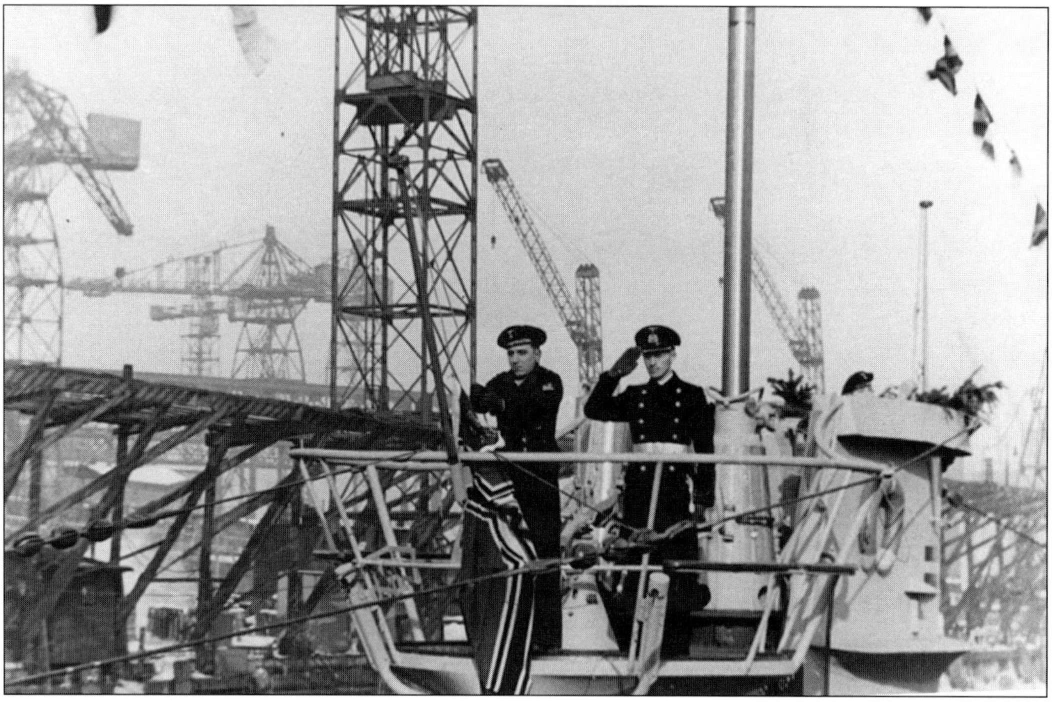

Hoisting the national ensign during the commissioning ceremony for *U441*, 21 February 1942. The tactical mark just visible on the side of the tower confirms that this is not *U442*. The myriad cranes in the background add an interesting dimension to this cold, but sunny February day. After it was established that the machinery inside a submarine was correctly installed and functioning properly, the boat would be handed over to the Kriegsmarine. Very often this was a far more ceremonial occasion than the launch. The crew usually assembled on deck while the national ensign was hoisted for the first time. This was followed by celebrations which required considerable irrigation with beer and wine. Dockyard workers, friends, members of the crew's families and survivors from the boat's First World War predecessor were often invited to such occasions.

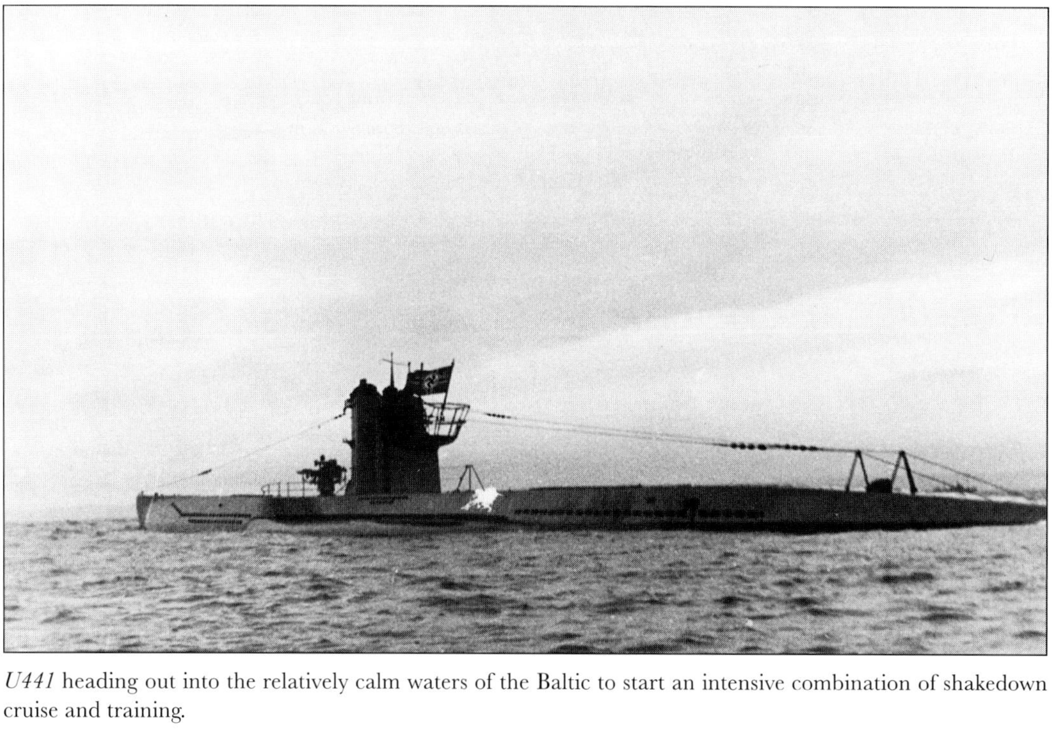

U441 heading out into the relatively calm waters of the Baltic to start an intensive combination of shakedown cruise and training.

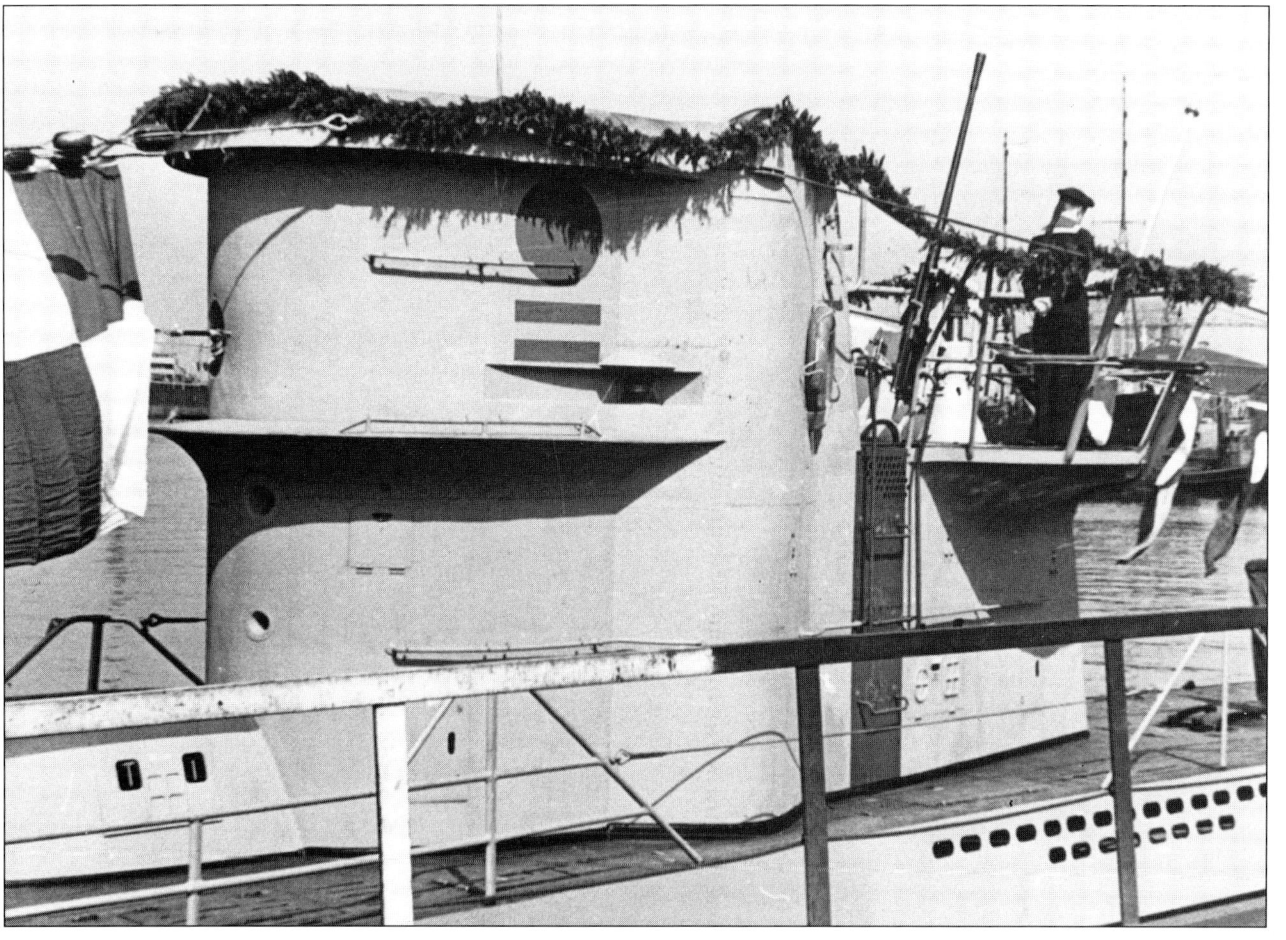

On 9 May 1942, *U444* was commissioned by OL Albert Langfeld with the tactical mark on the side of the conning tower. This mark served as identification during trials and training and the same symbol was reused by a number of boats. It would appear that these marks first appeared around 1940. Of course, they were unnecessary during the pre-war years because then U-boats had their numbers painted on both sides of the conning tower. Tactical marks for Type VII U-boats consisted originally of just four symbols – a circle, square, triangle or two small triangles, white in colour if the boats had been built by Germania Works and black for Deutsche Werke in Kiel. As more shipyards were drawn into U-boat construction a variety of bars were added to distinguish boats from different firms. Type IX boats used diamonds, hearts, clubs and spades from playing cards as a means of identification and the small coastal boats of Type II used another totally different set of symbols. The historian Karl Grützemacher classified the boats that used each tactical mark and these details can be found in Georg Högel's excellent book about U-boat insignia, *Embleme Wappen Malings deutscher U-boote 1939–1945* (Koehlers, Herford, 1987).

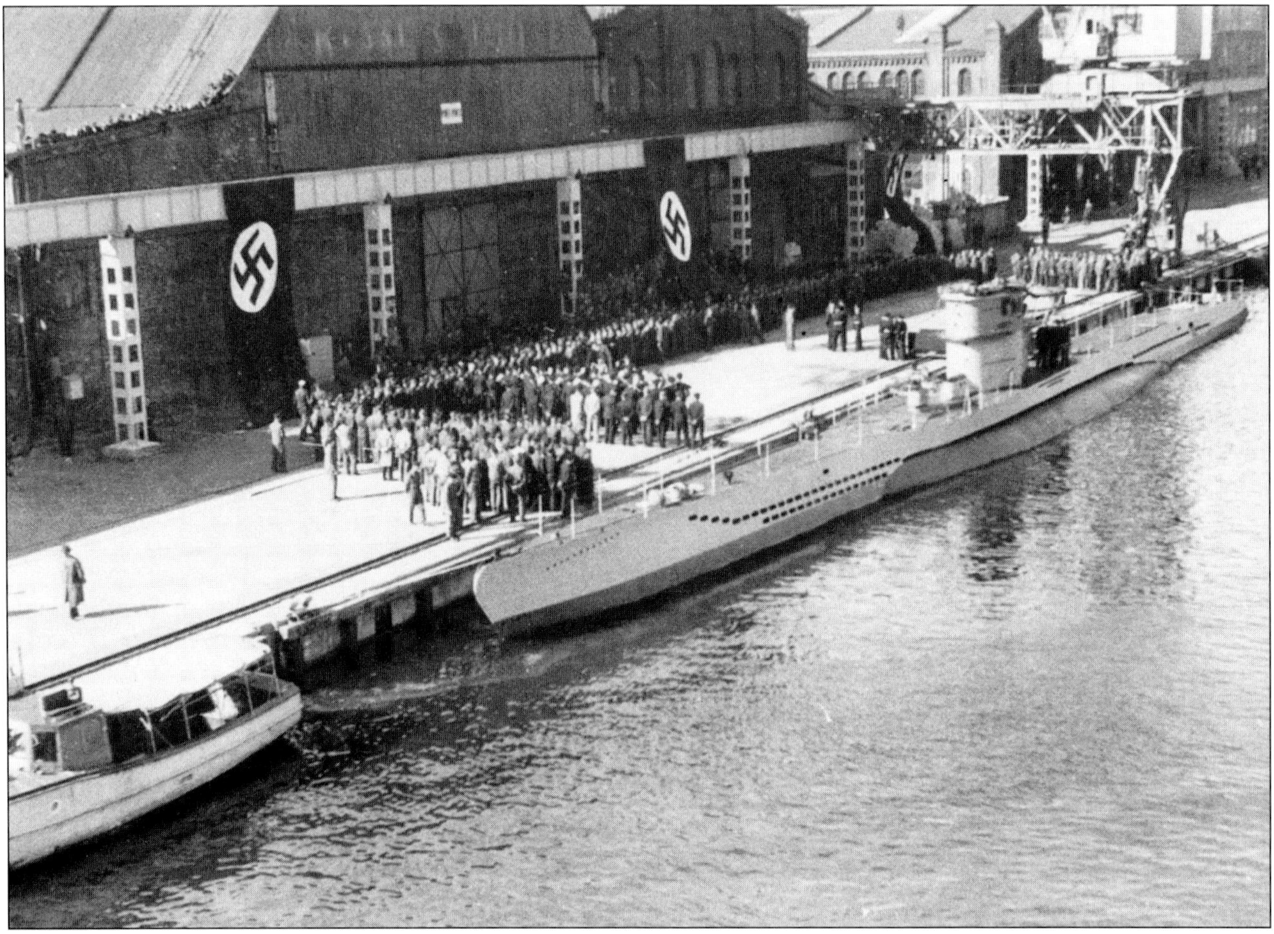

Danziger Werft on 17 September 1941 with KK Rolf-Heinrich Hopman commissioning *U405*. Hopman had already seen bitter action in the destroyer *Z19* and he had participated in the fighting around Narvik during the invasion of Norway. The senior rating in the bow torpedo room was Otto Giese, who had earlier been the Second Officer of the blockade breaker *Anneliese Essberger* and has taken a number of the photographs in this book. Although in charge of the bow torpedo room, he was not the most senior man there. The torpedo mechanic also had a bunk in those cramped quarters. He was the only non-commissioned officer to be accommodated with lower ranks so that he was close to his place of work.

The red flags with white circle and black swastika were the civilian version of the national ensign and were also flown aboard warships before they were commissioned. In this case they are hanging from a gantry which runs along the entire waterfront, allowing the crane in the background to travel the full length. This commissioning ceremony appears to be a somewhat low-key function compared to celebrations put on by some other crews.

Keen observers will notice that the boat is made fast to a permanently fixed quay, without a floating pontoon for accommodating tidal changes. The reason for this is that there is no tide in the Baltic, only a fluctuation in water levels of a metre or so caused mainly by winds blowing on or off shore.

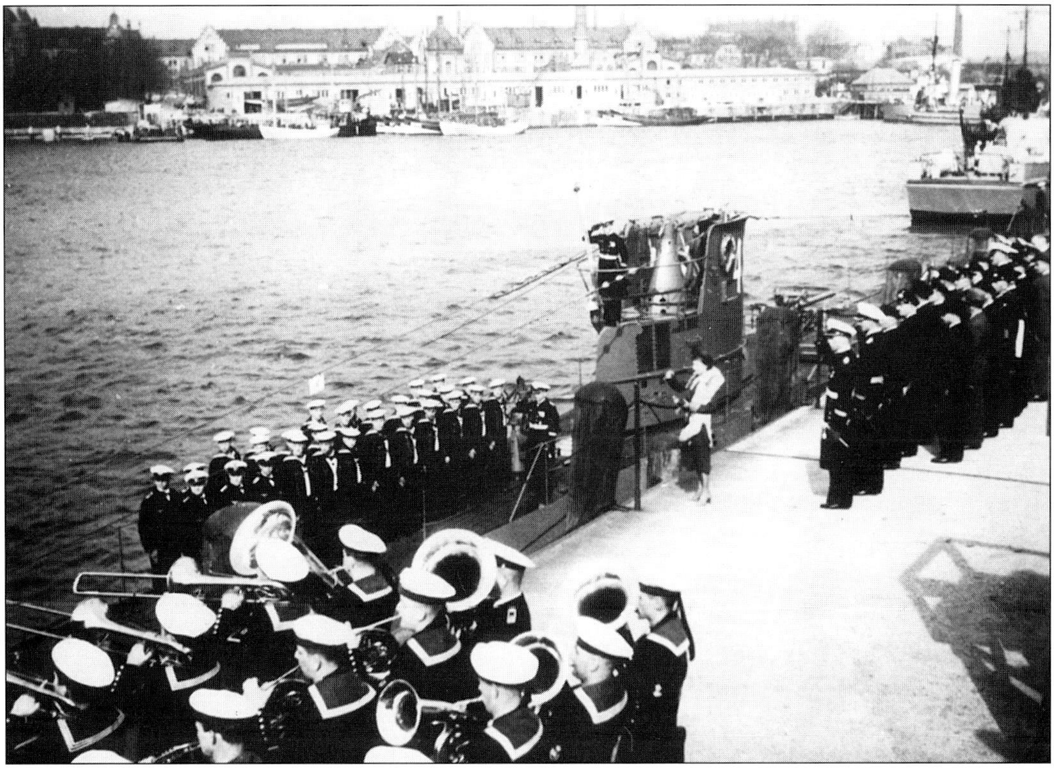

Commissioning *U48* on 22 April 1939 by KL Herbert Schultze in Kiel, complete with band, a vast number of visitors, onlookers and veterans from the First World War. This was a Type VIIB, which received only slight modification from its forerunner the Type VIIA. The most noticeable of these changes was the placing of an above-water torpedo tube lower down to eject between two rudders. Two of the main reasons for this were that after the modification the outside doors were less likely to be damaged by floating ice and could be reloaded from the inside, rather than from the upper deck on the outside.

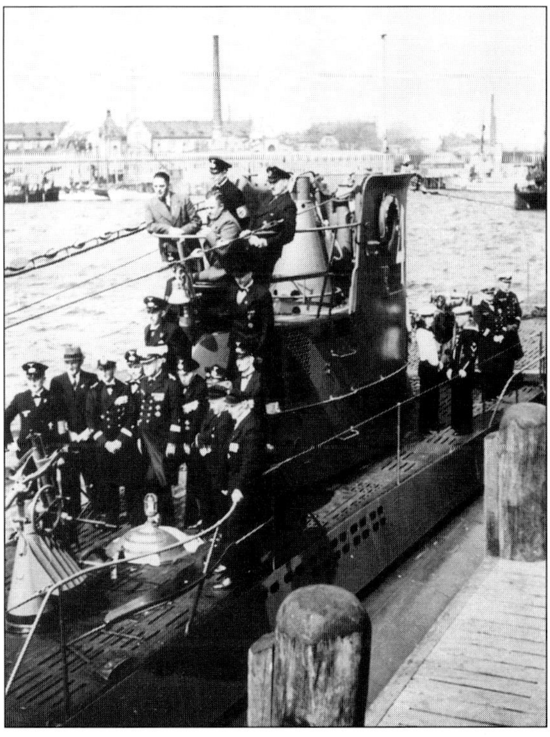

The proceedings for *U48* were followed by a semi-official photo-call to record the unusual event of men wearing their best formal uniforms. Note that the anti-aircraft gun, which has not yet been fitted to its mount (extreme left), was situated on the upper deck and not on the gun platform at the rear of the conning tower. Clearly *U48* appeared at a time when the German Navy had not yet given aircraft a great deal of thought. The device with a light bulb on the top by the men's feet is an emergency rescue buoy which could be released from the inside of the boat and remained connected to it by a stout cable. Tactical marks, which were mentioned earlier, were not yet necessary because pre-war boats had their numbers painted on the conning towers, as can be seen here.

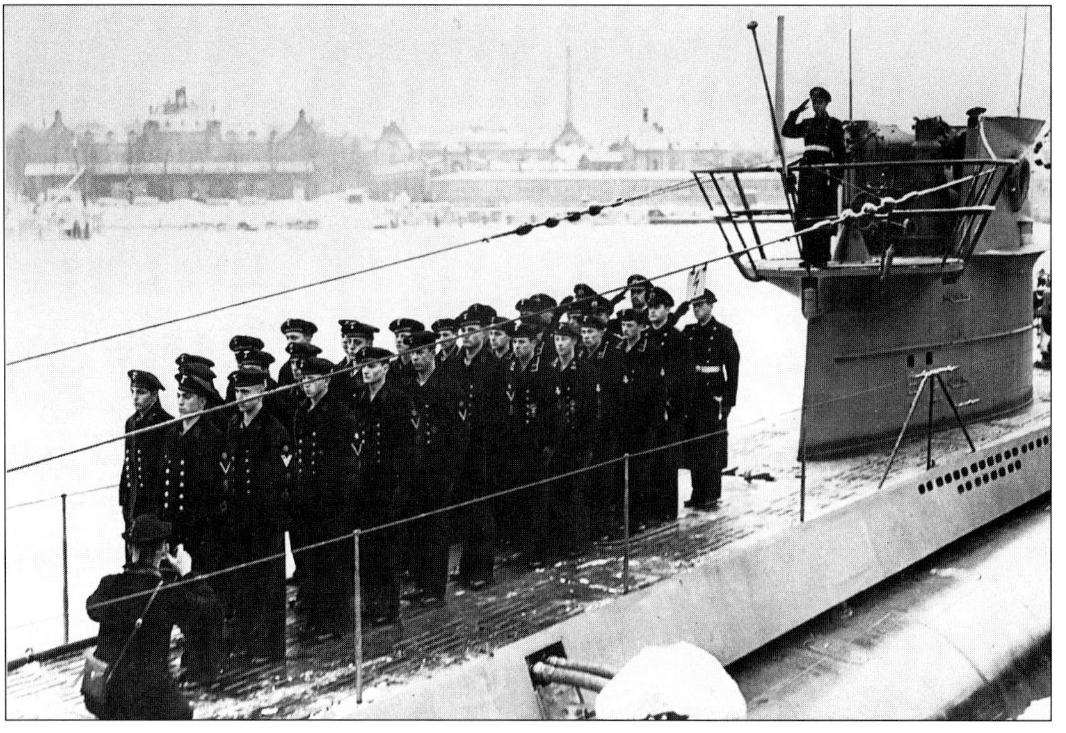

This probably shows *U201* being commissioned by KL Adalbert Schnee on 25 January 1941, not a good time of year for submarine activities because the cold surroundings added to the discomforts of living inside a submarine. It is interesting to note that this boat was commissioned in almost exactly the same location as *U48* (*see* p. 23). The pipes running into the boat by the men's feet provided electricity so that batteries could be charged without running the boat's own diesel engines. Also notice the yellow plate with lightning flash hanging from the jumping wire. This was to warn the unwary that both wires could be charged with a considerable current, enough to throw a man into the water. Obviously this was usually switched off when men worked on the upper deck because in rough weather the cables also served as an anchor for safety harnesses. The wire railings along the edge of the deck were usually removed once the boat went to sea. Notice that the petty officers towards the back are wearing the new type of pea jacket with the gold braid around the edge of the collar. This elaborate addition was introduced towards the beginning of the war.

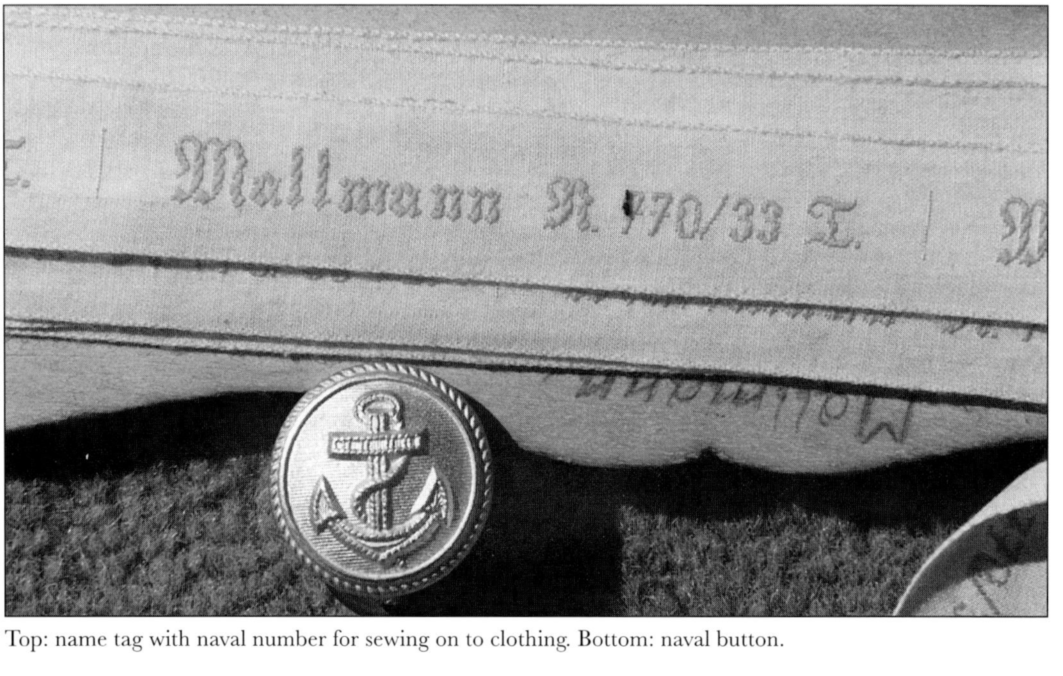

Top: name tag with naval number for sewing on to clothing. Bottom: naval button.

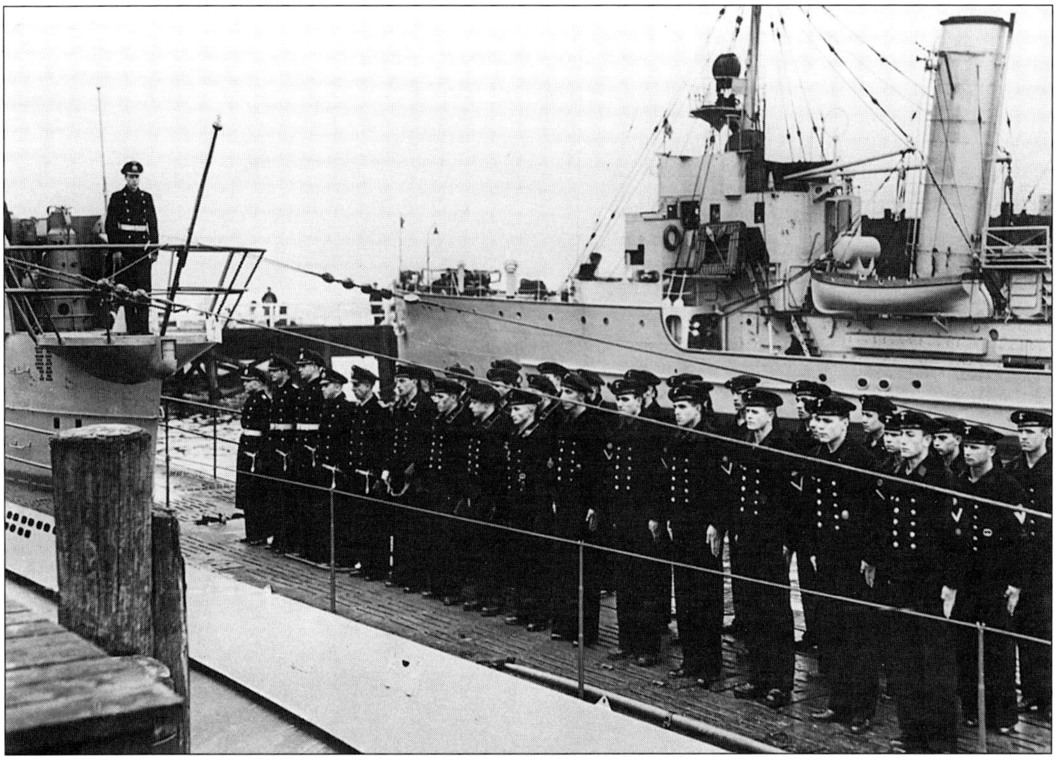

It is quite likely that this shows the commissioning of *U101* by KL Fritz Frauenheim on 11 March 1940 at the Blücher Pier in Kiel. Although the figure standing on the wintergarten does not look like the commander, it is possible that he has not yet come on board. The man second from the right is wearing a U-boat badge which indicates that this is not an entirely fresh crew. In the background is an M-class minesweeper. The portholes suggest it could be *M135*, which also served as submarine tender *Hela*.

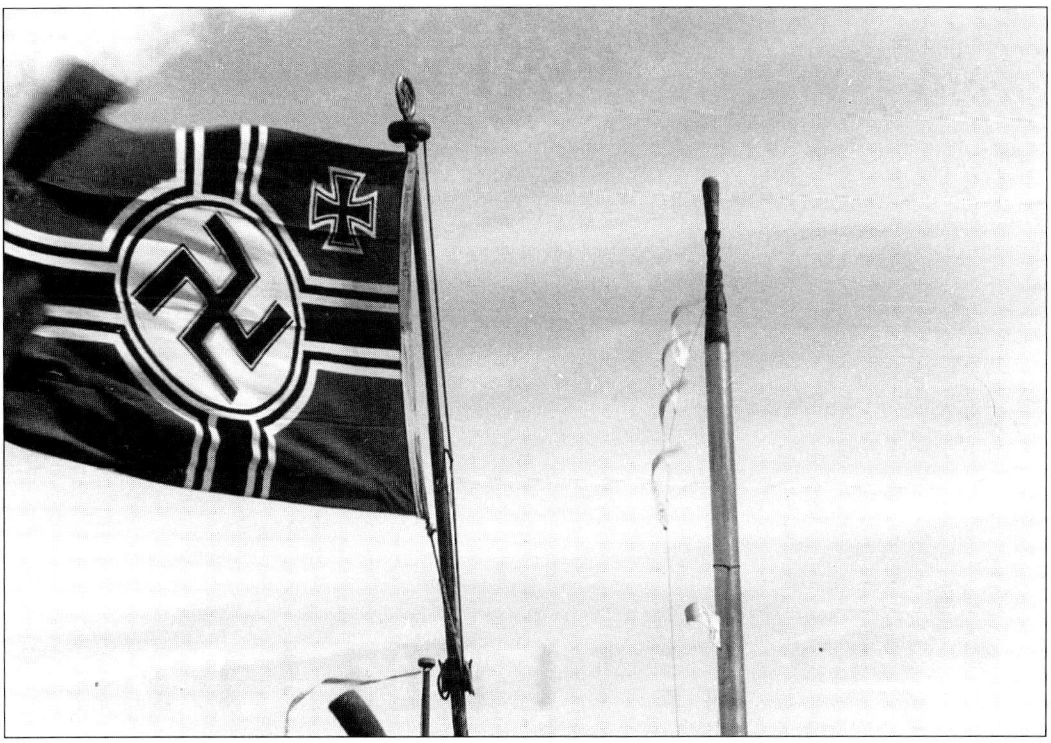

The reverse of the naval ensign.

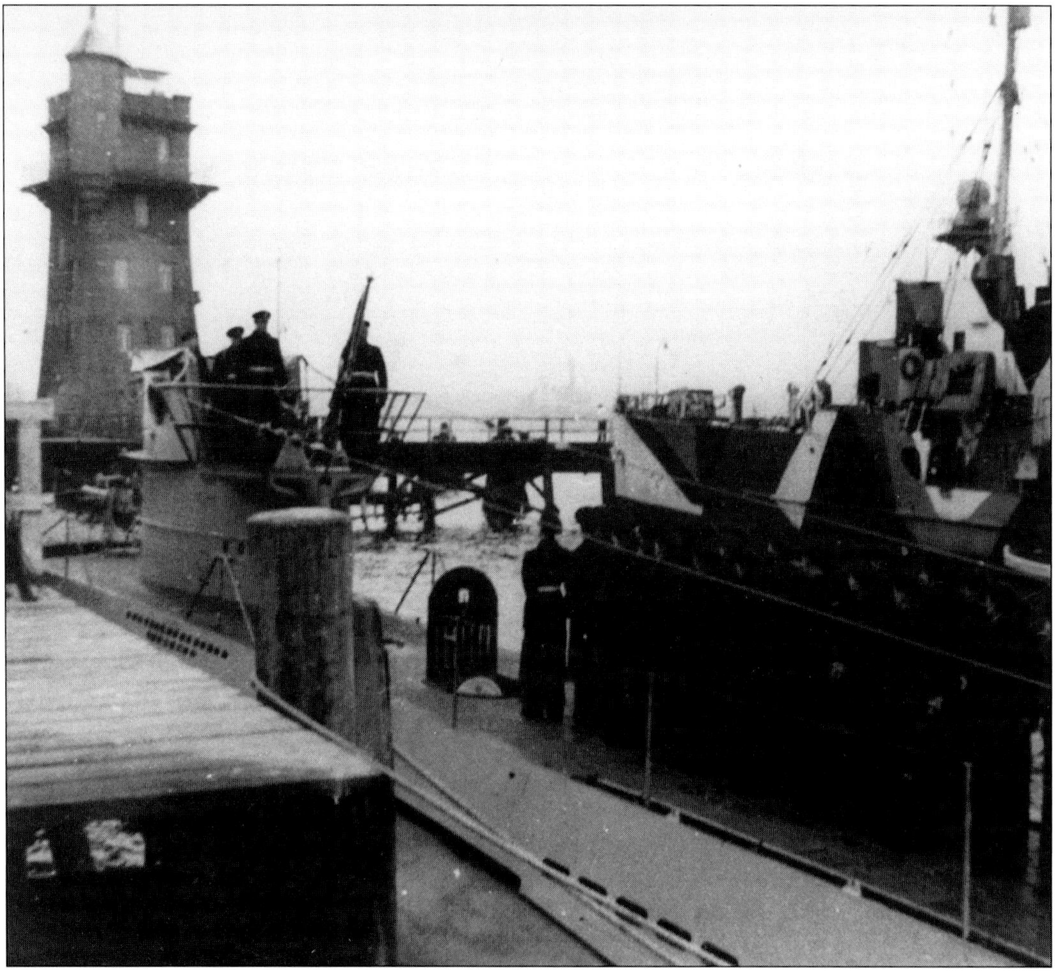

This somewhat blurred vision of almost the same scene as that on p. 25 shows the commissioning of *U69* – the first Type VIIC boat – by KL Jost Metzler on 2 November 1940. The wooden bollard in the foreground suggests that the photographers for both pictures must have stood in almost the same spot, but this view also includes the old signal tower which used to stand by the Blücher Pier until it was demolished because of excessive old age and the fact that modern technology had made it redundant. It could well be that the ship in the background is the tender *Hela* just as it was in the image of *U48*'s commissioning; if it is not it must be of a similar class. These two photographs demonstrate the effectiveness of disruptive camouflage. Just try distinguishing the details in the two pictures and then imagine yourself as a submarine commander who got only a few seconds glimpse before having to decide what the vessel was and what action he should take. The object with the round top protruding above the level of the deck between the men and conning tower is the covering over the hatch leading down to the galley.

The Blücher Pier has always been the traditional mooring for the sail-training ship *Gorch Fock.* Yet recently this long-standing tradition seems to have been broken and the modern sail-training ship with this name has been banished to the naval dockyard further away from public view.

Commanders Adalbert Schnee, Fritz Frauennheim and Jost Metzler became Knights of the Iron Cross. Indeed, Schnee was awarded the medal twice, receiving the Oak Leaves to the Knight's Cross in July 1942, almost one year after he got the first award. He also had the remarkable distinction of being on duty in a U-boat on both the day the war started and the day it ended. In September 1939 he was IWO of the small coastal boat *U23* and in May 1945 he commanded *U2511*, one of the new, large electro Type XXI boats. On 8 January 1981, as Chairman of the German U-boat Association, he headed the procession at Karl Dönitz's funeral by carrying a cushion holding the Grand Admiral's medals. Jost Metzler was also lucky enough to survive the war. Before volunteering for U-boat service, he held the prestigious position of First Officer of the state yacht, *Aviso Grille.* At the beginning of the war *Grille* participated in the unglamorous task of laying mines in the North Sea. Metzler started his specialized U-boat training in April 1940, just seven months before taking command of *U69.*

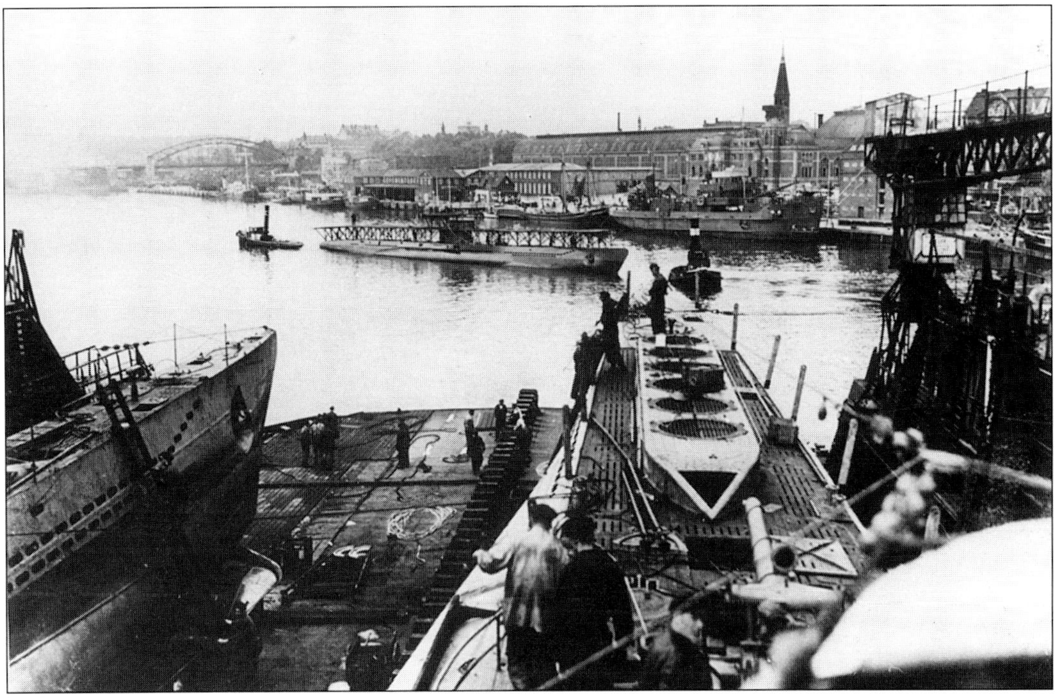

Another incomplete boat being manoeuvred by tugs in front of the Germania Works in Kiel. This photograph was taken from inside a floating dry dock and the famous glass house covering the slipways was situated to the left, which suggests that the boat might have just been launched. The metal arch in the background is a bridge and the railway station can be seen just above the boat in the water. The untidy foreground is also of special interest because it shows the mineshafts on the bows of a Type XB minelayer. Only eight of this large type were commissioned, making it quite a rare sight in photographs. This was the only U-boat type with a raised section containing the vertical mineshafts on the bows.

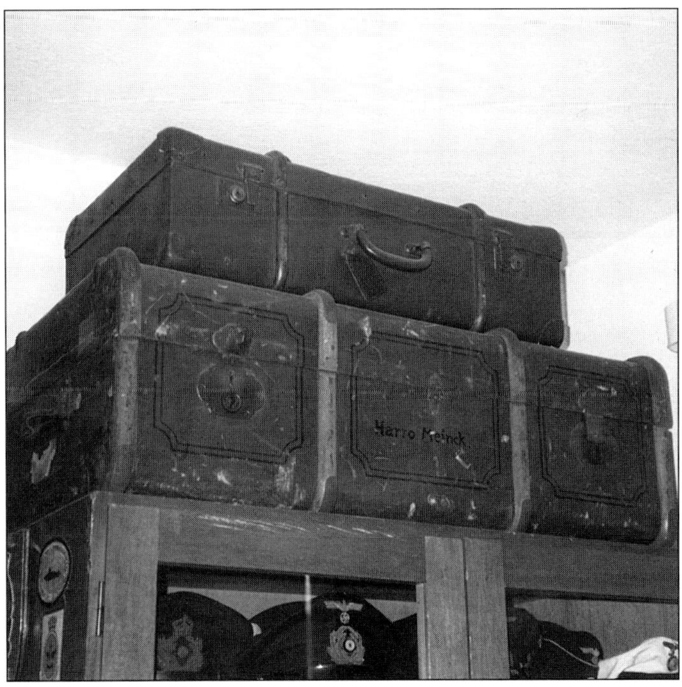

Photographs have been published of men carrying suitcases, patiently queuing to enter their new U-boat. It is difficult to guess who conceived such pieces of propaganda but it does not match reality. First, this trunk and suitcase on top of a uniform cabinet inside the U-Boot-Archiv never got into a U-boat because they would never have fitted through the hatches. Moreover, U-boat men would not have had the space to bring so many personal belongings. In port men usually lived in reasonably comfortable accommodation and once they went to sea, their personal belongings, as well as spare uniforms, were stored by the U-boat flotillas' administrative network. Usually the system was efficient enough for the luggage to catch up with men when they moved bases.

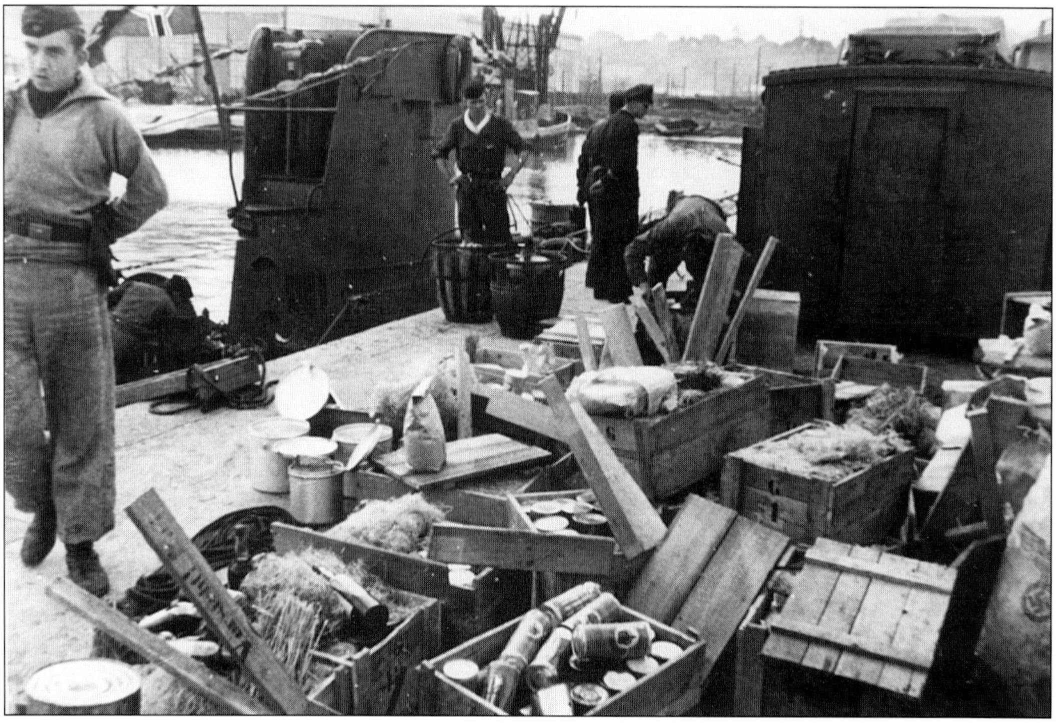

Getting stores into U-boats was a major undertaking. Many crates, as shown here, were too large for the hatches which meant they had to be unpacked on the quay. What was more, food had to be stored in the reverse order to that in which it was going to be consumed and neat arrangements for placing similar tins in the same place did not work. Some of the supplies were so inaccessible that they could not be reached until the layers above them had been removed. This caused some hardship in boats where food had been stored in the wrong order and men found themselves temporarily living on a monotonous diet until the more interesting food could be reached. The boat here appears to be *U24* in Pillau.

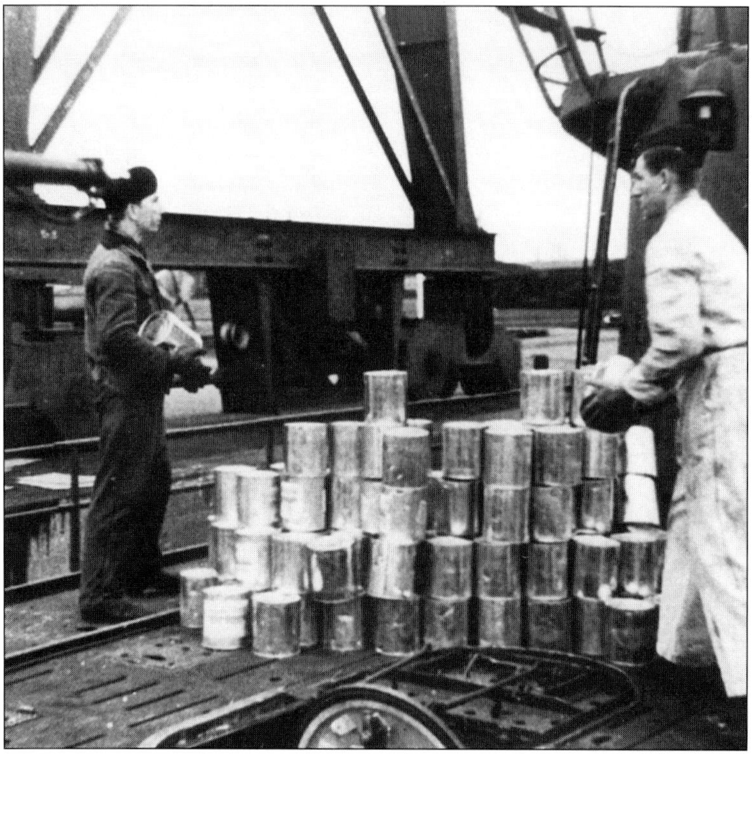

Moving stores below was not an easy matter either. The hatches were in the ceiling and a vertical ladder ran down from them. Men often arranged themselves as a chain-gang. Here tins are being loaded into *U172*.

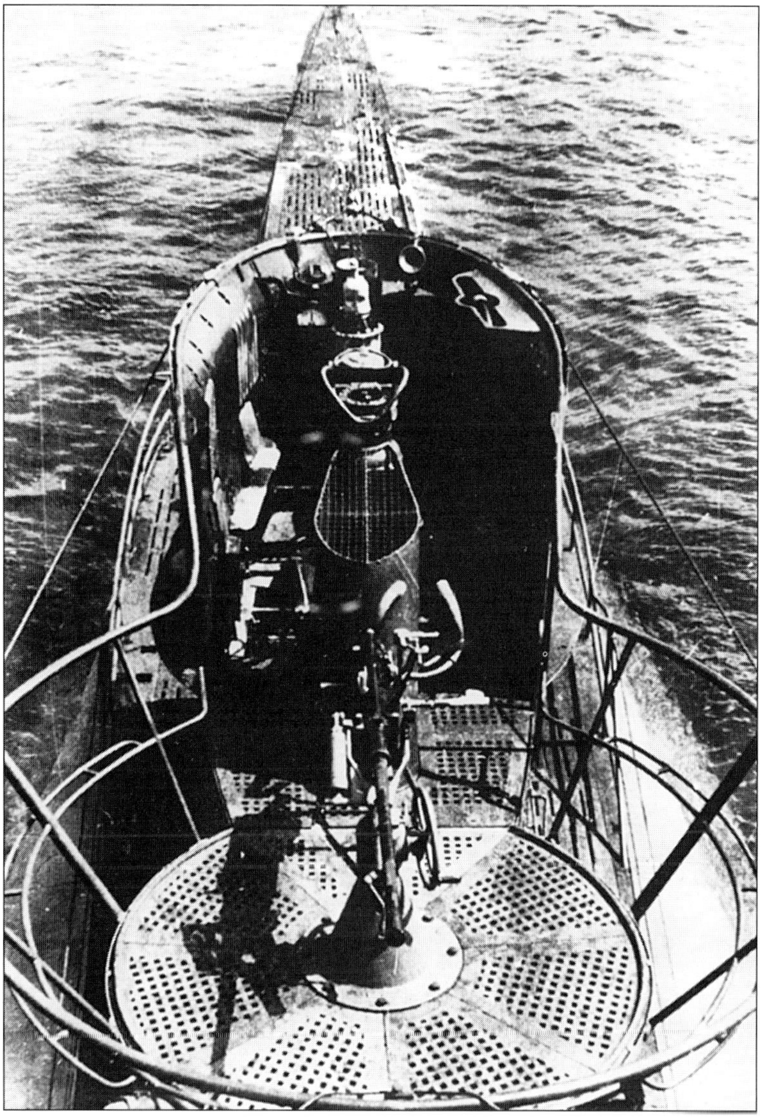

The first step for the majority of boats after being commissioned and loaded with stores was to receive a full test from the UAK (Unterseebootsabnahmekommando – Submarine Acceptance Command). Anyone confused by the long word must avoid the Marinenachrichtenhelferinnenausbildungsabteilung (School for training female communication assistants). Such long words were partly offset by the U-boat commander Hans Ey, whose family name consisted of just two letters and Dietrich Epp with three.

One of the first procedures, without which a submarine could not put to sea, was testing the trimming or balancing system and the valves on the diving tanks. The trick was to lower the boat gently until it was fully submerged and then adjust the displacement so that it would go neither up nor down. But this state of perfection was almost impossible to achieve, so U-boats were trimmed to be slightly heavy in order to sink very slowly. Correct depth was then maintained using the hydroplanes which functioned similarly to aircraft elevators. Of course, the desired depth could only maintained as long as there was sufficient power in the batteries to turn the propellers and push them through the water.

This is *U86* under KL Walter Schug during the summer of 1941 with an early type of conning tower layout. Note the thin walls with a slot for the circular radio direction finder aerial towards the right. Just forward of this is a speaking tube connecting the bridge with the helmsman down in the central control room. The torpedo aimer – furthest away from the camera – and periscope support with magnetic sighting compass can be seen just forward of the grid over the air duct. The gun on the platform is a 20mm.

U86, one of the earlier Type VIIBs, was launched on 16 May 1941 at the small Flender Works in Lübeck, some eight months after the first Type VIIC (*U69*) had been launched at the bigger, faster Germania Werft in Kiel.

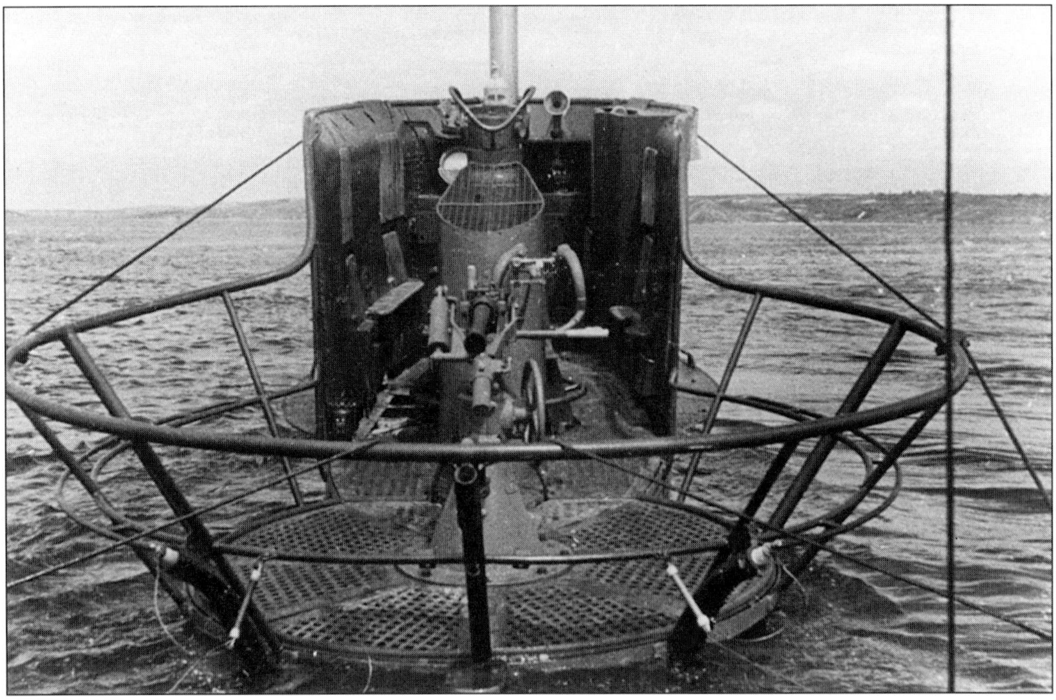

It would be rather interesting to know how the following sequence of images of *U86* was photographed. The camera is obviously over the submerged hull but there does not seem to be a great depth of water for a substantial boat to float on. Some blurred shots later in this sequence show the submarine moving at considerable speed. The air duct, gun and speaking tube can be seen clearly and some of the engine repeater dials have also come into view.

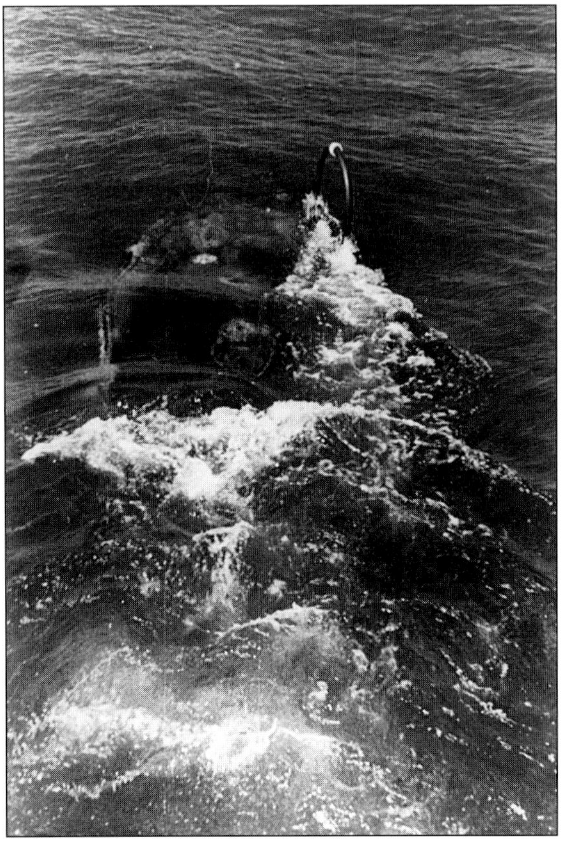

U86 almost fully submerged. The wake would suggest it is moving slowly though the clear Baltic waters. The circular loop of the radio direction finder is still above the surface. Is it being tested or is it there for effect? It certainly was not designed to be used from partly submerged boats.

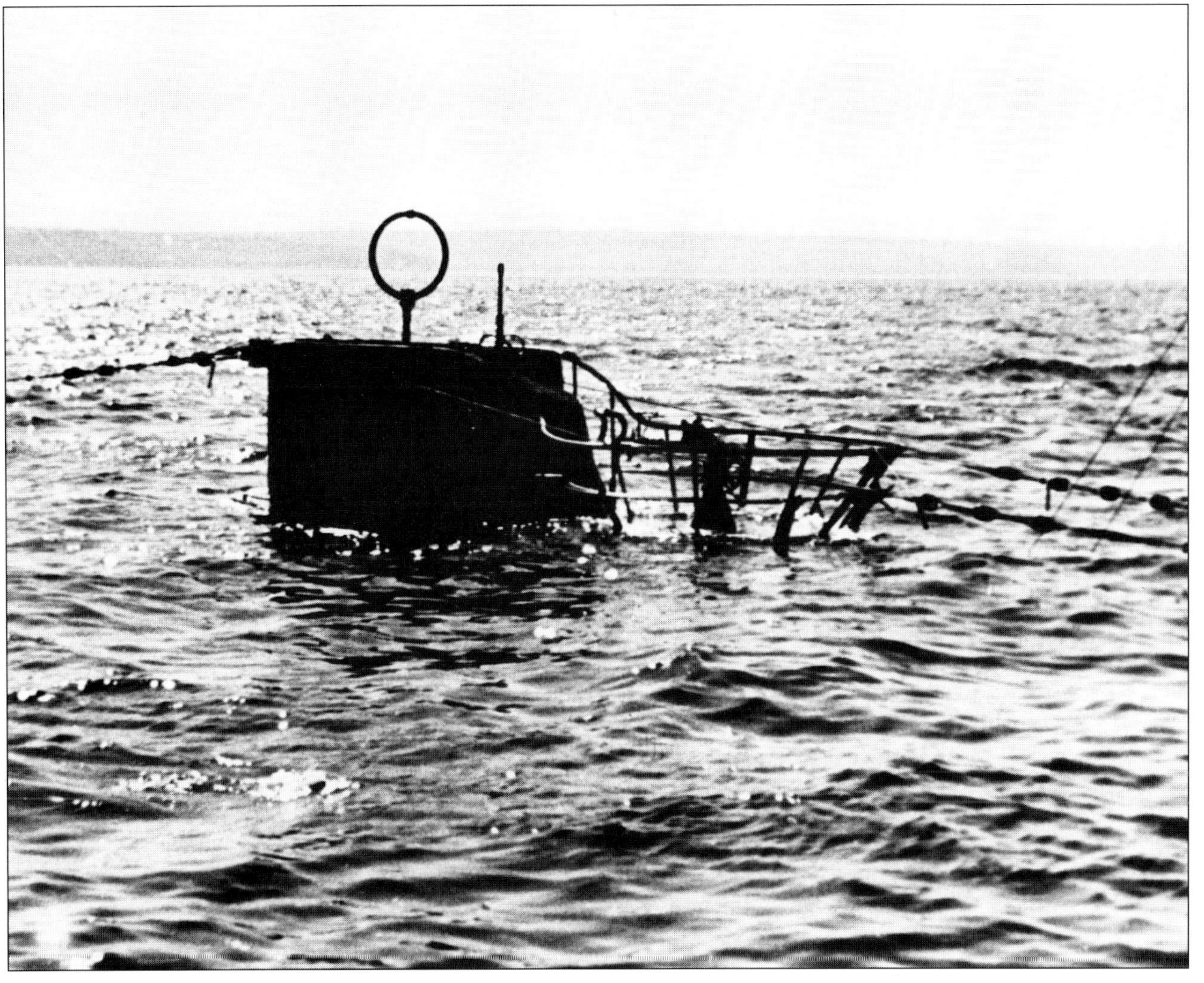

U86 has reappeared and almost revealed the secret of how the photographer got so close to a submerged submarine. Two wires on the right suggest a mast had been rigged for the purpose of filming the boat proceeding underwater. Anyone familiar with the excellent moving film footage shot during the war might recognise this sequence and realise it shows no diving trial but is in fact an attempt to capture some exciting motion on celluloid.

The author and war correspondent, Jochen Brennecke, took some remarkable photographs showing a submerged submarine moving through the water. In 1942, some of these won a major competition and were named 'Best Photographs of the Year'. It could well be that this image shows the camera rig used to obtain those unusual shots.

The circular radio direction finder can be seen. This was a pressure and water resistant aerial for determining the direction of radio signals and helped U-boats home in on beacons. Although it is not quite clear in this picture, *U86* chose quite a dirty part of the sea for this filming attempt because a mass of seaweed has been left hanging from wires and railings.

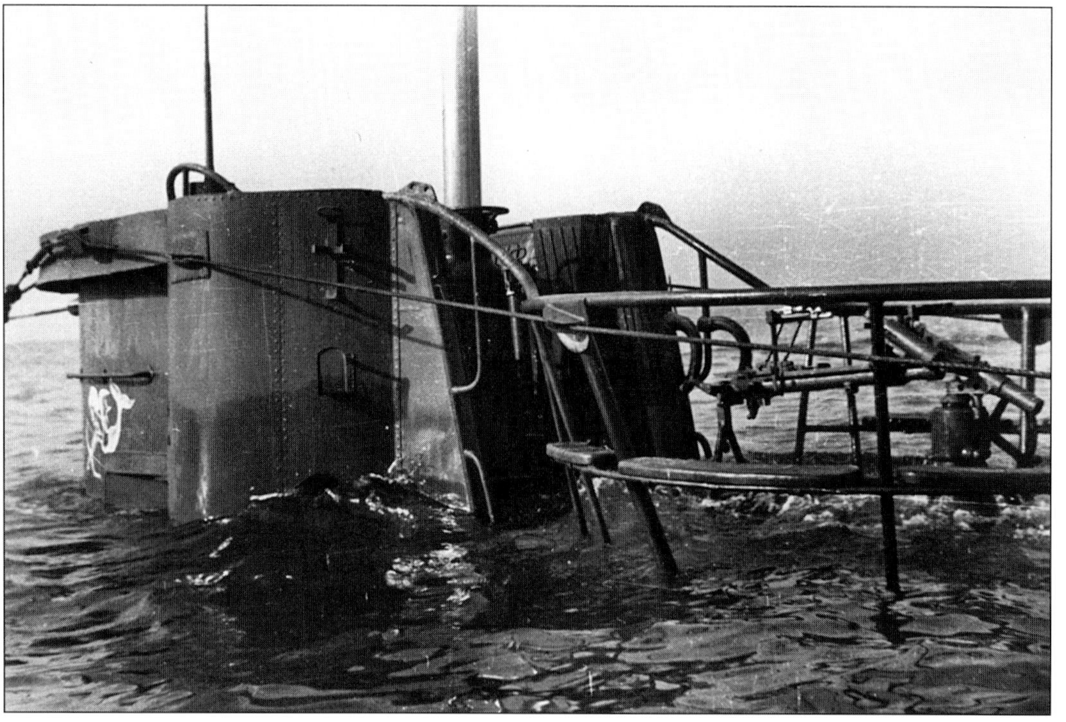

The emblem on the front of this Type VIIC conning tower confirms that these diving trials with *U332* were not carried out by the Submarine Acceptance Command because the winged mermaid did not appear until after the boat had arrived in La Pallice, France, on 16 December 1941. The design of the wintergarten has some interesting similarities with *U86* (*see* p. 47). Model makers will be interested to note that the steel plates appear to be riveted rather than welded. Both the attack periscope and the telescopic rod aerial have been raised. The bracket on the outside wall just above the jumping wire would hold a horseshoe-shaped lifebelt when the boat manoeuvred in port.

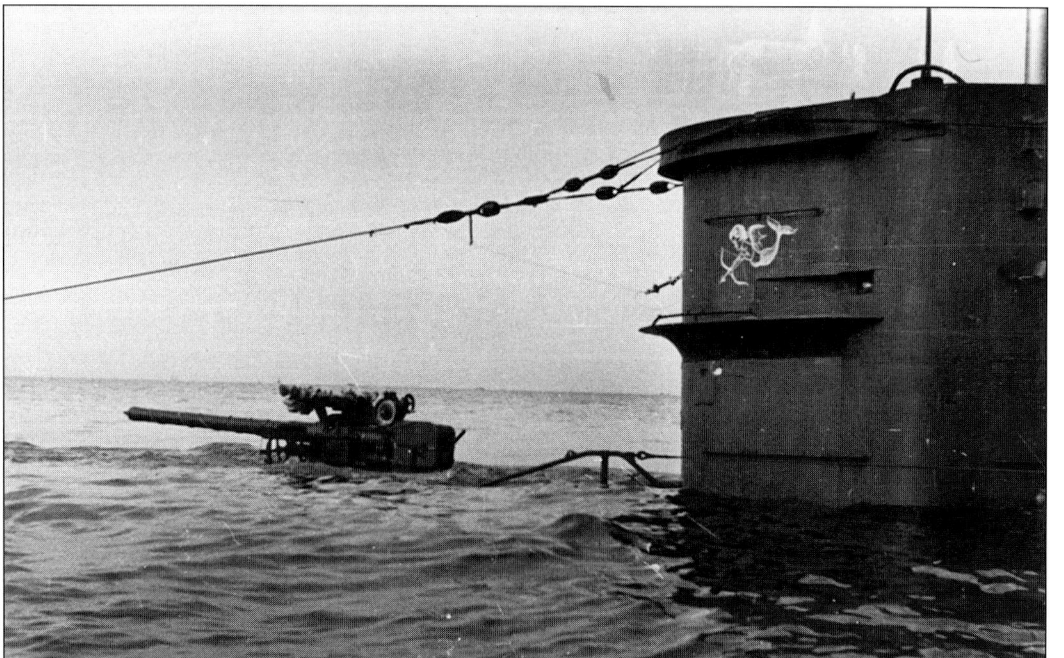

U332 under KL Johannes Liebe. The gun – an 88 mm – was developed from a tank weapon. Above it are a number of porcelain insulators to prevent the electricity in the aerial from making contact with the metal of the boat. The navigation light can be seen below the mermaid's tail and the lifebelt bracket is on the right.

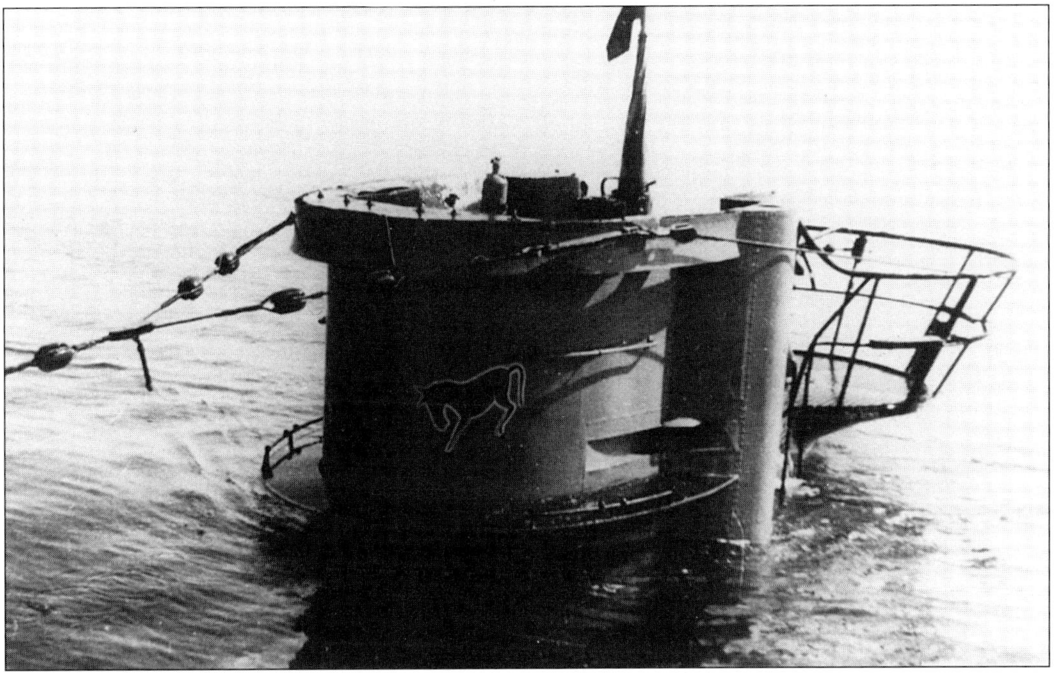

The emblem of the horse clearly shows that this is Type VIIC *U77* under KL Heinrich Schonder, which was launched on 32 November 1940 at Vulkan Works in Bremen. The flag on the conning tower would suggest that this diving test took place in fairly confined waters where passing boats might stumble upon the submerged submarine.

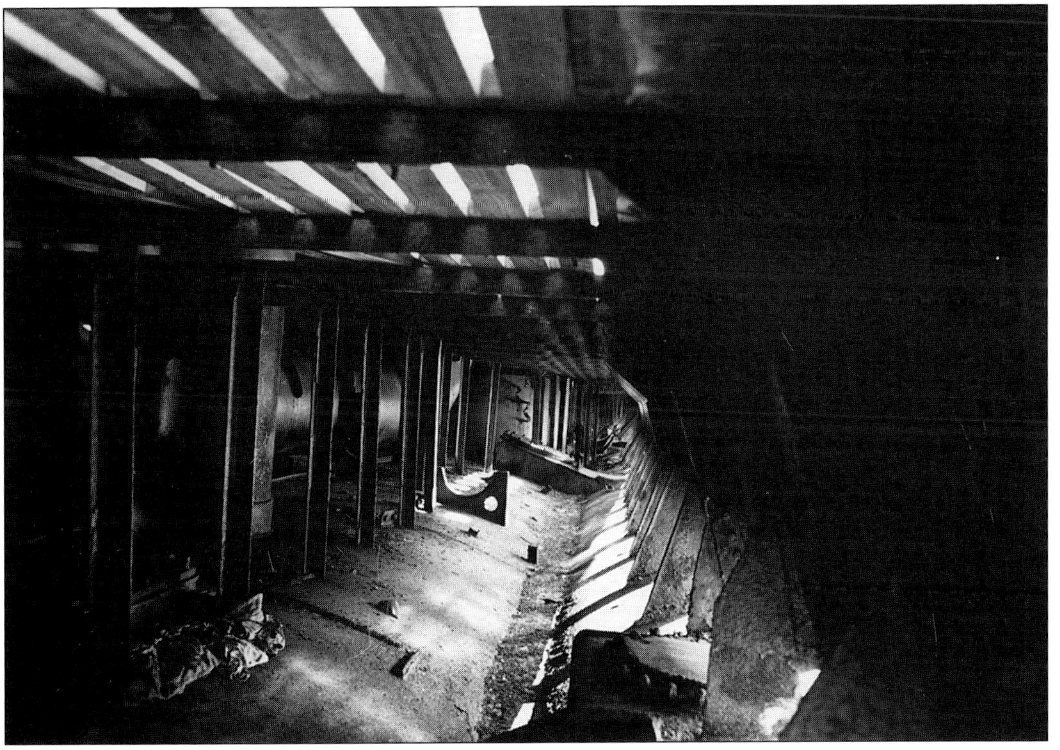

On a Type VIIC there was just about enough room for a man to crawl on all fours under the deck and vents along the sides provided sufficient light to take a photograph without flash. In many museum boats these vents provide excellent access for a variety of birds to nest under the deck planking. This image shows the wooden deck planking of *U995* at the top with vertical supports running down to the pressure hull at the bottom of the photograph. The pipe on the left is an air duct. When the boat was diving this space filled with water.

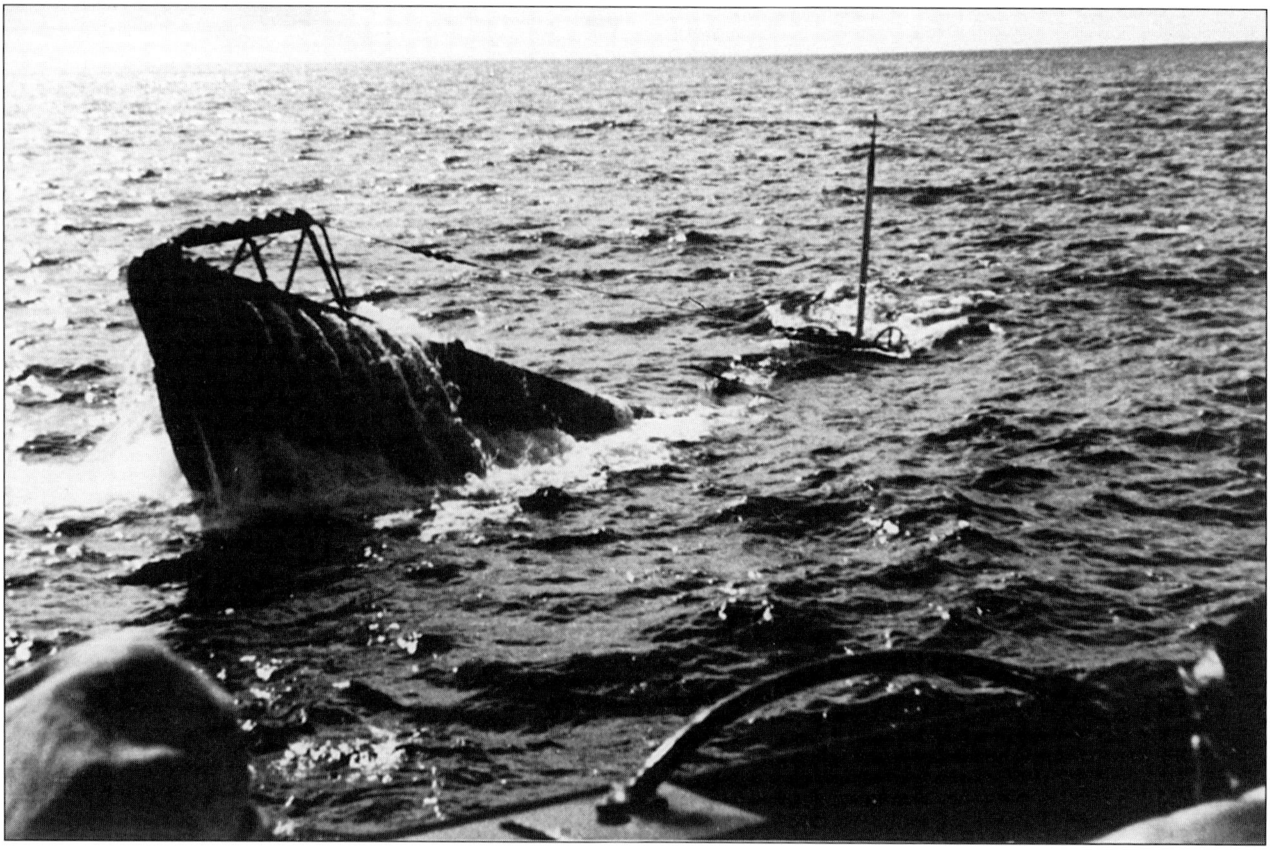

Water that filled the space beneath the decks when the boat dived (*see* previous page) poured out as the vessel surfaced. It appears that the surfacing sequence that begins here was filmed from another U-boat and the vessel's close proximity would suggest that the dramatic emergence was created for the benefit of the camera rather than to test the capabilities of the machinery. Although the commander could see through the raised periscope when submerged, even clear water would limit his vision. Surfacing so close to another ship involved considerable risk and these pictures suggest he was no novice.

The raised railing on the top of the conning tower was supposed to have been restricted to *U120*, *U121*, *U137* and *U158*, but photographic evidence in the U-Boot-Archiv indicates that the records are wrong because it was also fitted to several other boats. *U120* and *U121* belonged to a special group of Type IIB built for China by Flender Works in Lübeck but the war started before they could be handed over. The other boats mentioned above were standard IID from Deutsche Werke in Kiel and it could well have been that the railing was a feature from this shipyard. The Type IID was made by lengthening the original design and this increased the vessel's range from 2,000 to 5,600 nautical miles but the machinery did not allow for an increase in speed and there was still only room for the three bow tubes and two spare torpedoes.

Note the net-cutter on the bows and the water pouring from the vents in the side of the boat. The pressure hull – housing machinery and men – was constructed as a circular tube-like structure and a surfaced U-boat reveals mostly only the casing around this strong steel hull. The casing was designed to make life easier for men working on the upper (outside) deck and rendered the boat more streamlined. The metal of this casing was relatively thin and would have buckled under pressure when the boat dived, so water was allowed to flood into the space between the casing and pressure hull.

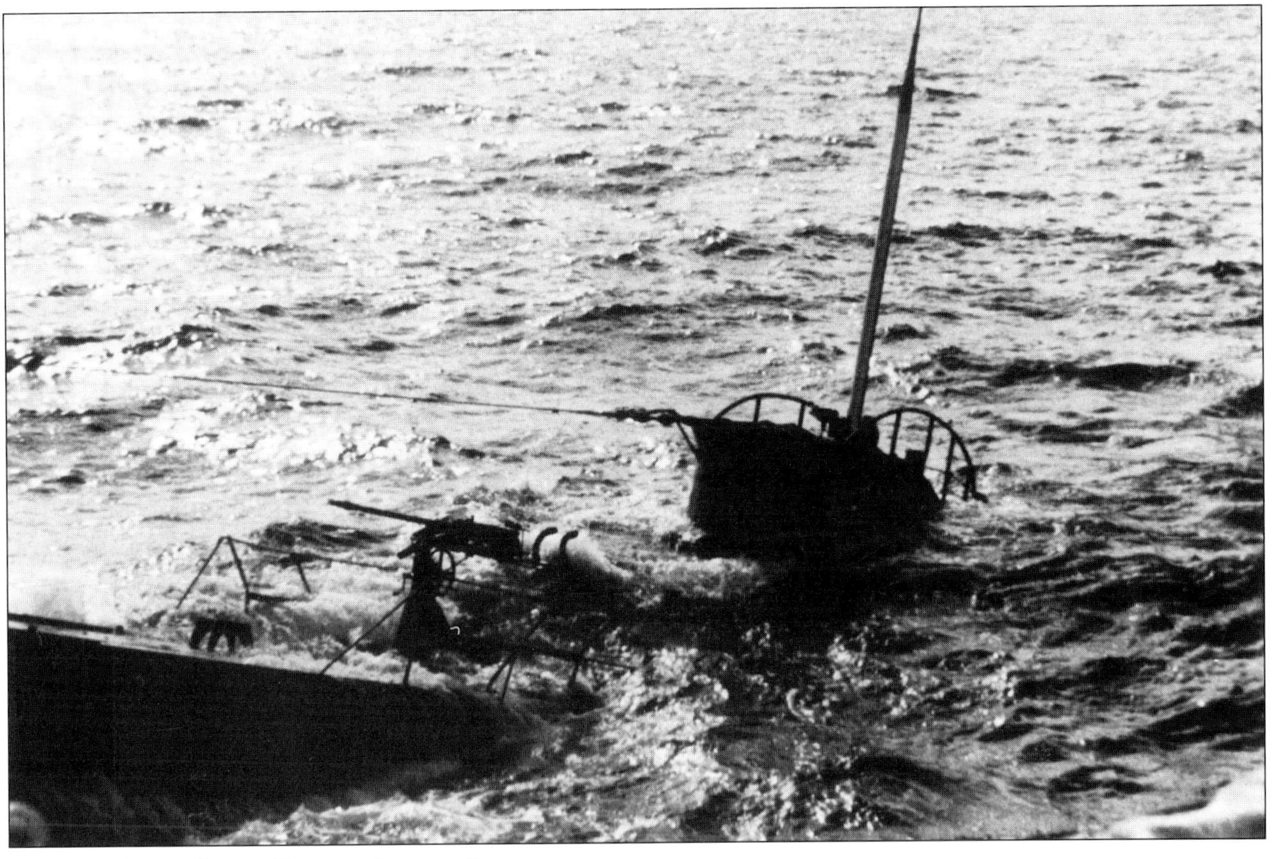

The small coastal boat breaks the surface . . .

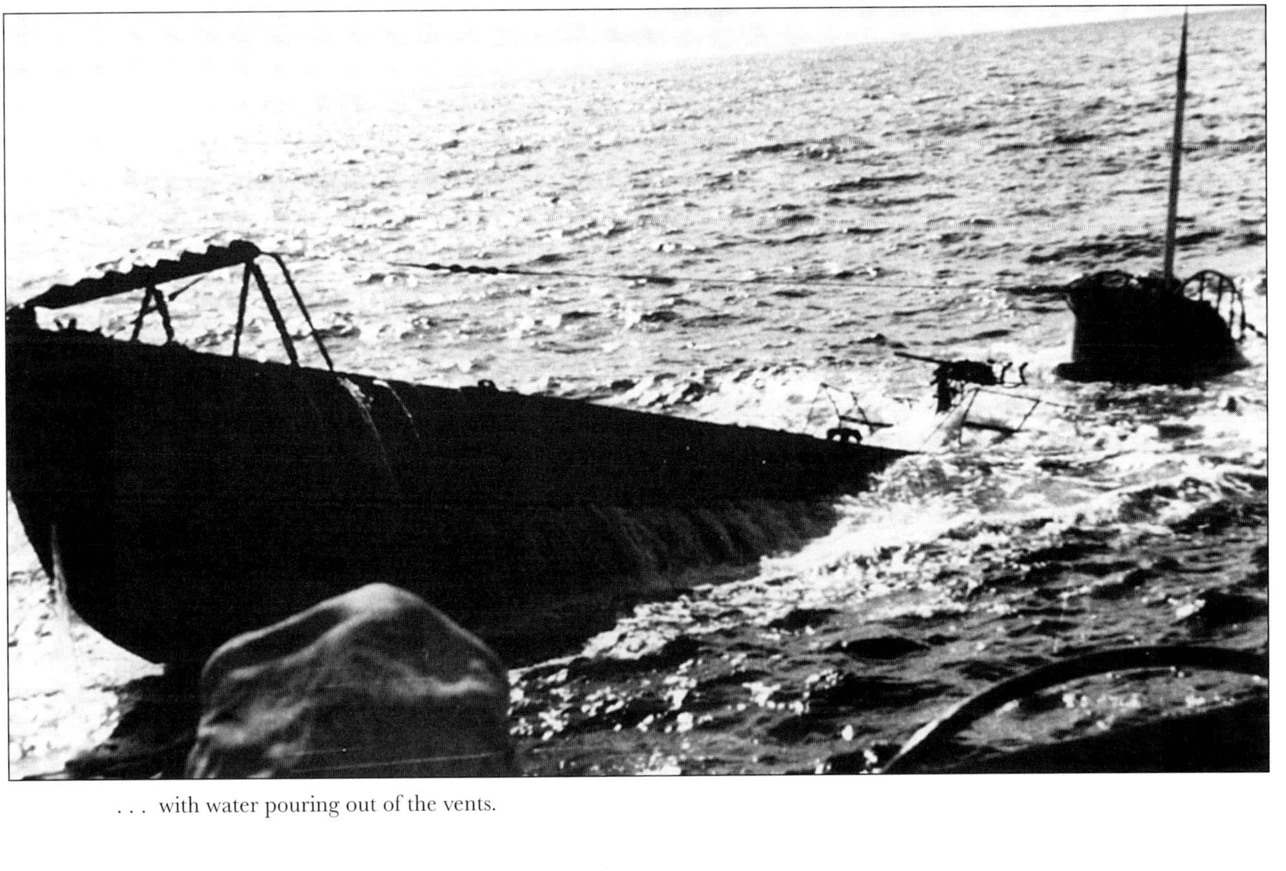

. . . with water pouring out of the vents.

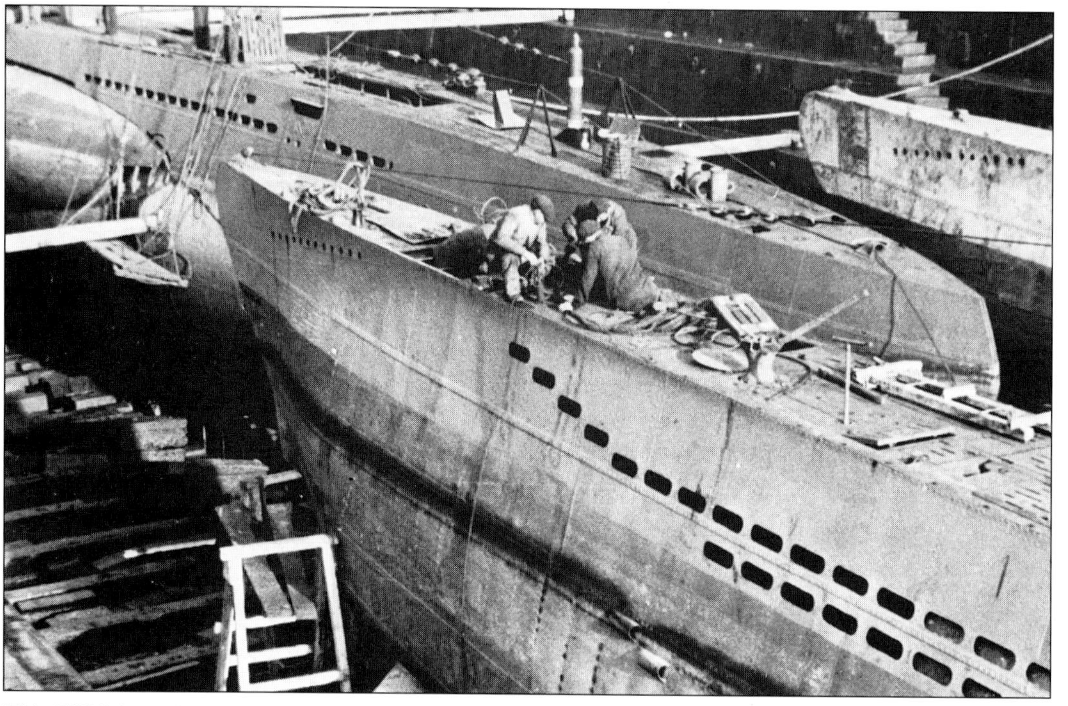

This VIIC boat in dry dock has free-flooding vents along the side. The pattern was not unique to an individual boat but often a small group shared a distinctive set of patterns and these minor differences can be useful when identifying old photographs. Some vent patterns have been classified by the Swedish historian Lennart Lindberg and published in Erich Gröner's book *Die deutschen Kriegsschiffe.* The port hydroplane for controlling depth is just visible at the bottom. These devices functioned similarly to elevators of aircraft and allowed the boat to cruise up or down. They were usually operated electrically from the central control room below the conning tower but in an extreme emergency they could also be adjusted from under the floor of the two torpedo compartments. A set of essential repeater dials were provided there for the purpose.

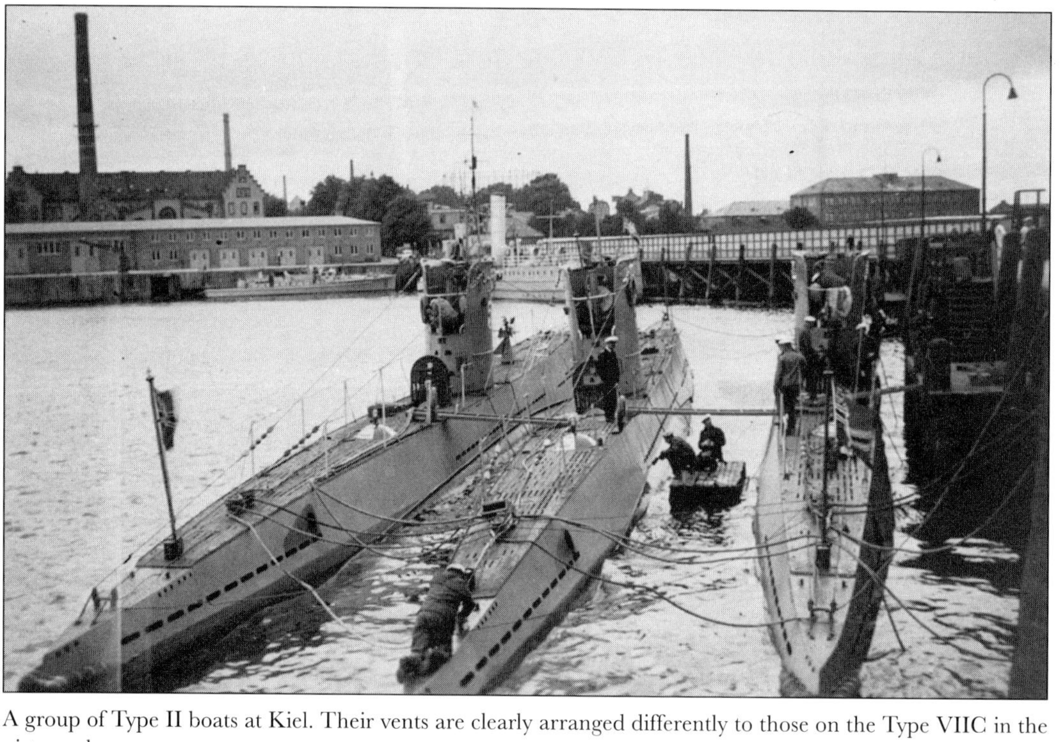

A group of Type II boats at Kiel. Their vents are clearly arranged differently to those on the Type VIIC in the picture above.

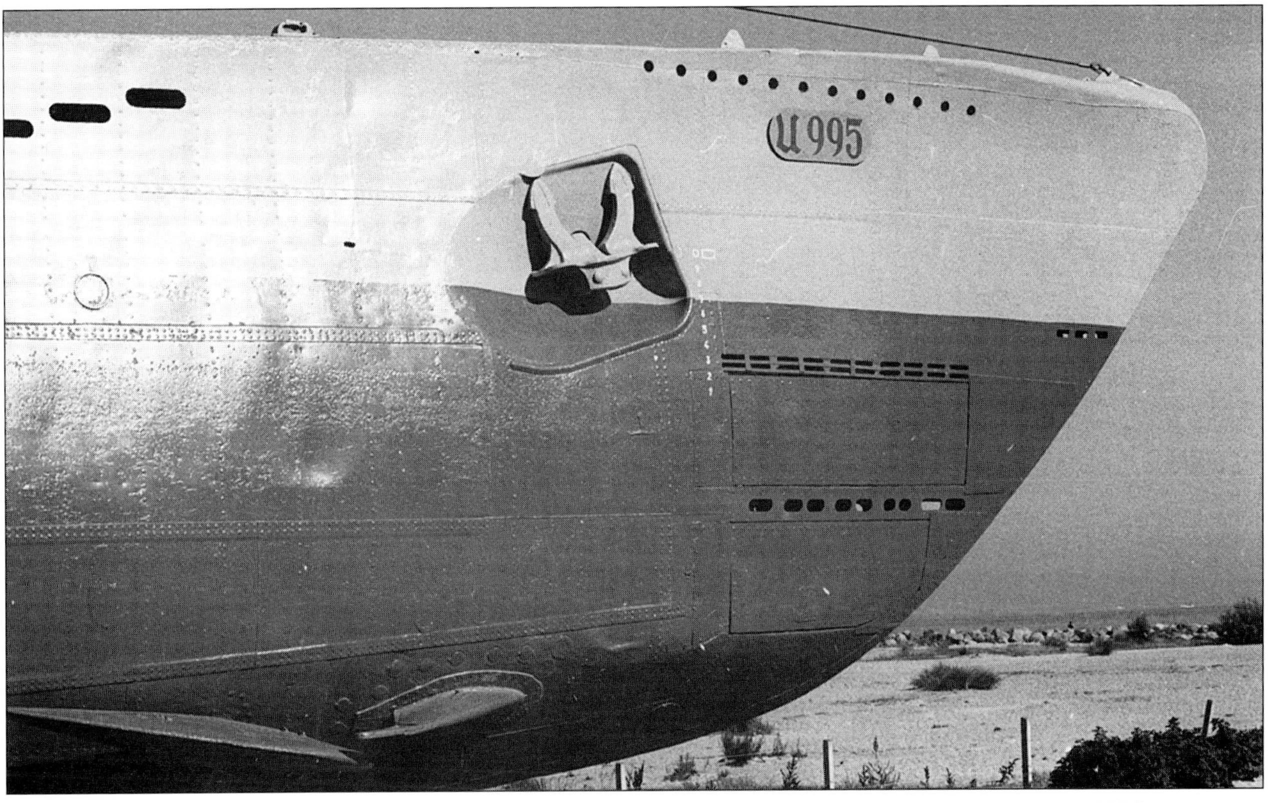

The bows of the museum boat *U995* at Laboe (Kiel) showing the arrangement of vents in the bows of a Type VIIC.

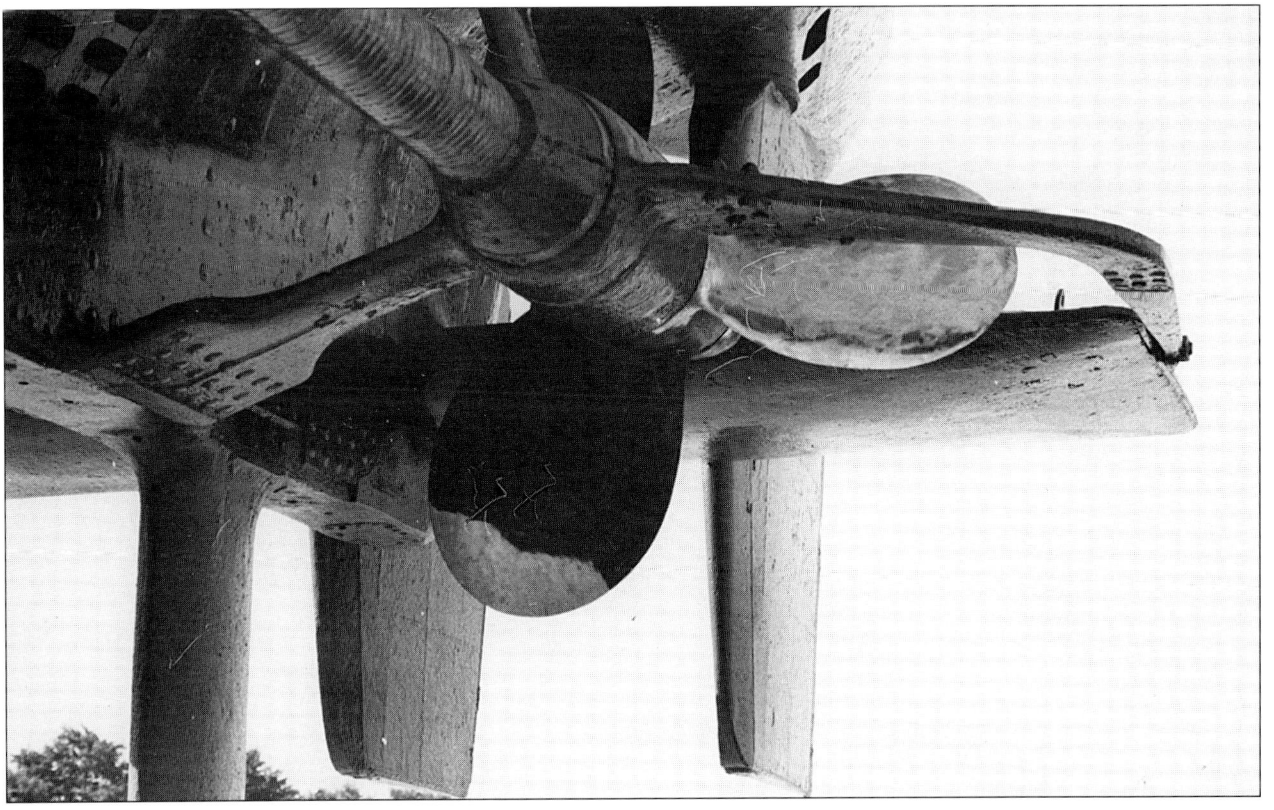

U995's hydroplane bracket behind the propeller but forward of the two rudders. The two rudders allowed the rear torpedo tube to be situated on the central longitudinal axis of the boat to eject between them.

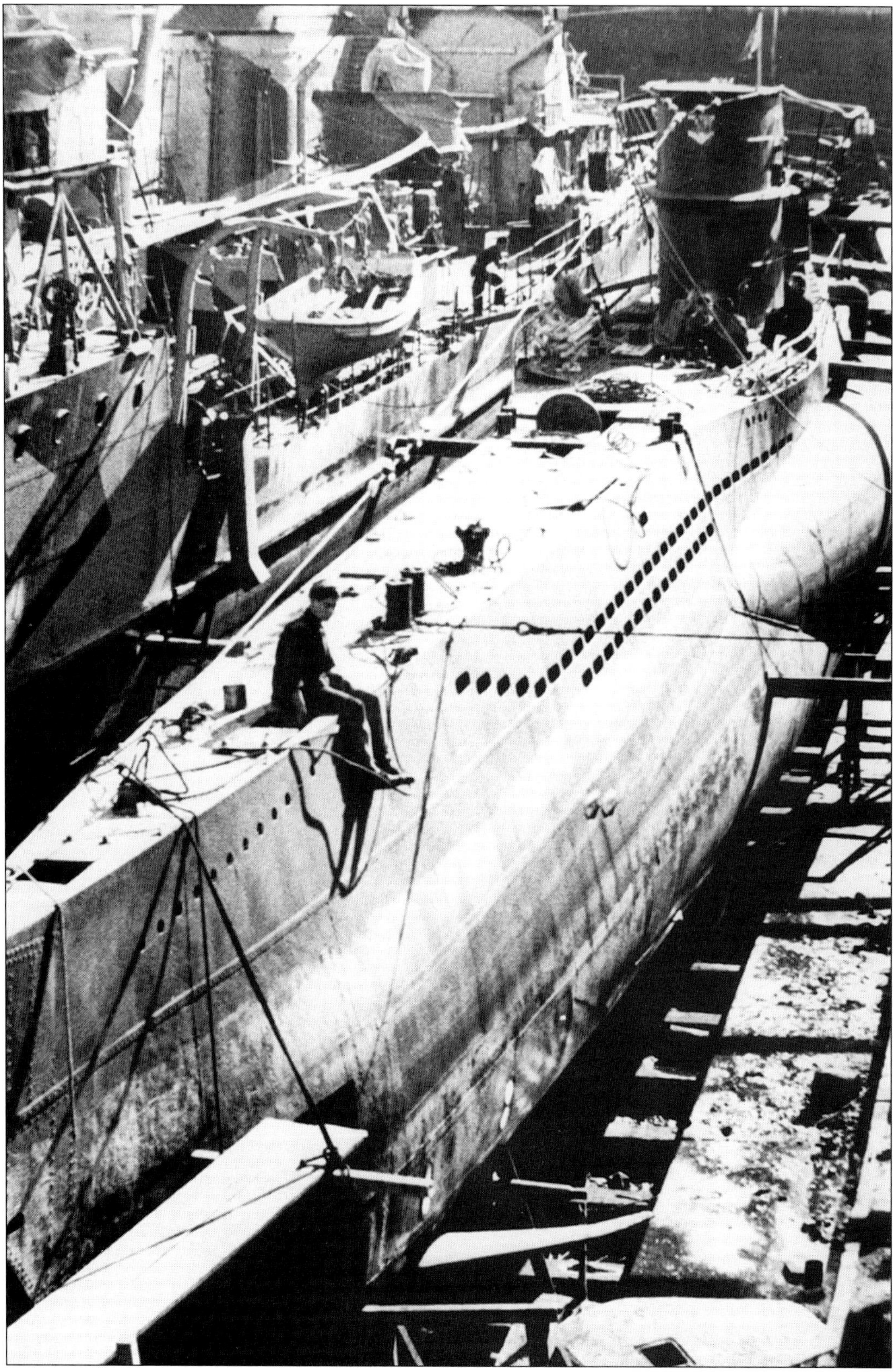

Another Type VIIC with a similar set of free-flooding vents to the boat at the top of p. 36. Although the big gun has been removed, the side of the hull can be seen curving around the platform where the gun used to be. The port saddle tank is also clearly visible by the side of the conning tower in this and in the next picture.

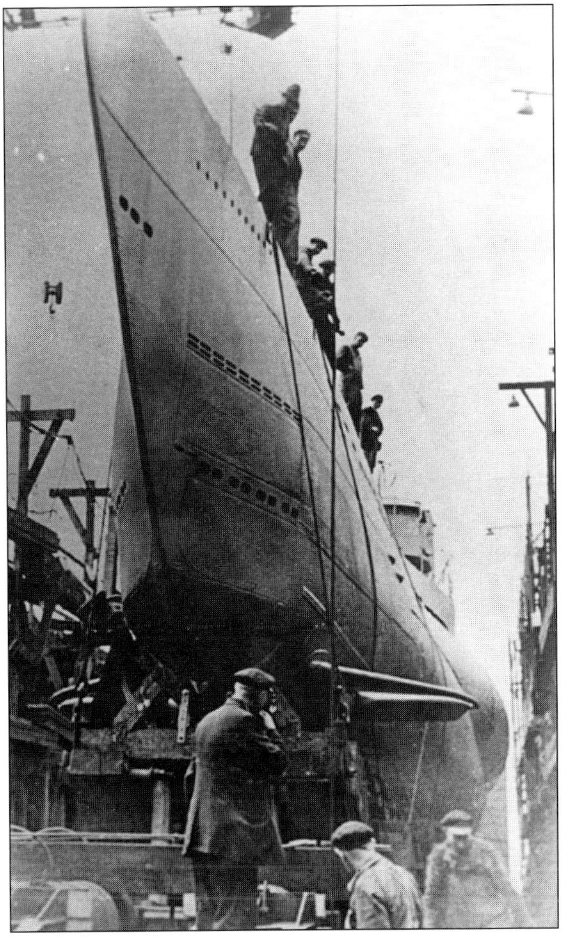

This picture was probably taken just prior to a launch and shows the streamlining around the forward torpedo tube doors very well. Again, the vents are free-flooding slots for allowing water into the space between the boat's casing and pressure hull. The port hydroplane with its supporting bracket can also be seen. These protrusions were quite a problem when making fast at jetties and special fenders were provided to prevent them from being damaged. There were a number of incidents in the locks of the Kiel Canal where mild collisions forced boats into dockyards. Once the war started, the U-boat Command insisted that submarines were locked through on their own to prevent such accidents. The problem has been overcome in modern boats by providing retractable hydroplanes.

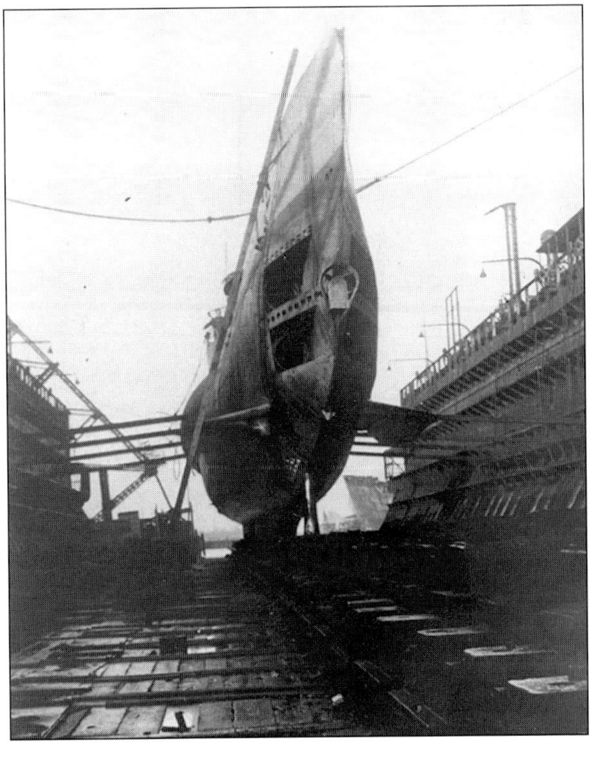

Another Type VIIC, this time *U703* with the outer torpedo doors open. *U703* was commissioned by KL Heinz Bielfeld, who was born in 1916 in Tientsin, China, and later served as naval officer with the Luftwaffe. He died in most unusual circumstances as commander of *U1222*, snorkelling to the west of La Rochelle, France. Apparently the boat's small wake was spotted by an aircraft on 1 September 1943 and the vessel was depth charged before it could reach a safe depth. *U703* also vanished under somewhat strange circumstances while under the command of KL Joachim Brünner. She was probably mined somewhere between Greenland and Iceland on 30 September 1944.

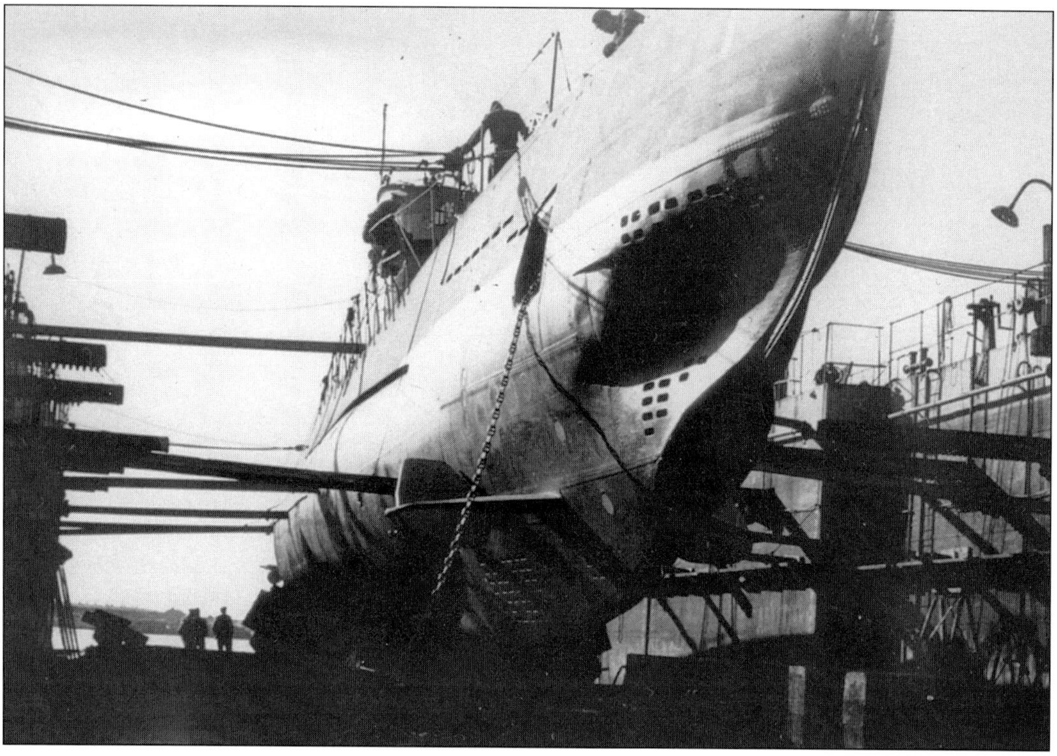

Although the smaller coastal boats of Type II had three bow torpedo tubes, they could carry only five torpedoes. This made their role far out at sea somewhat untenable and after the start of the war the majority were used for training. The chain hanging down from the bows has an anchor attached to it.

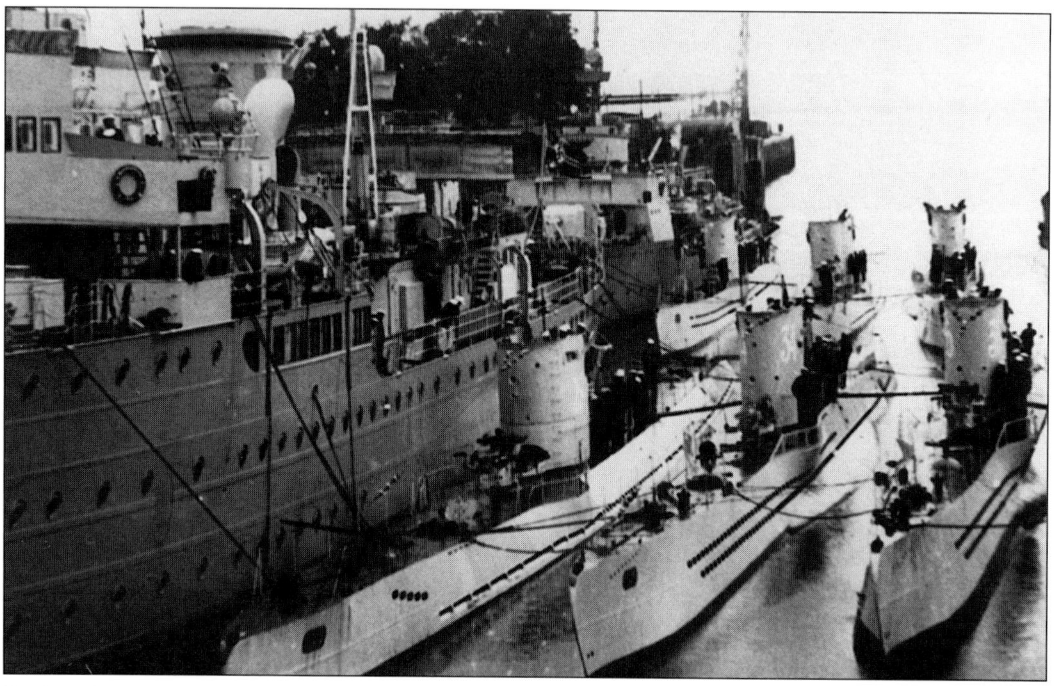

During the early trials in the Baltic, the crew often had the advantage of still living on land or being accommodated in one of the many depot ships. This shows the tender *Saar* with part of the flotilla alongside. The numbers on the side of conning towers indicate that the picture was taken before the beginning of the war because they were removed after hostilities started. On the right are two Type VIIA boats and on the left is a Type IA, which would suggest that the vessels were part of an operational flotilla, rather than a group of school boats. Only two Type IA boats were ever built – *U25* and *U26* – so photographs of them tend to be rare.

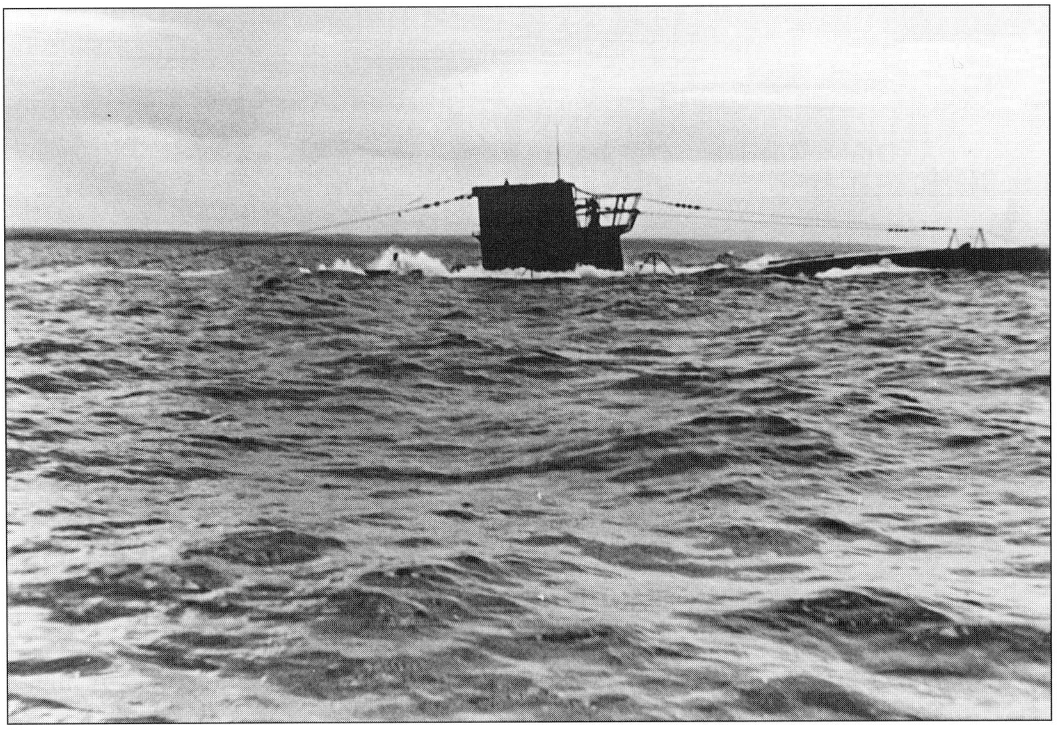

Of course, it would have been a rare occurrence for operational submarines at sea to dive by the method shown in the photograph on p. 17. Things happened much faster if the hydroplanes were also brought into operation and these only worked when the boat was moving. To get down quickly at sea, spare hands rushed into the bow torpedo room to make the boat front heavy. At the same time, engines were driven at the fastest possible speed and then, when all hatches and vents were shut, the hydroplanes helped force the bows under while water flooded into the diving tanks. Diving a stationary VIIC boat took at least one minute, while going down at speed during an emergency took only 30 seconds. The boat in this speed diving sequence is probably *U441* or *U440*.

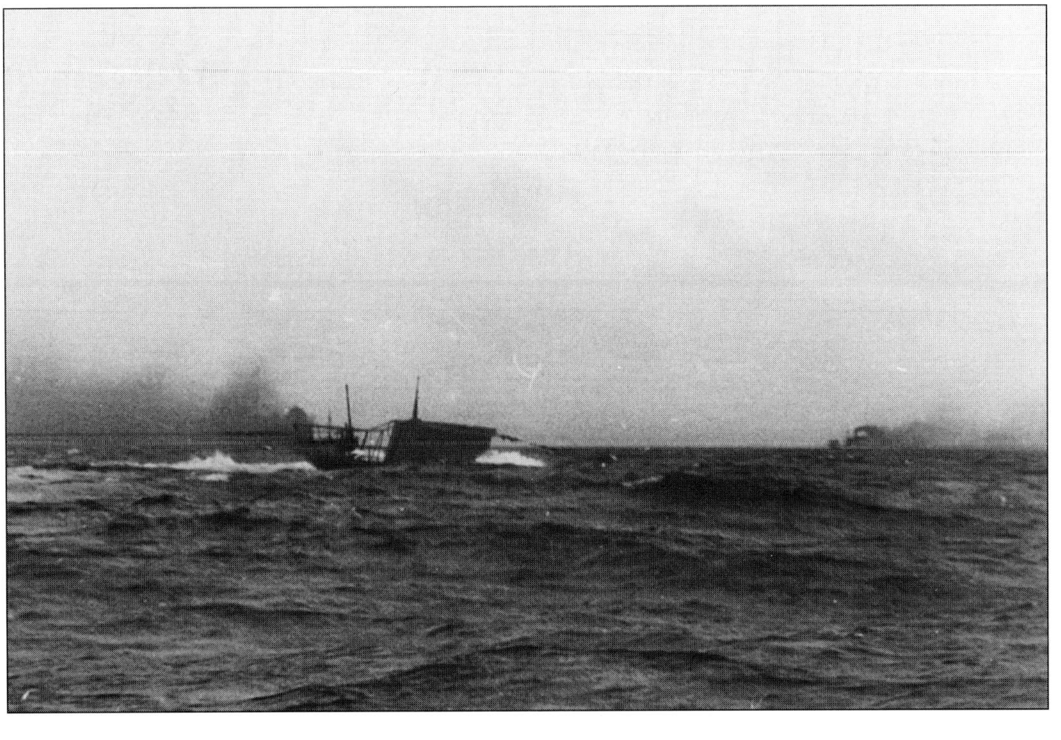

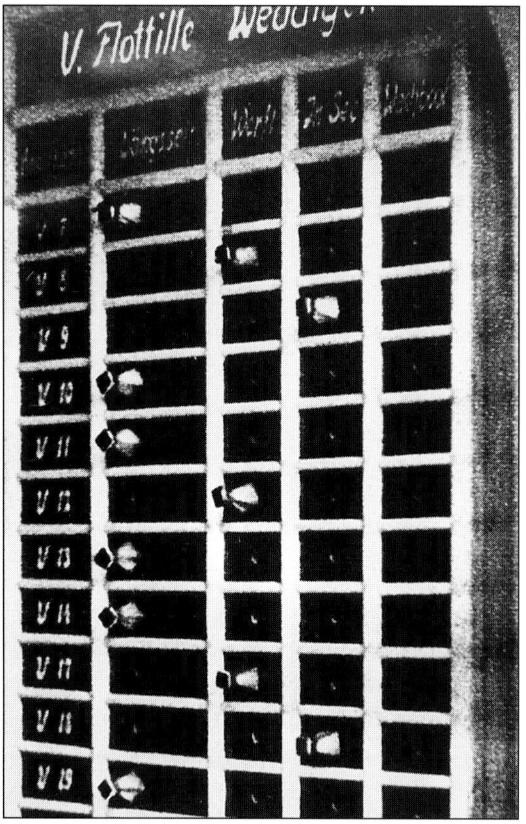

Keeping tabs on all the boats was a major problem and men aboard the depot ship and tender *Saar* recorded the whereabouts of the school boats by sticking pegs into a board. The headings for the columns are: Boat, Alongside, In the Shipyard, At Sea, Duty Guard Boat.

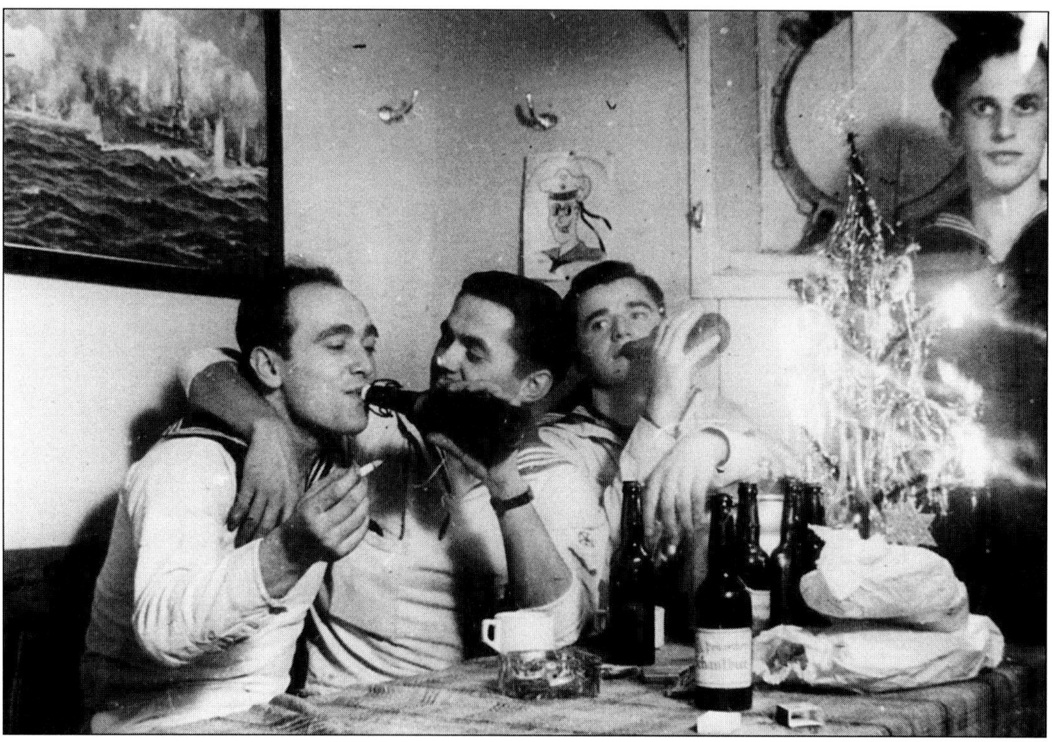

Christmas 1942 aboard the tender *Donau* with men from *U62* (commanded by OL Adolf Schönberg) letting their hair down. It is quite likely that at the beginning of the year some of these boys were still at school where they were not allowed to smoke or indeed consume alcohol. Both activities had to be learned rather rapidly in the navy.

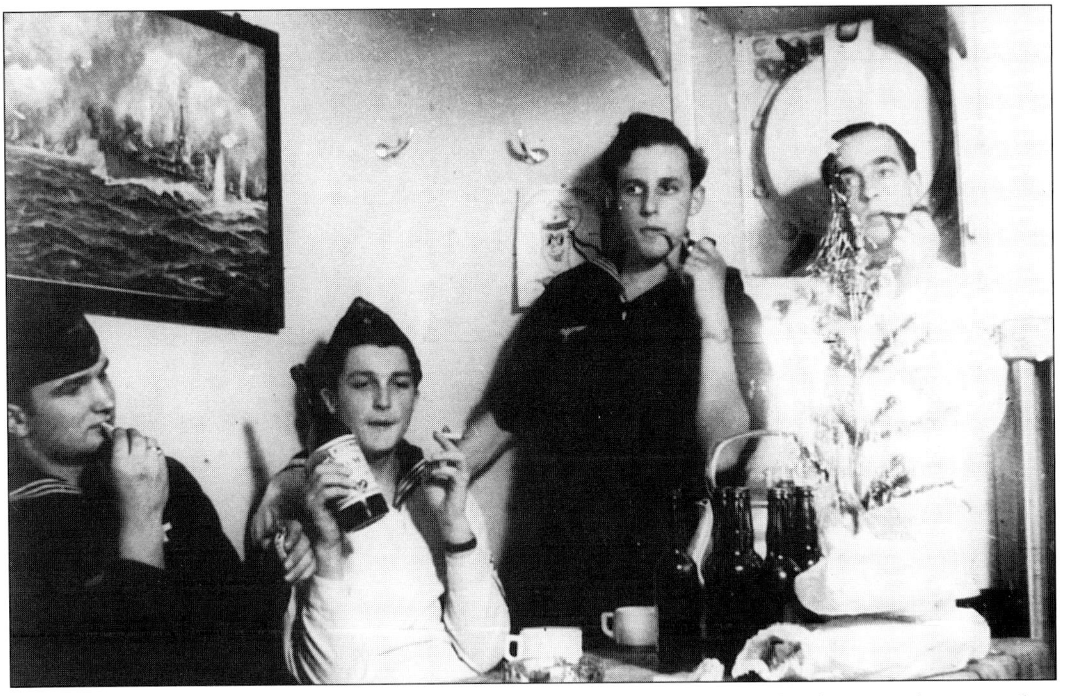

Lead–acid batteries fitted in submarines gave off a highly explosive mixture of hydrogen and oxygen when charging or discharging and therefore men were not allowed to smoke inside U-boats.

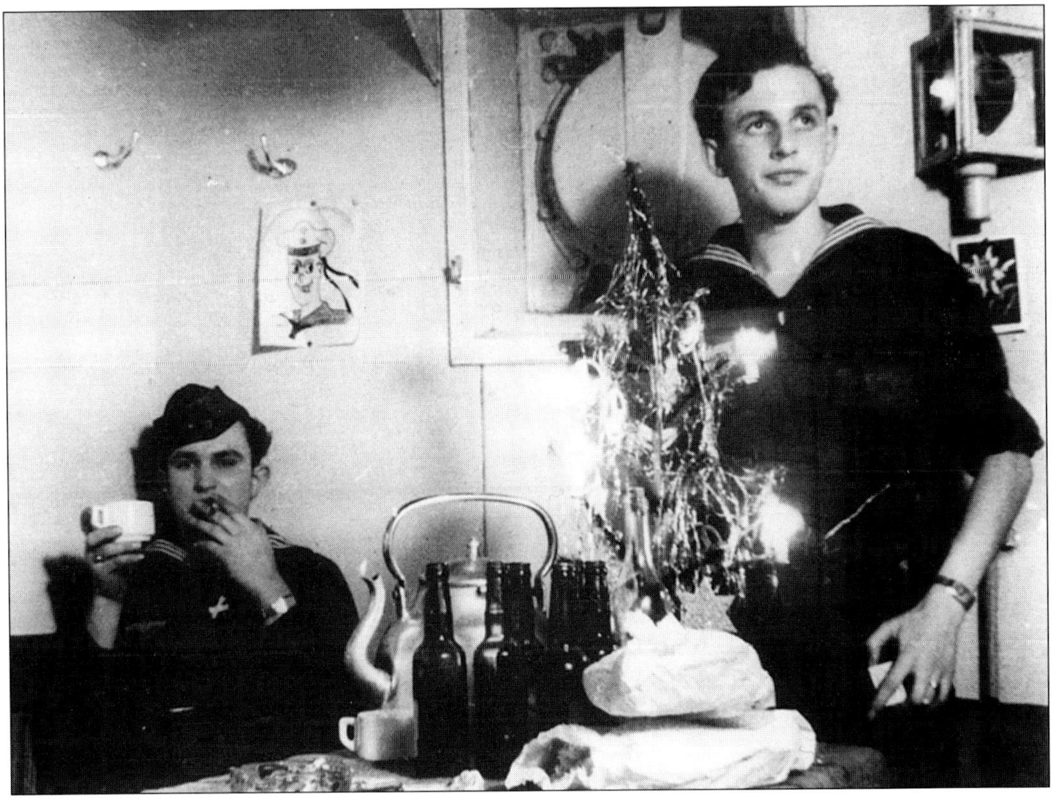

Smoking was usually allowed only inside the well-ventilated commander's control room while on the surface or, if conditions permitted, on the top of the conning tower. This was the only reason the majority of men had for asking permission to leave their cramped quarters and consequently a number of non-smokers quickly took up the habit in order to see the light of day at least occasionally during patrols.

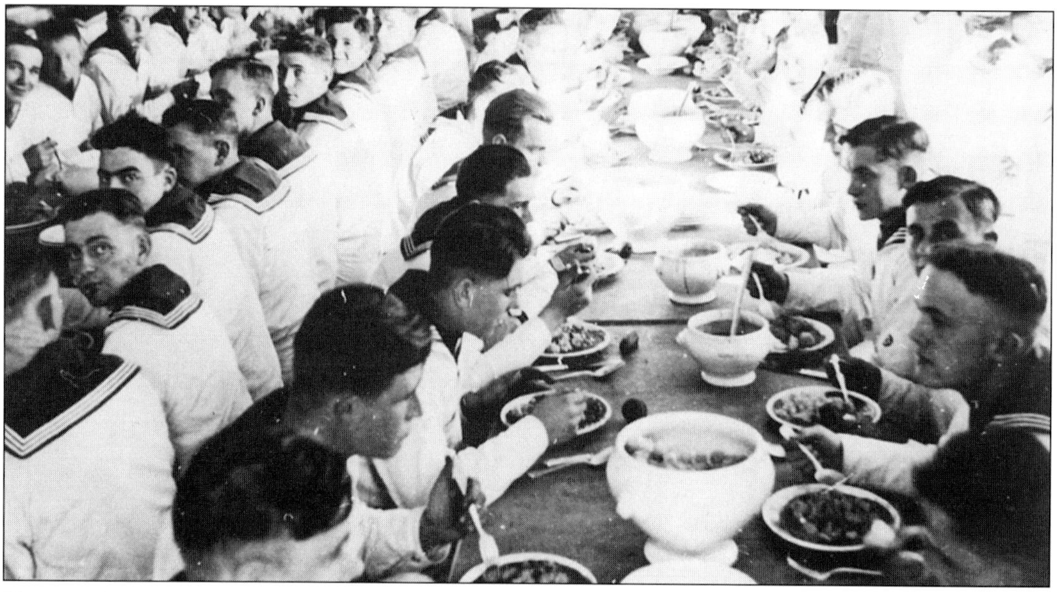

Pictures of semi-wild parties aboard ships or on land, often the only time when men could photograph, tend to give a wrong impression of what life was like in the institutional existence of naval shore establishments. This picture shows the mess hall for seamen at the U-boat school in Neustadt. The meal looks to be of a simple nature in keeping with the government preaching of the time which suggested that 'Eintopf' (a nutritious meal cooked in one pot) should be eaten for at least one day each week. The propaganda system ensured that there were a good number of photographs in circulation showing such meals being served to Hitler and the high-ranking officials of the government. Generally U-boat men received the best rations and fared considerably better even than the majority of rich or high-up people on land. Warrant and commissioned officers had white mess jackets for wearing on land but these sailors are clothed in the usual white summer or tropical version of the ordinary blue naval uniform with large Nelson collars.

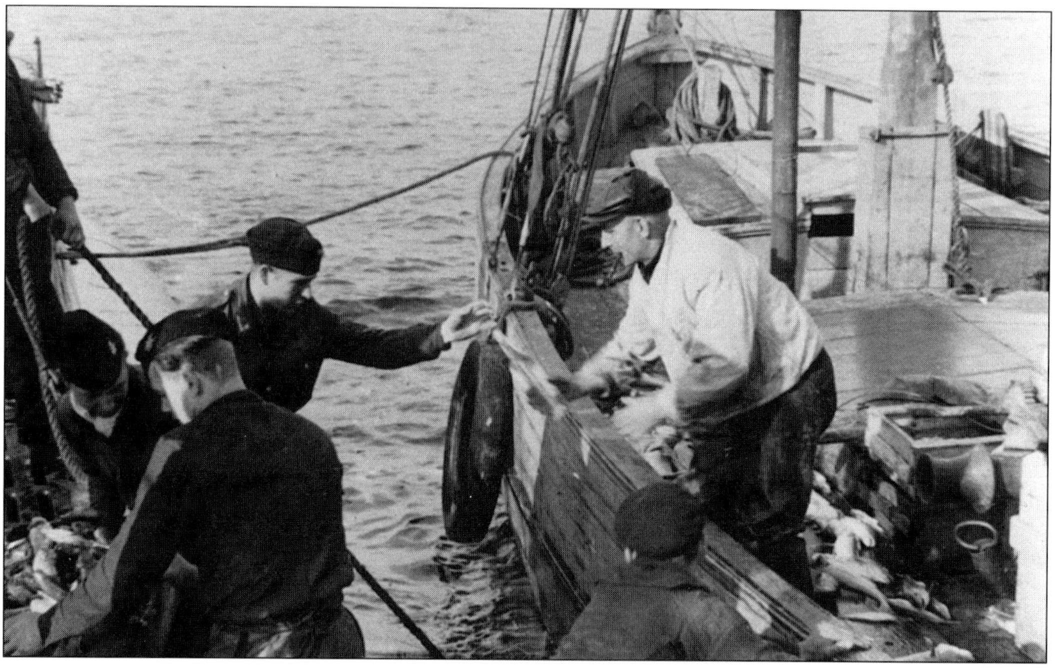

Before the war there were ample opportunities for some relief from the monotony of daily routine and from a tin-rich diet by chatting up coastal fishermen, who were usually willing to exchange some of their catch for alcohol, tobacco or other goodies. Once the war started this mutual help stopped because every small ship had to be treated with the greatest of caution; sighting a fishing vessel presented the U-boat commander with a choice of remaining out of sight or checking the boat's credentials.

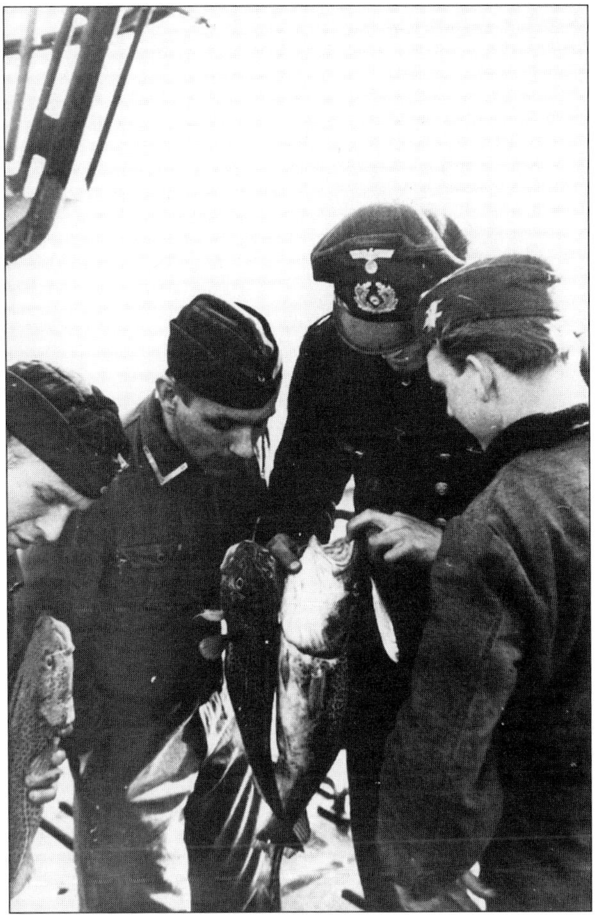

For many U-boat men it was not so much a case of checking the freshness of the catch, but of studying the anatomy of fish. The majority of U-boatmen came from far inland where they hardly ever had the opportunity of handling sea fish. Here there seems to be some detailed discussion going on about the startling differences between cod and dogfish. Fish formed a large part of the North German diet but refrigerators were still exceptionally rare and even the majority of shops did not have such modern conveniences. Therefore, fresh sea fish were only transported short distances inland. Hamburg – some 100 km inland from the nearest sea fishing grounds – had a harbour for trawlers, drifters and shrimpers together with an active fish market until the early 1960s when the widespread use of refrigeration made the long voyages by individual small boats unnecessary.

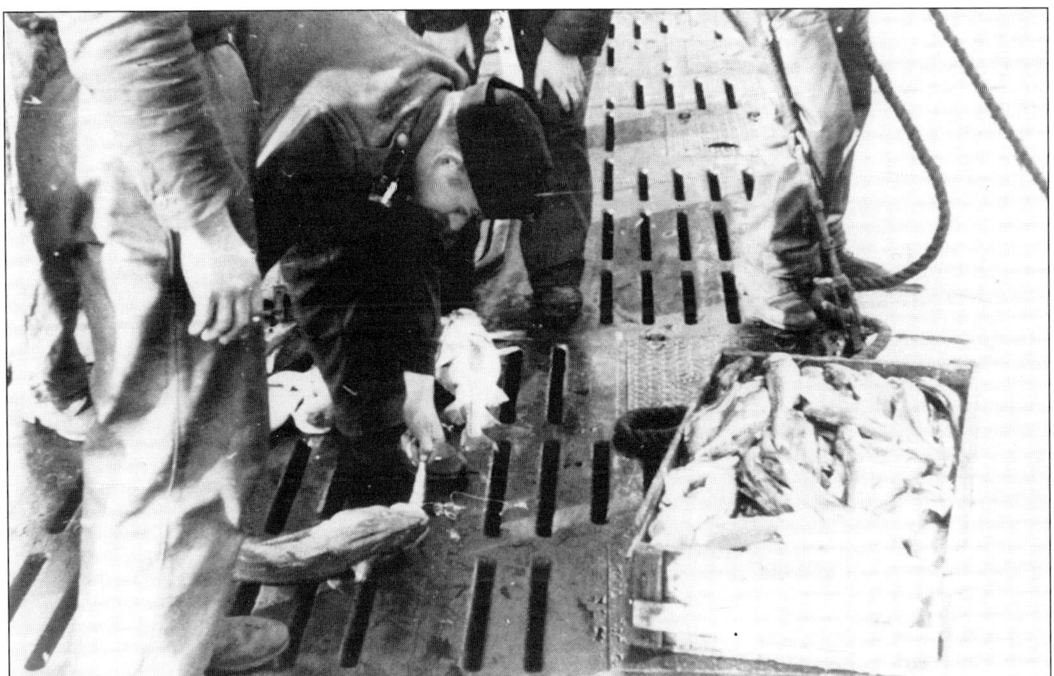

Fish brought on board from fishing boats were usually still alive and testing the sharpness of teeth seems to have been an activity which filled every sailor with curiosity.

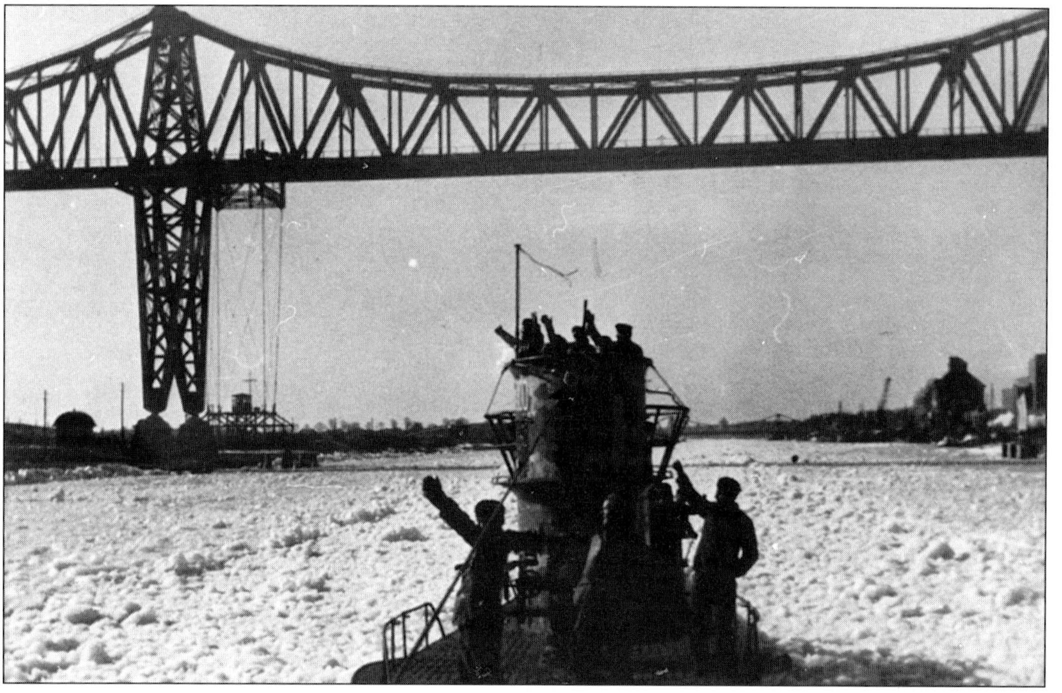

U48, which became the most successful U-boat of the Second World War, on the Kiel Canal. One of the conditions imposed on the builders of the canal was that they should provide free crossing points but in those days there was little traffic and no need for many bridges. This is the massive steel girder bridge near Rendsburg carrying the railway over the canal. Hanging from it is a small, mobile platform for ferrying road vehicles over the water. The bridge is high enough to allow ocean-going ships underneath and the flat land meant a long incline was required so that trains could reach that dizzy height of 42 m. In those days, two of these bridges crossed the canal – this one and another near the western end – each of about 2.5 km in length and significant examples of the technology of the time. Even today, one cannot help but be awe inspired when travelling over the top of these magnificent structures.

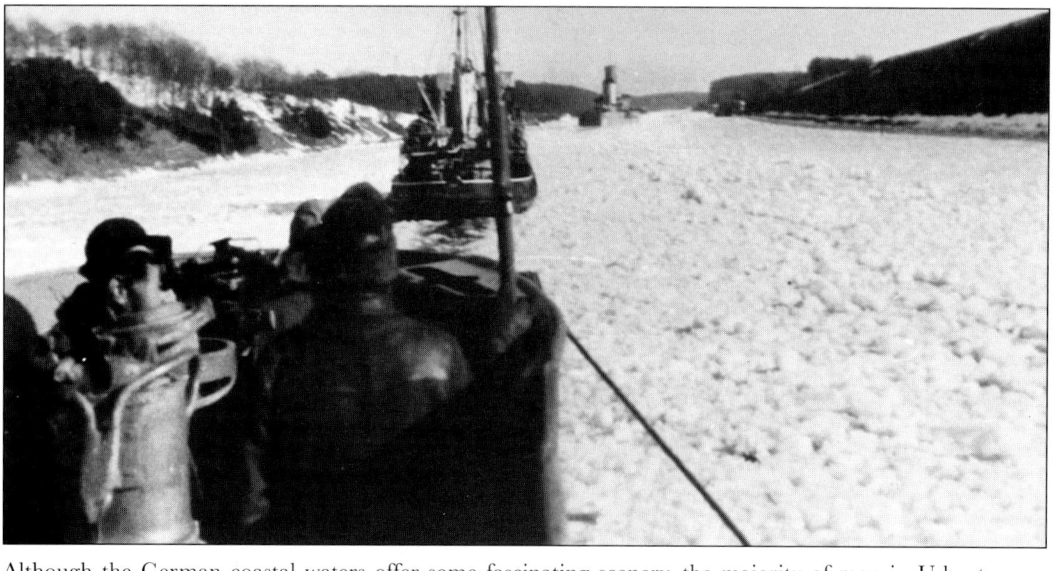

Although the German coastal waters offer some fascinating scenery, the majority of men in U-boats were unable to take advantage of the sights because only a few could be allowed out onto the upper deck. In this case it looks as if the crew were not terribly keen on fresh air – it must have been pretty cold. It is quite likely that the tug ahead of *U48* in the Kiel Canal was there to act as ice breaker. The strange shape in the distance appears to be the old battleship *Hessen*, which served as remote-controlled artillery target but was here also used to cut through the frozen waters.

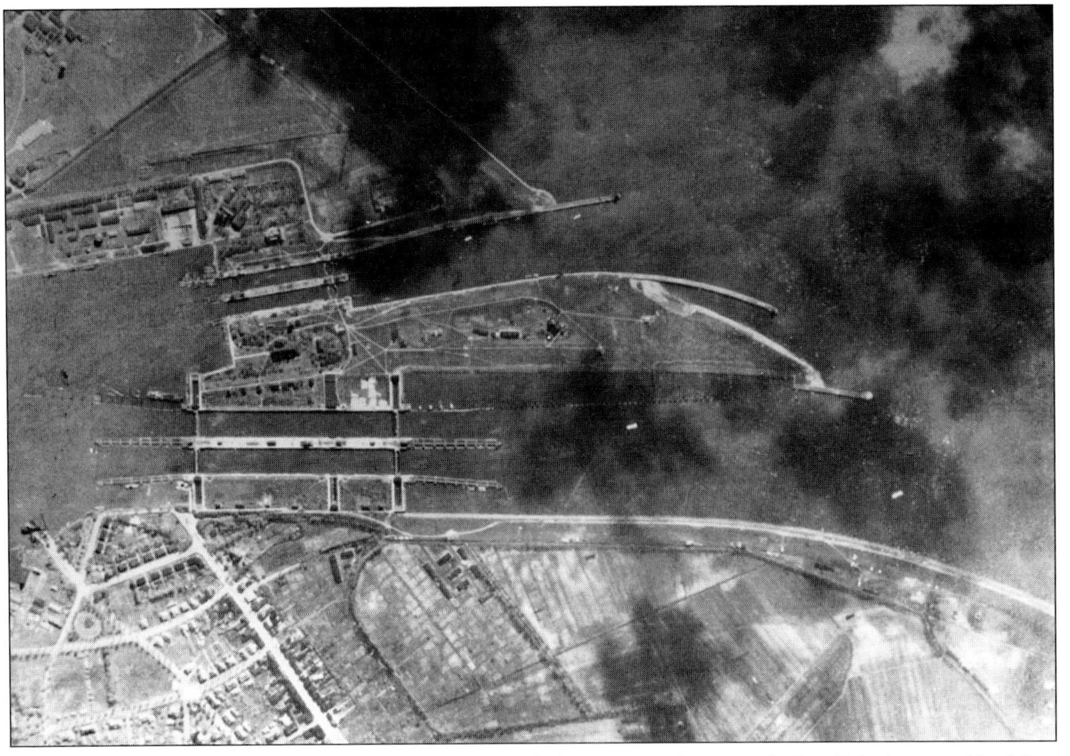

The Kiel Canal was completed at the turn of the twentieth century, a few years before Britain started building large Dreadnought battleships and forced other nations into an unprecedented arms race. This newer and bigger generation of ships could not fit through the canal, so the waterway was enlarged and a second set of locks was built. This is the western end of the canal as it emerges into the River Elbe at Brunsbüttel. The original locks are towards the top and the bigger set, which were finished shortly before the beginning of the First World War, nearer the bottom of the picture. Keen-eyed observers will also spot the small silver shapes of several barrage balloons, suggesting that this photograph was taken during the Second World War.

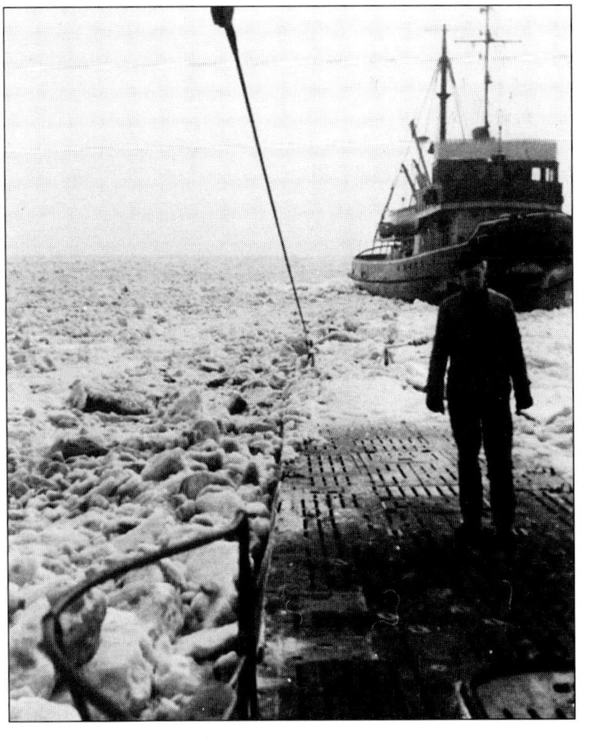

People living in Germany are used to severe continental winters and the Kriegsmarine usually remained operational until ice-breaking became an impossibility. This shows *U48*, under KL Herbert Schultze, in the North Sea while on her way to Heligoland where it was discovered that her propellers were damaged beyond repair and she had to put into the dock yard at Wilhelmshaven to have a new pair fitted. Ice was indeed a major problem for U-boats and disrupted more training activities than the enemy. It was also responsible for the massive increase in U-boat numbers thrown against convoys during the latter months of 1942. The reason for this was that construction continued throughout the exceptionally cold previous winter, but training was curtailed for a period of five months, meaning there was a large bulge waiting to burst out to the front during the summer and autumn of that year.

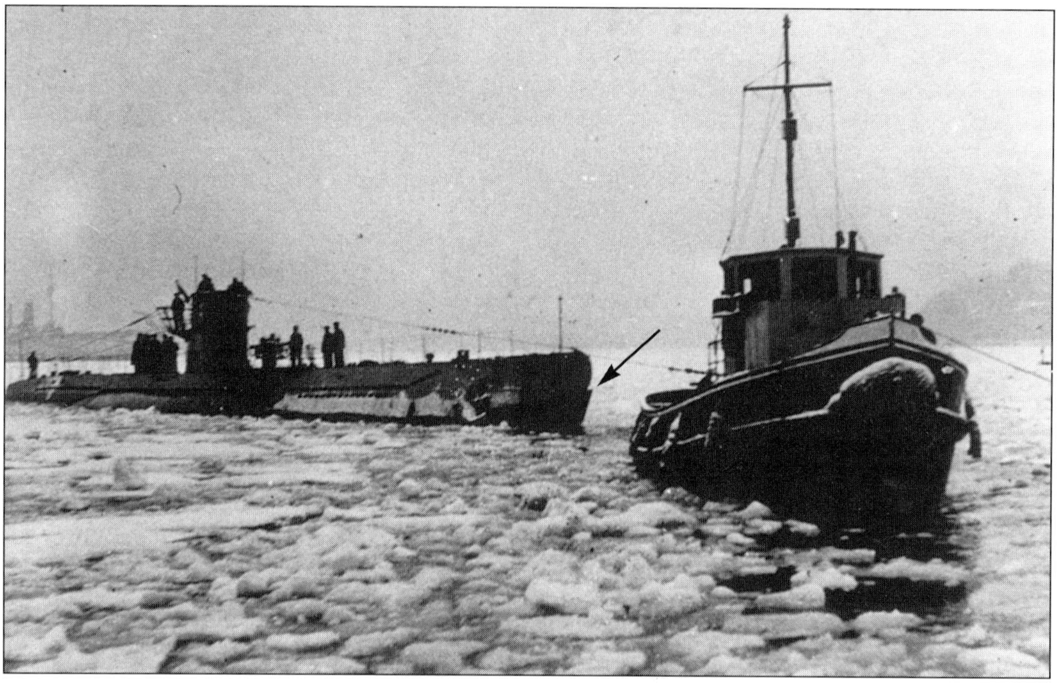

U201 in Kiel under KL Adalbert Schnee. It appears that the boat is under tow and this picture could well have been taken during the first two months of 1941, shortly after the commissioning. A small kink in the bows (*see* above) gives some clue as to how relatively delicate submarines negotiated thick ice without damaging the upper deck casing.

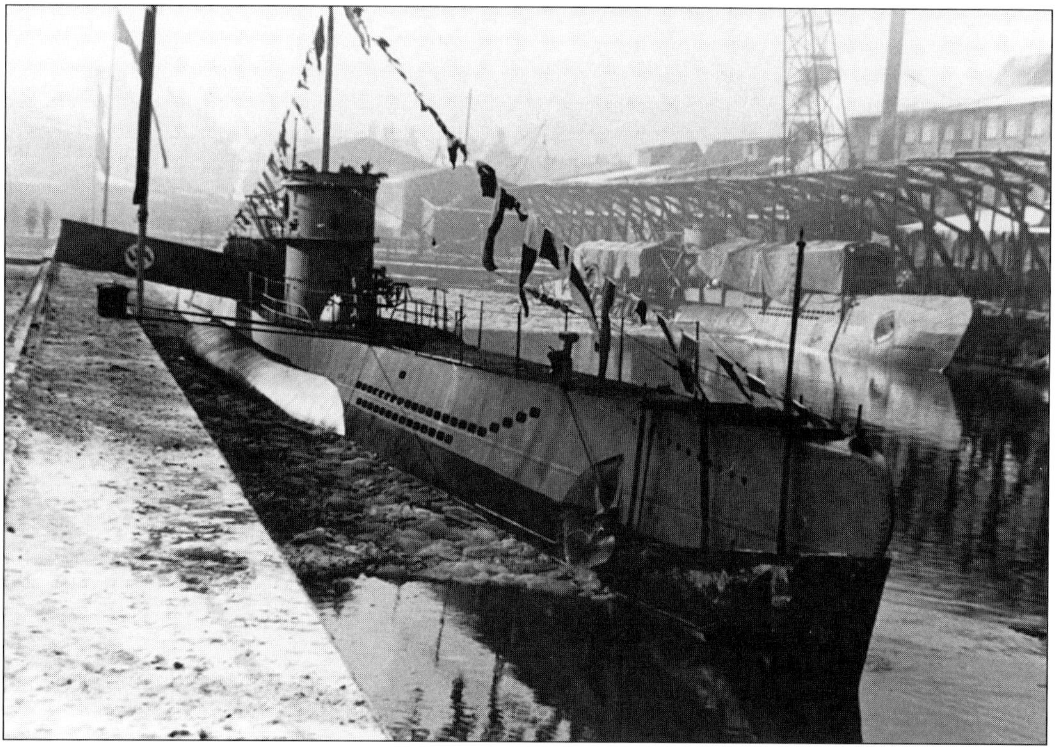

U441 in Danzig with the steel bow protection cap in place. The boat in the background is covered with tarpaulin to protect the workers from the extreme cold. The flags running up to the top of the extended periscope suggest that this photograph shows the boat's commissioning on 21 February 1941, some time before enemy long-range aircraft could reach the far eastern Baltic which means the camouflage was somewhat superfluous at this time. The light is reflecting rather well off the saddle tank along the side of the boat. These were originally a means of stabilising the boat on the surface but they were also used as fuel tanks.

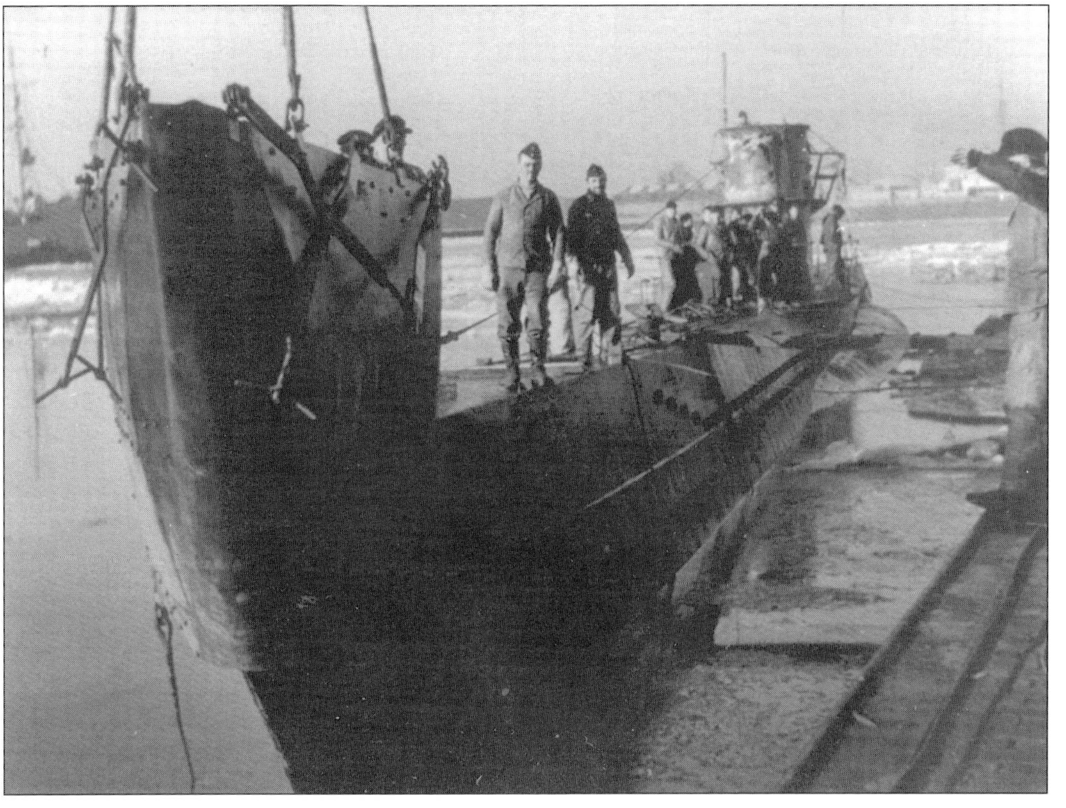

U48 with the heavy steel ice cap partly raised.

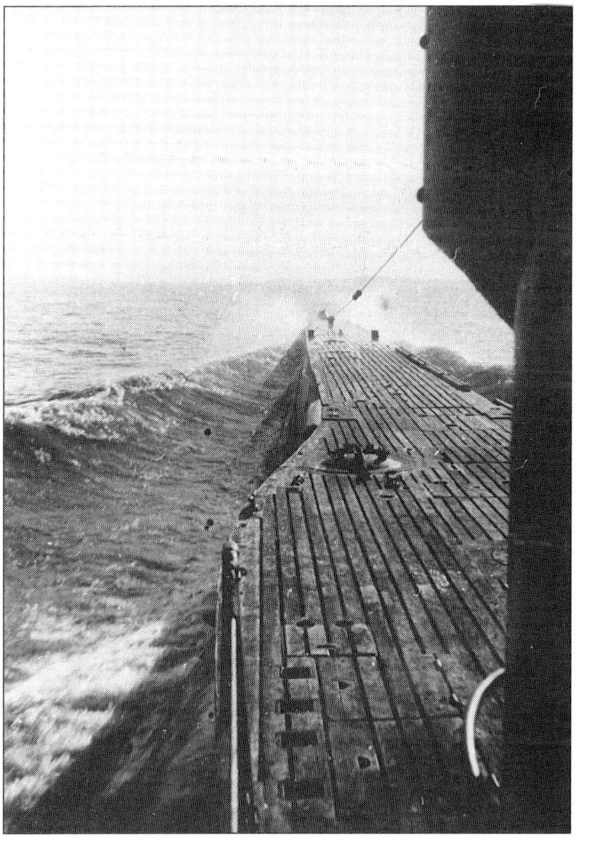

Every U-boat seems to have been photographed from the conning tower while ploughing through the water but this lack of variation in subject matter has helped postwar model makers because there are a large number of deck views, showing the different types of surfaces. The entire decks of some boats were made from metal while others had wooden slats held in place with double-ended copper nails – usually good quality teak was used in preference to timber grown in Europe. When new, this had a dull brown colour, but quickly weathered to shiny silver. This is *U473* under KL Heinz Sternberg, who was born in Freiburg on the edge of the Black Forest. The top of the conning tower is somewhat wider than the bottom, which would suggest anti-aircraft armour had been fitted and this theory is further supported by the absence of the large deck gun. These were removed from 1942 onwards when boats were modified to carry additional anti-aircraft guns. The hatch visible by the port edge is the cover of a pressure-resistant container originally intended for storing a few rounds of large-calibre ammunition and later for inflatable life-rafts. This was only about a metre or so deep and did not lead into the interior of the boat.

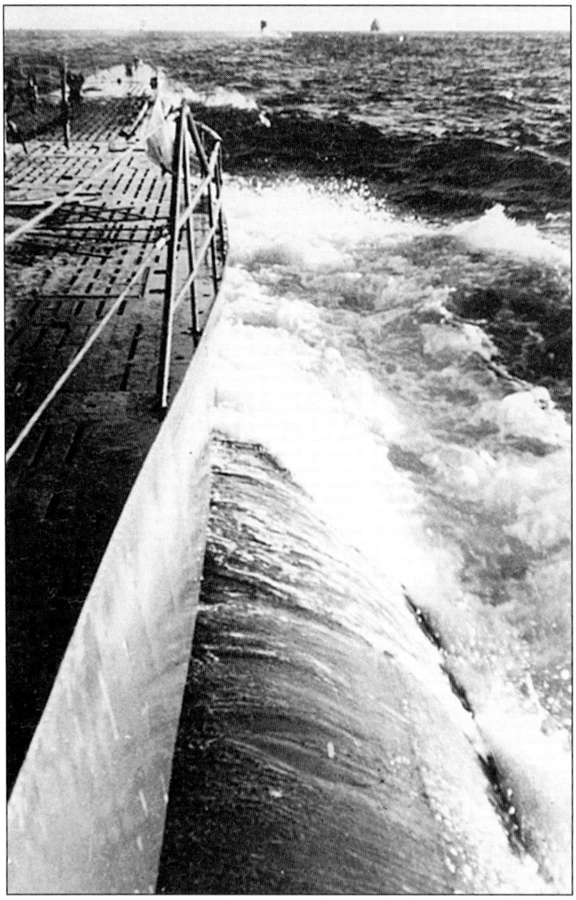

A VIIC on the move (left and below) through the water at the measured miles. Such facilities were buoyed near Eckernförde and in several far eastern Baltic locations and enabled boats to get an accurate indication of speed or calibrate gauges by timing themselves along measured nautical miles. The exact position of the start and finish lines, as well as buoyed marks in between, were further identified by lining up pairs of dominant markers on the land.

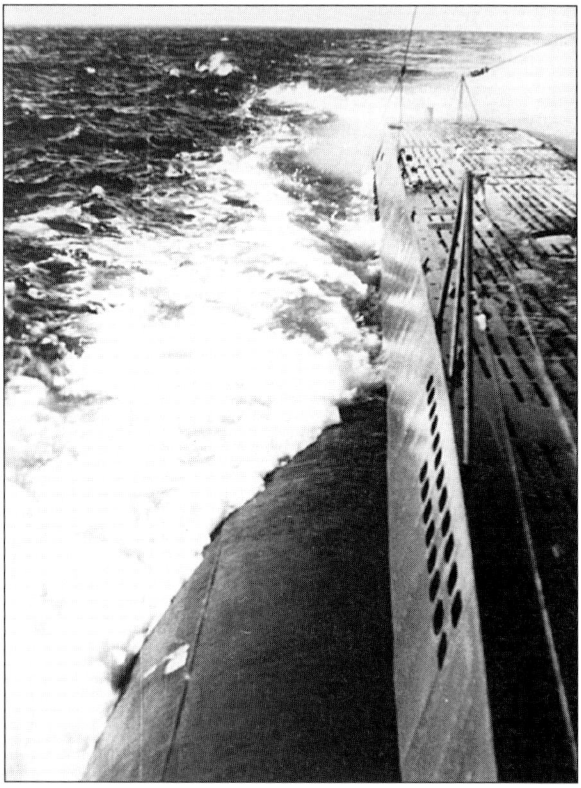

U-boats operating in the Atlantic had top speeds of around 17–18 knots. One knot is one nautical or sea mile per hour which means boats could travel at the land equivalent of about 30–33 kmh or 20–21 mph. However, this consumed vast quantities of fuel and for most of the time they moved at more economical speeds. There were several options for this and the exact procedures were not worked out until the middle of the war when Type VIIC made long distance voyages for operations along the Canadian and North American coasts. Cruising speed was about 10 knots, which more than doubled the range achievable when moving at 17 knots.

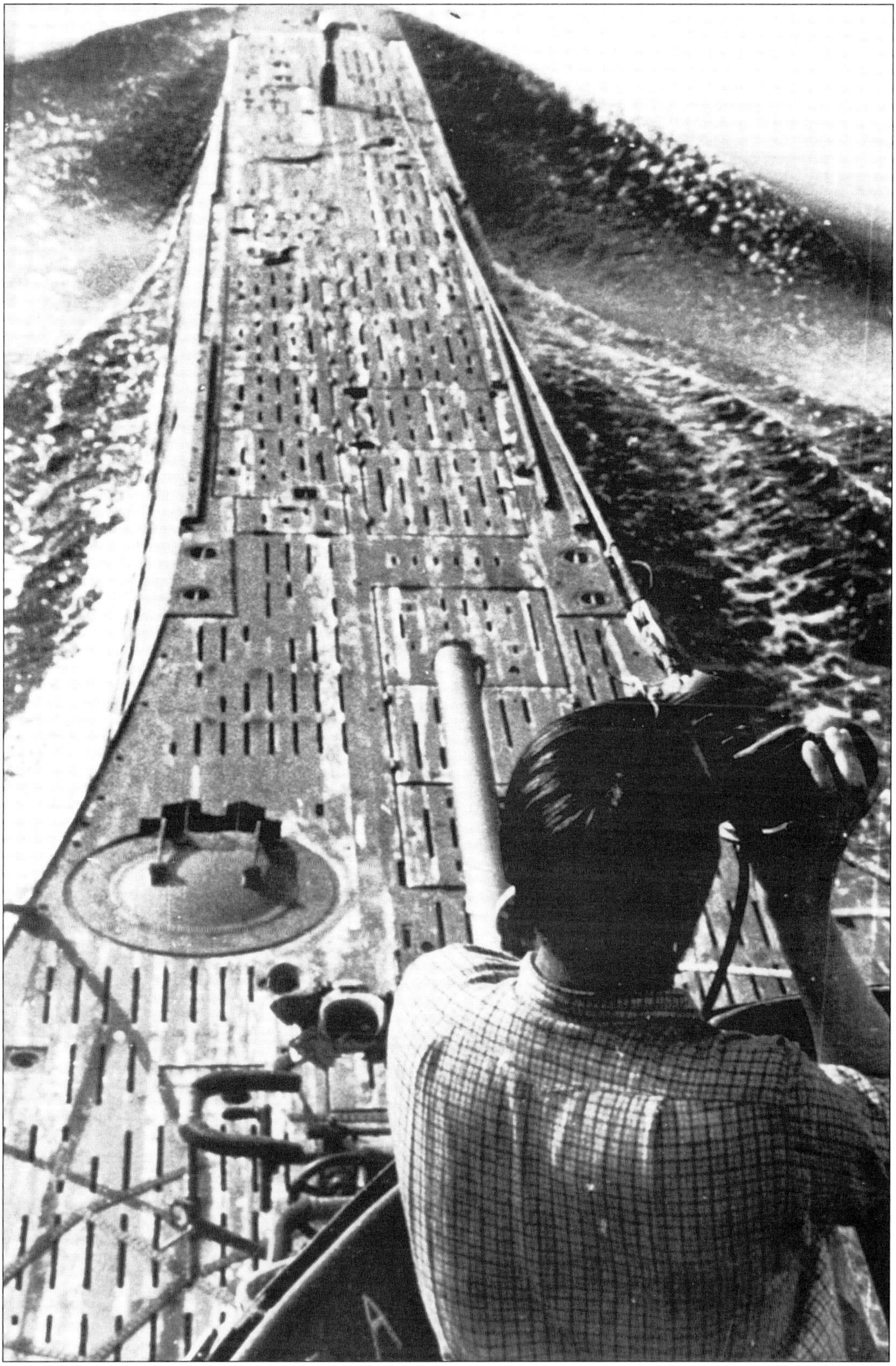

Another view of a different VIIC showing the large 88 mm quick-firing gun still in position. The chequered, cowboy style shirt was standard naval issue. Such patterns appeared in large numbers around the time of the invasion of Norway.

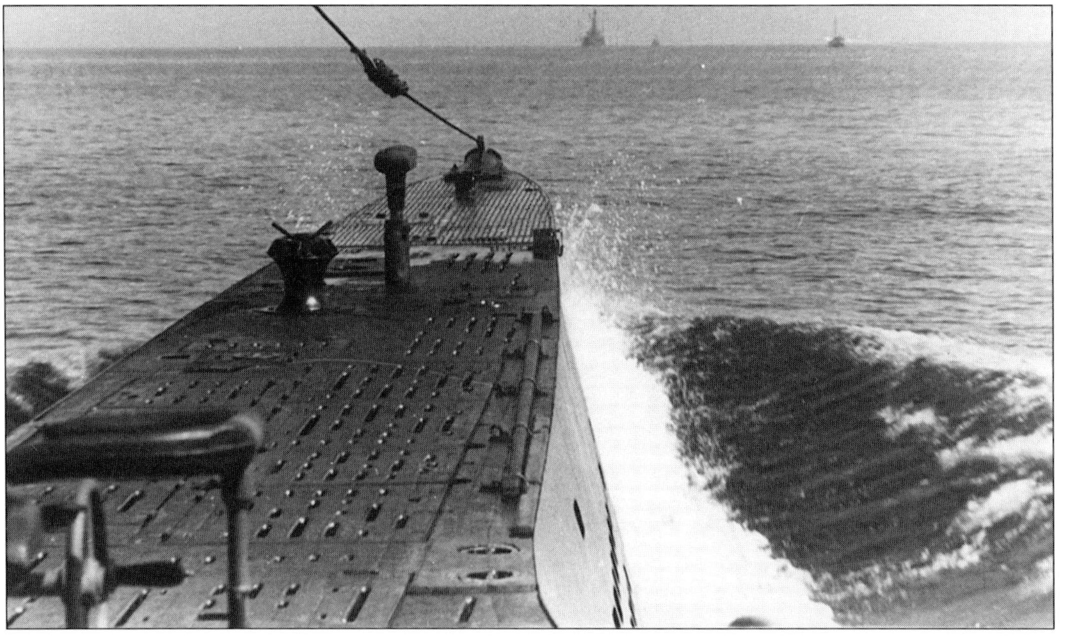

The objects at the front of the bows are of interest. Retractable bollards, which can also be seen in the next picture, have been lowered into the deck casing to make the boat more streamlined. The thick object towards the left is the capstan head of an electric winch. There are holes in the top for inserting wooden poles in case a power failure makes it necessary for the device to be turned by hand. The mushroom-shaped stalk – also detachable and therefore not always visible – is the head of sound detection apparatus.

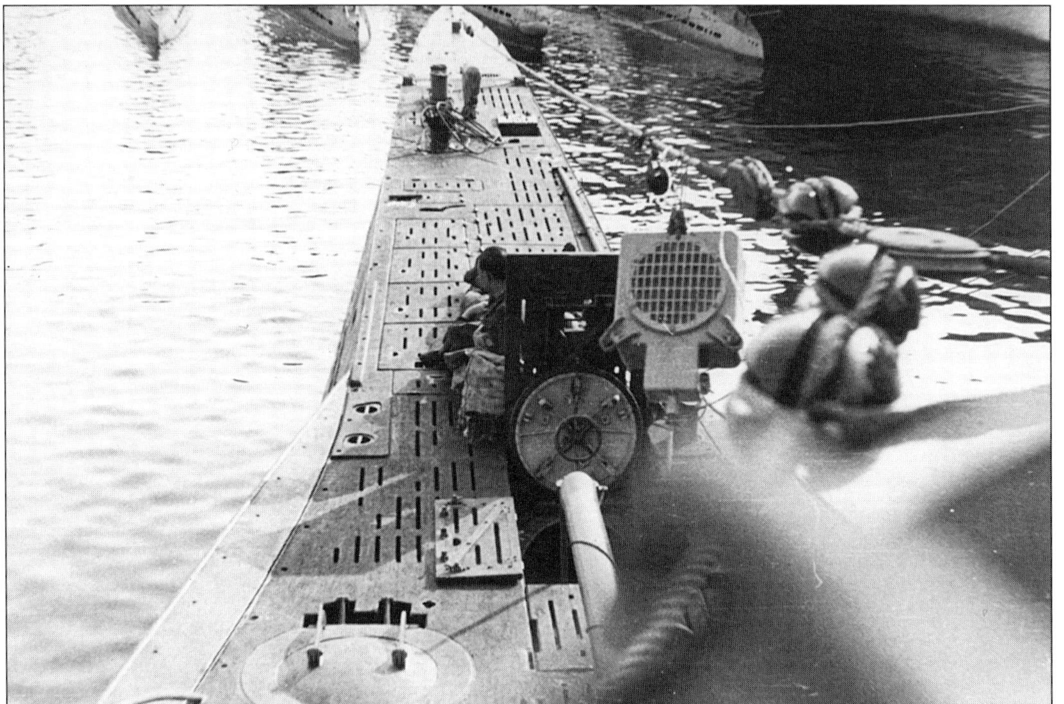

The bows of *U71* with covered sound detection head, capstan and two raised bollards towards the front. The tops of two bollards lowered down into the casing can be seen to the left, just forward of the gun barrel. The thick bulges supporting the jumping wire are insulators to prevent electricity in the aerial from being earthed by the boat. Hanging from the jumping wire is an armoured loudspeaker. Listening to the radio formed an important part of entertainment on board and was the men's only contact with the outside world for long periods. The locking mechanism of the forward hatch can seen by the front of the gun barrel.

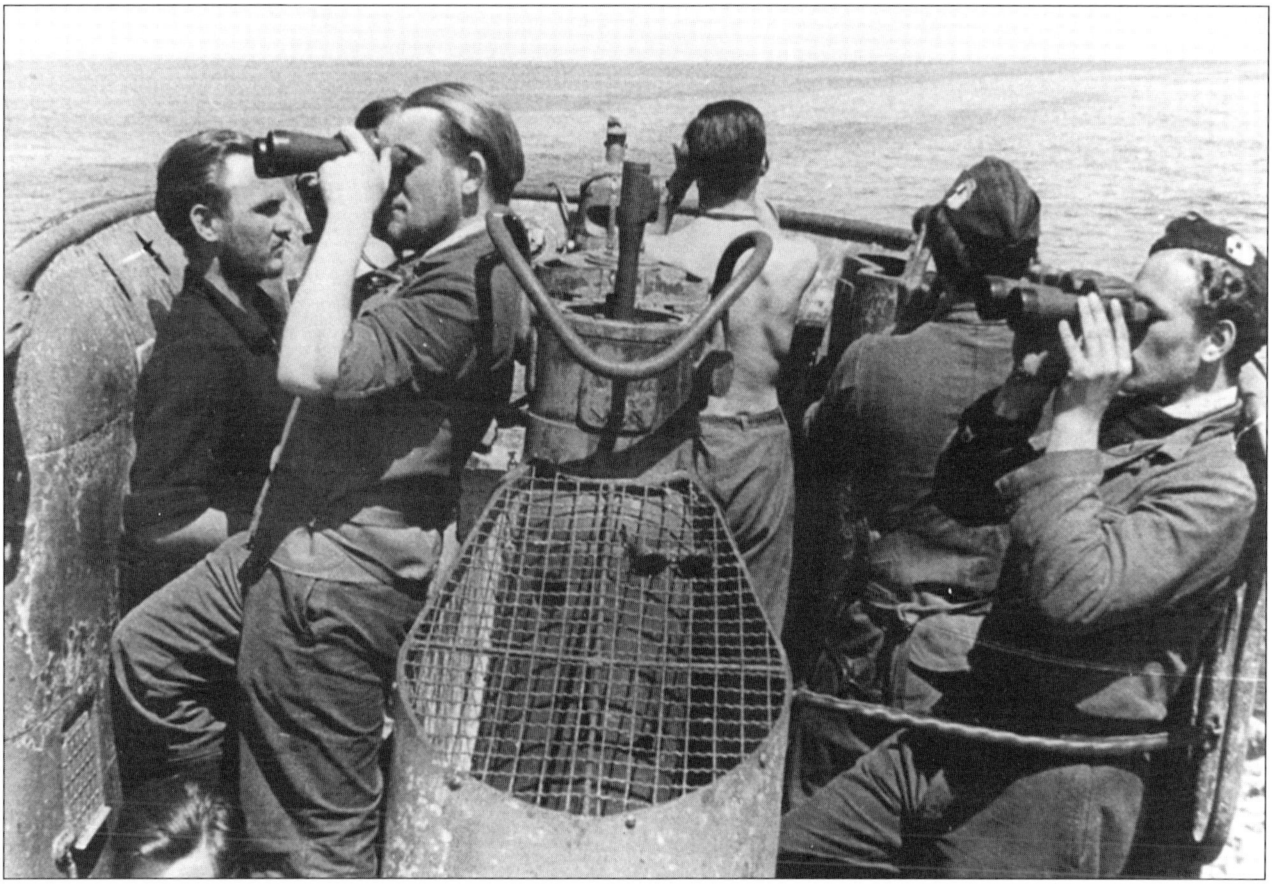

U86 under KL Walter Schug with the head of the attack periscope just visible. Keeping lookout in good weather was a treat indeed and much better than being confined to the inside of the stinking boat. The majority of boats operated semi-formal watch duties, where men were often allowed to conduct their own private conversations and to smoke. Although the sea looks dead calm, a safety chain has been fastened to prevent the man on the right from falling out of the conning tower. In rough weather he would have been wearing a full harness with chains attaching him to the side of the boat. The possibility of being washed overboard was indeed a major hazard. Hundreds of men must have lost their lives this way and thousands more were picked up again a little worse for the experience of the enforced swim. During hectic attacks on dark nights some men were not even missed until long after they had disappeared. Anyone who has seen the film *Das Boot* will appreciate how easily this could happen during the chaos of an alarm dive followed by depth charge attacks. The grid in the foreground covers the top of the ventilation shaft of this Type VIIB.

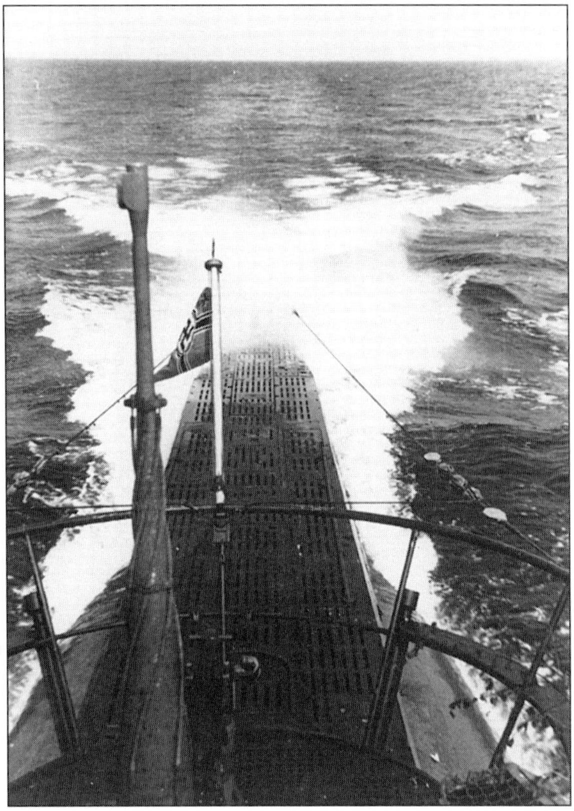

The rear view of the boat was just as monotonous as the bows, except here there were two jumping wires running down to deck level. A system of one wire over the bows and two over the stern was common practice until the middle of the war when rigid radar aerials were fitted to a few conning towers. This meant that the whole boat had to be rotated for a circular sweep. The single jumping wire would have interfered with these signals and boats with such apparatus were modified for a brief period to have two jumping wires at the front, one on each side of the radar aerials. This cumbersome system was quickly replaced by more sophisticated equipment, making photographs of this emergency phase somewhat rare. This picture also shows the attack periscope with the smaller head lens. The bottom end terminated in the commander's control room inside the conning tower and the spiral of wires strung around the top allowed water to wash past the raised head more easily thus reducing the foam generated when moving.

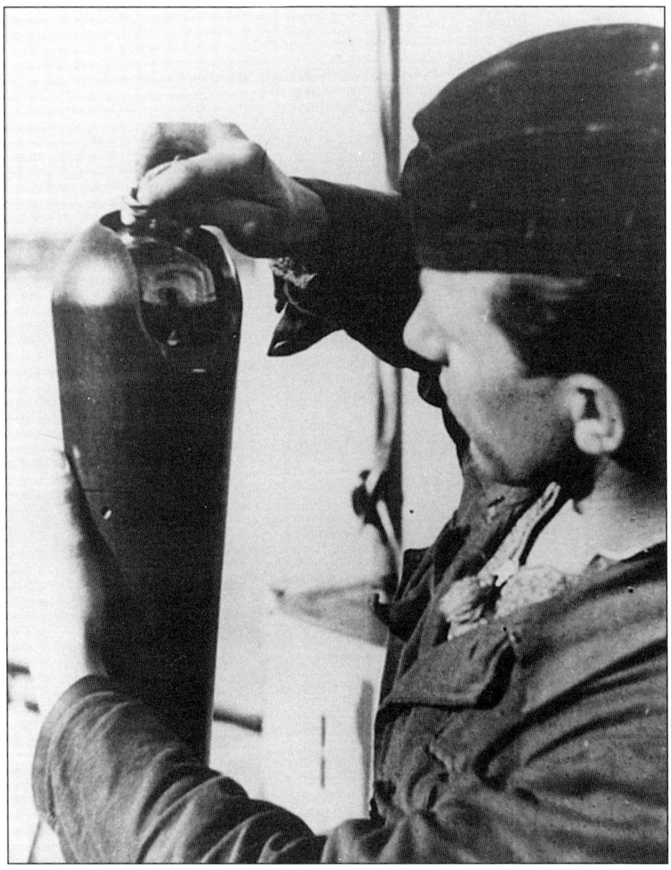

The sky or navigation periscope of *U110* (under KL Fritz-Julius Lemp) being cleaned. Although the head lens could be trained to look at objects at sea level, it could also be used for looking at the sky. Technically it would have been possible to see aircraft through it but such small, fast-moving objects would have been very difficult to spot unless the commander knew roughly where they were. This periscope was hardly used during attacks because the large head lens could easily have been spotted.

U56 under KL Wilhelm Zahn during the summer of 1939 with Willi Drews on the left and IWO Herwig Collmann on the right. Collmann went on to become commander of *U562* and later training leader for the 21st U-boat Flotilla. This picture shows another useful device on the top of the conning tower – the radio direction finder. This could be rotated from the radio room down below to detect the direction of in-coming radio signals. It was particularly useful when approaching convoys, especially at times when bad weather made it difficult to get an accurate fix on the sun or stars. At such times a shadowing U-boat near the target would transmit special homing signals to help draw in other boats. Before the war the radio direction finder was used to take bearings on the numerous known radio transmitters, and boats carried an almanac of their frequencies and transmission signals.

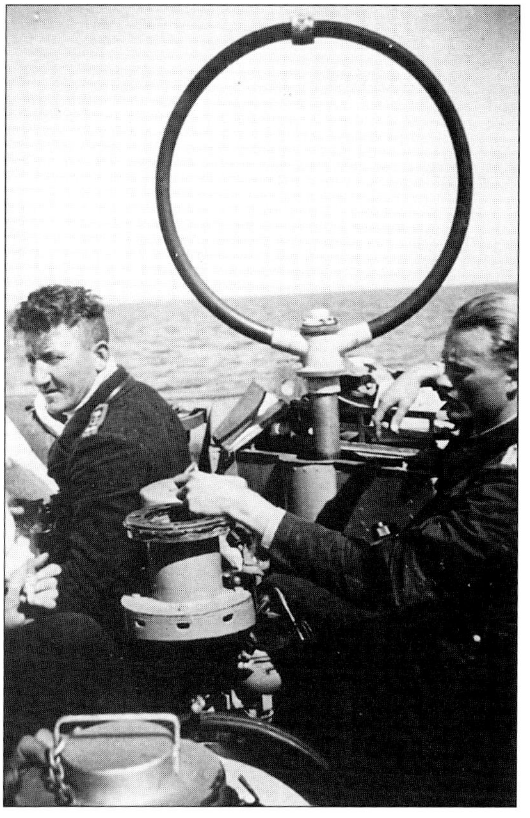

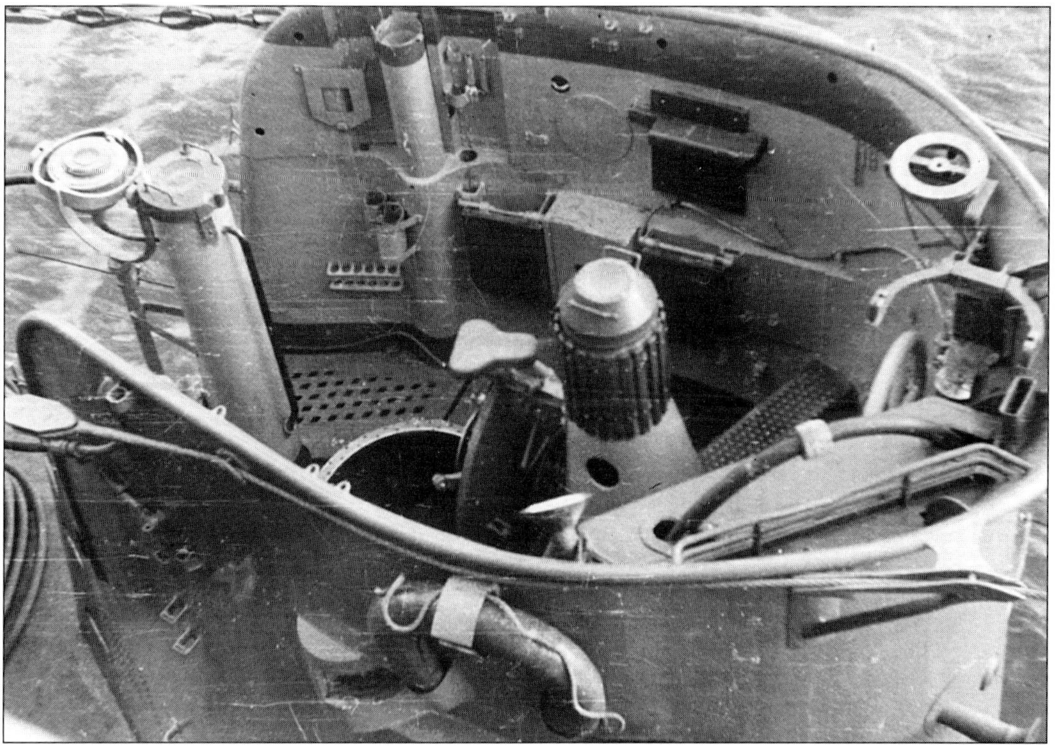

U24, a small coastal boat of Type IIB, showing just how much clutter was fitted inside conning towers. To the left is a magnetic sighting compass attached to a covered periscope support. The torpedo aimer (to the right of the saddle) has also been protected with a cover and the hole for the radio direction finder is just visible in the foreground. On the outside of the tower is a navigation light and lifebelt and towards the right a trumpet shaped fog-horn or typhoon.

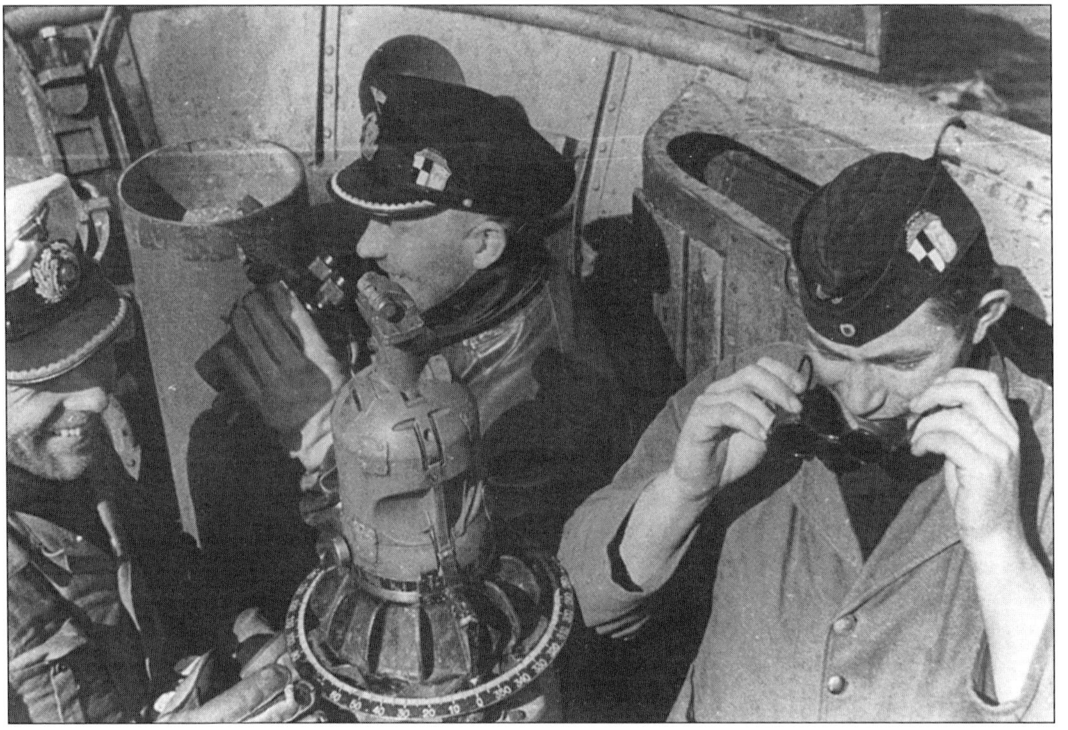

U86 under KL Walter Schug showing (centre) the head of a torpedo aimer which is more modern than the one in the previous photograph. Naval binoculars butted directly onto the special sunglasses worn by the man on the right. This method had the advantage over optical equipment with internal filters inasmuch as there was less change in light intensity when the lookout cleaned the lenses or took a rest from peering through the binoculars. Note the unofficial boat badges on the sides of the men's hats.

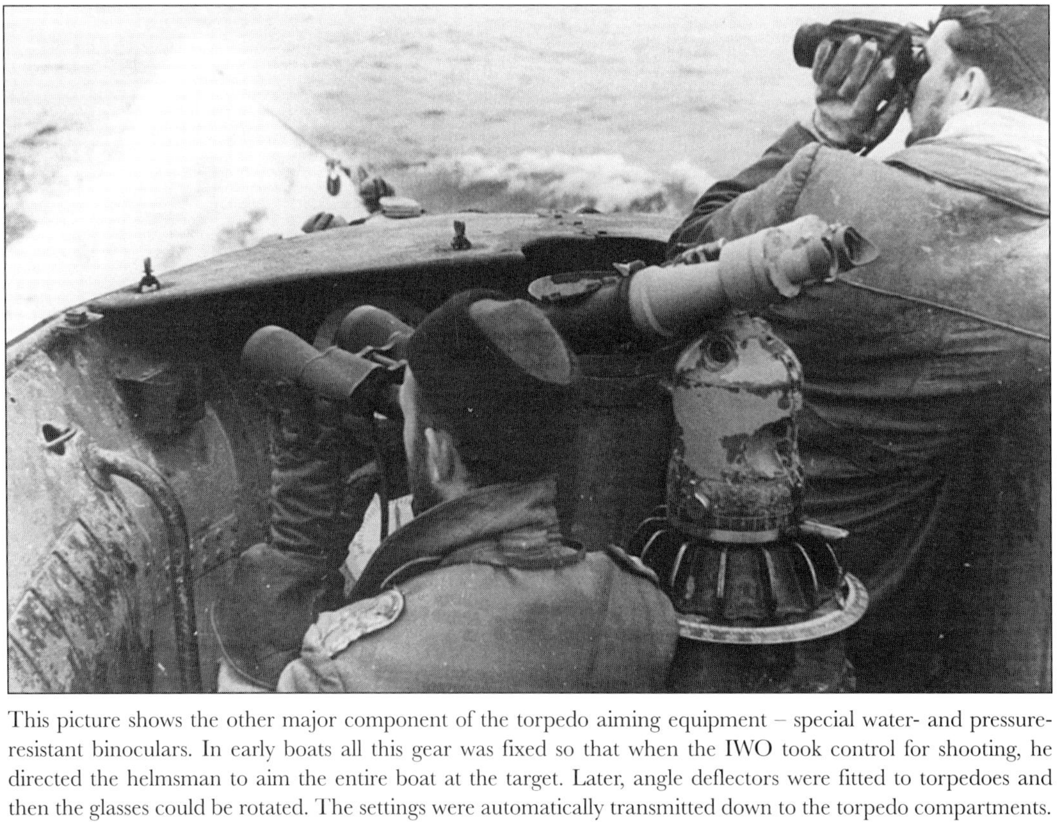

This picture shows the other major component of the torpedo aiming equipment – special water- and pressure-resistant binoculars. In early boats all this gear was fixed so that when the IWO took control for shooting, he directed the helmsman to aim the entire boat at the target. Later, angle deflectors were fitted to torpedoes and then the glasses could be rotated. The settings were automatically transmitted down to the torpedo compartments.

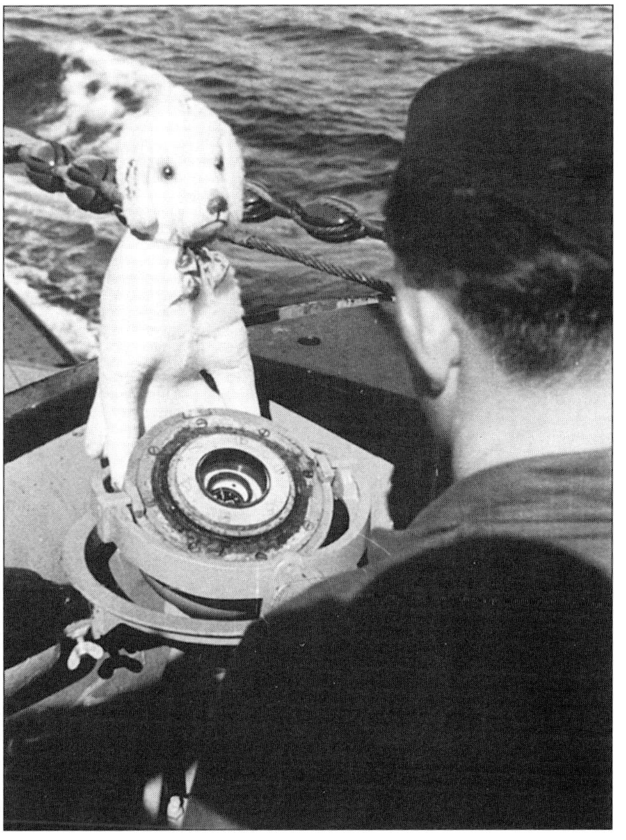

This close-up clearly shows the working of the gimbals holding the magnetic sighting compass. Although some boats had real live mascots on board, this dog from *U123* is of the toy variety.

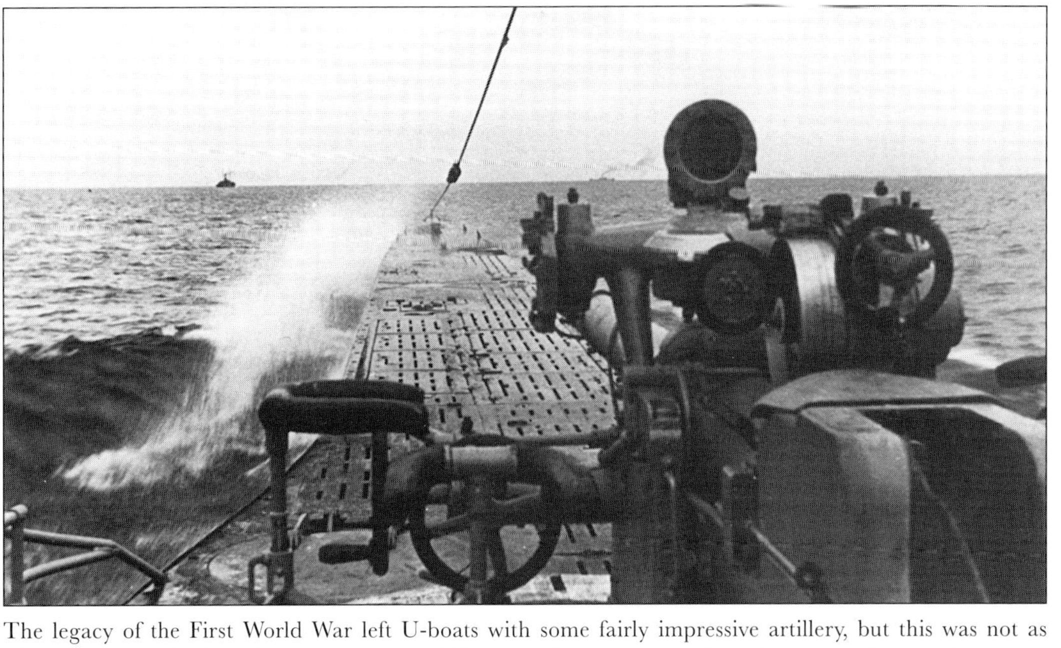

The legacy of the First World War left U-boats with some fairly impressive artillery, but this was not as effective as it might look in photographs. A U-boat rocking on even a slight Atlantic swell moved about so much that gun aiming became very difficult. In addition, cartridges had to be brought up from a locker below the floor of the radio room. This presented many problems and caused so many injuries that many commanders considered it criminally irresponsible to order the gun crew on deck except in the mildest of conditions. Yet, despite these problems, some U-boats fought some impressively long gun duels, expending in the region of 100 shells in a single action. Generally Type VII (seen here) had an 88 mm and Type IX a 105 mm quick-firing gun forward of the conning tower. This picture shows *U441*.

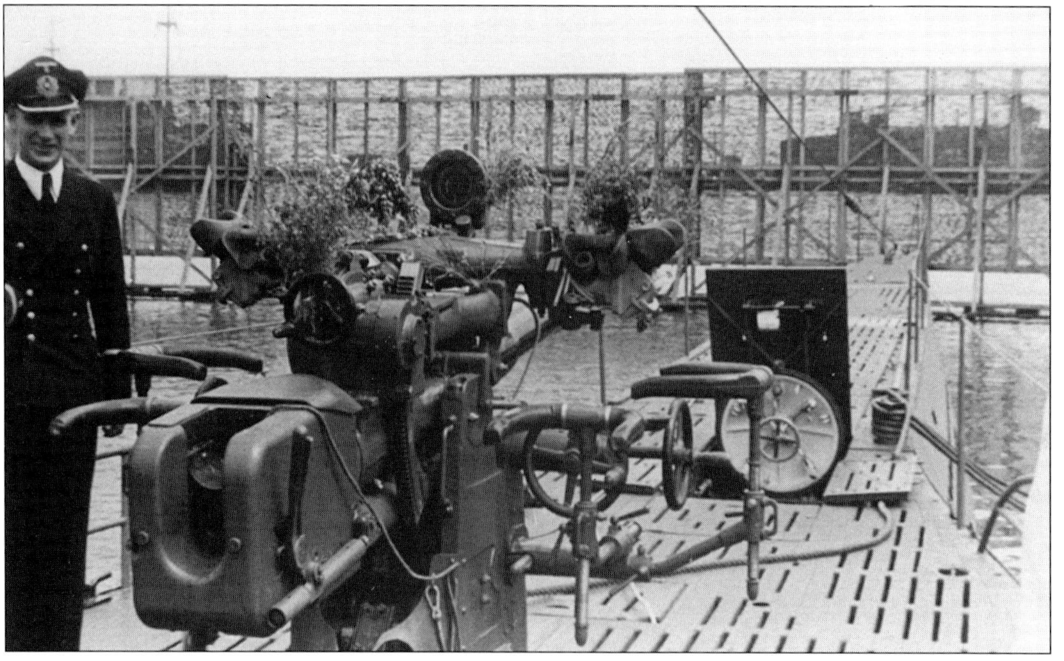

U440 or *U441*.The breech had a watertight locking mechanism and four men could work together at the same time to aim the gun, although only two of them were usually required for each shot. The U-shaped brackets enabled men to stand by the gun in rough weather and use both hands to work the hand-wheels. This photograph shows both the double gun sights, although they have been partly hidden by bunches of flowers. The brackets on the extreme right and left have been reversed to prevent the deck being obstructed. The fence in the background is a semi-see-through screen to hide the naval activity from prying eyes.

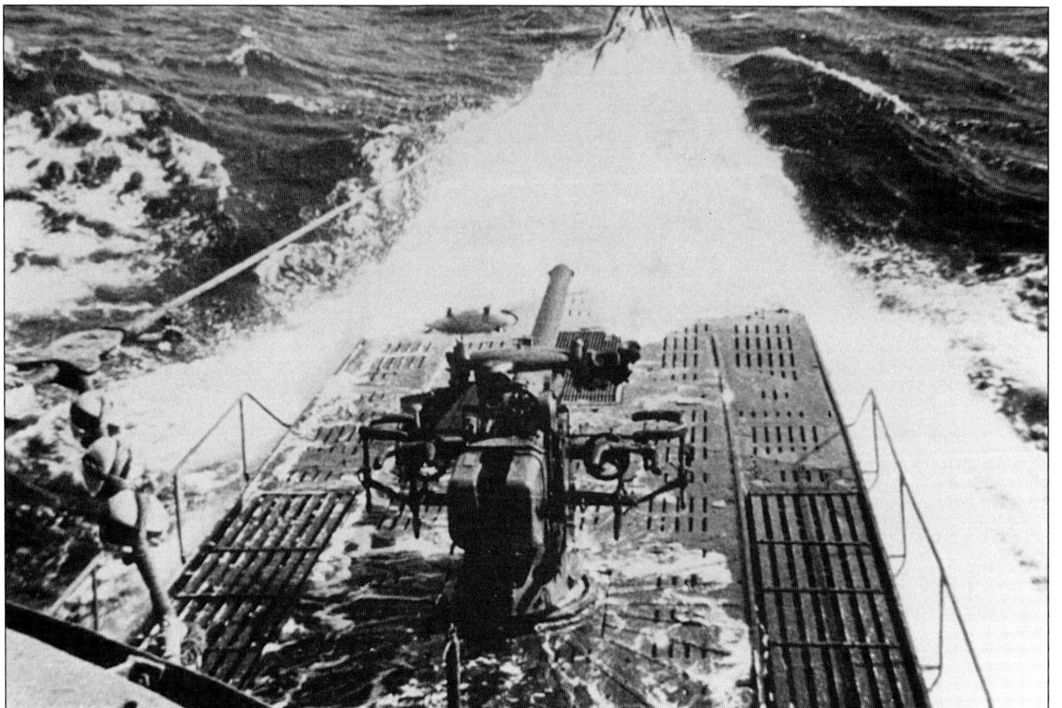

At first glance this 105 mm aboard the much larger Type IXA *U37* looks very similar to the slightly smaller gun shown in the previous pictures. The main distinguishing feature between the two major boat types VII and IX is the much wider deck with a graceful curve from bow to stern on Type IX vessels. Type VIIs had a bulge around the large gun or the part of the deck where it used to be.

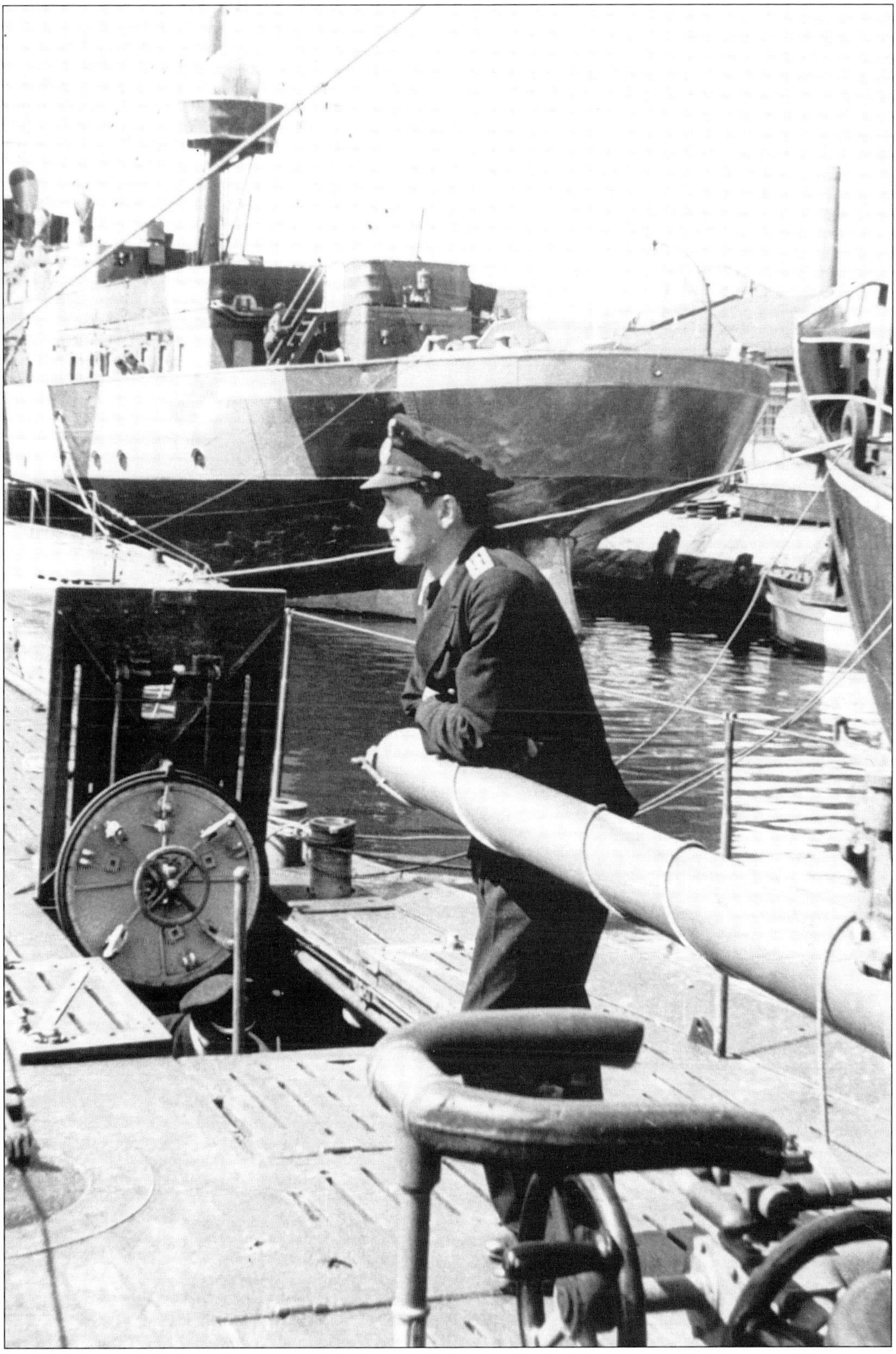

U72 under KK Hans Werner Neumann from Berlin – later killed when he was commander of *U117* – with Obermaschinist Hannefarth demonstrating that the 88 mm could also be used for dreamy poses. The rope around the barrel prevented the water-tight tampon at the end from getting lost. Note that the large, padded bracket for supporting the gun aimer has been turned inwards to prevent it from obstructing the deck.

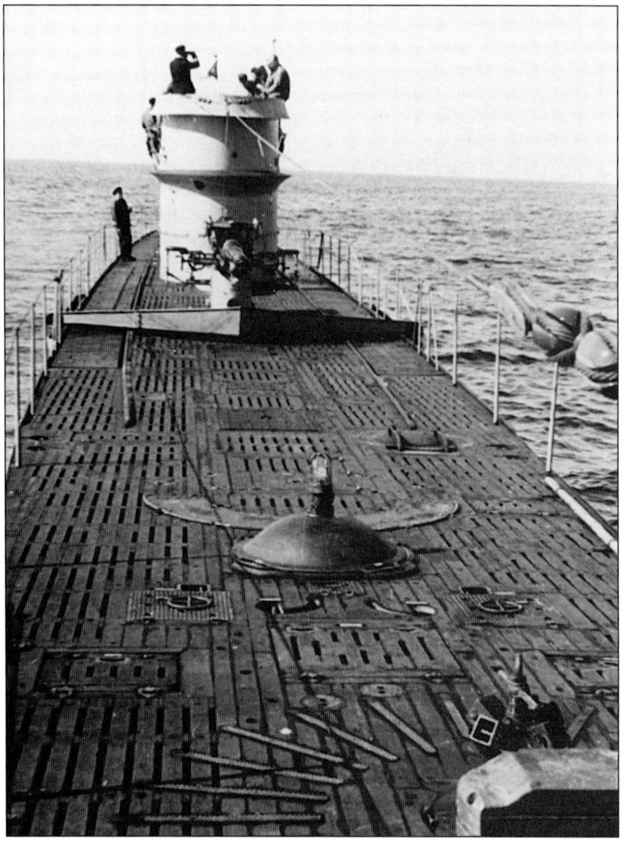

U123, a large Type IXB. The spray deflector just forward of the gun was not terribly effective and was not fitted to many boats. In the foreground is a rescue buoy with a light on the top.

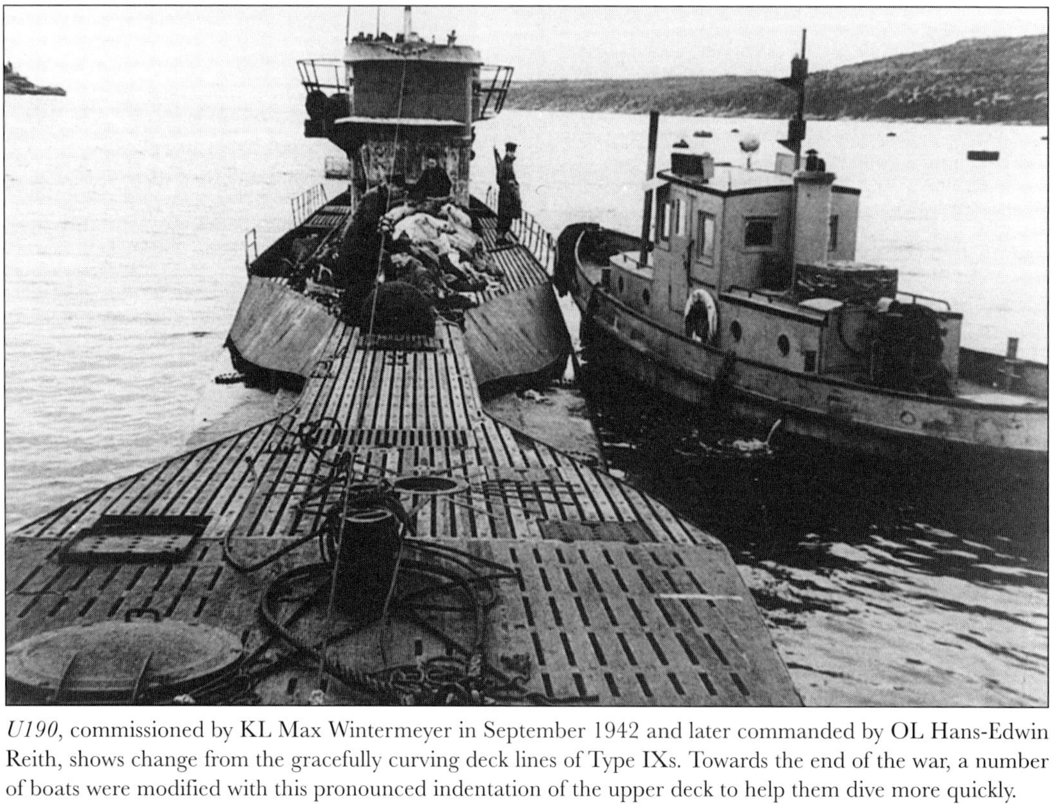

U190, commissioned by KL Max Wintermeyer in September 1942 and later commanded by OL Hans-Edwin Reith, shows change from the gracefully curving deck lines of Type IXs. Towards the end of the war, a number of boats were modified with this pronounced indentation of the upper deck to help them dive more quickly.

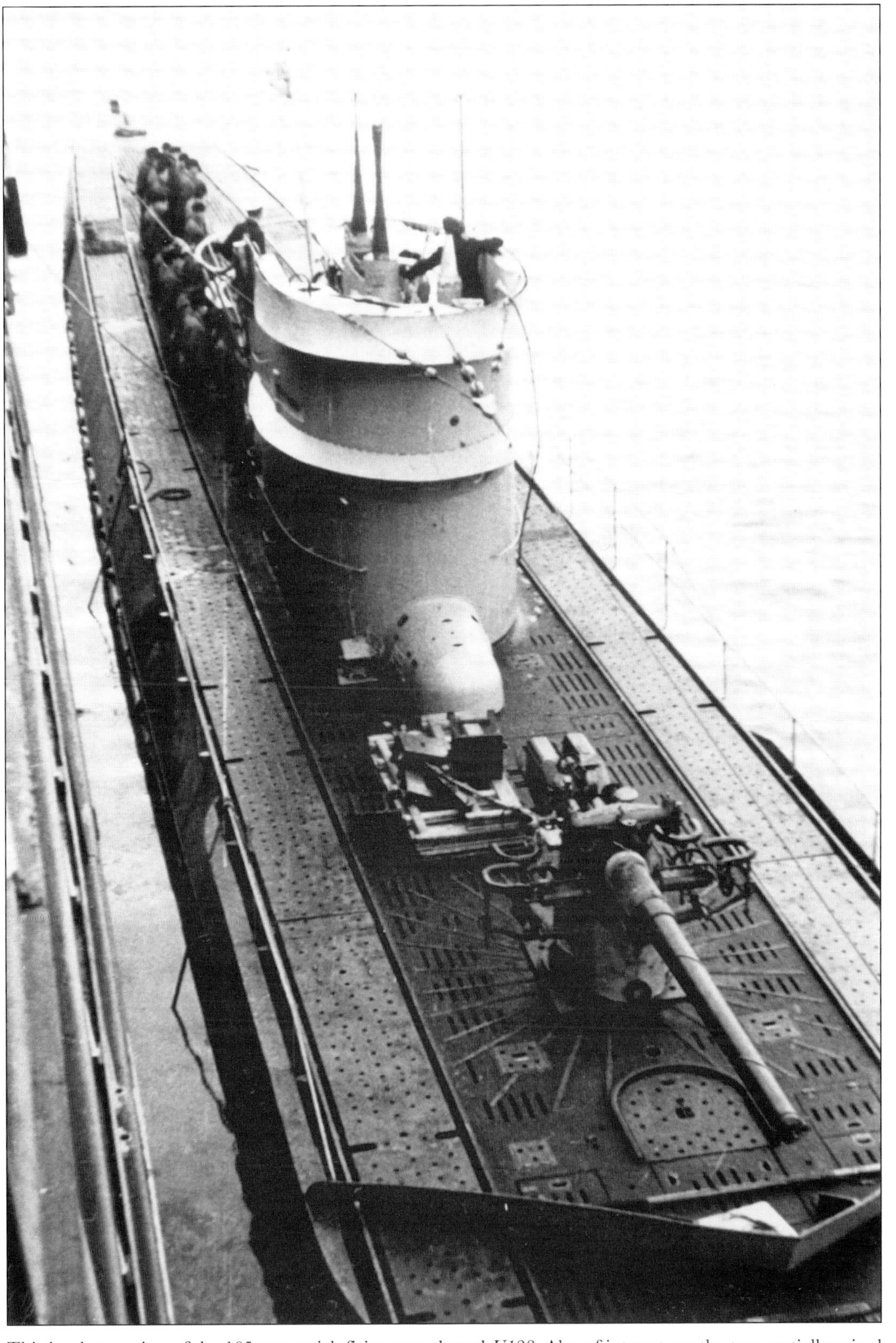

This is a better view of the 105 mm quick-firing gun aboard *U123*. Also of interest are the two partially raised periscopes, with the thick head lens of the navigation or sky periscope on the right and the very much smaller attack periscope on the left. The huge bulge at the base of the conning tower housed a magnetic compass which was viewed from the central control room through an illuminated periscope.

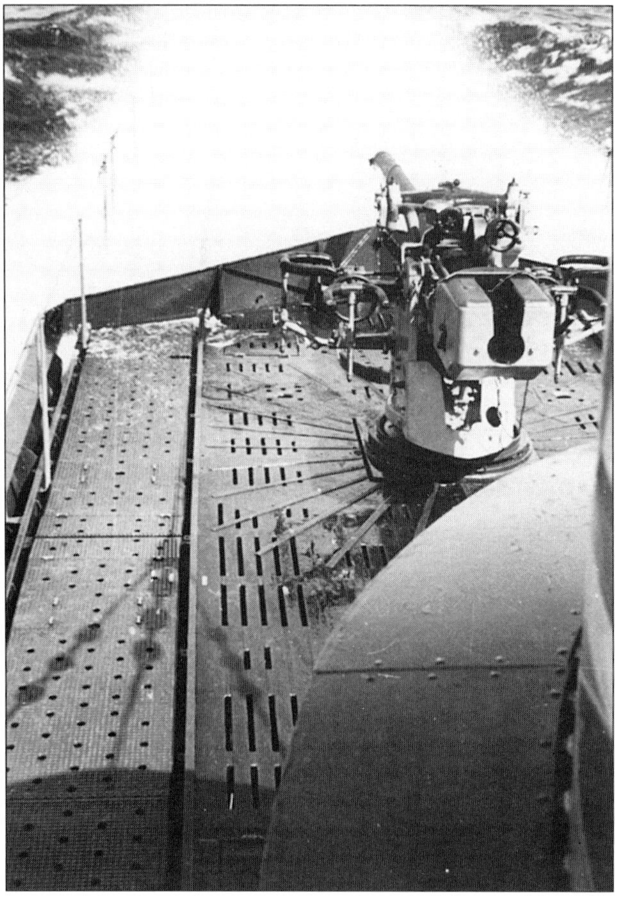

U123's 105 mm quick-firing gun. The wave deflector across the upper deck did have some effect in moderate seas. This photograph was taken from the spray deflector, halfway up the conning tower.

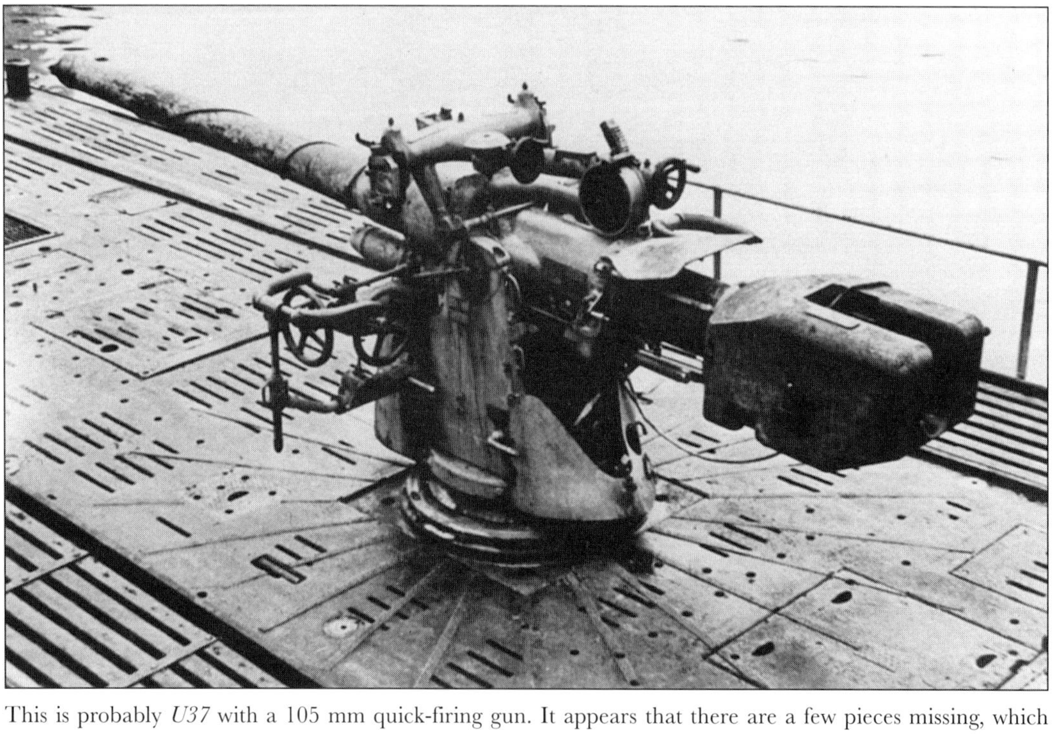

This is probably *U37* with a 105 mm quick-firing gun. It appears that there are a few pieces missing, which makes this gun look different to those in other photographs. However, many of the fittings were detachable and sometimes temporarily removed.

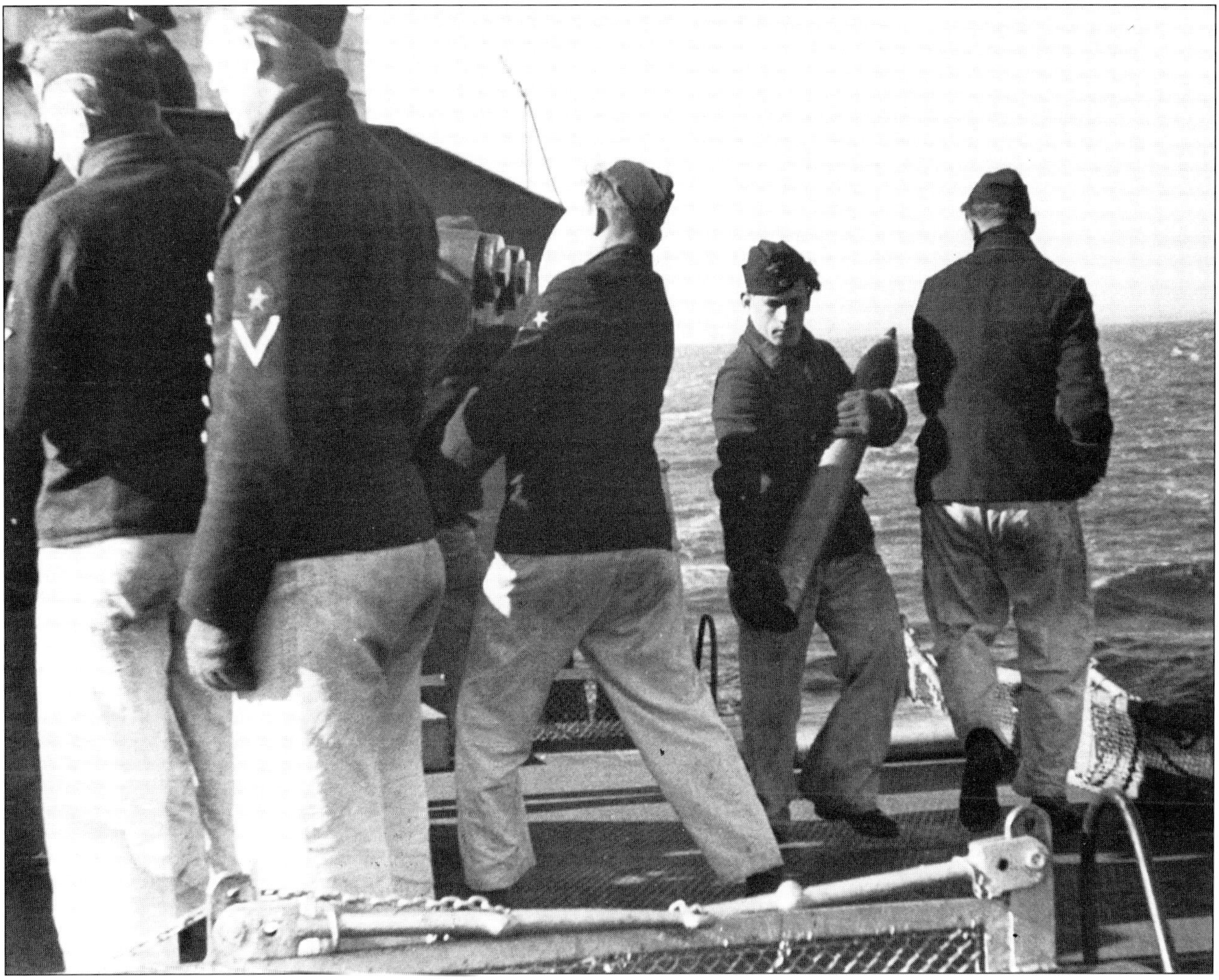

Gun crews were often trained while the boat was conducting trials on which they were not required or when vessels returned to shipyards for finishing off work. There were a number of specialist schools and this picture shows men practising using weaponry at the Naval Artillery School in Swinemünde. Practise cartridges were often filled with a small quantity of explosives and then topped up with what looked like old socks full of compressed sawdust. This meant that they had the feel of the real thing but did not force the shells out very far. Another trick for economy was to slide a steel jacket down the inside of bigger barrels so that they could fire smaller shells. The men are wearing standard working pea or blazer-style jackets with white denim trousers. The sleeve chevron is a rank badge for Matrosengefreiter with the star indicating that he is a seaman by trade.

Gun training usually worked well, although in his splendid book *Make another Signal* (William Kimber, 1973), Captain Jack Broome reports a rather irate signal from a pilot who saw a practise shell explode ahead of him, 'Please remember that I am PULLING this target. Not pushing it.'

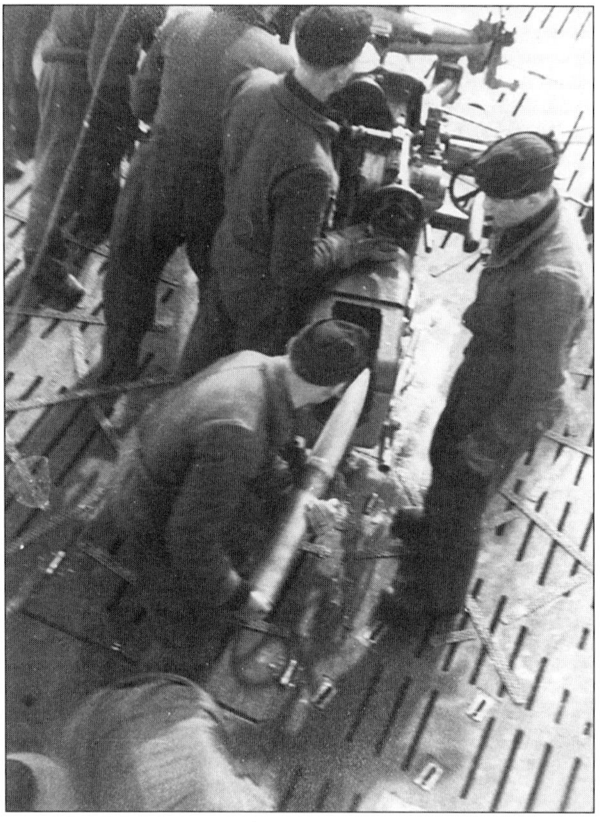

Cartridges were stored in a locker below the radio room and had to be man-handled through the central control room, up the vertical conning tower ladder, past lookouts, down the back of the conning tower, around the side and then manually pushed into the breech. This operation often had to be performed while the boat was rocking and water washed around the men's feet; it is a wonder that the guns achieved any successes at all. This boat is probably *U215* under KL Fritz Hoeckner, who went down with her in the North Atlantic to the east of Boston, USA, in July 1942. The boat is of special interest because it was a Type VIID, with five mineshafts immediately aft of the conning tower. Only six of this type were ever built.

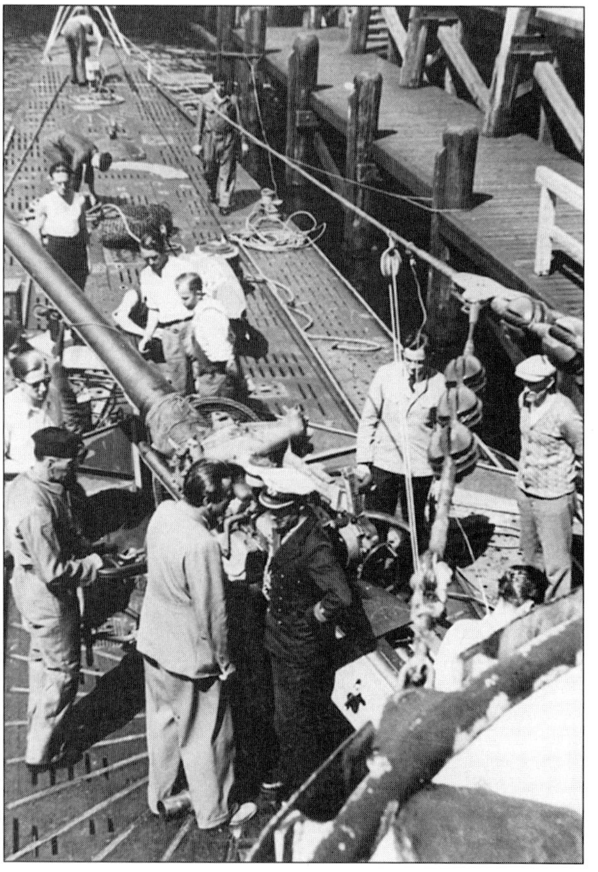

Men aboard *U172* under KL Carl Emmermann testing the deck gun in port. Firing in this location was not recommended because the noise and blast would have been too offensive.

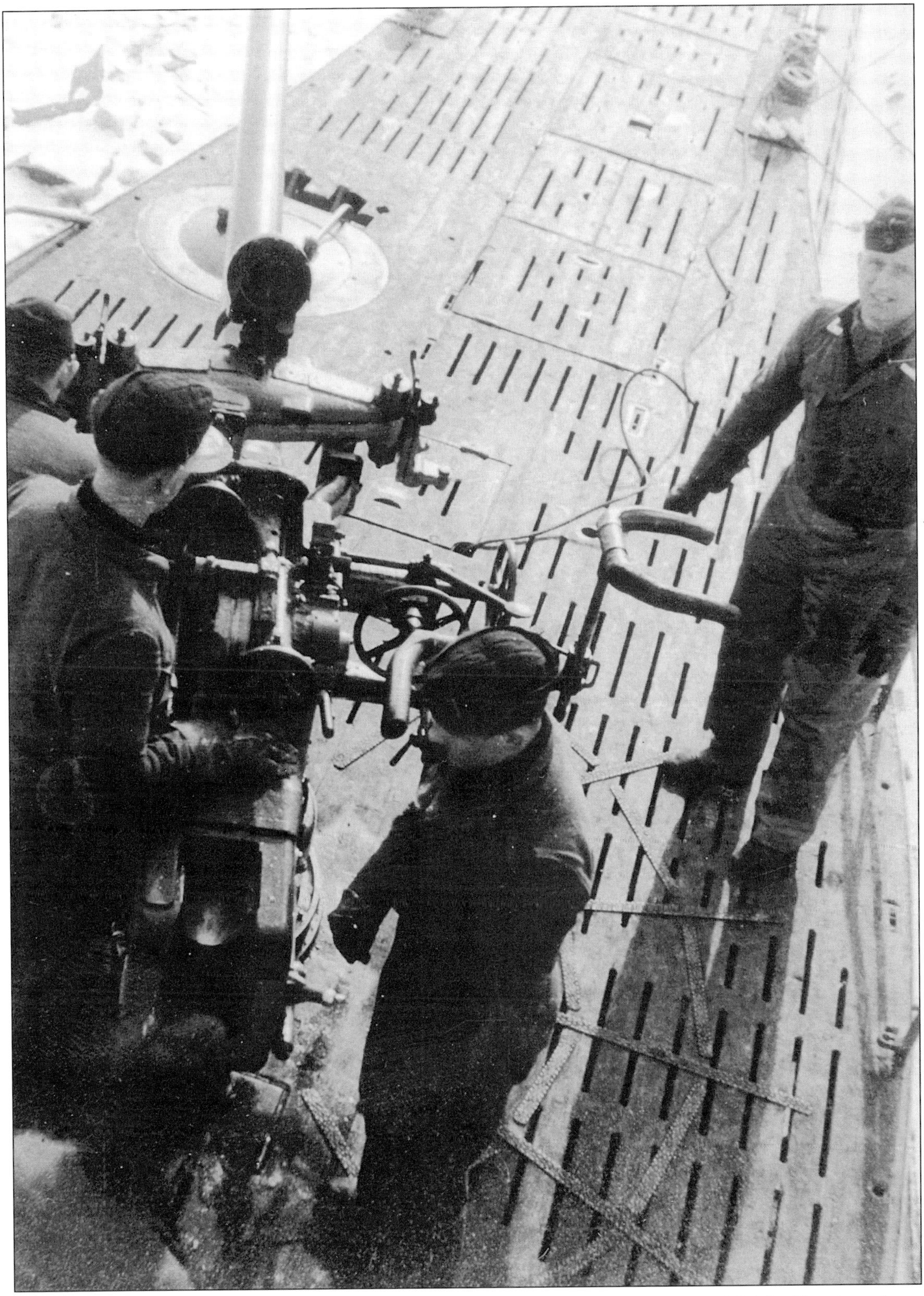

Does this show the 88 mm gun aboard *U215* in action at sea? The man on the extreme left is looking through the sights while the right-hand bracket for holding these optics on the other side of the gun is clearly visible. Eagle-eyed readers will notice that the first sentence of this caption cannot be correct because the bollards in the background are raised and show the boat made fast.

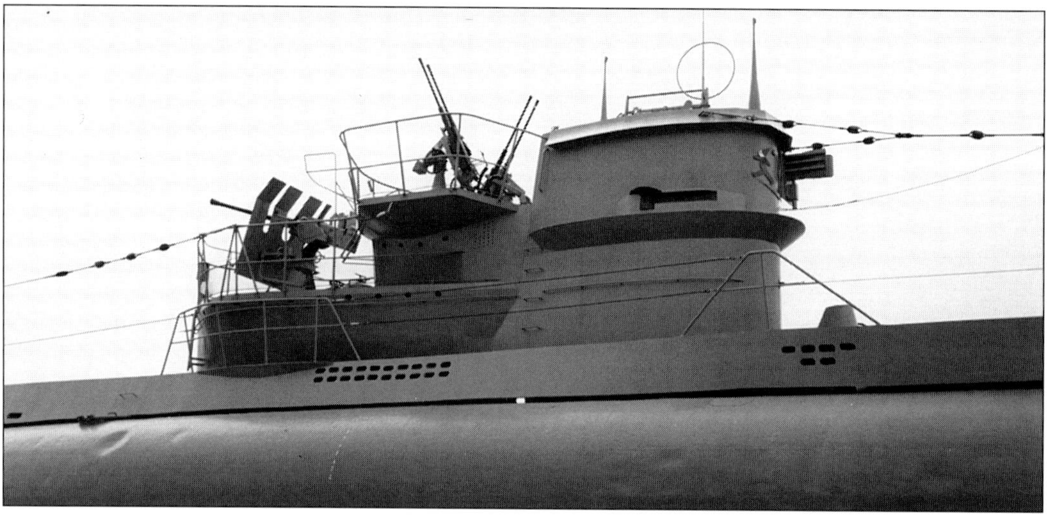

U995, March 1998. Type VII boats with 80 mm guns carried a maximum of approximately 250 rounds and Type IX about 180 for the bigger 105 mm calibre. Some boats sent out to the Caribbean and North Russian shores with the objective of attacking land installations probably stored more ammunition. Large deck guns saw a limited amount of use at the beginning of the war then their importance declined rapidly and they were dismantled in ever-increasing numbers from 1942 onwards. At the same time conning towers were modified to carry more powerful anti-aircraft weapons and armour was added to protect lookouts from aerial gunfire. This photograph of the museum boat close to the Naval Memorial in Laboe, Kiel, shows the basis of the modified conning tower design. The existing gun platform to the rear of the tower was enlarged to carry two 20 mm twins and a lower platform was added to accommodate either one 37 mm or a quadruple 20 mm anti-aircraft gun. The circular device near the front of the tower seems to have replaced an earlier genuine radio direction finder. A number of the original fittings have been removed from the inside of the boat and it could well be that the loop was also stolen. It is a pity that everything which could be unscrewed has been taken away by eager collectors. The German Naval Association (Deutscher Marinebund) made a considerable effort to replace losses but now it also seems to have run out of original spare parts. Since opening as a museum, the boat has always had two attack periscopes protruding above the tower, probably because there were no original navigation periscope head lenses to be had. The horizontal rail protruding above the conning tower wall, was an aerial for a combination radar and radar detection apparatus. The rectangular bracket just below the top edge at the front (right) of the tower used to hold the raised snorkel in position.

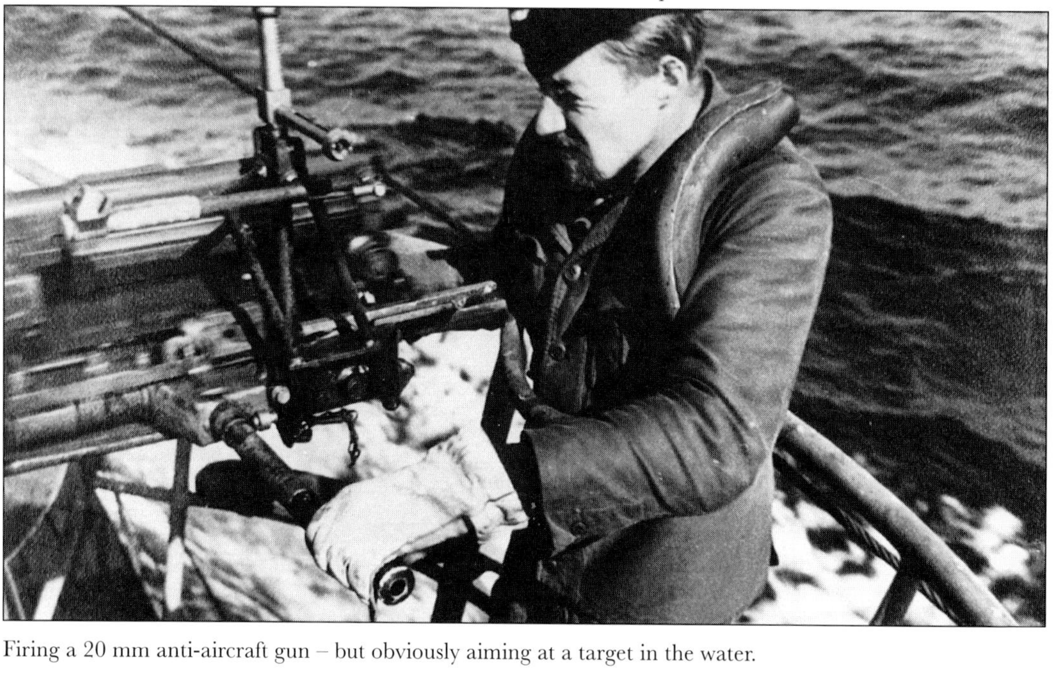

Firing a 20 mm anti-aircraft gun – but obviously aiming at a target in the water.

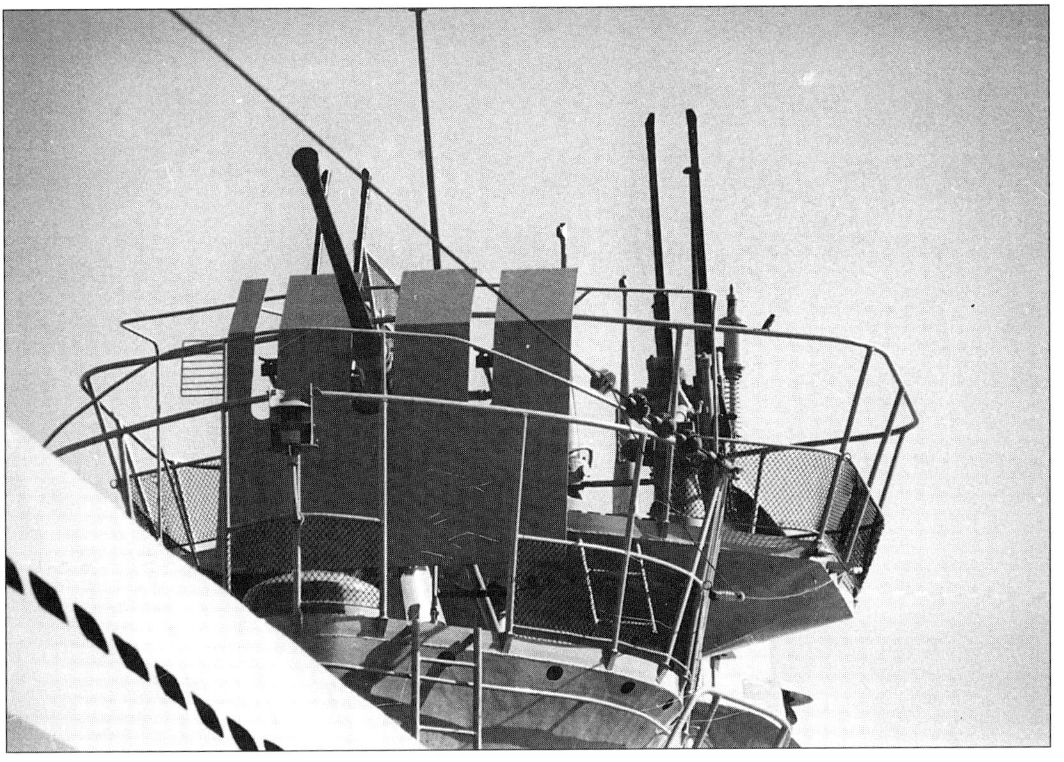

U995's 37 mm anti-aircraft gun with the twin 20 mm towards the right.

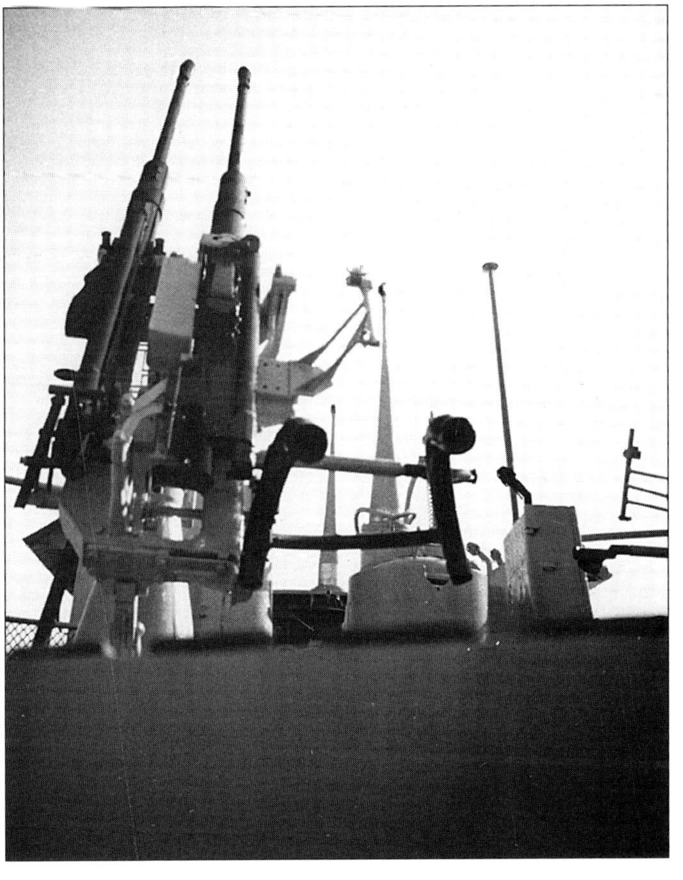

A gunner's view of the 20 mm twin.

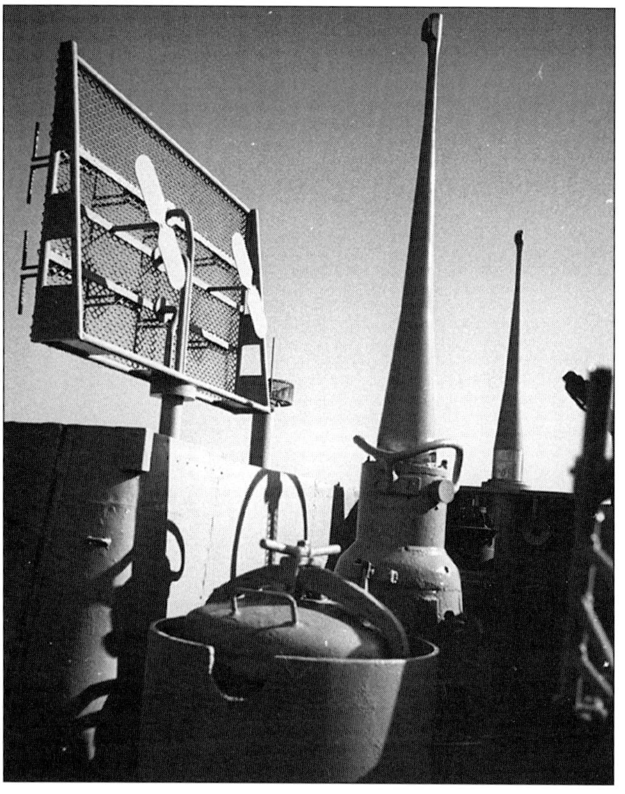

The bedstead-like, Hohentwiel radar aerial with a circular dipole aerial for detecting enemy radar transmissions behind. A shadow of *U995*'s earlier radio direction finder, with a spiral-like vertical aerial attached, has been thrown against the coning tower wall by the early morning sun. In the foreground is another later addition, a water- and pressure-resistant ammunition container for the anti-aircraft guns.

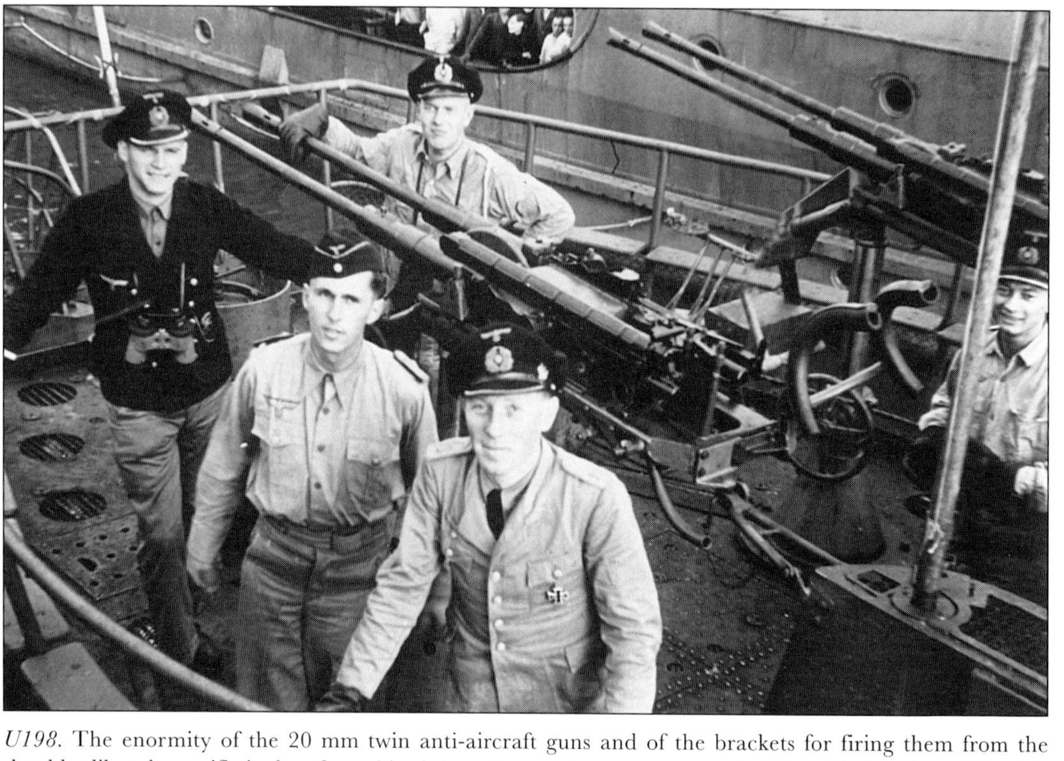

U198. The enormity of the 20 mm twin anti-aircraft guns and of the brackets for firing them from the shoulder like a large rifle is clear from this picture. A second person was required for adjusting the height. It is easy to see that there was no protection from an aircraft's returning fire and this helps to explain why there were so many casualties during combat with planes. *U198* had rather an interesting start in life: it was one of the few, perhaps the only, boat not to have been commissioned by her first commander but by KK Werner Musenberg from *U180* who stood in for KK Werner Hartmann.

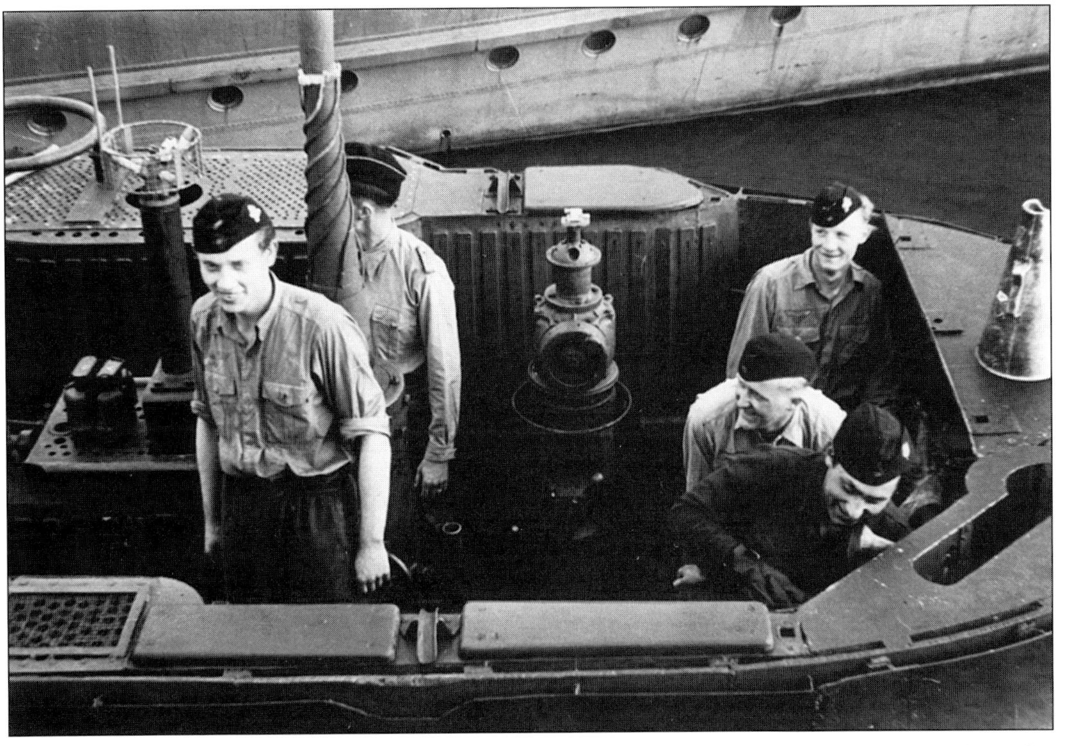

U198's conning tower. The circular aerial with two prongs sticking up on the left replaced the earlier rough wooden Biscay Cross aerial of the Metox radar detector. The partially raised periscope can be seen in the middle and to the right is the torpedo aimer. The cone-shaped object sticking out from the wall on the right is a megaphone. *U198* was one of the few very large, long-range boats of Type IXD2 that undertook voyages to the Far East.

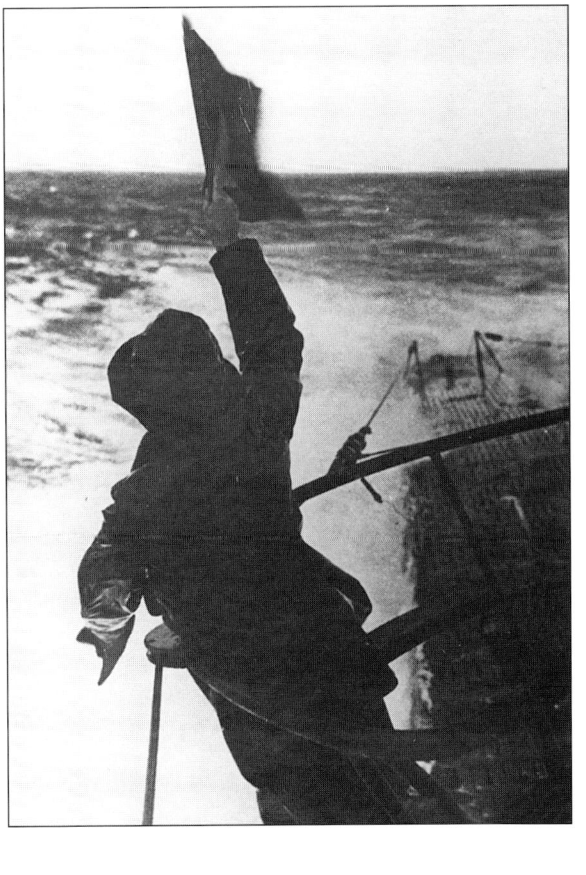

Cone-shaped megaphones were made of plain tin tubes and were employed for shouting orders to men on deck or on the quay when docking. They were also used on rare occasions when two boats met at sea. Semaphore was the other common communication method between U-boats when radio silence had to be maintained. A fear of being detected by enemy radio direction finders prevented transmissions unless the boat's position had already been compromised.

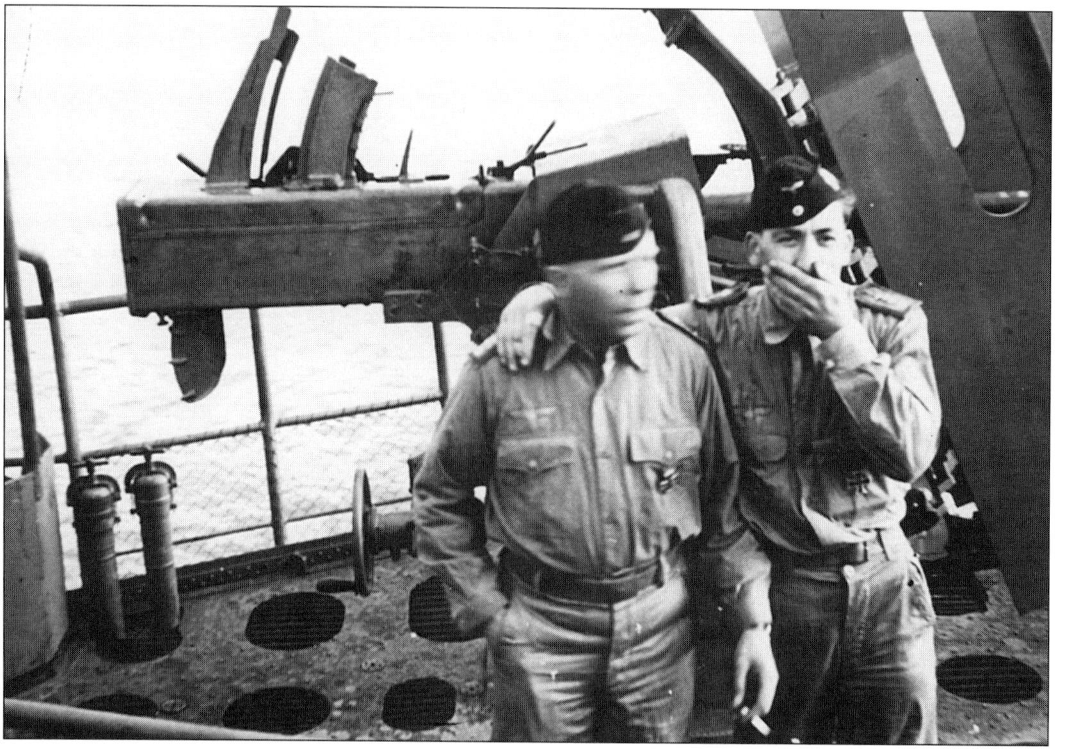

U198 showing the breech of the 37 mm anti-aircraft gun with a clip for inserting a magazine of cartridges. The 37 mm quick-firing deck guns, which were fitted on some boats towards the beginning of the war, differed from the anti-aircraft guns in that they had a breech where cartridges were fed in singly.

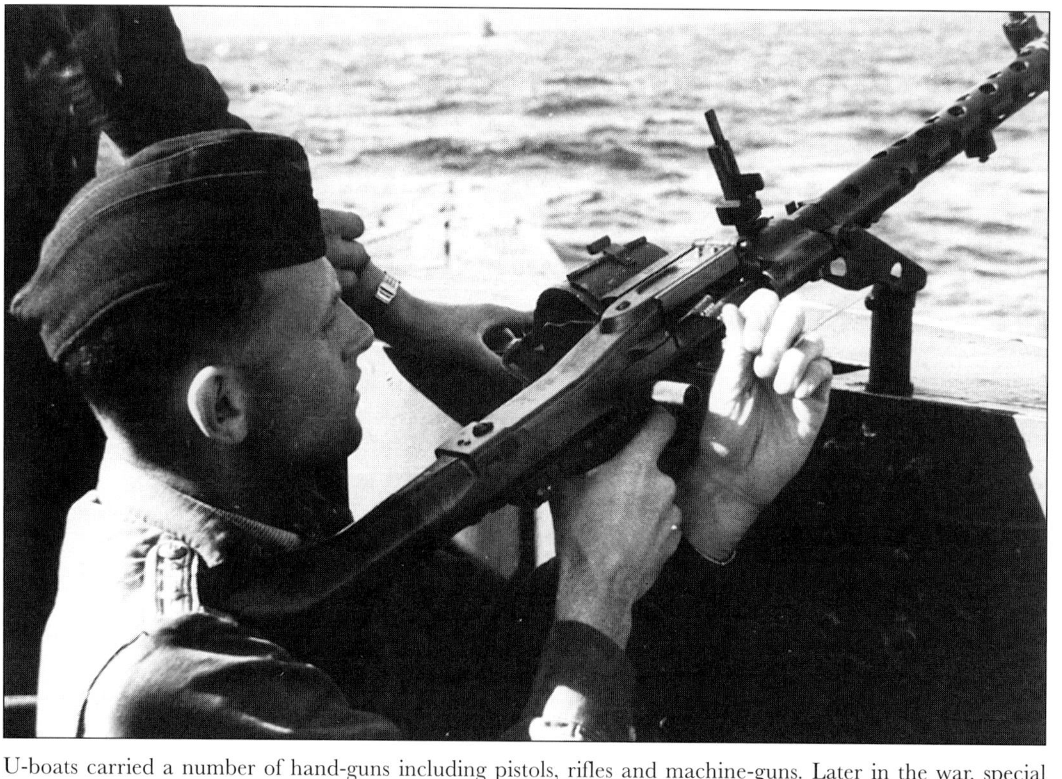

U-boats carried a number of hand-guns including pistols, rifles and machine-guns. Later in the war, special fittings were provided for a variety of different fast-firing machine-guns with a view to aiming them at attacking aircraft.

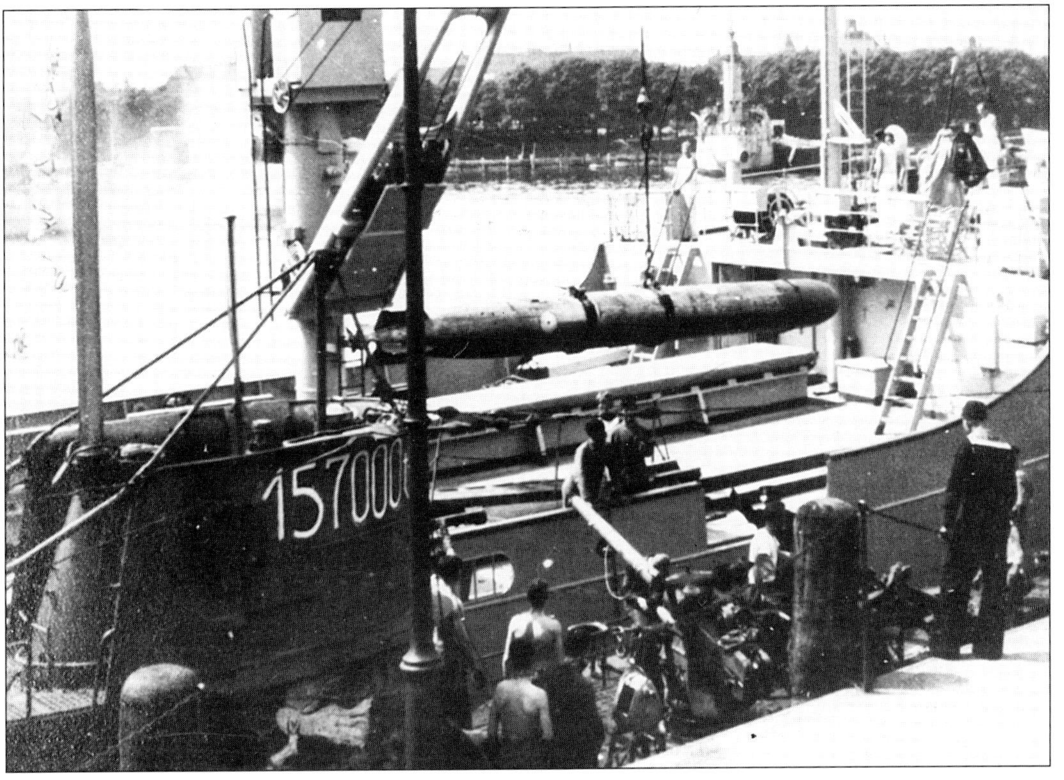

There was no standard method for delivering torpedoes to a boat but each weighed 1.5 tons which meant a crane was usually needed to bring them on board. At sea they were often transferred by attaching fenders and additional flotation aids and then diving the boat underneath before surfacing hopefully to leave the eel on the deck. Here *U48* is receiving the genuine article with explosive warhead.

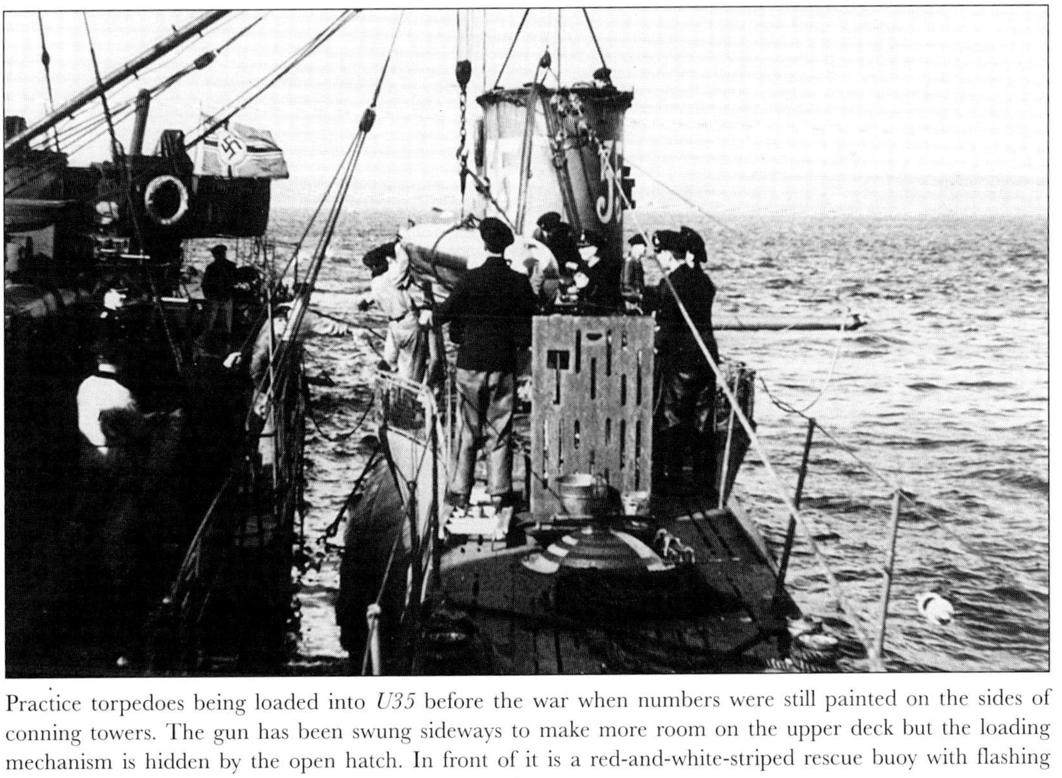

Practice torpedoes being loaded into *U35* before the war when numbers were still painted on the sides of conning towers. The gun has been swung sideways to make more room on the upper deck but the loading mechanism is hidden by the open hatch. In front of it is a red-and-white-striped rescue buoy with flashing light on the top. Railings were usually removed when boats went to sea.

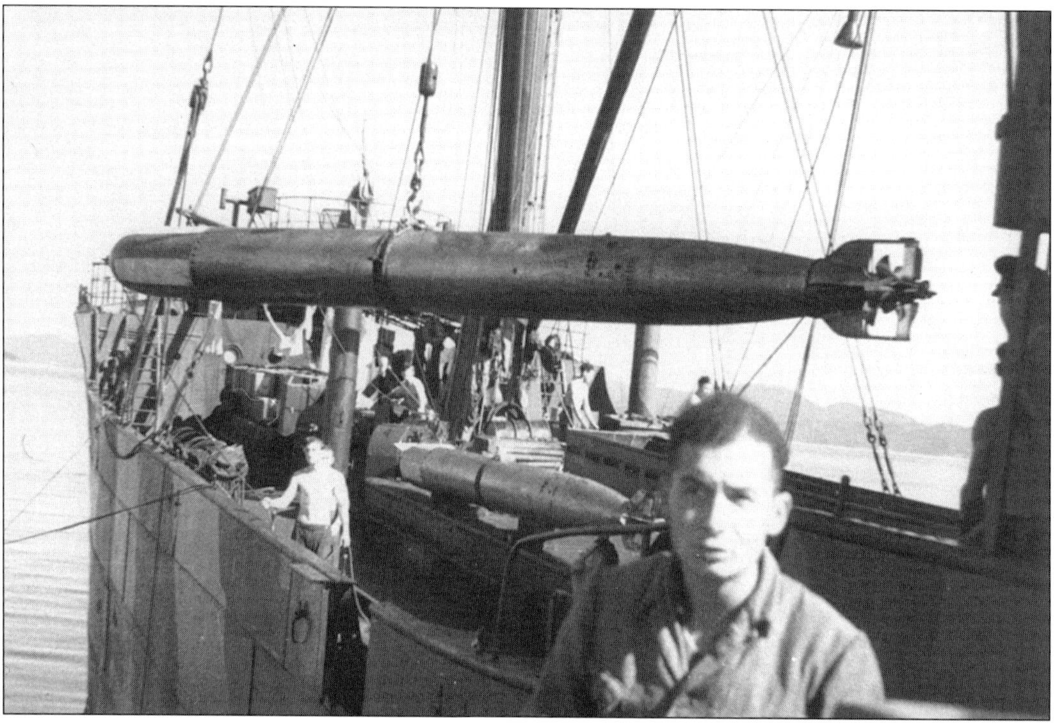

Practice torpedoes had a white-and-red-striped warhead without explosives. These arrived in very much the same fashion as those with bite but they surfaced after shooting so that they could be caught again to be reused over and over again. Many also had a lamp on the top so that observers could watch their progress at night.

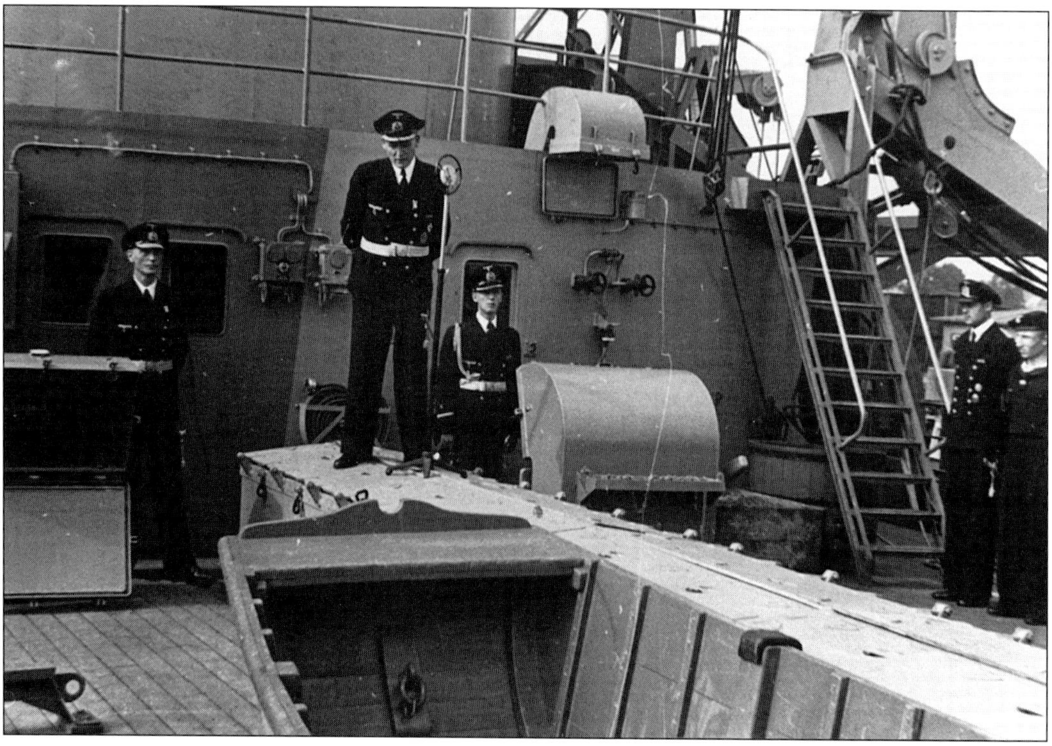

Many of the rudimentary skills for dealing with torpedoes were learnt before men arrived at their U-boat. This is the torpedo training ship *Hugo Zeye*. The third man from the right is wearing the so-called 'monkey swing' or adjutant's lanyard, which suggests he is the commanding officer's right-hand man.

Anlaufskizze mit Schußbild: 1.) Wie sind Schußunterlagen erworben? 2.) Besondere Beobachtungen, 3.) Abwehr, 4.) Erklärung für Fehlschuß, 5.) Begründung für den Fall, daß mit „MZ aus" geschossen oder die „Kleine Prüfung" vor dem Schuß nicht durchgeführt wurde, 6.) Feindwirkung vor dem Schuß (Wabo - Flibo)

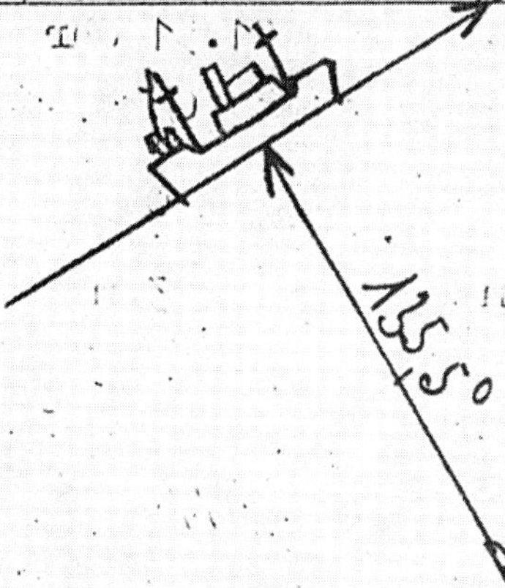

1) Durch Schätzung

2.) Nach dem Treffer erfolten 21 Wabodetonationen in der Untergangsstell

3.) keine

4.) entfällt

5.) entfällt

6.) keine

1.) Wirkung am Ziel, 2.) Höhe und Aussehen der Sprengsäule, 3.) Zeit bis zum vollkommenen Untergang, 4.) Wahrnehmungen im eigenen Boot:

1.) Treffer hinten 15. Schiff sakte über das Heck sofort ab.

2.) 20 m Breiter Rauchpilz.

3.) c.20 sec

4.) Treffer wurde deutlich gehört. Keine großen Erschütterungen. Kurz nach dem Treffer flog Artl.Mun. in die Luft. 21 Wabodetonationen nach dem Untergang in der ~~Tauchstelle~~. Untergangsstelle.

gez. A r e n d t	gez. Fleige
Lt.z.See und I.W.O.	Oblt.z.See und Kmdt.
Unterschrift des Schützen	Unterschrift des Kommandanten - gegebf. beglaubigt

Gutachten der Torpedoinspektion

Shooting torpedoes was not a straightforward matter of just pressing a button. At today's prices, one cost about the same as a dozen or so medium-sized family cars and such expensive items had to be accounted for. This is just the first page of a torpedo shooting report. The torpedo mechanic would also have had a log to record the servicing he carried out. The information asked for includes:

Sketch of the attack. How were the torpedo settings calculated? Any special observations. Any defences. Explanations for having missed. The enemy's reaction to the attack. Effects of the attack on the target. Height and appearance on the detonation. Time until the target actually went down.

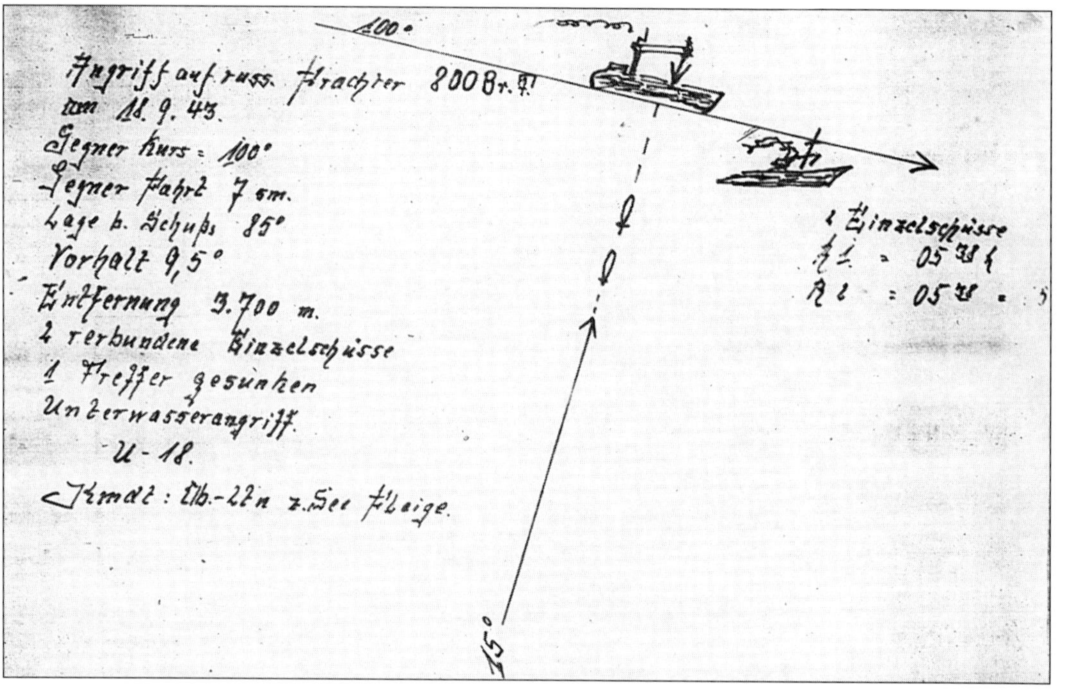

Torpedo shooting reports were usually accompanied by a variety of diagrams showing the details of the attack. They formed a major supplement to the boat's log. Despite this complicated paperwork, it was still possible for some boats to lose a torpedo or two. The easiest way of doing this was to check the tube mechanisms without switching off the firing circuits first. In such cases anyone pressing the crucial button caused a launch. Some commanders took rather a dim view of such accidents; others shrugged their shoulders and cooked the books.

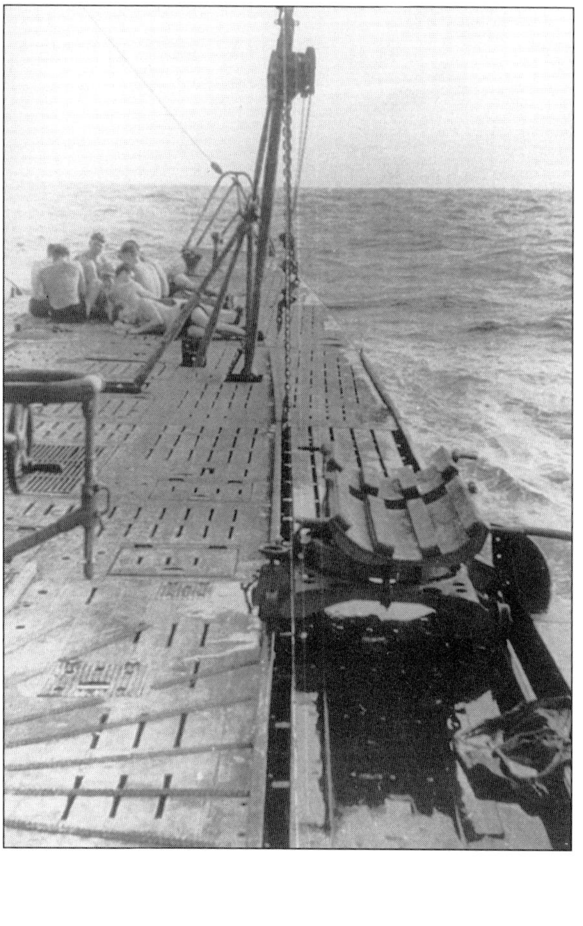

U107, a Type IXB, at sea with torpedo transfer equipment assembled on the upper deck. KL Günter Hessler had the distinction of having conducted the most successful single war cruise of the Second World War with *U107* and he married Ursula Dönitz, daughter of the U-boat chief and later Grand Admiral. After the war he was locked up by American authorities in the witness wing of Nuremberg jail for almost a year without being charged for any crime.

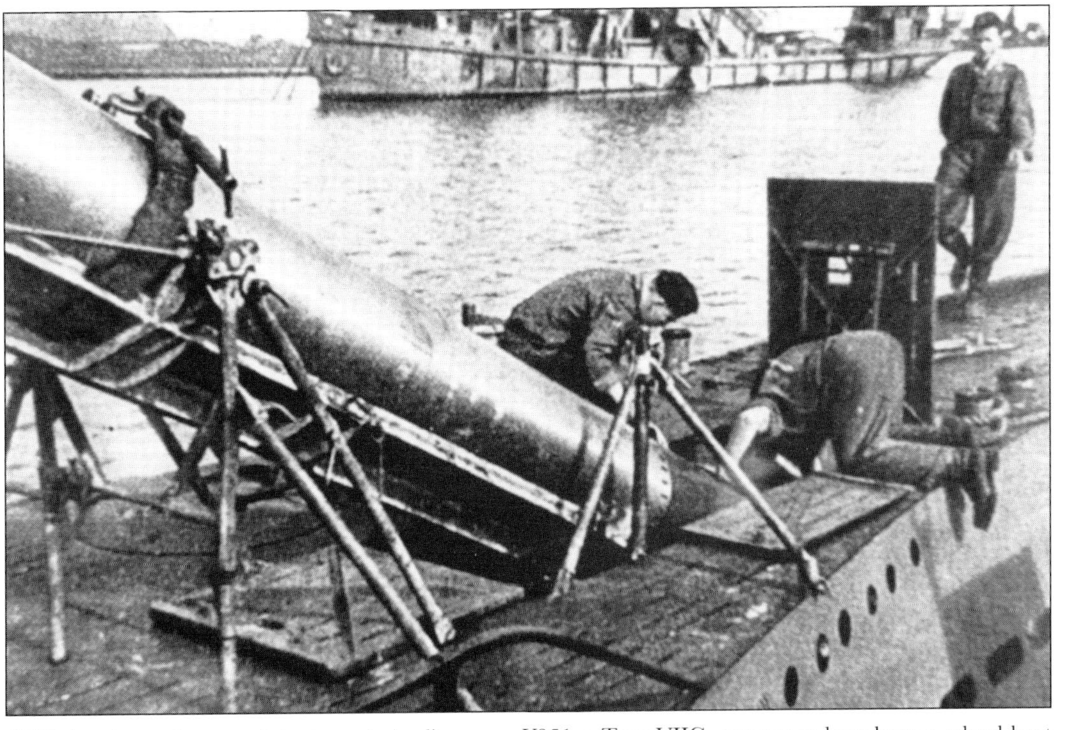

U351 showing a close-up of the torpedo loading gear. *U351*, a Type VIIC, appears to have been a school boat from its commissioning to the end of the war and had seven different commanders. Such a high number was not unusual for training boats, with some of them having had a dozen or so commanders during their short existence.

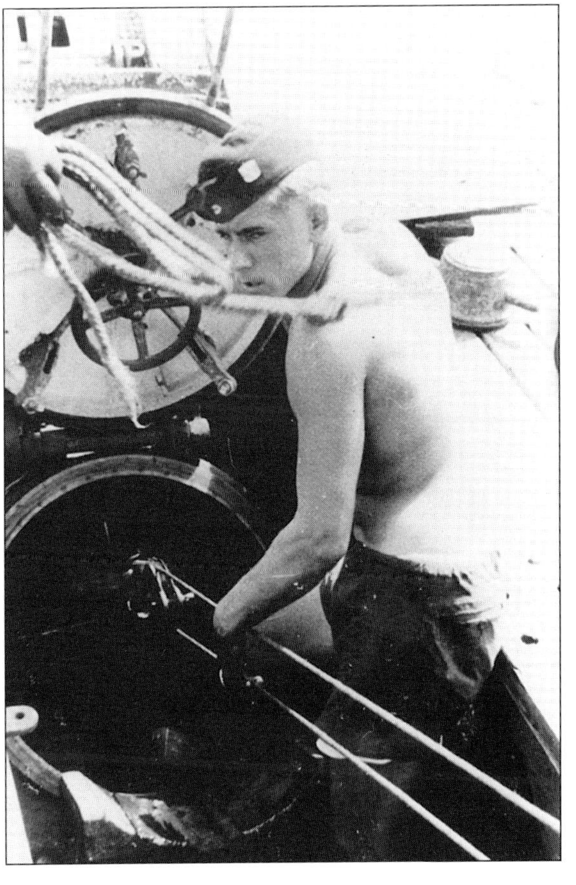

U172 with the torpedo almost down in the forward compartment.

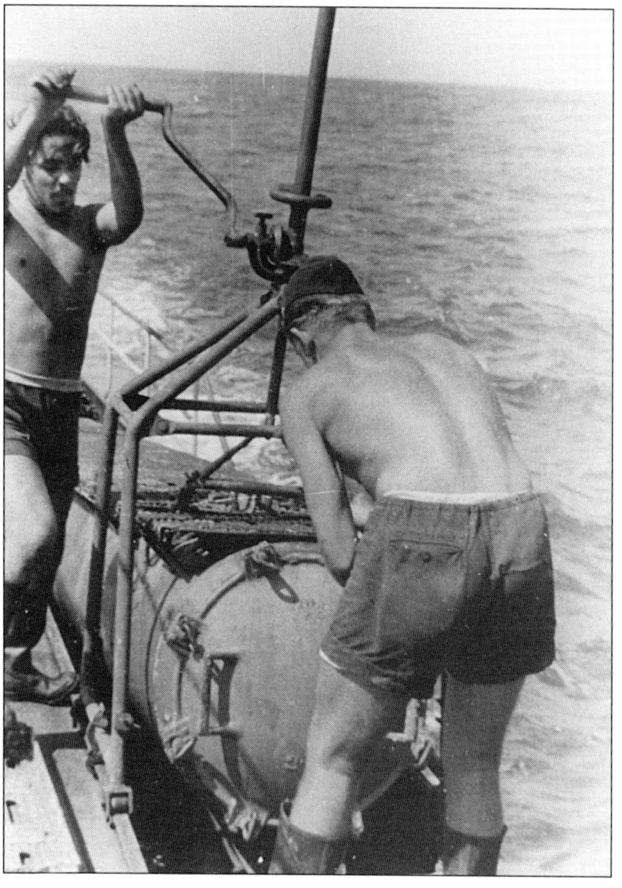

U172, a Type IXC, raising an external torpedo container. Type VII carried two and Type IX four of these pressure- and water-resistant storage tubes. Transferring their contents into the boat for ejection was a long and somewhat complicated business which often required calm weather, a good number of swear words and produced a fair share of bruises. Here one end of the storage container is being raised . . .

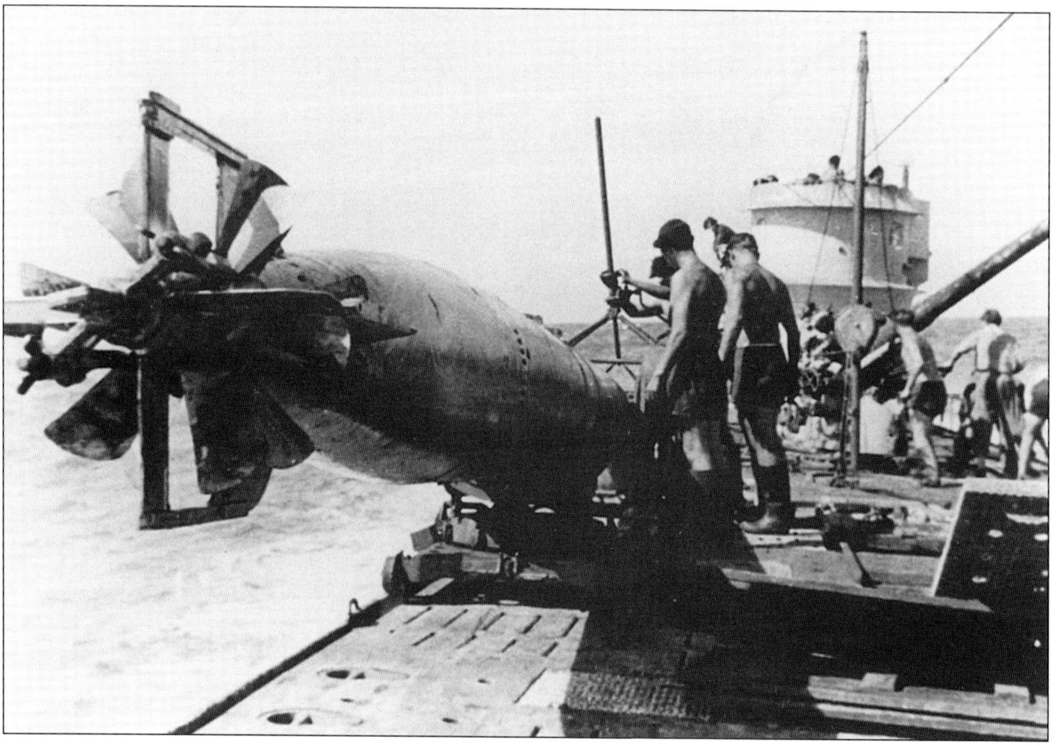

. . . so that the torpedo could be pulled onto the transfer trolley and brought over to the hatch . . .

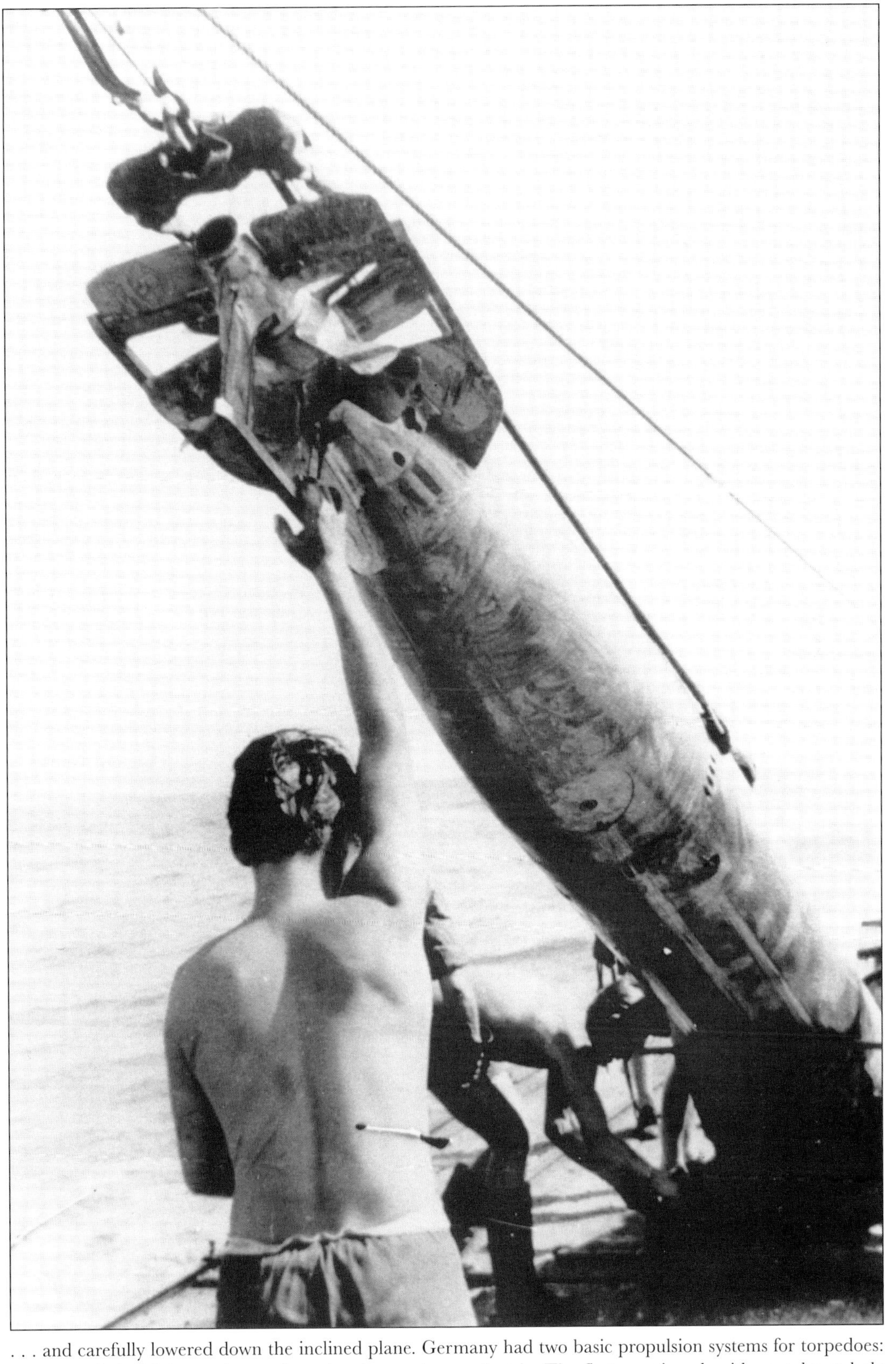

. . . and carefully lowered down the inclined plane. Germany had two basic propulsion systems for torpedoes: compressed air driving an internal-combustion engine or electric. The first mentioned, with an exhaust hole at the back, can be seen here. Torpedoes with closed-circuit Walter turbines, developed towards the end of the war, did not see general operational service.

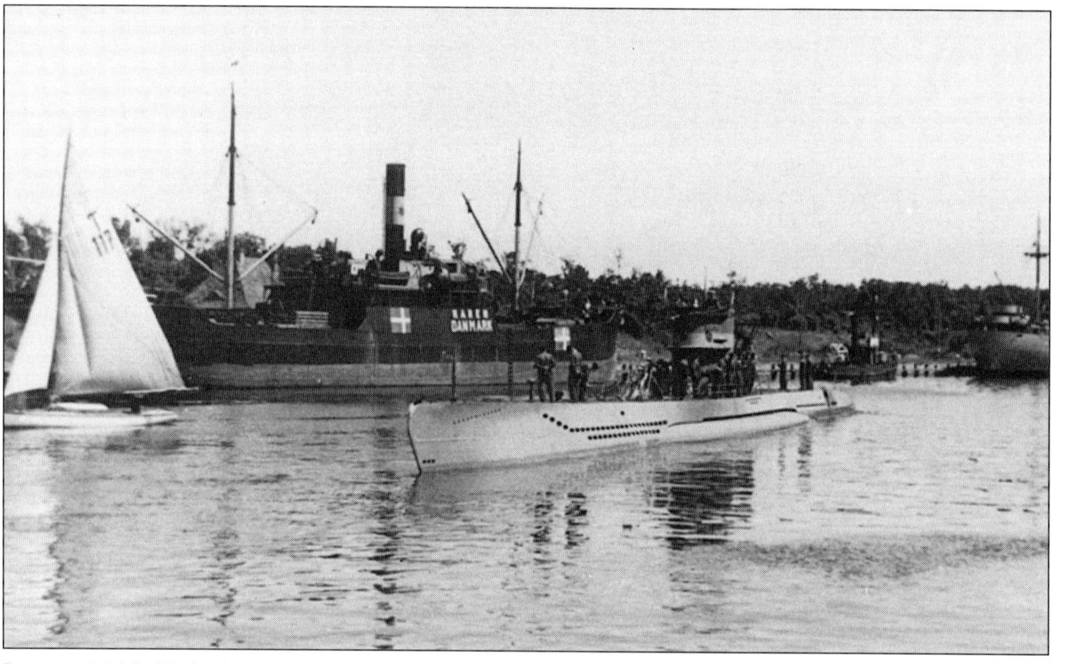

It seems highly likely that the boat in the following docking sequence is *U441*. Docking was usually a tense procedure that required considerable training because it was something U-boats did not have to do very often. It was very easy to damage protruding structures such as the hydroplanes.Although there are a good number of photographs of U-boats, many of them were taken without regard for postwar model makers! This sequence appears to be an exception. The photographer has caught a variety of different angles in a good light showing up details with exceptional clarity.

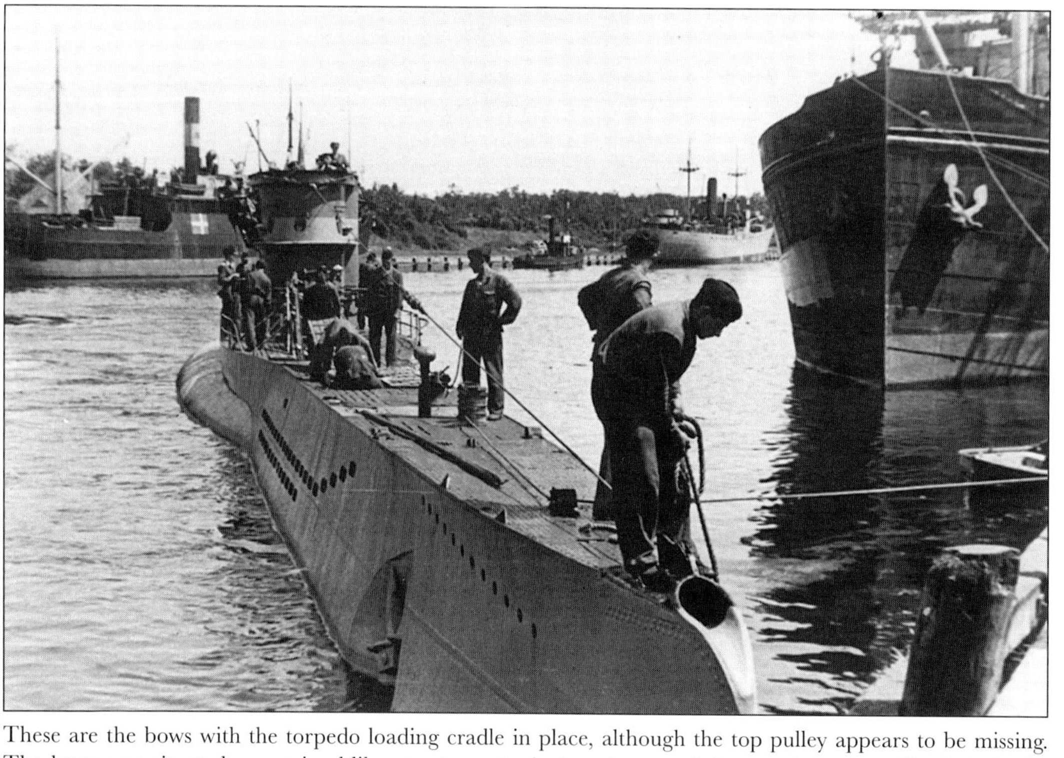

These are the bows with the torpedo loading cradle in place, although the top pulley appears to be missing. The latter was situated on a tripod-like structure attached to the top of the conning tower. The hole in the bows by the man's feet was used to secure a tow-rope. Attaching the line was a great challenge, especially in rough weather, and in some conditions the operation was virtually impossible. The rope ran through this hole and fastened to an eyelet on top of the pressure hull, underneath the deck casing.

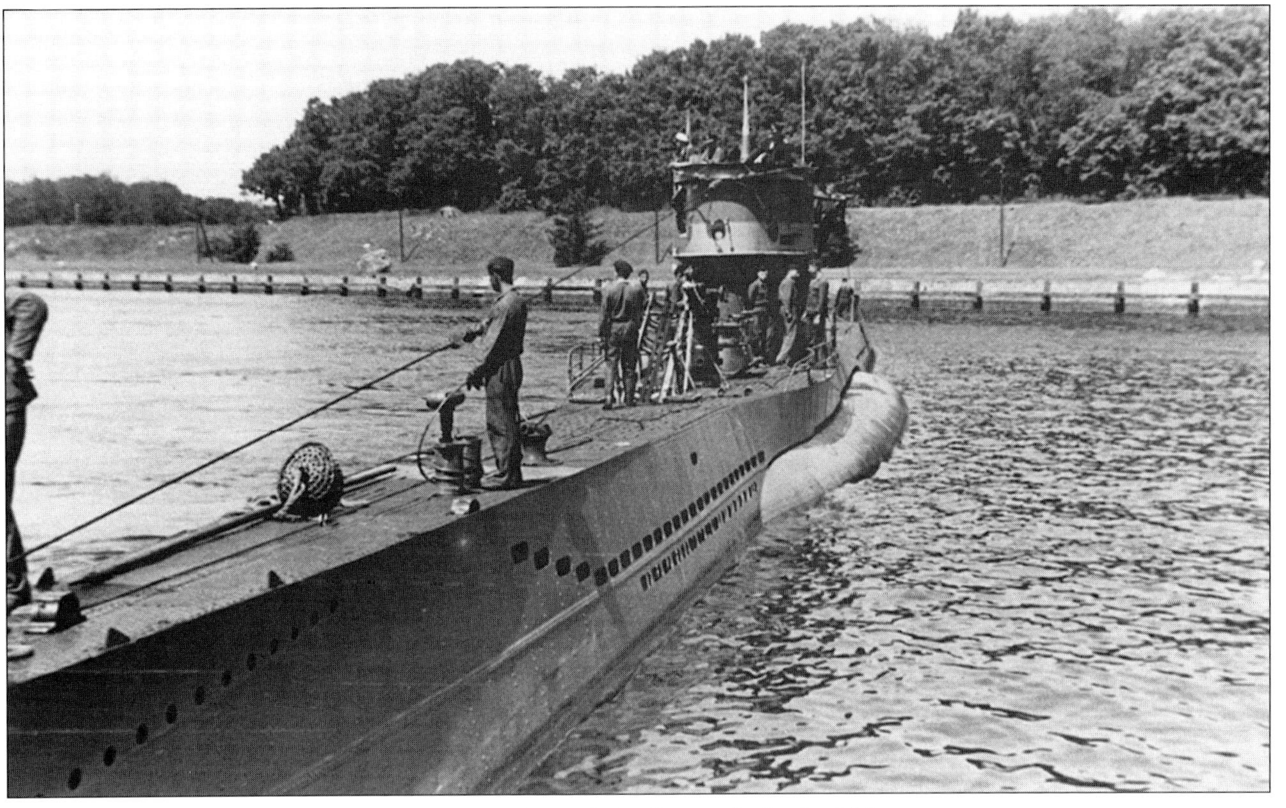

The port side of *U441* with saddle tank and torpedo loading cradle clearly visible.

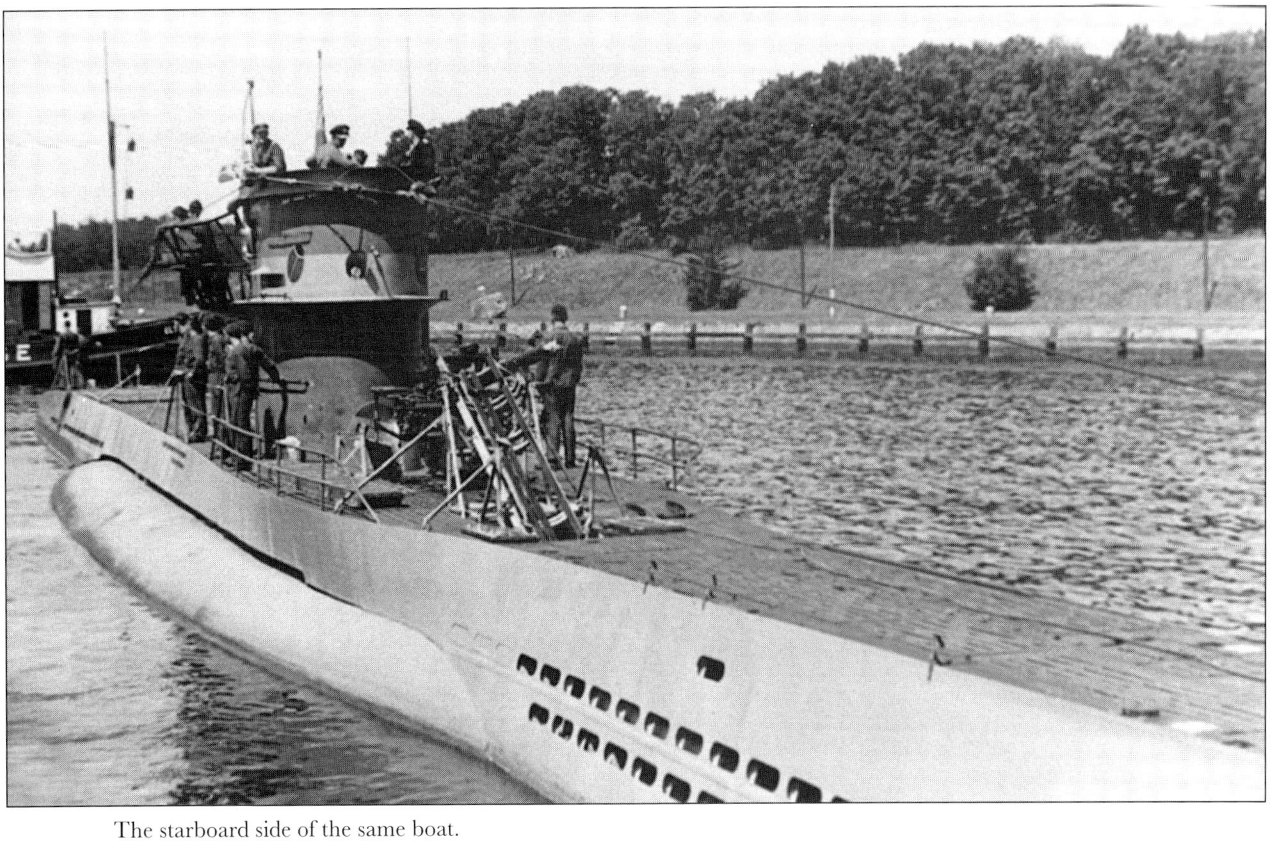

The starboard side of the same boat.

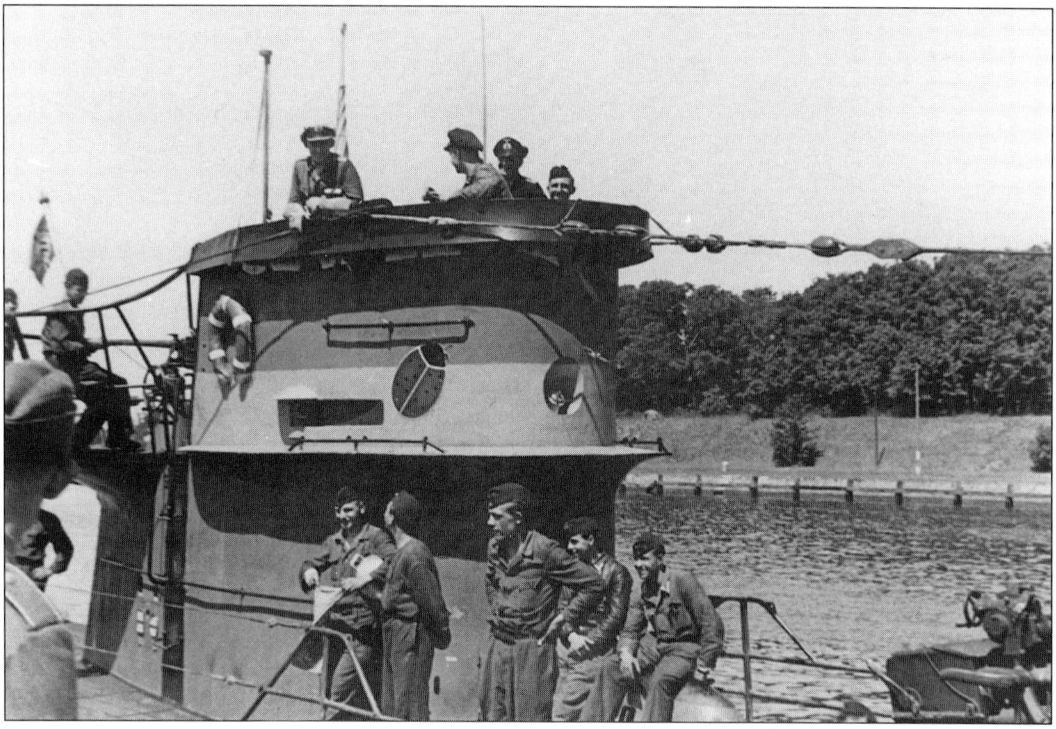

The conning tower of *U441* with a later arrangement of wind and spray deflector. The navigation light by the painting of the ladybird was, of course, green and the other one, on the port side, red. A good way to remember which colour belongs to which side is 'You will never come across a green port wine'! The large hole at the front of the tower is the inlet for the radio aerial.

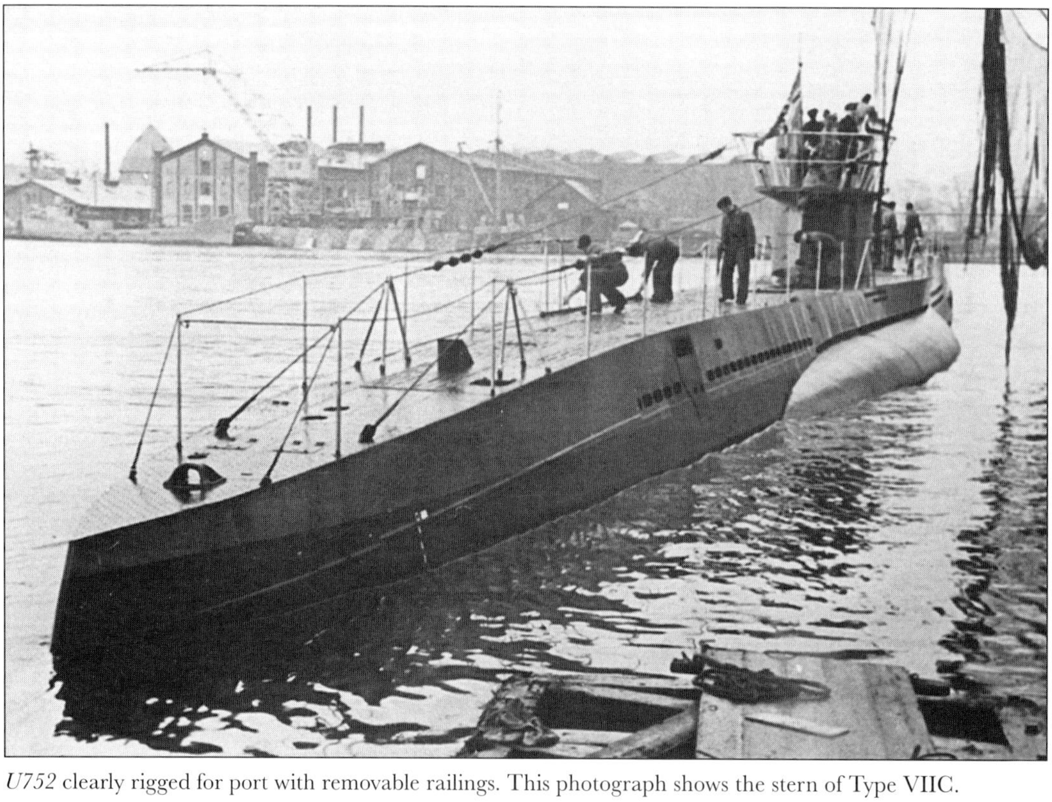

U752 clearly rigged for port with removable railings. This photograph shows the stern of Type VIIC.

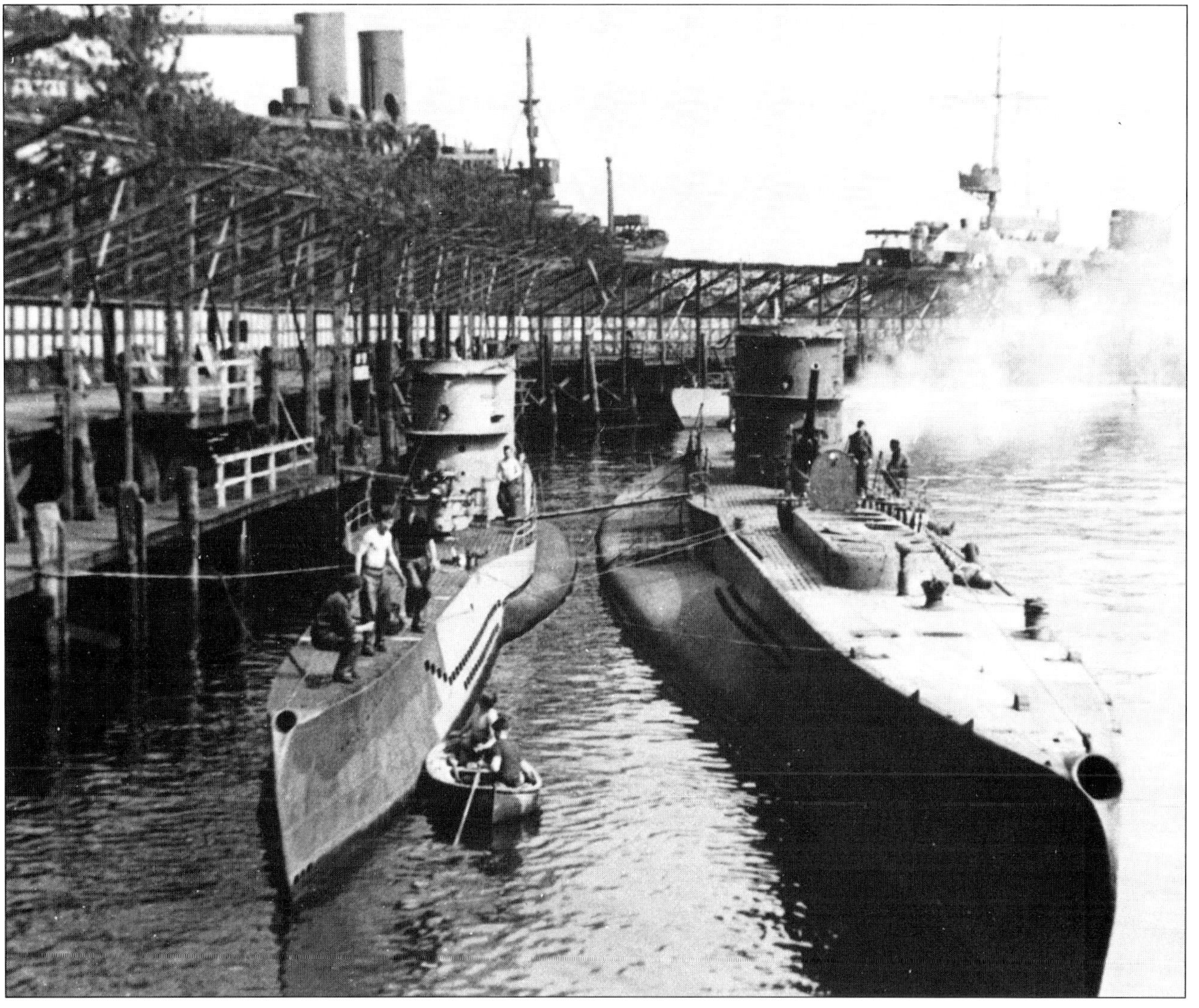

The stunning difference in size is clearly visible between a Type VIIC and the large minelayer – Type XB – with a row of mineshafts in the bows. The massively fat waistline along the side of the boat held another row of vertical mineshafts. It appears this photograph was taken in the naval dockyard in Kiel with the Tirpitz Quay in the background and the accommodation ship *Berlin* on the other side. Another accommodation ship, the *Milwaukee*, was moored at the other end of the harbour for part of the war. *Berlin* was a First World War cruiser and the *Milwaukee* went to Britain after the war, was renamed *Empire Waveney* and was totally gutted by fire at Liverpool in 1946.

Type VIIC had a displacement of about 770 tons on the surface and 1,070 tons when submerged while the bigger boat on the right was about twice the size and displaced between 1,616 and 2,150 tons. However, Type XB was by no means the biggest in the Kriegsmarine. Supply boats of Type XIV displaced 1,763/2,710 tons and the large electro-boats, which appeared at the end of the war but hardly saw operational service, displaced 1,688/2,300 tons. By comparison, the small coastal boats of Type IIC displaced only 314/460 tons.

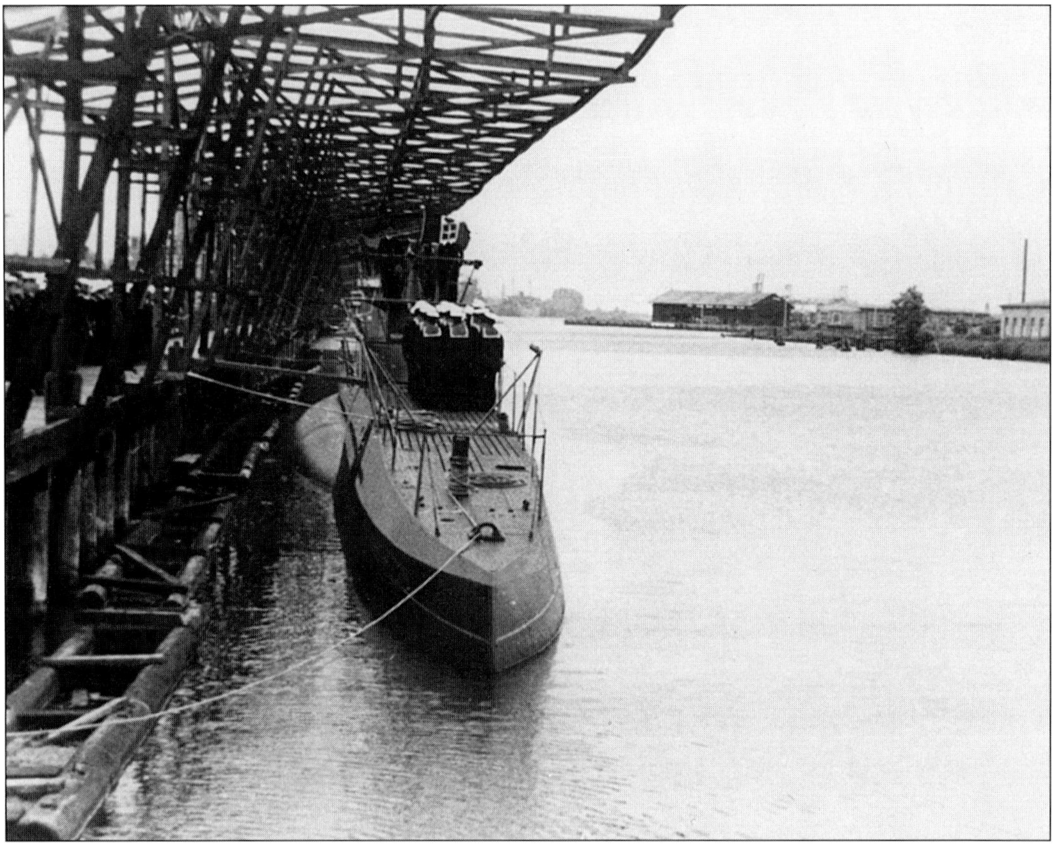

Another good view of a Type VIIC's back side. The large number of people assembled on the quay and the crew standing to neatly on deck would suggest that this boat might be in the process of being commissioned. This scene is most interesting: the flag flying from the conning tower would suggest that this is one of the German U-boats which was handed over to Italy. The combination of blue shirts and white hats is not necessarily foreign because the mixture of different seasons' uniforms was common during the transition time from spring to summer and again in autumn.

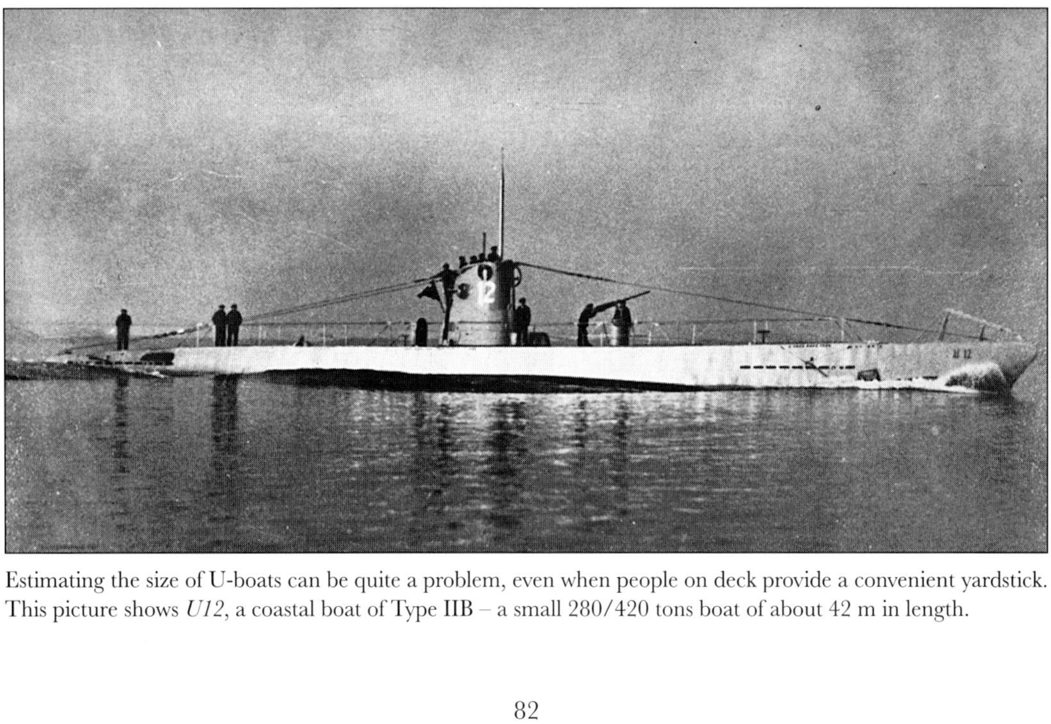

Estimating the size of U-boats can be quite a problem, even when people on deck provide a convenient yardstick. This picture shows *U12*, a coastal boat of Type IIB – a small 280/420 tons boat of about 42 m in length.

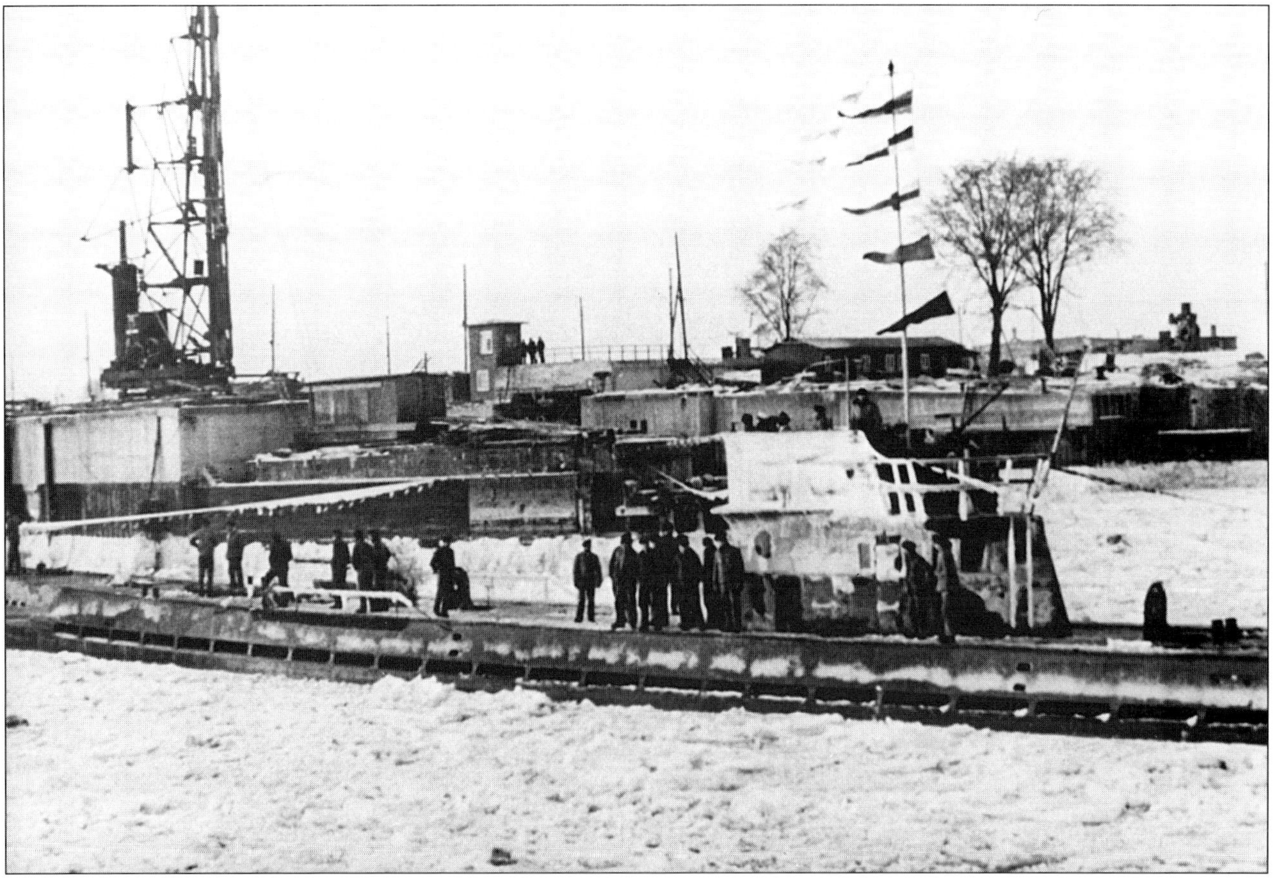

This ocean-going Type IX was the largest U-boat commonly seen in the shipping lanes of the North Atlantic. Germany commissioned over 600 Type VIIs, making it the largest submarine class ever to have been built and there were about 165 of these larger Type IXs. The metal structure on the quay is not part of Germany's war machine but a steam-driven pile driver.

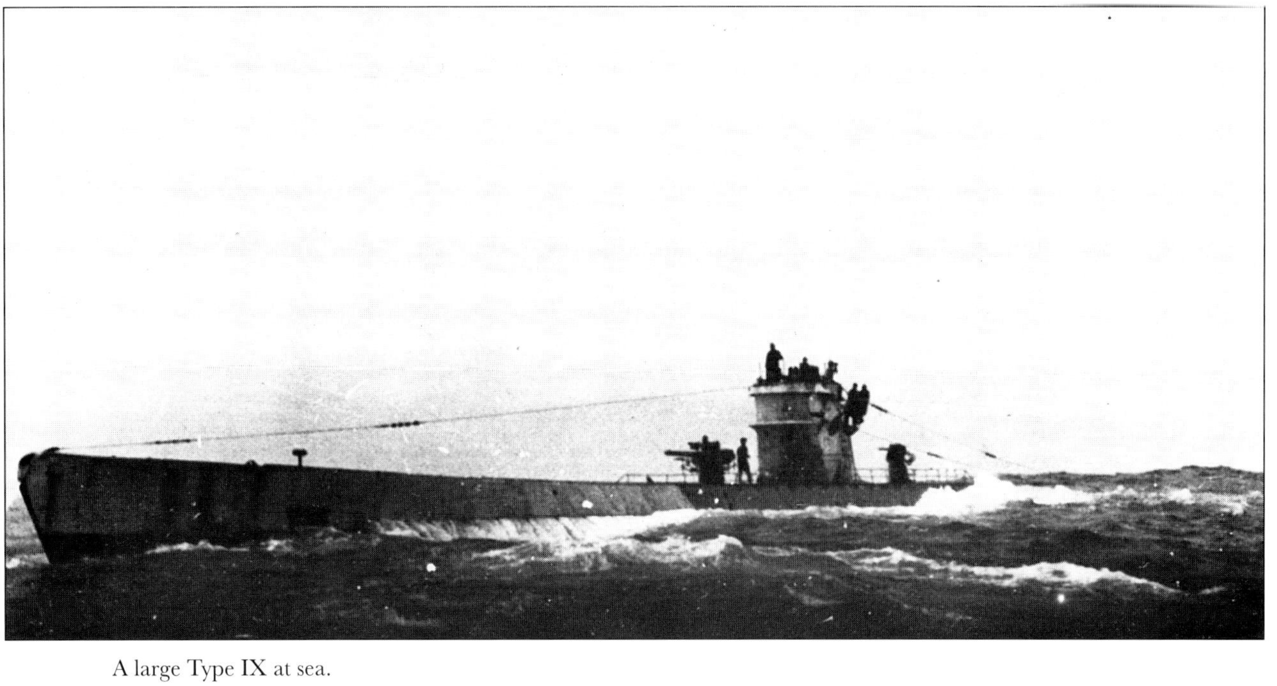

A large Type IX at sea.

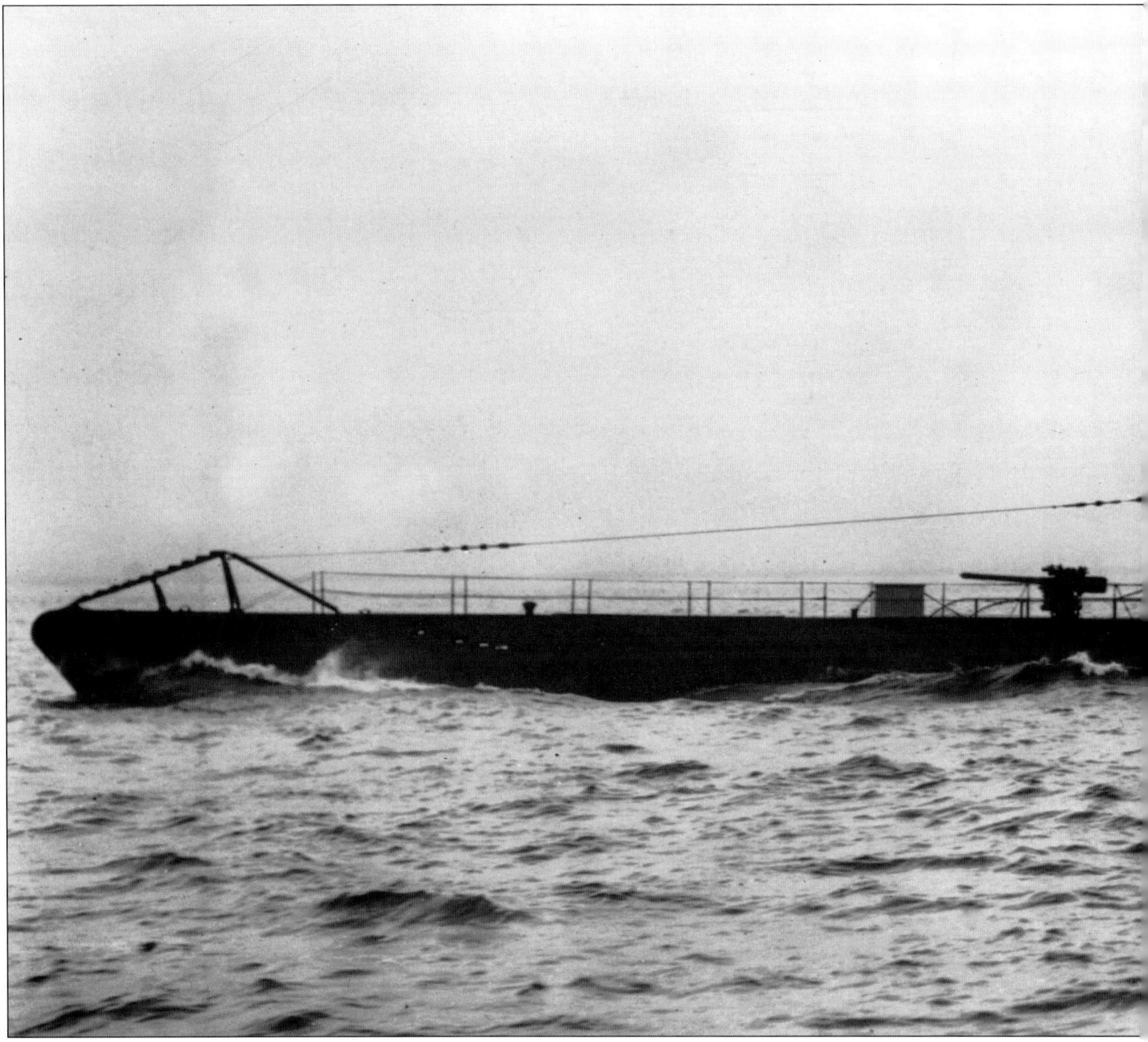

U551 under KL Karl Schrott during early trials towards the end of 1941. The rectangular, box-like roofs over the hatches would suggest the boat is not intending to dive. In any case, this particular boat did not do that many times. It was commissioned in November 1940 and was sunk south of Iceland just four months later by depth charges from the armed trawler *Visenda*. This total loss without survivors took place two days before Schrott's thirtieth birthday. Note the light shining through the forward free-flooding vents. The man on the back is probably there for a good reason: he is saved the climb down to the 'head' (lavatory) and the

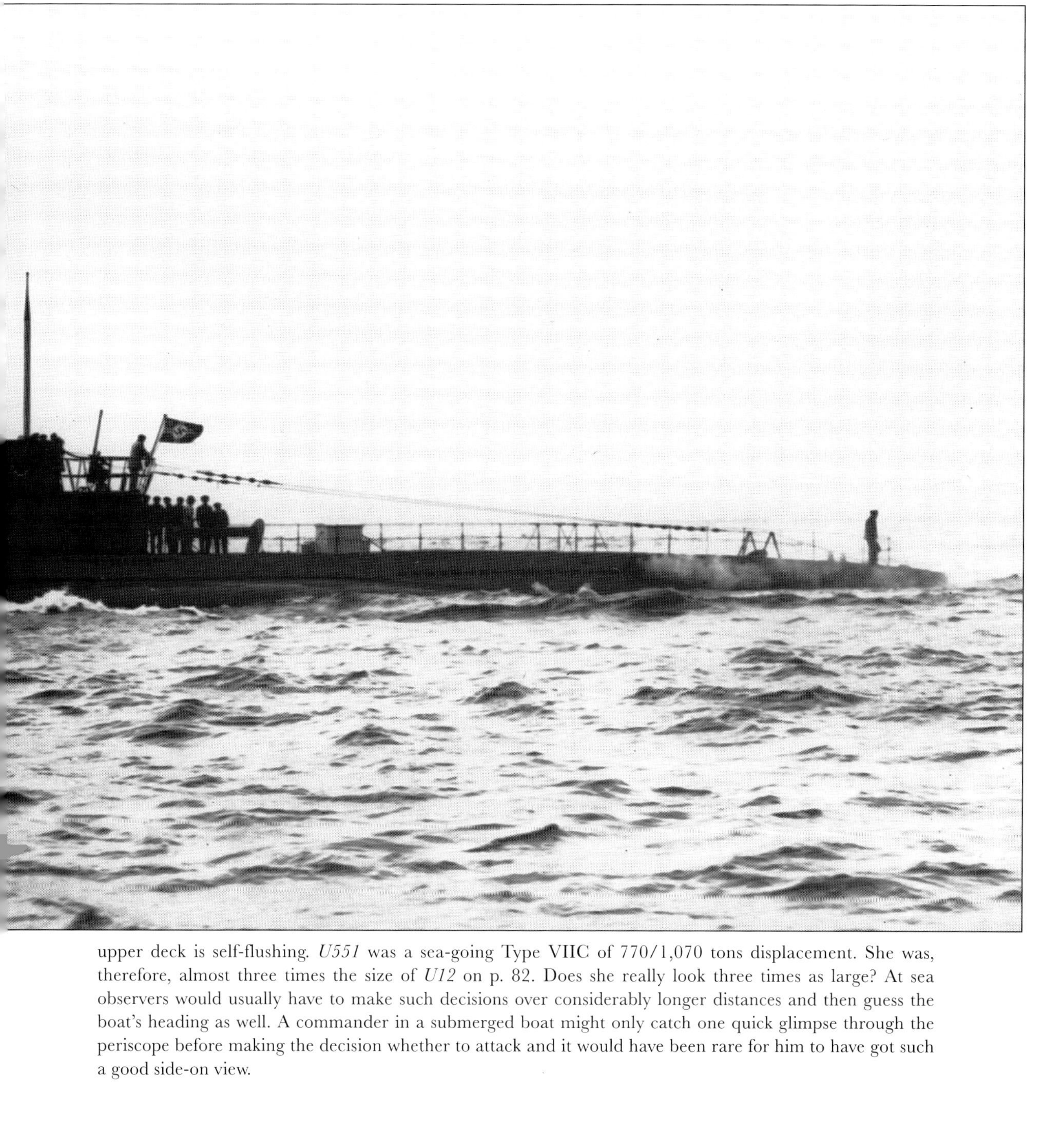

upper deck is self-flushing. *U551* was a sea-going Type VIIC of 770/1,070 tons displacement. She was, therefore, almost three times the size of *U12* on p. 82. Does she really look three times as large? At sea observers would usually have to make such decisions over considerably longer distances and then guess the boat's heading as well. A commander in a submerged boat might only catch one quick glimpse through the periscope before making the decision whether to attack and it would have been rare for him to have got such a good side-on view.

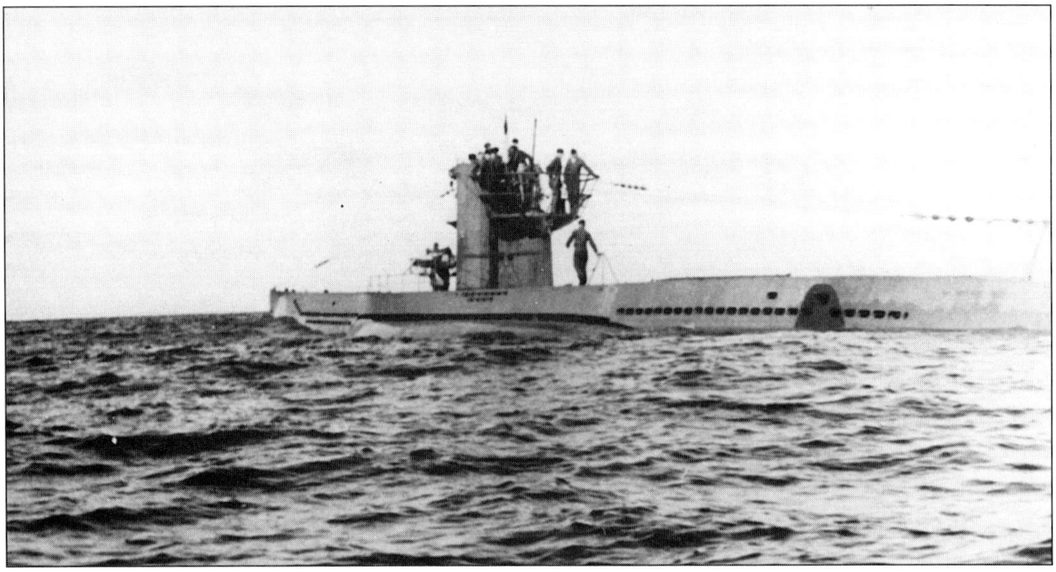

Have a quick look at this and then decide whether it is a small coastal boat, a sea-going type or a large ocean-going variety. What is its heading? In fact it shows *U581*, a sea-going Type VIIC of about 770/1,070 tons displacement and a length of 66 m. *U581* was commissioned by KL Werner Pfeffer in July 1941 and depth charged six months later by HMS *Westcott*. The exact location of this incident is somewhat disputed. British authorities claimed that the boat was sunk 3.1 miles off the neutral Portuguese Pico Island in the Azores, while the Germans claim their boat was inside territorial waters. Despite an argument at the time, the majority of survivors were sent to a British prisoner of war camp, although one man evaded the rescue attempt by swimming to the island, being interned and later repatriated to Germany.

This image of *U581* shows that the viewing angle can give a totally false impression of a conning tower's size. During the war, this problem was made more acute by observers often getting only fleeting glimpses of the enemy and false impressions were made worse by distractions from the surroundings.

Many aircraft reported that U-boats were capable of firing their guns while partially submerged. At first, one might think that this impossibility was made up by frightened airmen who looked for an excuse to keep away from enemy guns, but anyone with an understanding of the situation will realise the reason for this wild exaggeration. A U-boat forced to take on an aircraft in combat would go up to the fastest possible speed for quicker manoeuvring and also to make the eventual dive faster. Of course, this would help in breaking up waves, causing the water to wash over the top of the exposed deck, making it look as if it was partially submerged.

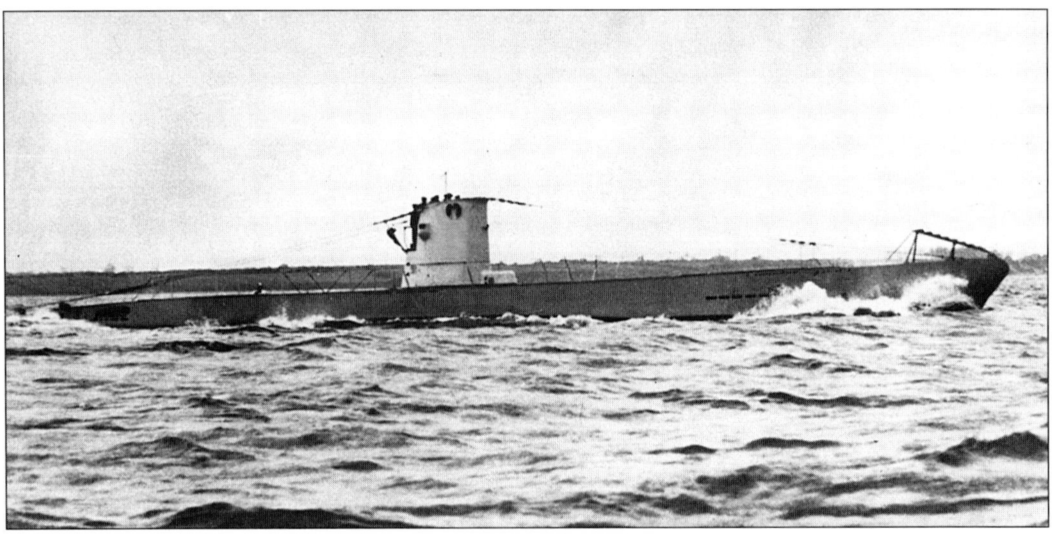

Try the same with this! What size is it? The picture shows *U20*, a coastal boat of Type IIB. *U20* was one of half a dozen boats moved overland to the Black Sea where it was scuttled in September 1944 and the crew interned in neutral Turkey.

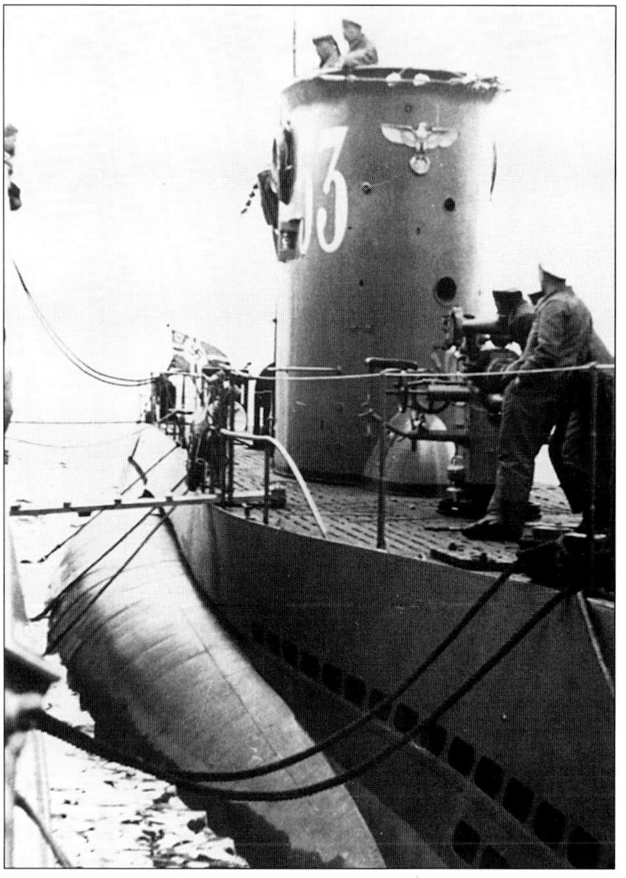

U53 (Type VIIB) commissioned by KL Dietrich Knorr, showing the pre-war type of conning tower with number painted on the side and a bronze eagle on the front. This combination usually also included two bronze plates with the boat's number, one on each side near the bows. These – along with the painted number and eagle – were removed after the beginning of the war. Note that this boat built at Germania Works in Kiel already has the side casing running around the outside of the gun platform, while other boats had the additional deck space for the heavy gun sticking out over the side, which can be seen on p. 9. The outward-bending lip of the tower top was supposed to act as wind deflector but was not terribly effective.

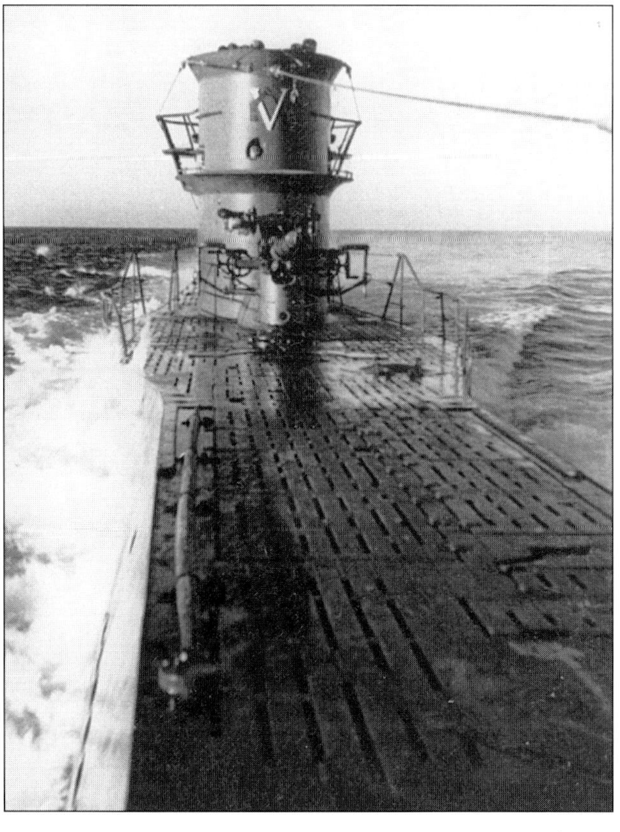

A Type VII boat with emblem of the 24th (Training) U-Flotilla, showing the modified conning tower, still with outward-curving wind deflector but with a spray deflector added halfway up. The 'V' emblem stood for the English word 'Victory'!

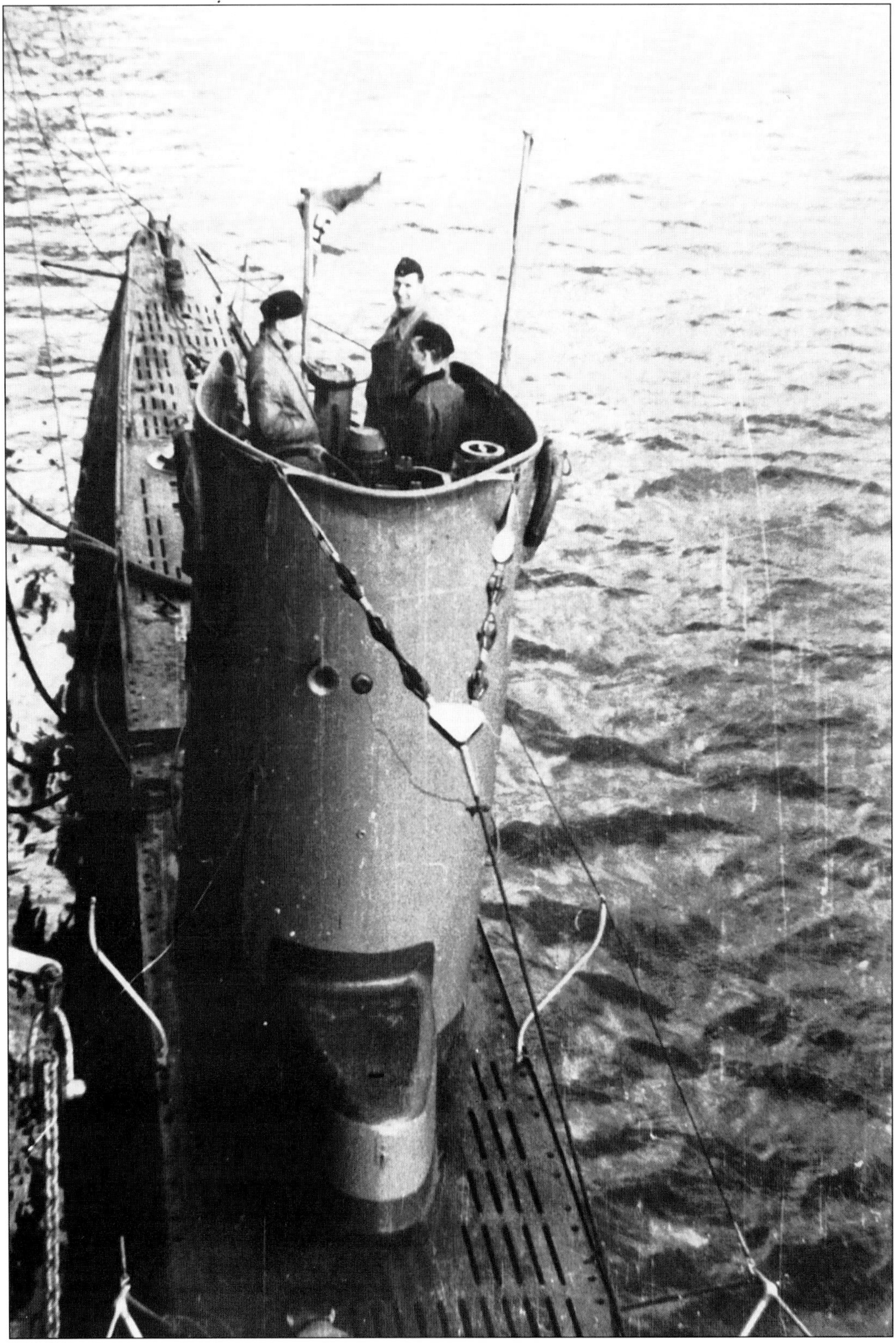

These two photographs help to illustrate how misleading perspective can be. At first glance it is easy to agree that both of them show similar submarines, yet the boat above is *U24*, a small coastal Type IIB and the picture opposite shows *U29*, a sea-going Type VIIA. *U29* is almost three times the size of *U24*. The descriptions 'coastal', 'sea-going' and 'ocean-going' were attributed to boats long before the beginning

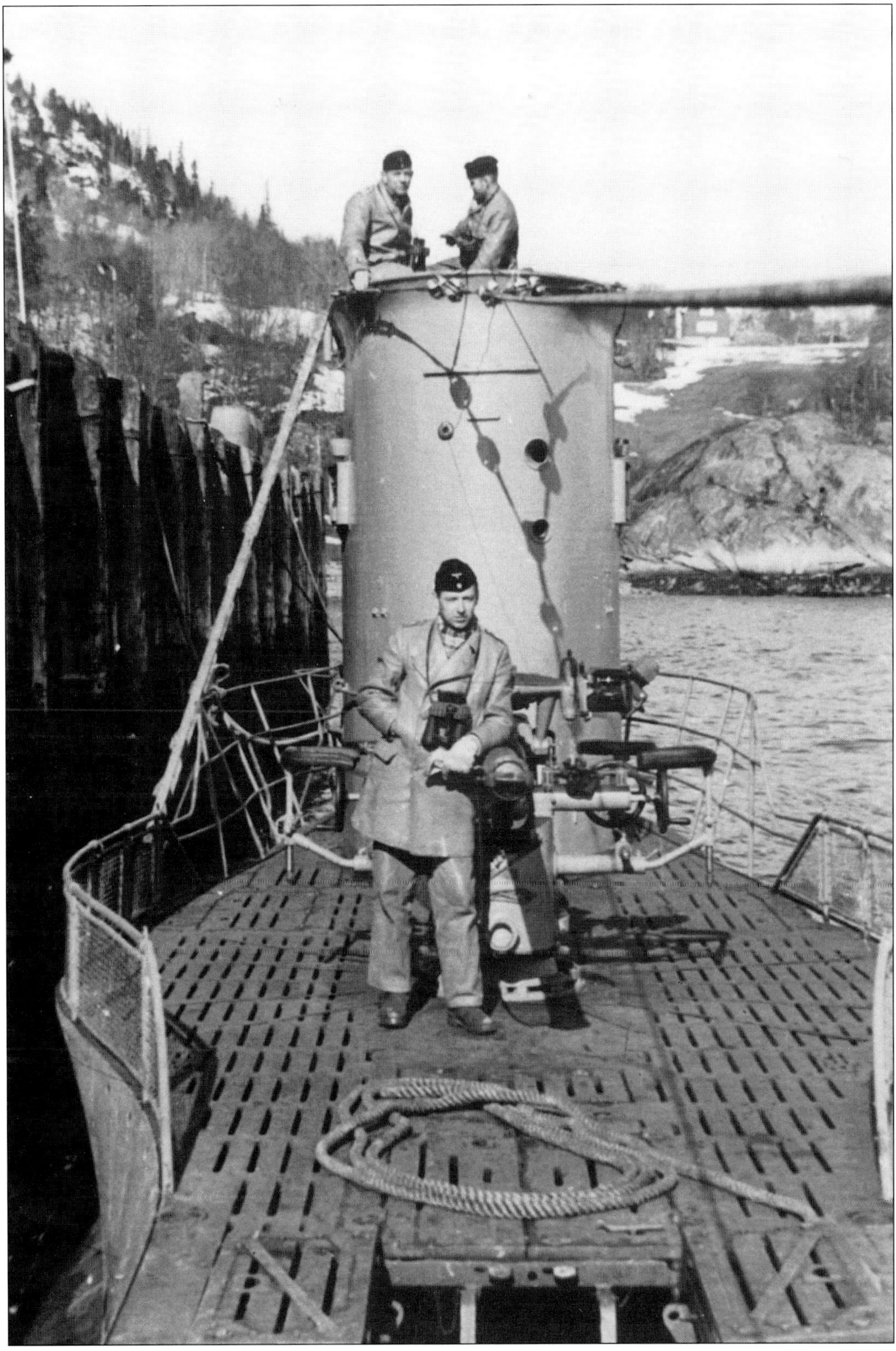

of the war. The medium-sized, sea-going Type VII formed the backbone of the Battle of the Atlantic and made voyages as far as the eastern seaboard of the United States, so 'sea-going' is a rather misleading term. This picture was taken on the coast of Norway.

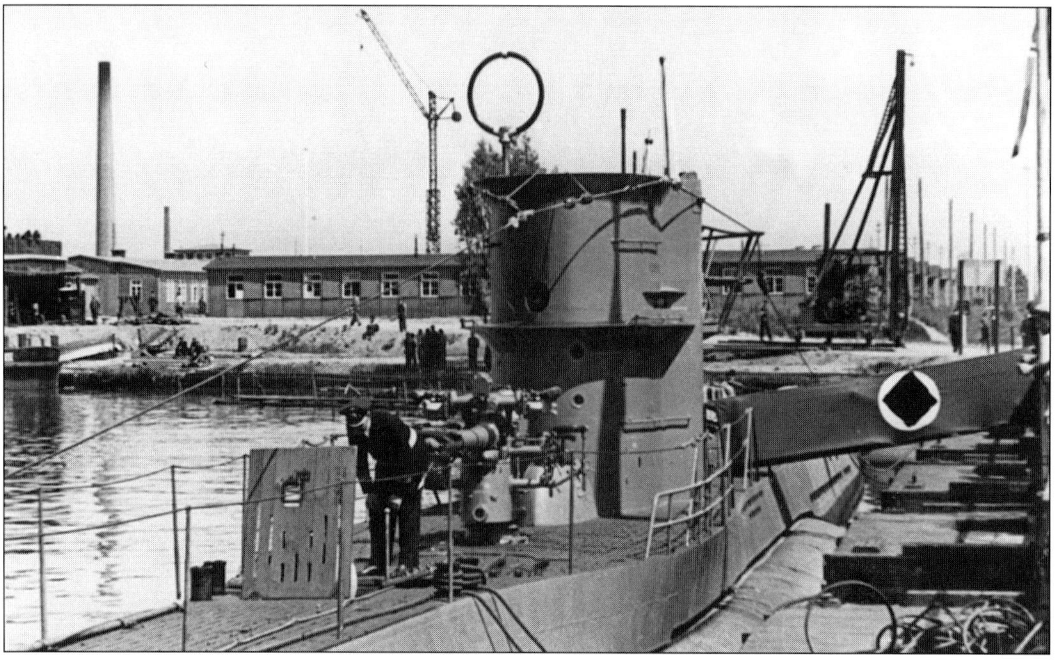

Another view of the spray and wind deflectors with the man by the gun offering ample opportunities for a humorous caption. The black square on the flag by the side of the gangplank was added after the war by touching-up the picture with ink; this was done because it is now against the law to display swastikas and rune symbols in Germany.

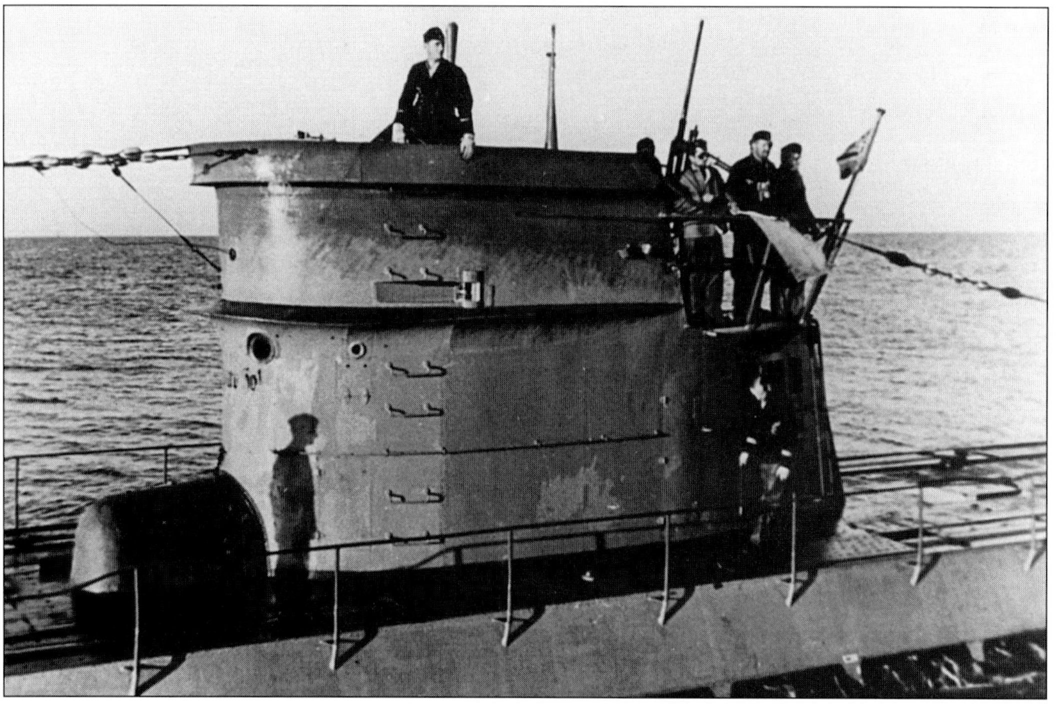

U37 with an addition to the spray deflector at the top of the conning tower. Such lips were first attached to the top of the outward-curving design seen in previous photos but they were later added as standard feature to other types of conning tower. This picture shows quite plainly how little the threat from aircraft had been considered before the war. There was hardly any provision for the fitting of significant anti-aircraft armament and from 1942 onwards conning towers had to be completely redesigned to meet airborne threat. The sailor at the base of the tower is not a ghost but the shadow of a man standing further forward on the upper deck. The difference in size of the large navigation and the smaller attack periscopes is also visible.

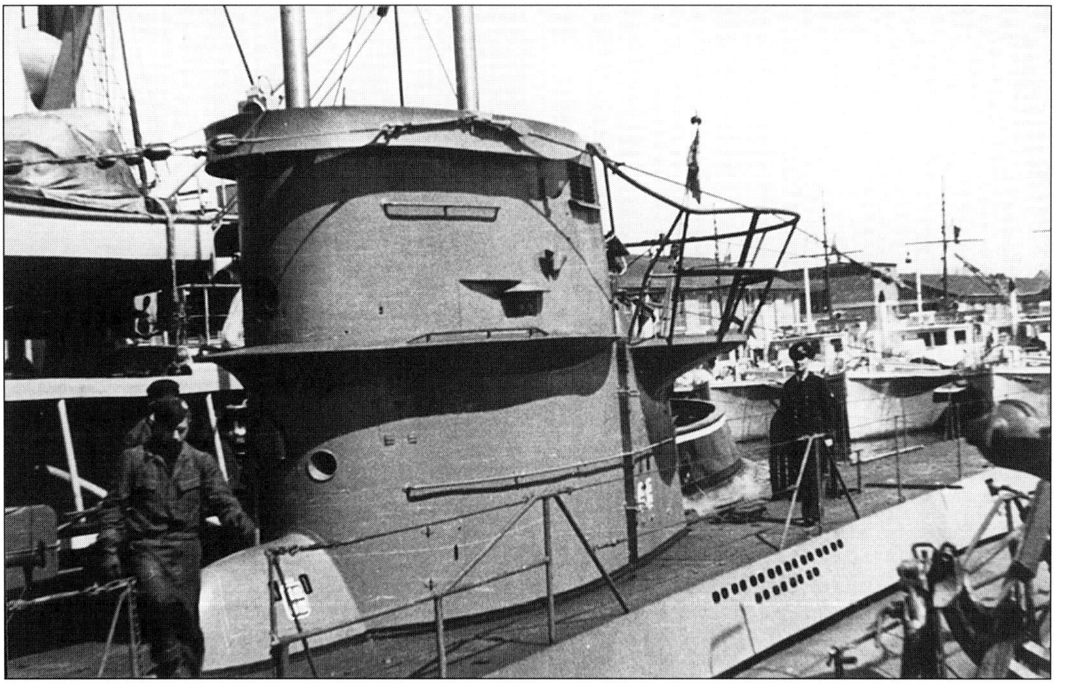

This is either *U71* under KL Walter Flachsenberg (who was born at the home of the famous postwar football team, Mönchengladbach, and retired to Westerland on the Island of Sylt) or *U72* (commanded by KK Hans-Werner Neumann) showing the later design of wind and spray deflectors. It is difficult to see whether the top edge was purpose-built or consisted of the original, outward-curving deflector with modification over the top.

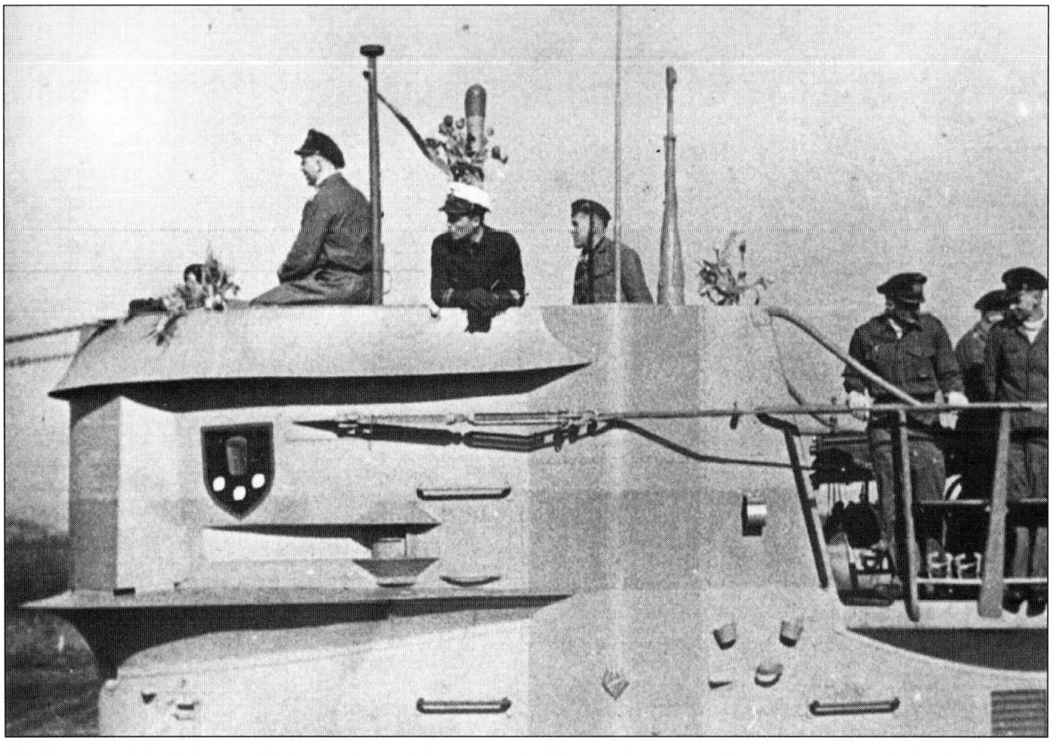

U168 under KL Helmuth Pich (another of those naval officers who served for some time with the Luftwaffe), showing the later type of spray deflector as an integral part of the conning tower. The projections above it are, from left to right: the commander's flagpole, which was detachable and stored either under the deck casing or inside the pressure hull; the large navigation periscope; an extendible rod aerial; and the attack periscope. The cup-shaped devices on the wall just to the left of the gun platform are brackets for a lifebelt.

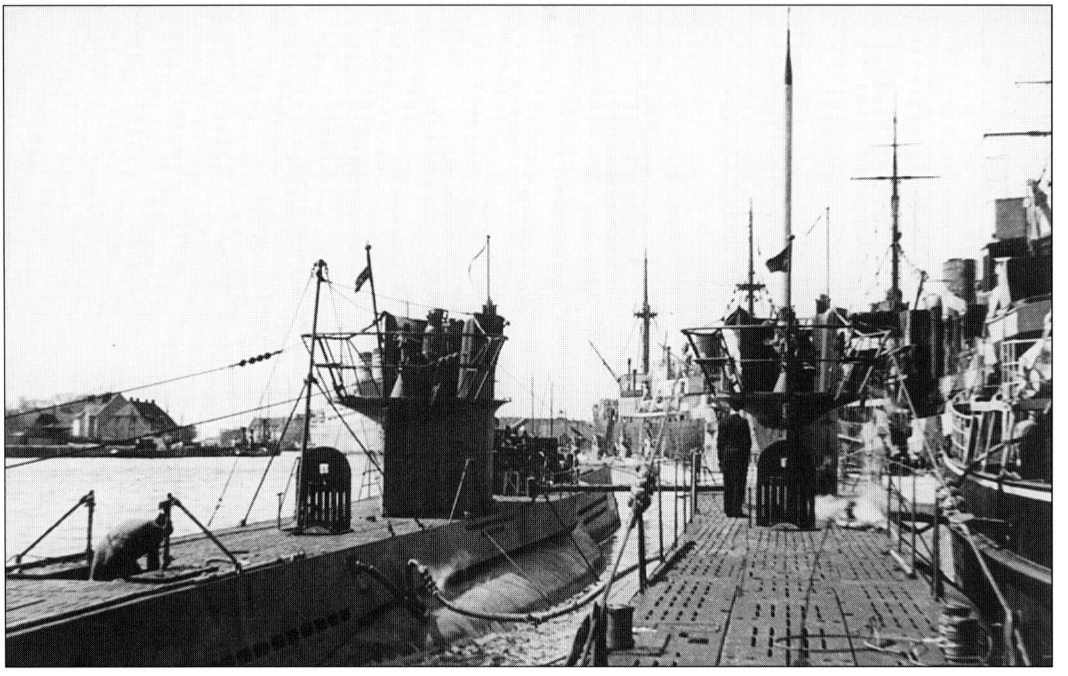

When seen from the rear the majority of conning towers looked identical, although their detail varied considerably. Here are two Type VIIC boats, *U71* and *U72*, both from Germania Works in Kiel. The boat on the left has a pole rigged for holding the uppermost pulley of the torpedo loading gear; on the right one can see an extended attack periscope. Both the covers above the hatches leading down to the galley are open.

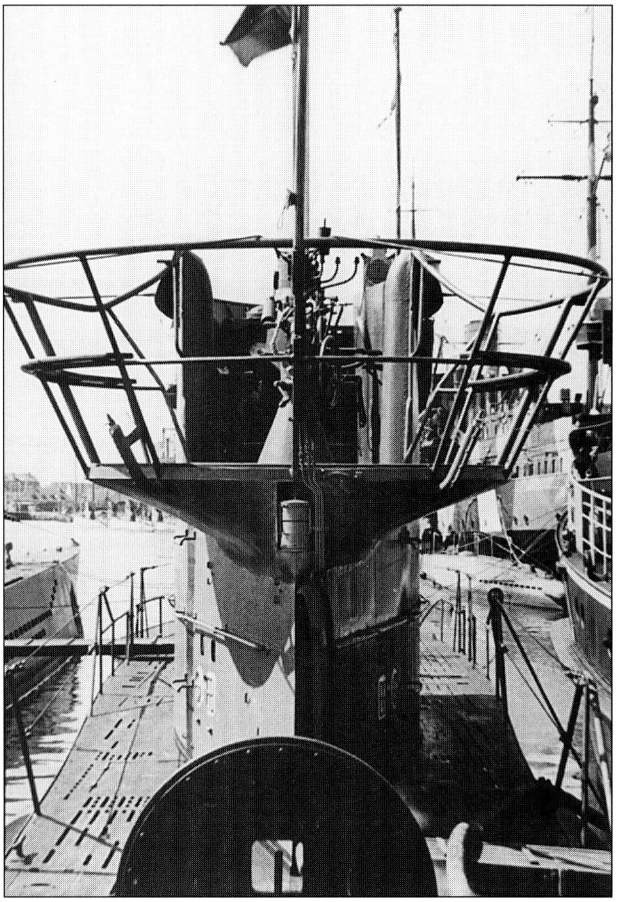

Either *U71* or *U72* showing the typical conning tower before the anti-aircraft armament was strengthened from 1942 onwards. At the base of the flagpole is a navigation light with narrow slit for when progress might be interrupted by enemy aircraft flying overhead.

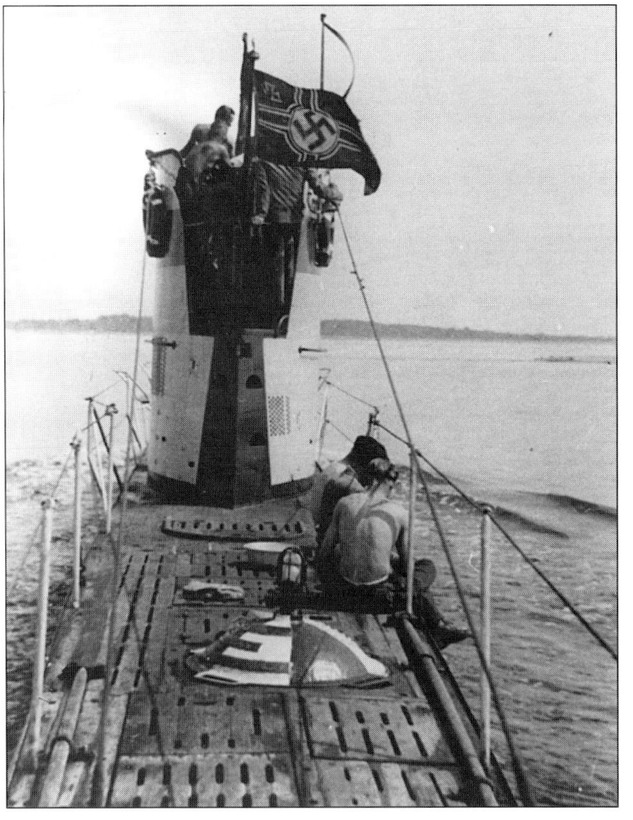

A similar view of a small coastal boat of Type II with national ensign flying from the main flagpole and, in the foreground, a red-and-white rescue buoy with a light on the top. Towards the right is the commander's flagpole flying a long, thin command pennant that looks like a D-shaped contraption.

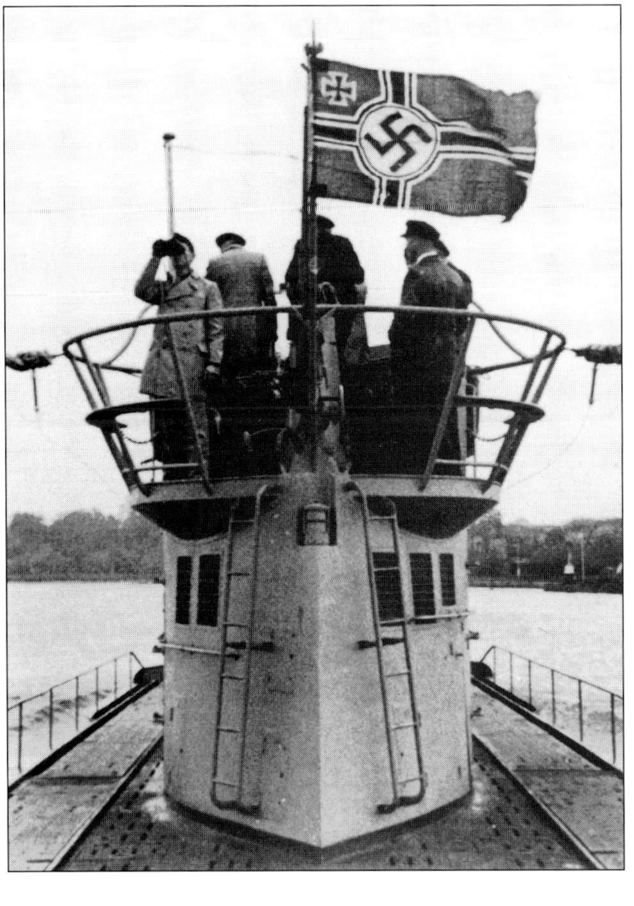

A very much larger boat of Type IX, also flying the national ensign and a long, thin commander's pennant.

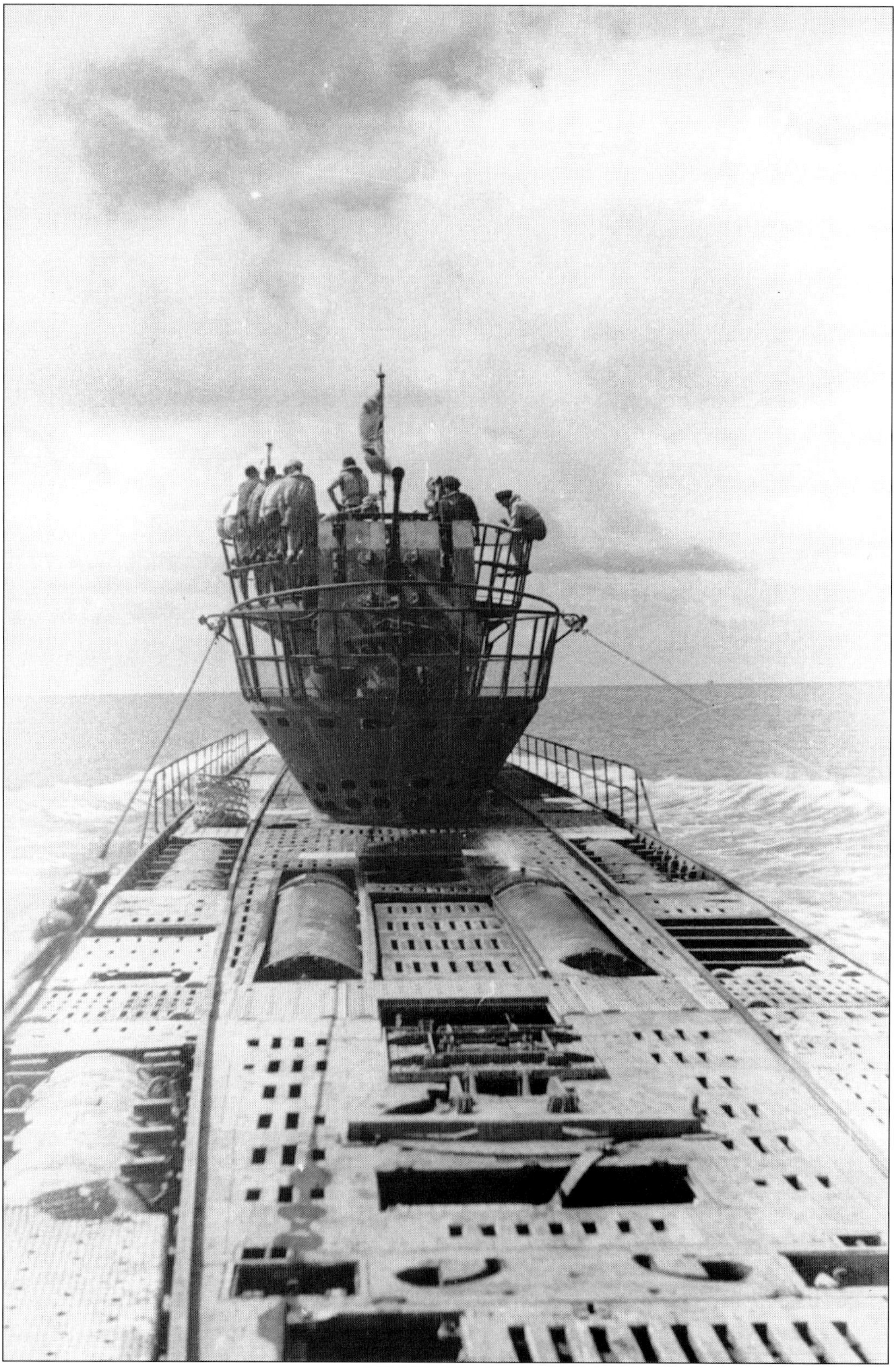

U181 under KK Kurt Freiwald on its way to the Far East towards the end of the war. This picture shows the modified conning tower with strengthened anti-aircraft armament and the tops of several water- and pressure-resistant storage containers under the deck casing.

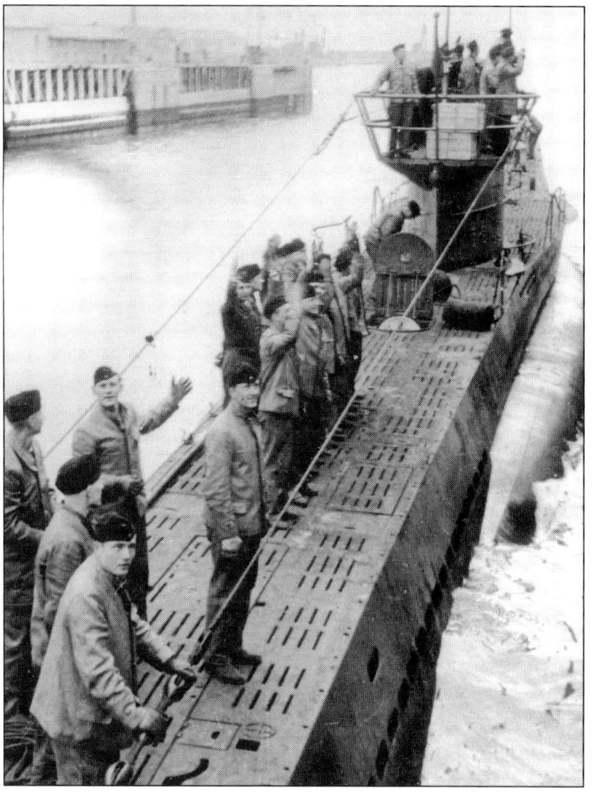

It seems highly likely that this is either *U48* under KL Herbert Schultze or *U47* under KL Günter Prien, both Type VIIB boats with an early kind of conning tower. There are a couple of orange crates on the gun platform. In those days oranges were still left to ripen on the tree and therefore provided a valuable source of vitamin C. It looks as if the photograph was taken inside the sea locks at Wilhelmshaven.

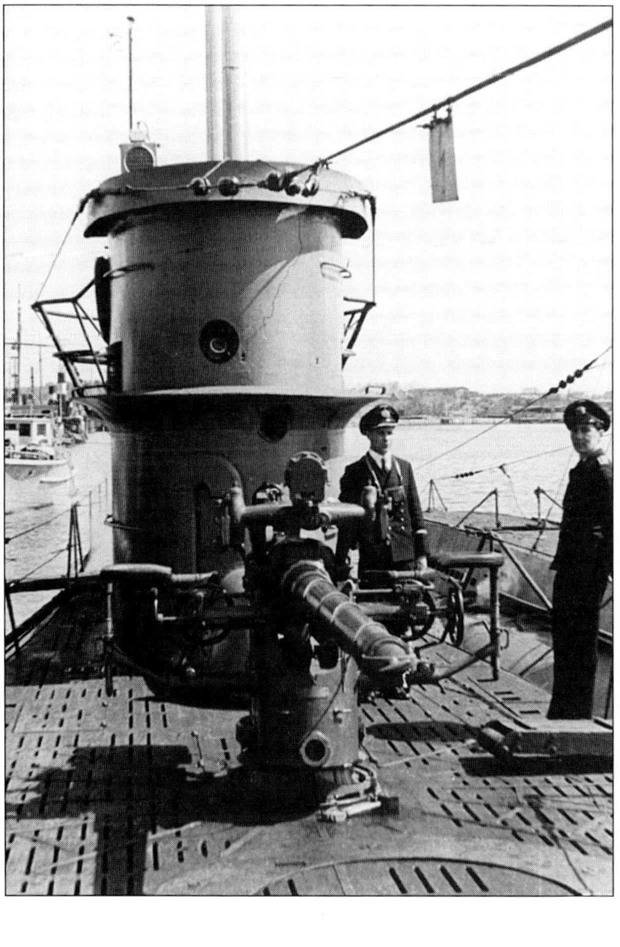

Either *U71* or *U72*, shortly after commissioning in January 1941 and still in pristine condition, showing the typical Type VIIC conning tower with a later version of the spray deflector at the top. The shield with lightning flash hanging from the jumping wire, warns the unwary that they could get a considerable shock if they touched it. The thin wire connecting the thick jumping cable with the radio aerial inlet is also just visible and so is the fog-horn or typhoon just below the wind deflector halfway up the tower. Both periscopes have been raised and there is a portable radio standing to the left.

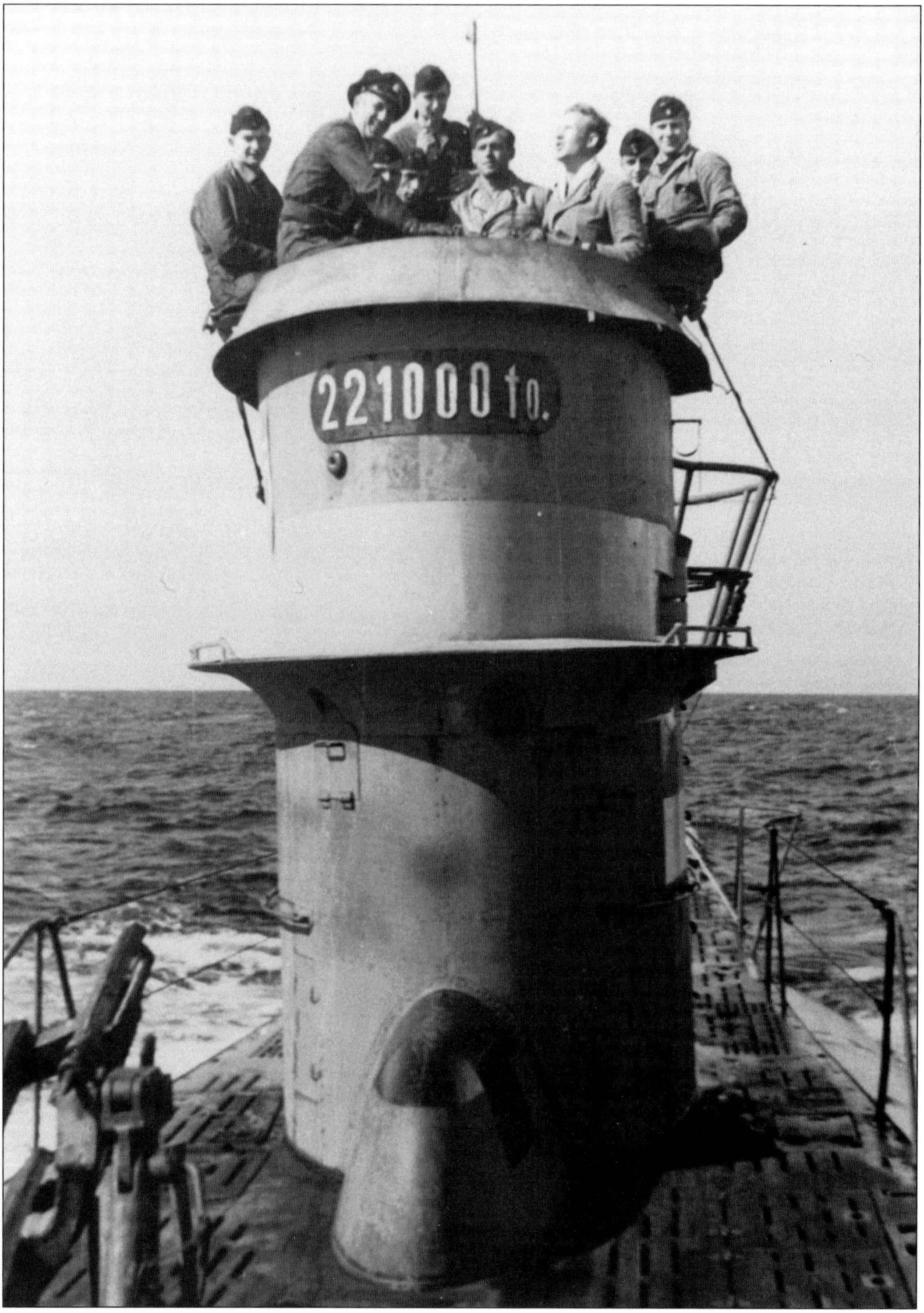

This image is especially interesting. The captain on the rear of this photograph says that it is of *U46* on the torpedo firing ranges after she had been pensioned off as an operational boat. However, the conning tower does look to be rather typical for a Type VIIC and *U46* was a VIIB. Could it have been modified? It also looks rather new! And notice that the forward jumping wire is missing. The number on the front could be the tonnage sunk earlier while in operational service. One of the boat's earlier commanders had been KL Engelbert Endrass who had served as IWO of *U47* under Günter Prien and was responsible for firing the torpedoes inside the Royal Navy anchorage at Scapa Flow which sank the British battleship *Royal Oak*.

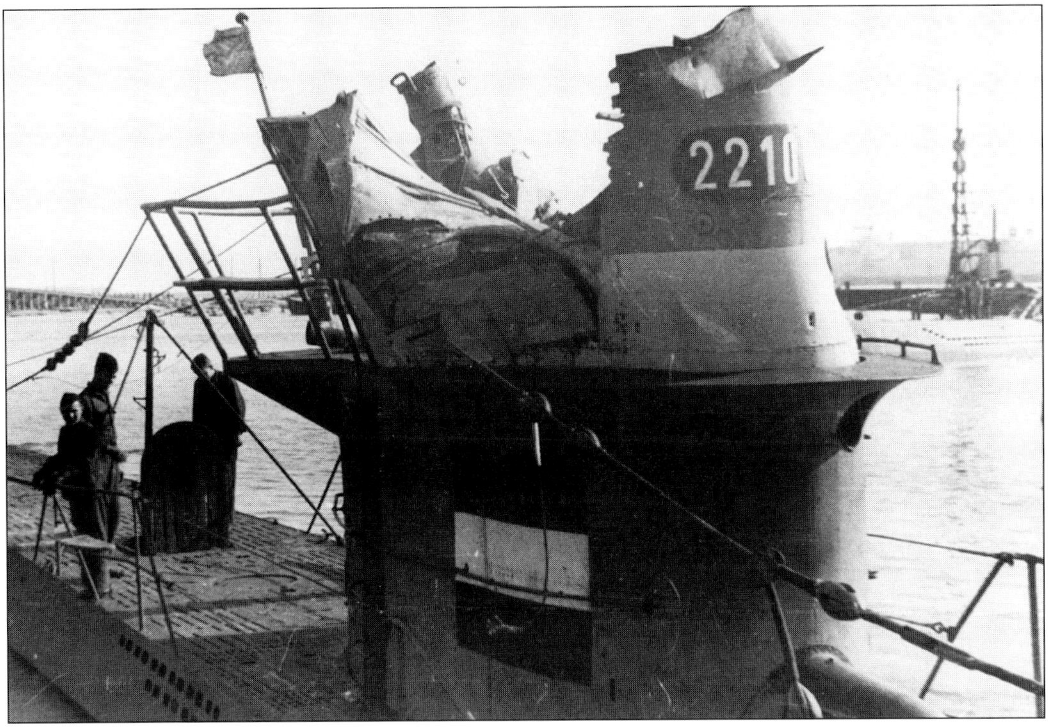

U46. This is what happens when a U-boat follows its torpedo too eagerly and also hits the target ship itself. Such damage would render an operational boat useless because neither of the periscopes were likely to function but it was not life-threatening to the crew. The pressure hull inside the conning tower casing appears to be undamaged. Notice the forward jumping wire with insulators in the foreground. This might suggest that the previous picture with the rather pristine conning tower was taken after this damage had been repaired! The 1 m sq emblem was an identification mark to help recorders at the torpedo ranges where a number of boats frequently shot at the same target simultaneously. Note that the old emblem '22100' was fitted to the new conning tower.

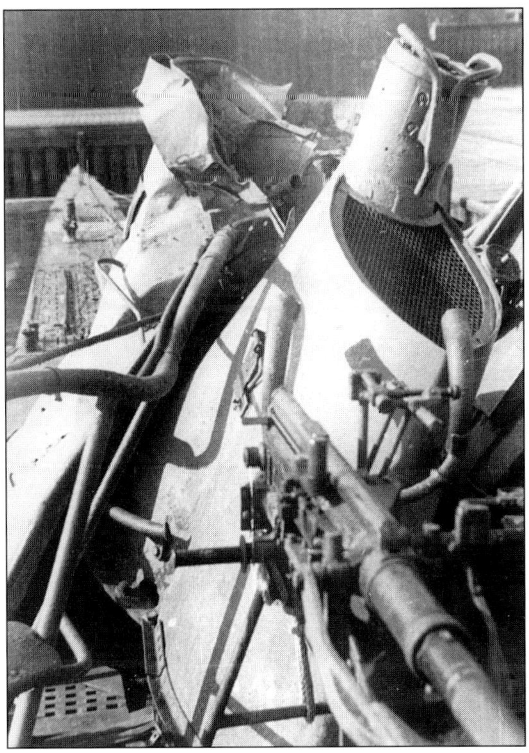

A close-up of *U46*'s crumpled conning tower. Strangely enough, despite a large number of U-boats milling around convoys in the Atlantic during dark nights, there was only one 'operational' collision throughout the entire war. This is quite remarkable because there were several cases of two boats attacking the same target at the same time. The problem of colliding with steel were far more acute during training when dozens of collisions, some of them fatal, marred the proceedings.

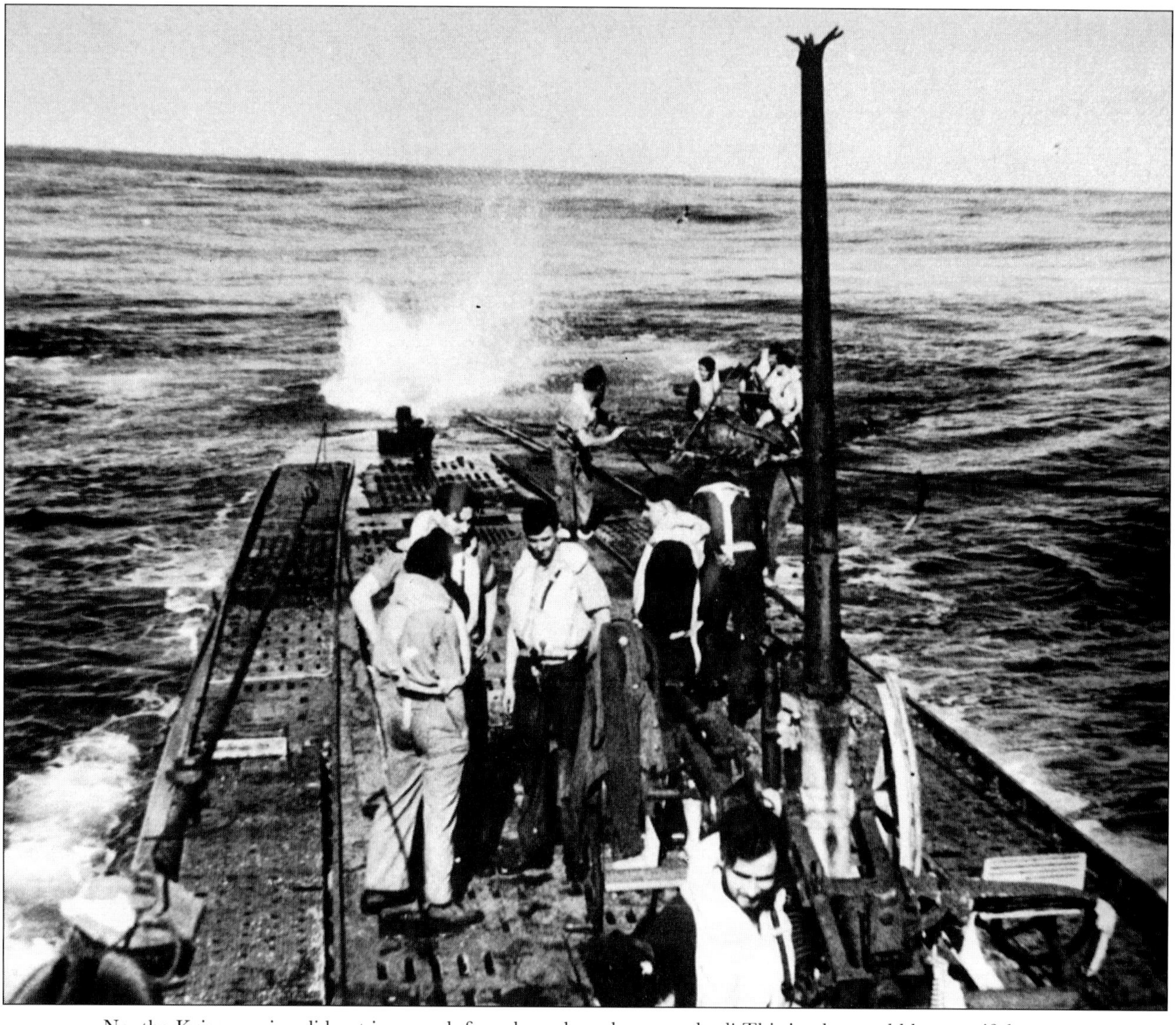

No, the Kriegsmarine did not issue such frayed gun barrels as standard! This is what could happen if the gun was fired without removing the watertight tampon at the end. The exact nature of the damage depended on how tight it was screwed but such action always produced a very loud bang. There were similar cases where the entire breech was blown off, killing some of the gun crew. This is *U181* with a 37 mm quick-firing gun to the rear of the conning tower.

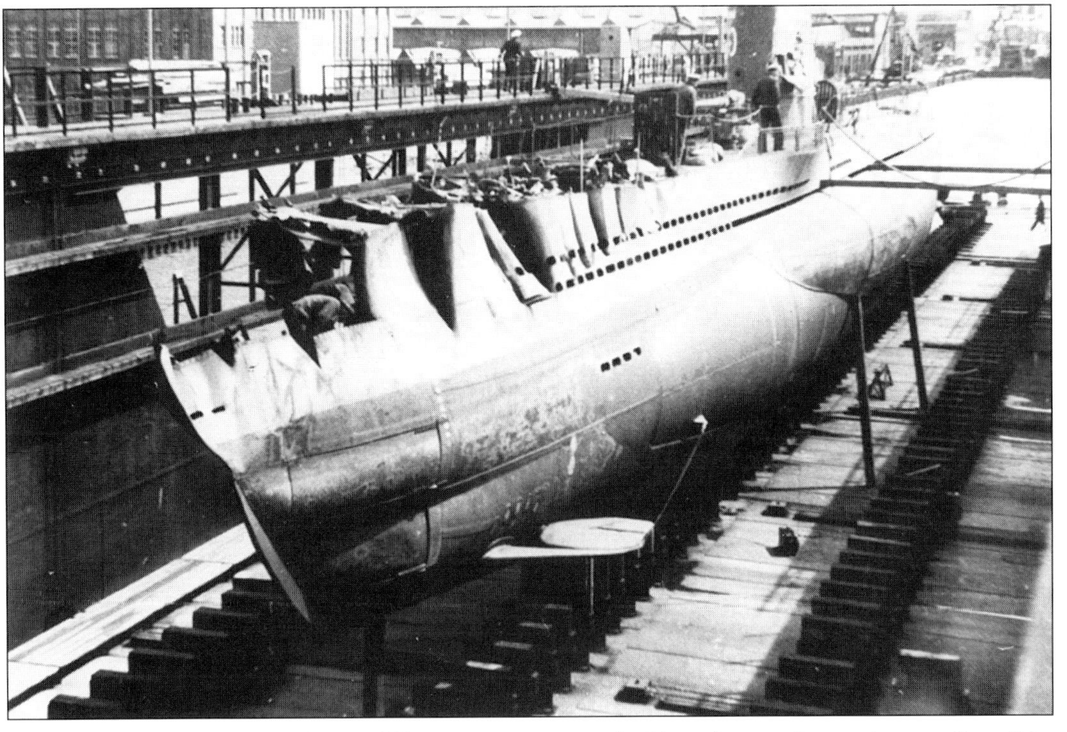

This rather unusual and exceptionally delicate pattern was acquired by going too close to the propellers of the pocket battleship *Graf Spee* while they were rotating.

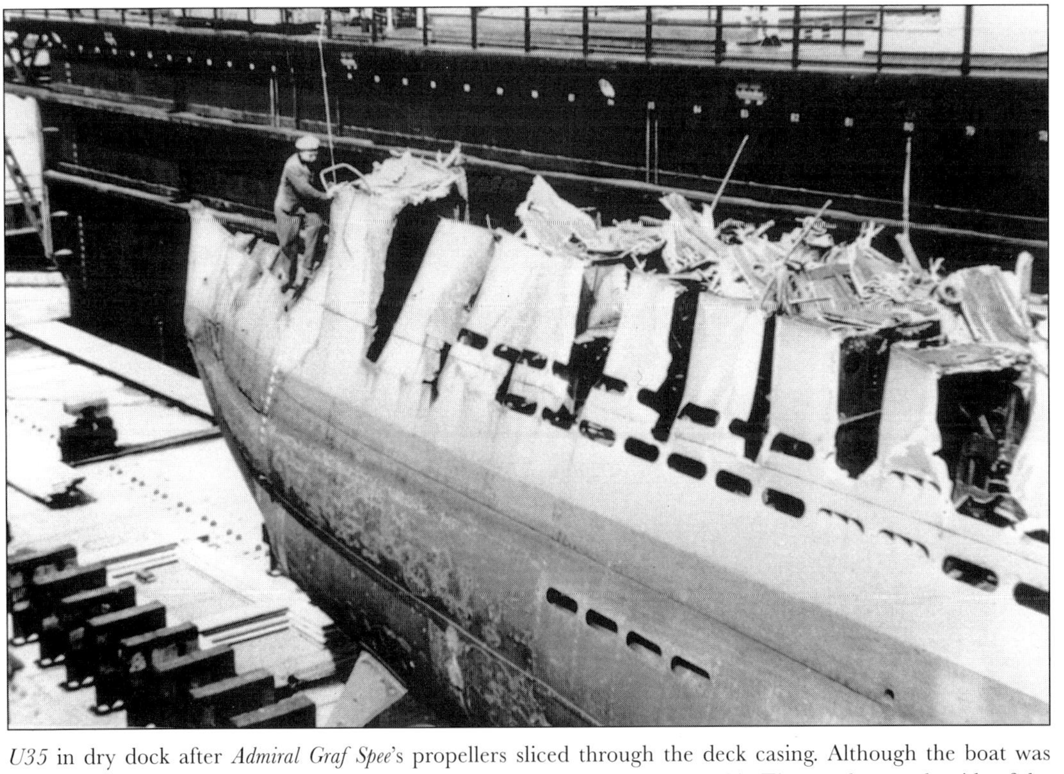

U35 in dry dock after *Admiral Graf Spee*'s propellers sliced through the deck casing. Although the boat was somewhat battered, this picture clearly shows the vent pattern of a Type VIIA. The number on the side of the conning tower indicates that this happened before the war. Of course, *Graf Spee* was never in Germany during the war. She left in mid-August 1939 and was scuttled in La Plata estuary at Christmas that year having spent most of her time in the South Atlantic.

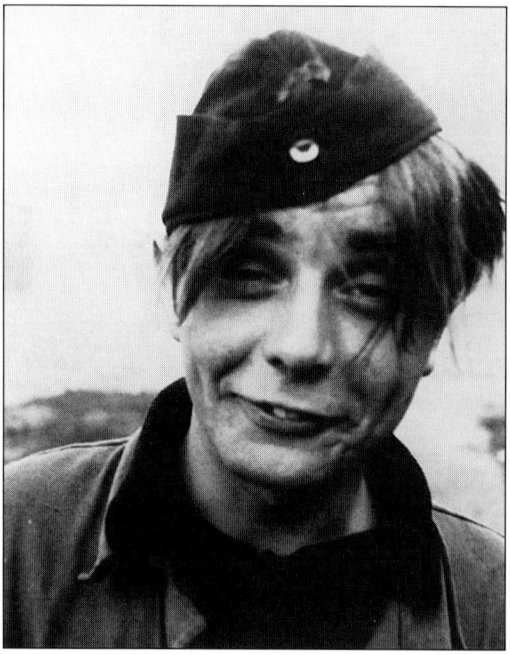

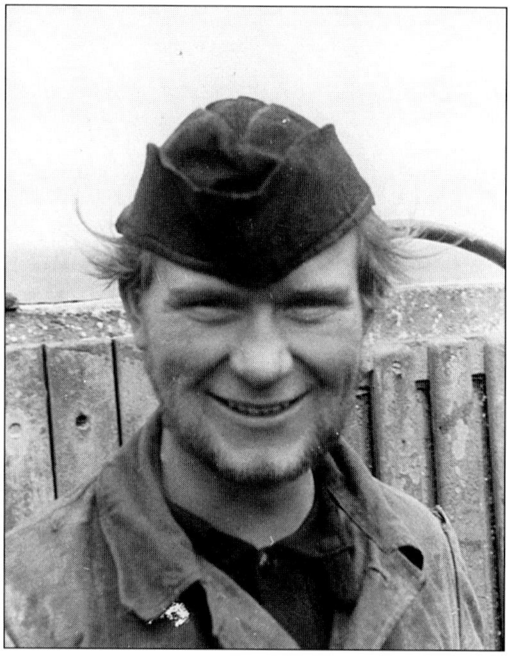

A number of American authors and historians have described rather gruesome characters aboard U-boats and have called them 'Killer Nazis'. Considerable proportions of books have been devoted to this type of man, but unfortunately none of those named feature in German Navy records. This discrepancy makes it exceptionally difficult, of course, to illustrate such a vital part of the U-boat Arm in this book. However, Horst Bredow's archive contains a vast number of photographs and during my research it looked as though there might be some examples of this 'Killer Nazi' type in his files. On the left is Maschinengefreiter Henkel of *U405*. Could he be a vicious 'Killer Nazi' of the kind referred to in American books? Or could the man on the conning tower of *U181* (right) be the object of American writers' hatred?

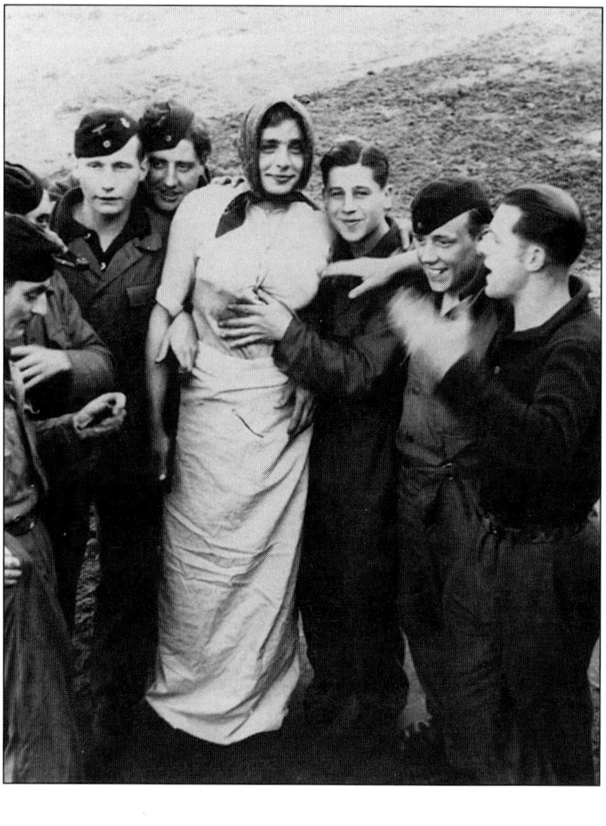

During the war, American Naval Intelligence devoted an incredible amount of time to studying and publishing information about the sex lives of these 'vicious' U-boat men. Indeed, some American intelligence reports give details of the number of prostitutes in named brothels used by the U-boat men as well as recording the costs and frequency of visits. When interviewing U-boat survivors, American Intelligence also made a considerable effort to grade brothels in some order of popularity and even mentioned one place where officers and men were forced into sharing the same women because there was only one centre for such entertainment. The American Naval Intelligence's enthusiasm for sexual activities in occupied France possibly spurred a number of postwar authors into telling their readers how girls were press-ganged into U-boats to provide pleasure for sex mad crews. Could this be one of those unfortunate damsels, caught by a bunch of desperate men? (In fact, it appears that this is in fact Maschinengefreiter Henkel wrapped up in a tablecloth or bedsheet.)

The Americans, who invented the 'Killer Nazis', also described a number of 'cruel' U-boat commanders who ill treated their crews. Again, it was impossible to find the names mentioned in the naval records . . . but could this be one of the cruel commanders who tortured his men by playing them awful music? Even stuffing a cigar into his mouth does not seem to have stopped him. For the serious minded I should point out that it is actually KL Adalbert Schnee aboard *U203* trying his hand at something creative with a borrowed accordion. The grid over a ventilation shaft is visible by the side of his head and a magnetic sighting compass can be seen by the raised periscope.

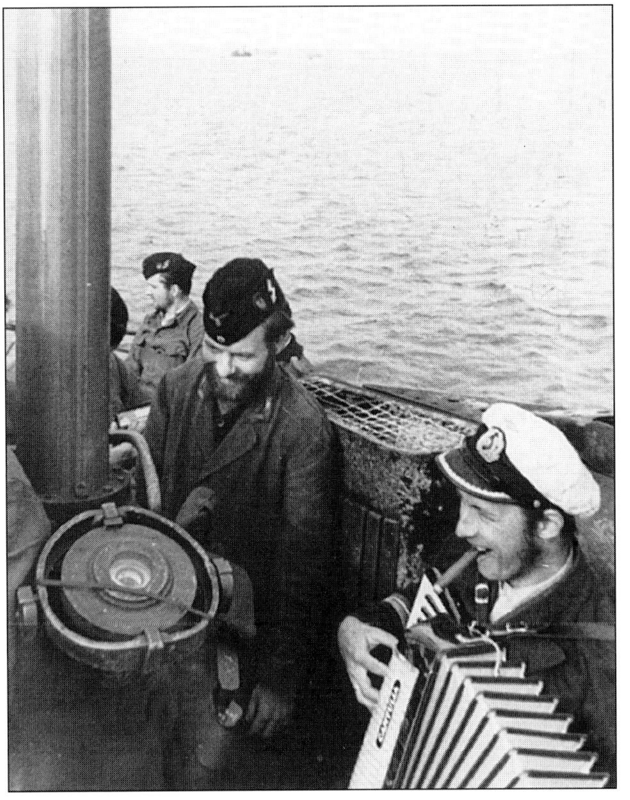

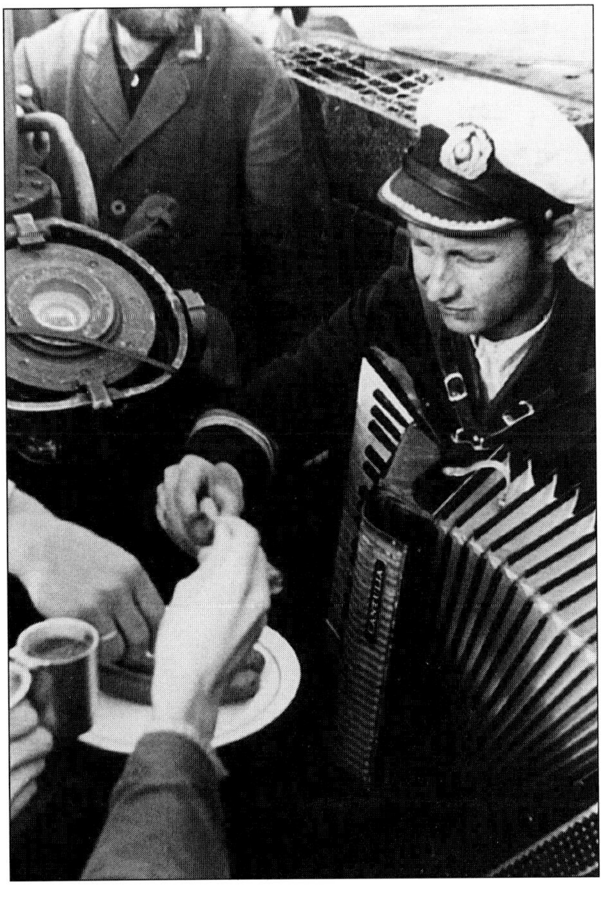

The German Navy had a secret procedure for commanders who insisted on playing the squeeze-box on the conning tower: exchanging that cigar for a spicy frankfurter and a mug of coffee seems to have put a stop to the music. But does the expression on Adi Schnee's face suggest that there is something suspicious about the humble German naval sausage?

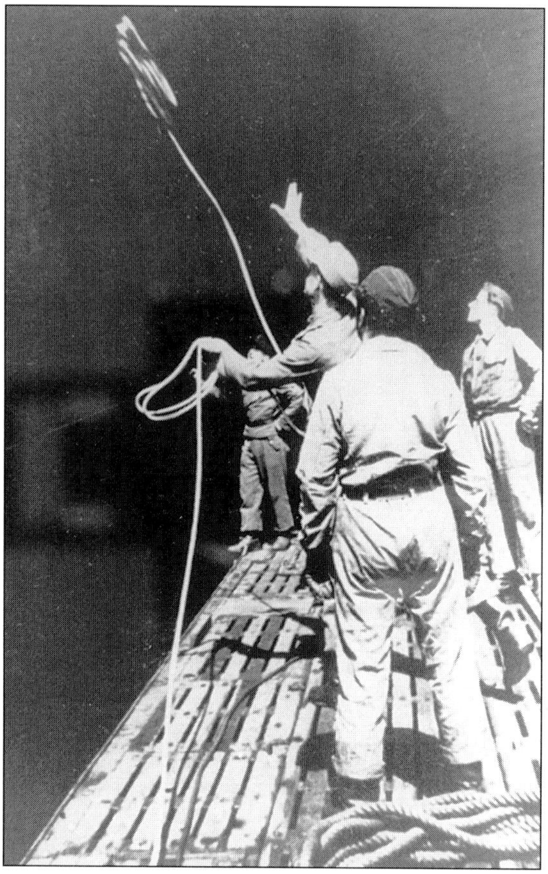

An American author has described a number of callous U-boat commanders and has said that one of them insisted his men stood to attention, saluted and then took three steps backwards before they were allowed to speak to him. Although the commander has been named, he cannot be traced in German records. One is left wondering how such feats were supposed to have been performed. It is not totally impossible on the outside deck, but conning towers were so small that men would have fallen off or collided with a metal wall. Anyone taking three steps back inside the majority of boats must have had a means of diffusing through solid steel bulkheads. Could *U373* also have had some of those callous officers who insisted that the men threw a rope at a bollard over a considerable distance before they were allowed ashore? A number of postwar authors have displayed their ignorance of naval procedures and the social life in Europe during the 1940s by describing what they claim to be unacceptable hardships suffered by men in the navy without realising that the majority of workers of the time struggled under equally bad conditions.

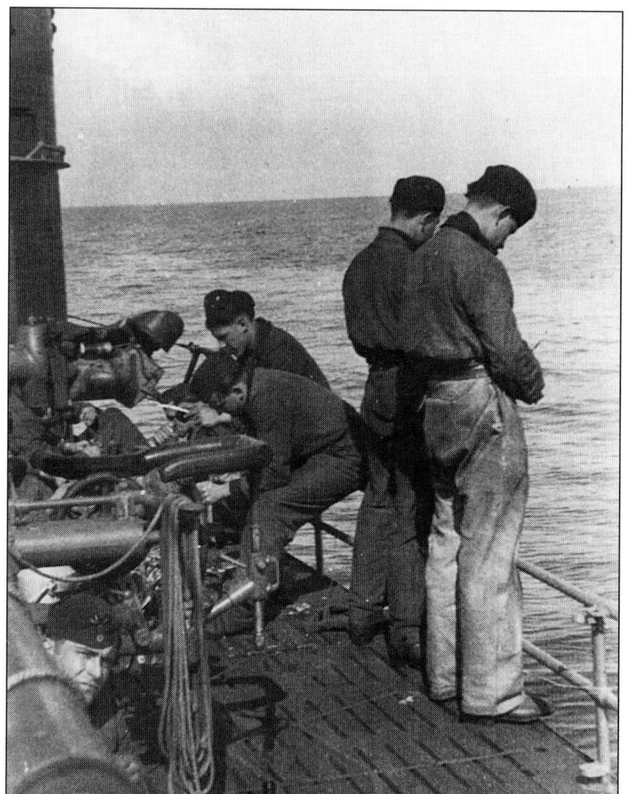

Here it looks as though these two men from *U441* have been naughty and made to stand in the corner. Or could they be playing hide-and-seek and cannot find the man under the 88 mm quick-firing gun?

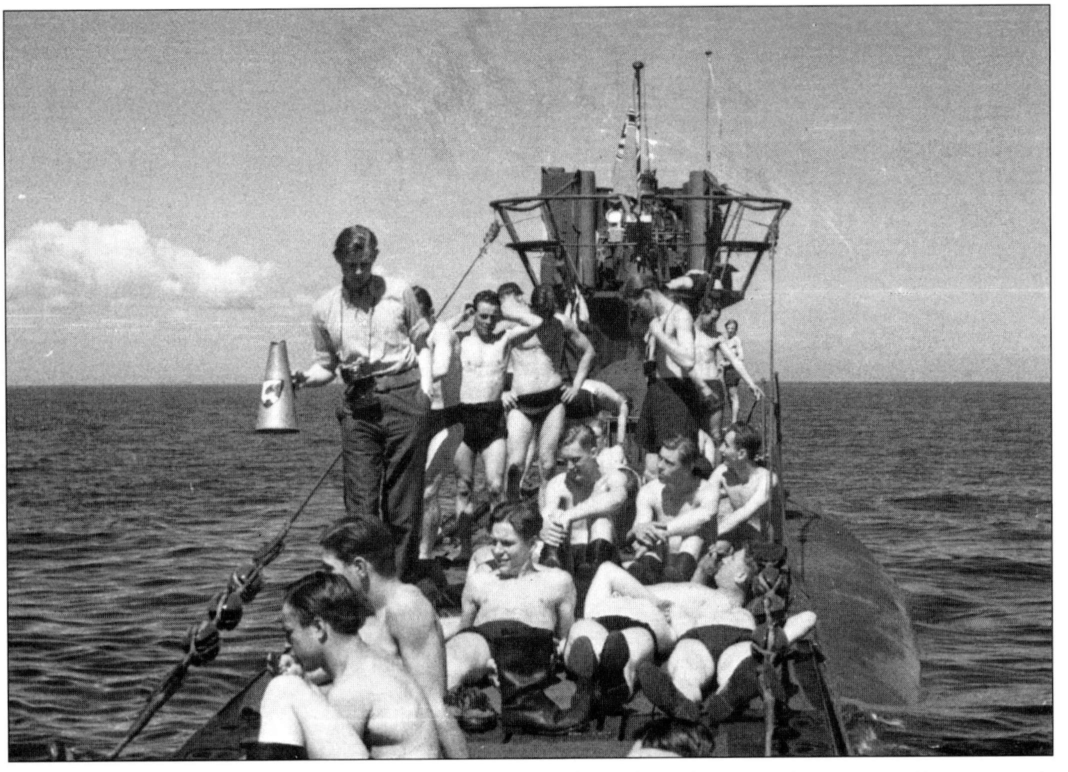

U223 in the role of a pleasure cruiser. Note the massive saddle tank on the right. The man standing on the left is holding a megaphone made from a tin funnel.

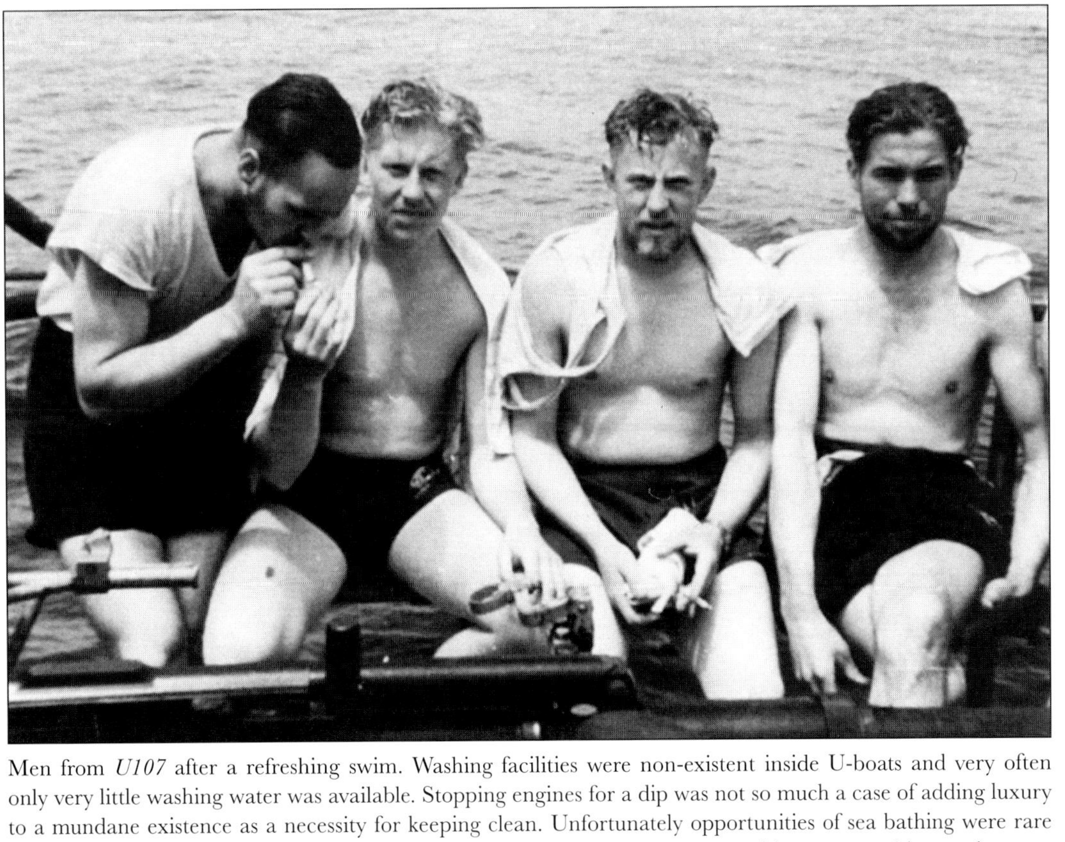

Men from *U107* after a refreshing swim. Washing facilities were non-existent inside U-boats and very often only very little washing water was available. Stopping engines for a dip was not so much a case of adding luxury to a mundane existence as a necessity for keeping clean. Unfortunately opportunities of sea bathing were rare because mostly it was too cold – and judging by their expressions, it was not terribly warm on this occasion.

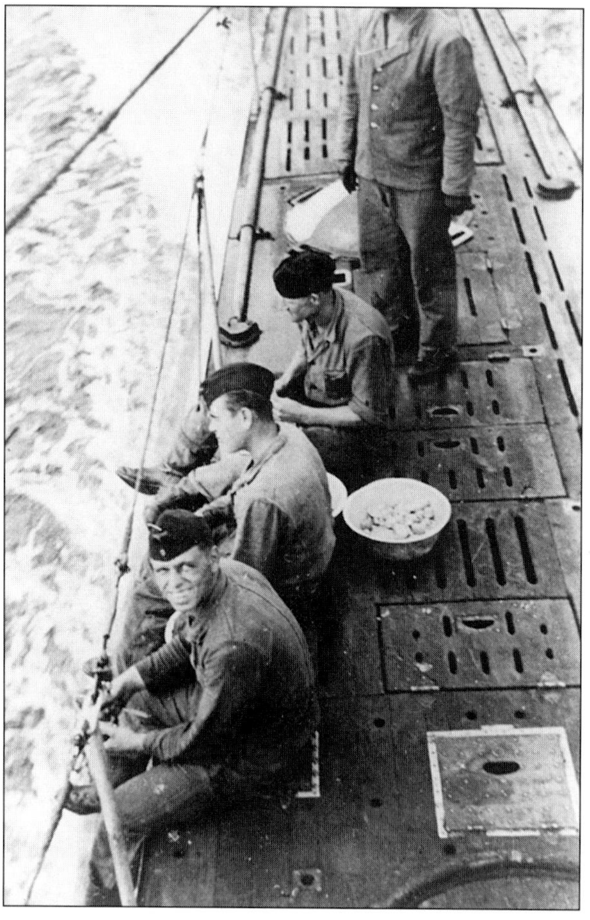

U62. Domestic chores such as washing-up and peeling potatoes always dominated the drudgery of daily life and the Kriegsmarine saw no reason to supply mechanical aids when there was an abundance of spare hands. Men often preferred the open upper deck to the cramped conditions inside, yet this luxury was denied to them once the boat became operational and might, therefore, need to dive quickly. This is the narrow deck of a small coastal training boat. Note the rescue buoy in the background.

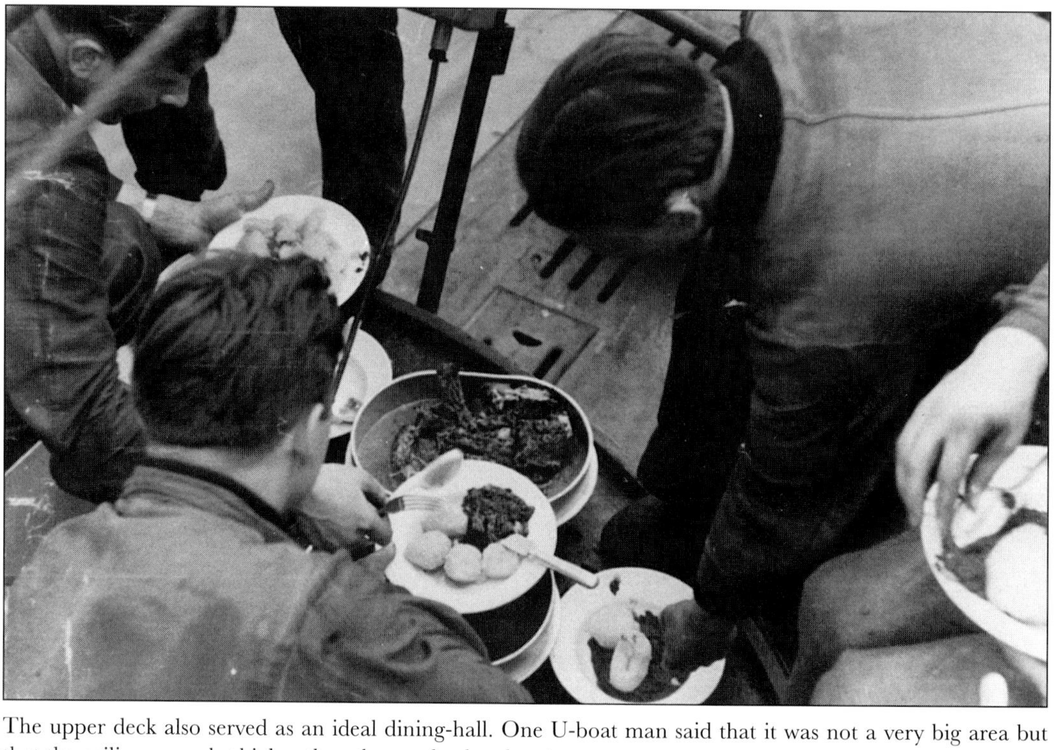

The upper deck also served as an ideal dining-hall. One U-boat man said that it was not a very big area but that the ceiling was a lot higher than the one back at base!

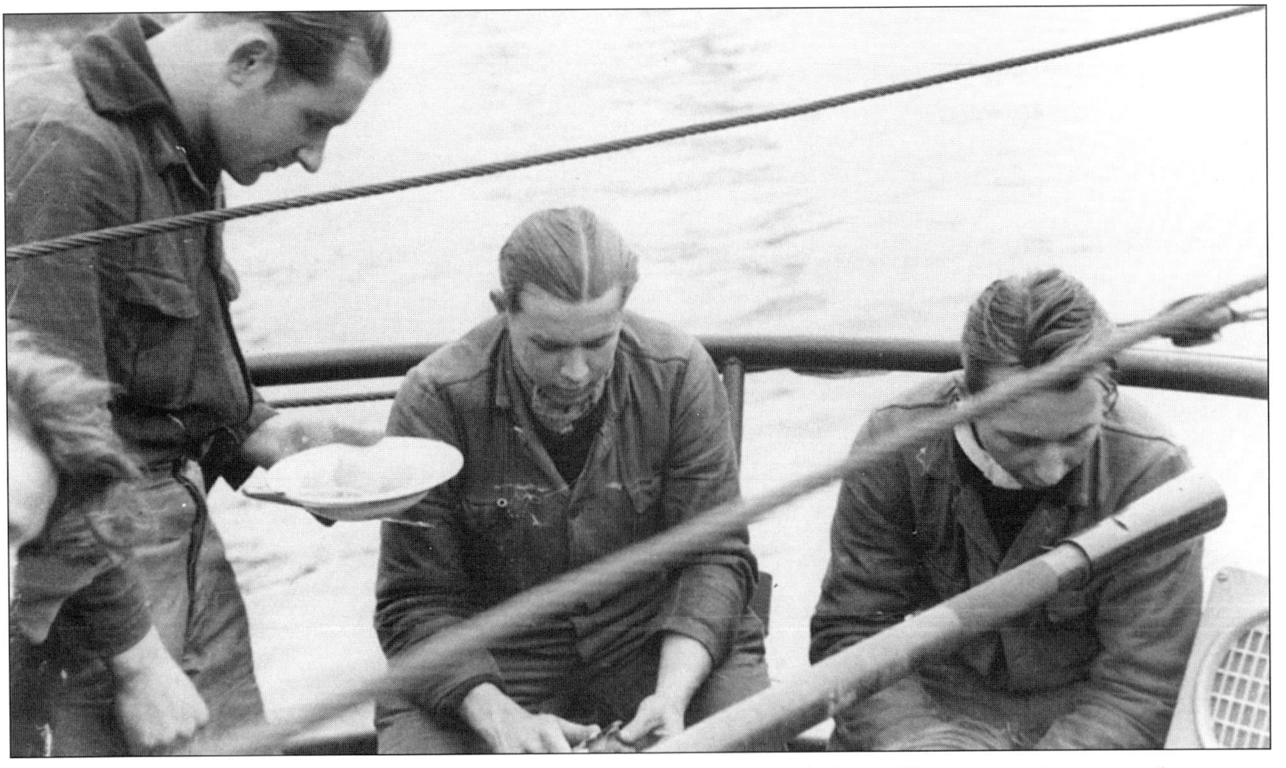

The galley was incredibly tiny and one man usually prepared all the meals for the fifty or so crew in an area of only a couple of square metres and with hardly any work-surfaces. However, U-boat men, like these on a Type VIIC, were among the groups of Germans who received the very best rations and often had luxuries of which other soldiers or civilians never even dreamed.

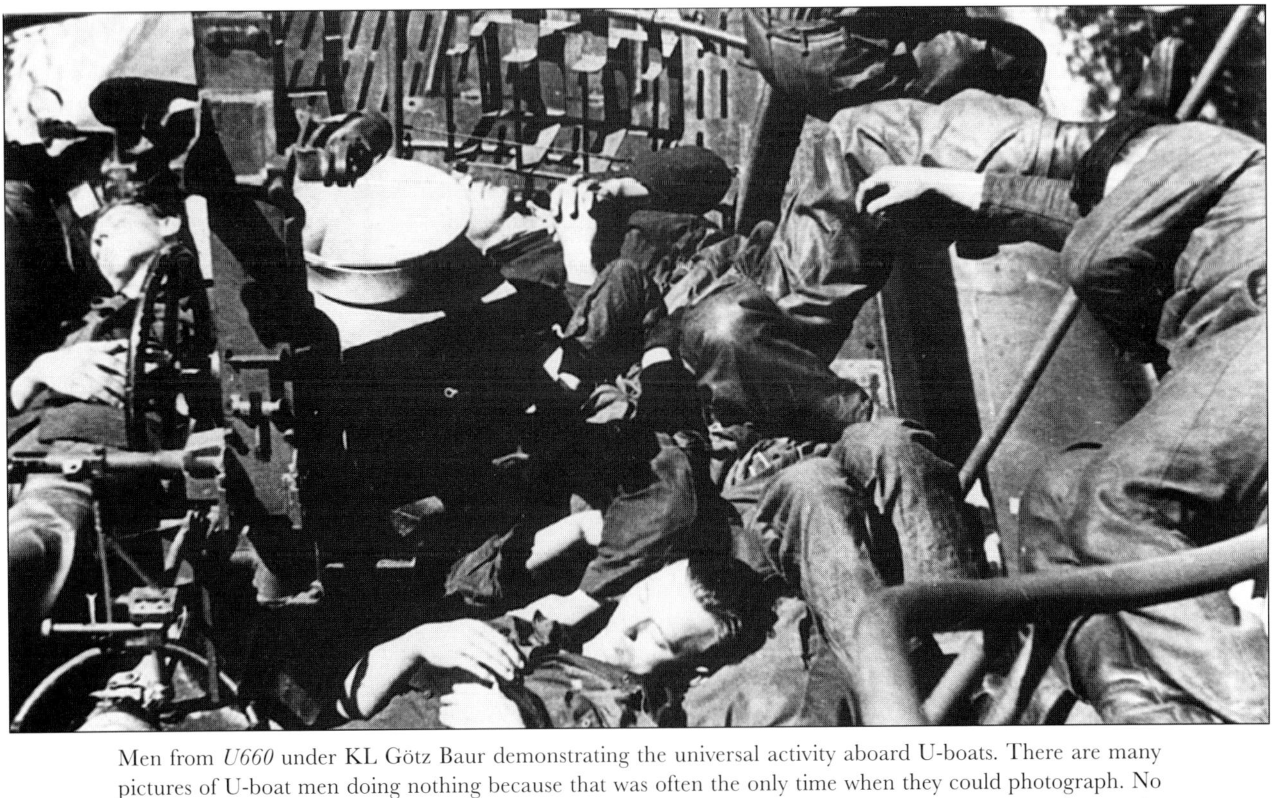

Men from *U660* under KL Götz Baur demonstrating the universal activity aboard U-boats. There are many pictures of U-boat men doing nothing because that was often the only time when they could photograph. No one, except the odd war correspondent, was stupid enough to stand around with a camera while under attack.

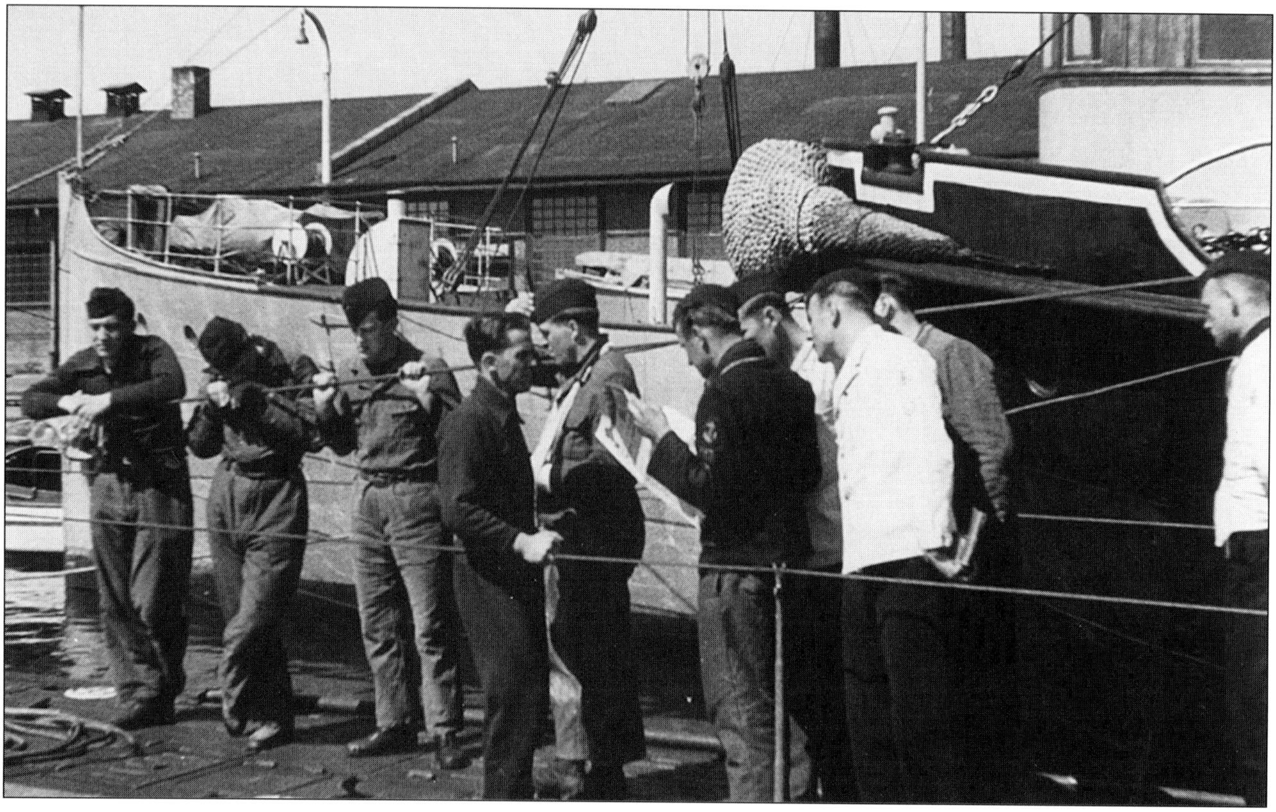

Men from *U69* passing the time of day and also demonstrating one use for the stout jumping wire. New newspapers were a rarity, although quite a few boats and flotillas produced their own.

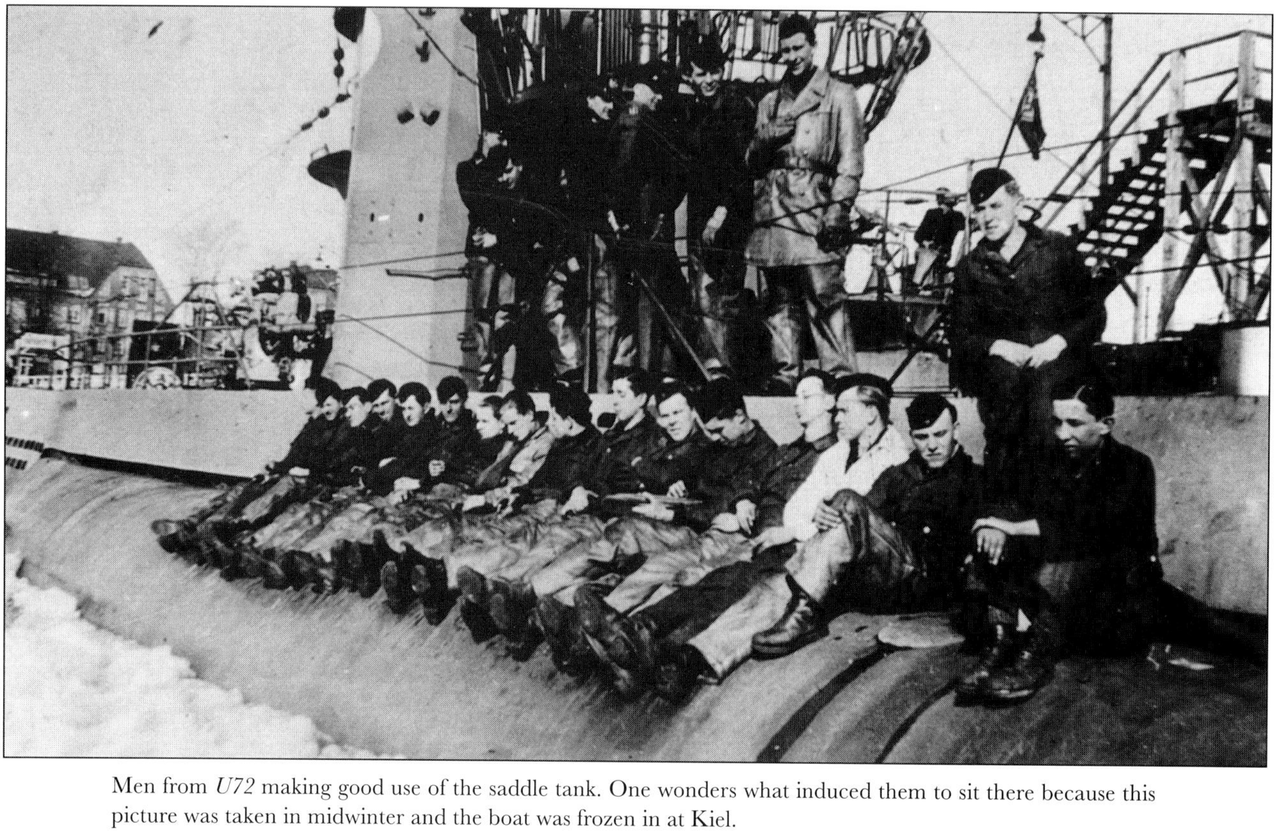

Men from *U72* making good use of the saddle tank. One wonders what induced them to sit there because this picture was taken in midwinter and the boat was frozen in at Kiel.

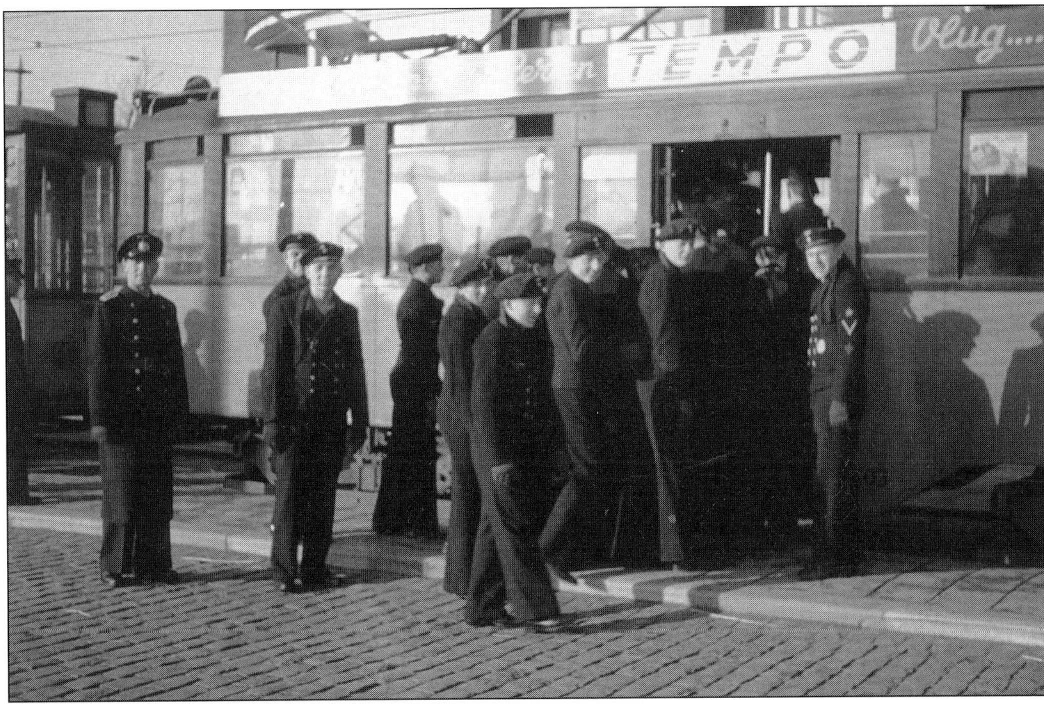

One advantage of training in the Baltic was that some activities were confined to the day, leaving the men free to take a tram into town to seek out some local night-life and the majority of ports provided plenty of it. Although contrary to reports in some American books, these facilities were not laid on by the navy but by private entrepreneurs.

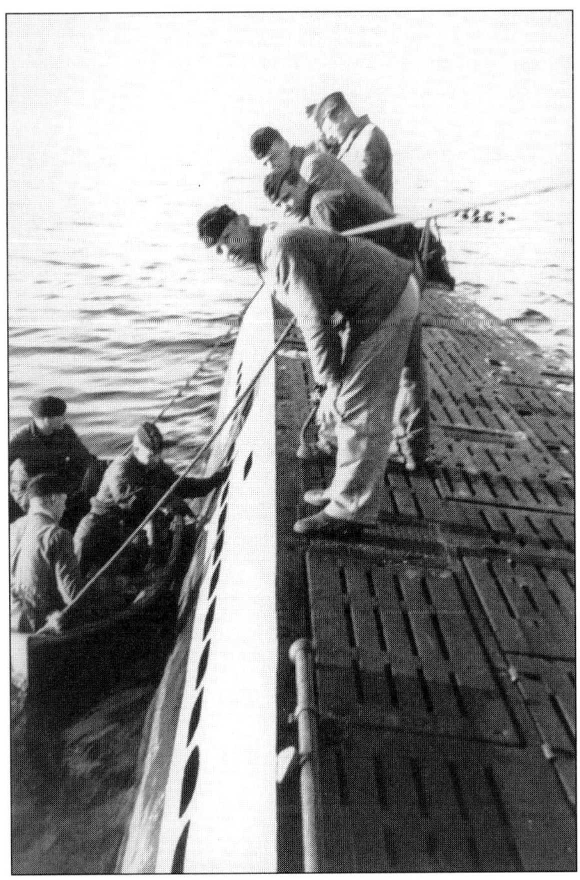

A common feature of many energetic naval recreational activities was that there were always a few chaps doing it and a large number of others offering encouragement and advice. This somewhat innocuous photograph is of interest because it shows that diving tanks could lift the stern of a Type VII a considerable distance clear of the water, much further than indicated by the majority of the pictures in this book. Usually boats were rigged for quick diving, leaving them somewhat lower in the water.

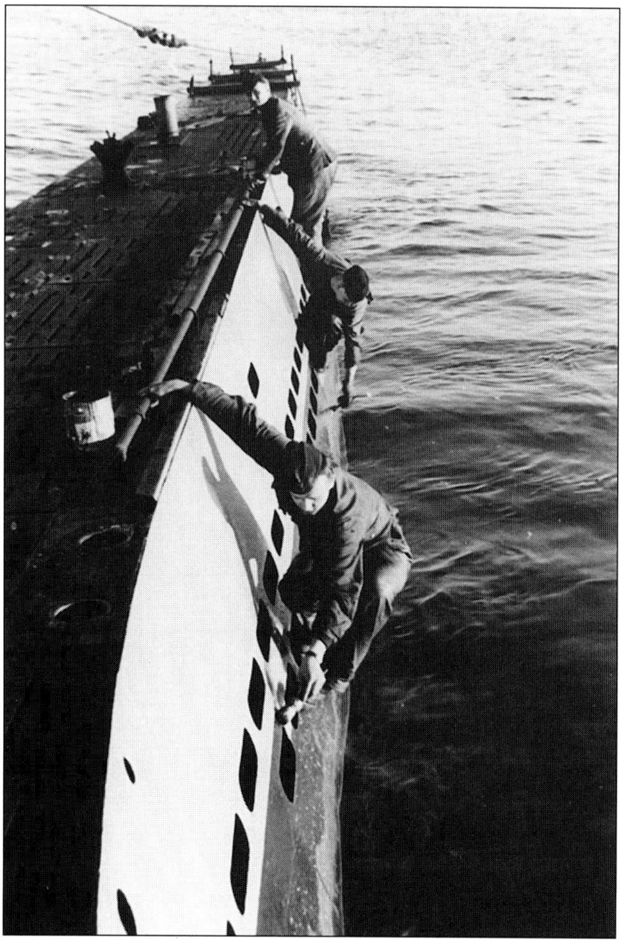

No doubt readers have been wondering why some U-boats had a low rail along the edge of the deck. Well, this photograph has the answer. This work must have been a quick patching-up job rather than a serious attempt at painting the whole side of the boat. Rather strangely, the steel cap for protecting the bows seems to be in place but there is no sign of ice and the weather does not appear to be terribly cold either.

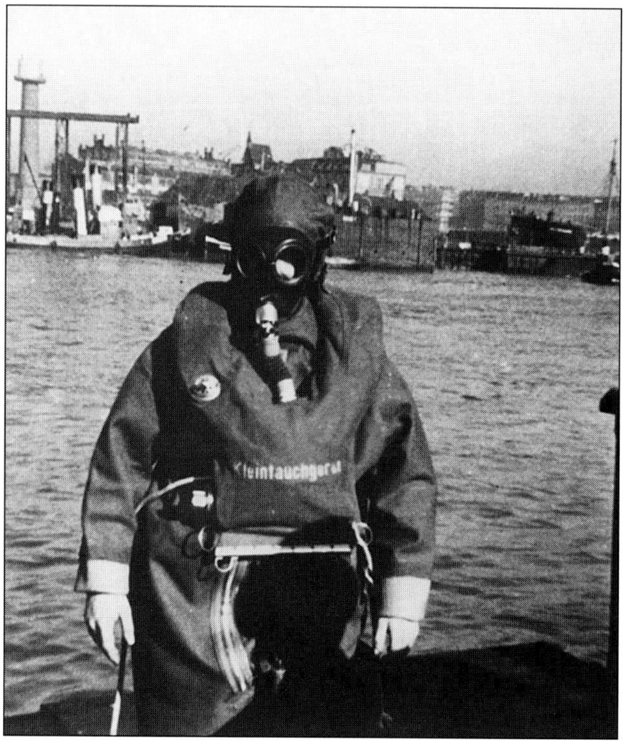

Training in the Baltic was designed not only to help men come to terms with their boat but also to enable them to learn how to cope with the variety of gear inside it. In the early days they had to get used to cumbersome breathing apparatus for removing carbon dioxide from the air. Initially this was worn by individuals but it hampered activity so much that designers later provided boats with purification cartridges attached to the walls. This is Maschinenmaat Holzke from *U172* with a small diving lung for inspecting the lower parts of boats. It was modified from the Dräger Lung or U-boat Escape Apparatus and only allowed the wearer down if he was wearing a heavy lead belt to compensate for the extra buoyancy of the partly inflated breathing bag. This allowed dives of up to about half an hour. The suit was also part of the diving gear and was essential in cold northern waters.

Roger Suiters at the U-Boot-Archiv demonstrating U-boat escape apparatus. Each man was issued with his own personal set. Inside the bag was a container for absorbing carbon dioxide and a cylinder for topping up the air with oxygen. This closed-circuit system enabled men to breathe for about half an hour while escaping from submerged boats or when the interior filled with poisonous gases. On the surface it could be inflated to act as life-jacket. There were a number of basic variations to the design and while these were being used in U-boats, British miners used gear from the same firm for coping with poisonous gases in coal pits.

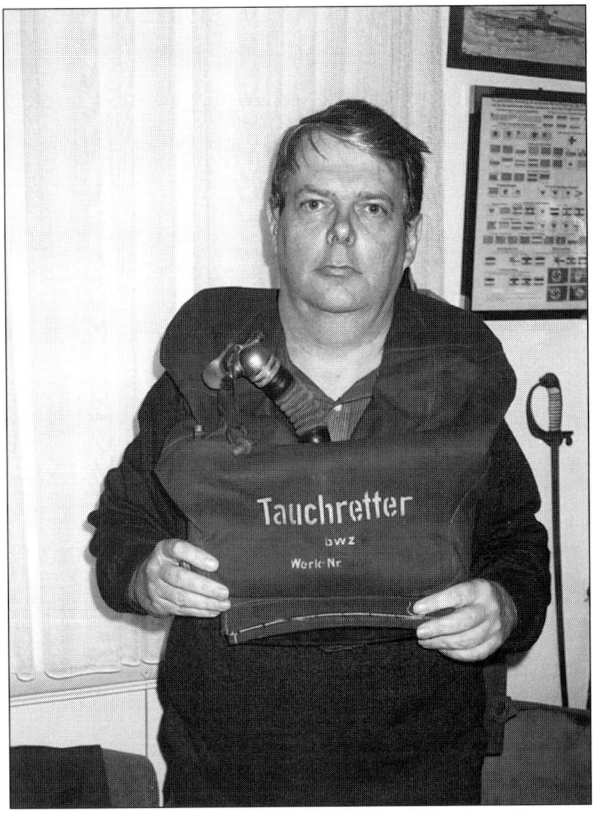

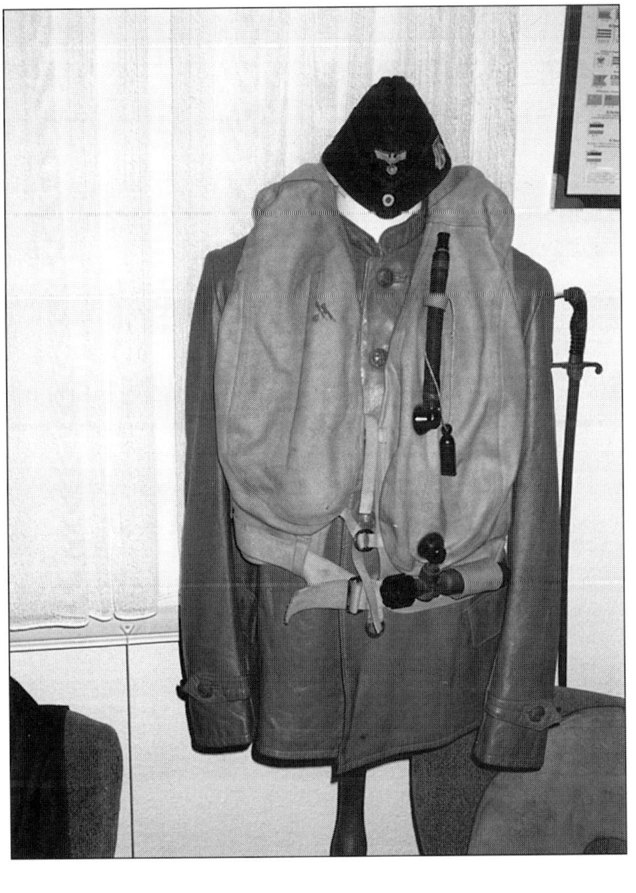

A life-jacket in the U-Boot-Archiv which could be inflated from a gas cylinder or by blowing down the pipe at the front. It is hanging over an engineer's leather coat and on top of the stand is one of the hats much favoured by U-boat men because they folded flat. Engineers often wore coats without lapels while men working on deck were provided with especially wide collars to help protect them from the weather.

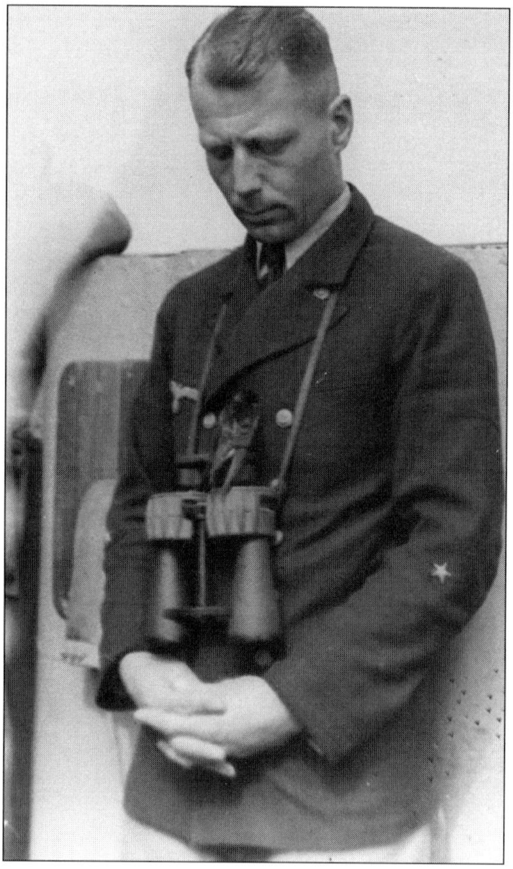

KL Otto Schuhart of *U29* wearing an old jacket without piston rings and carrying a passenger. The worn out swallow remained with the boat for some time and was revived with standard naval rations before flying off again. Commanders and Obersteuermann usually had their own binoculars, but there was often only one general set to be shared among the lookouts. Binoculars were supplied by a number firms and there were no standard types, although the majority were of the night glass variety with magnification of 7 × 50 and of superb quality. One dark night when the surface raider *Atlantis* passed two British warships, the men found that these ships could hardly be seen through captured glasses but stood out clearly through German night binoculars. Luckily for *Atlantis*, the British lookouts did not seem to have had captured German glasses.

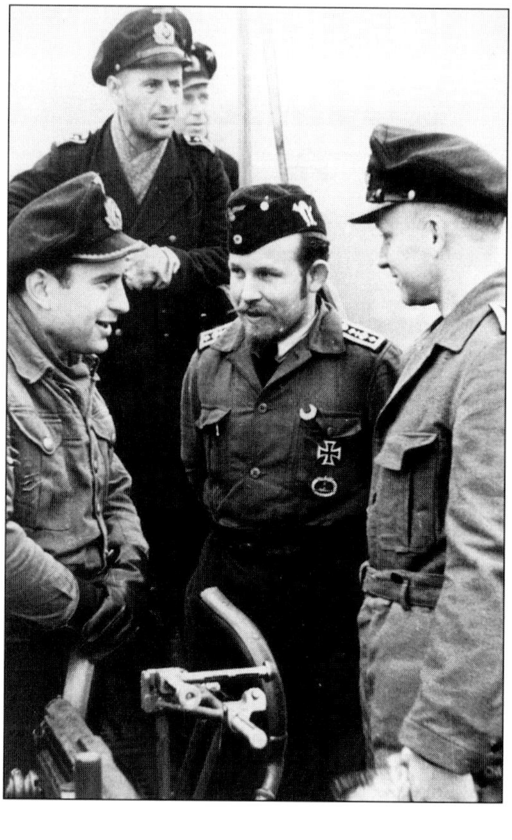

The men here are wearing U-boat overalls. This design was based on British battledress and the badges indicate that they were not novices when they commissioned *U564*. On the left is Reinhard ('Teddy') Suhren who had been second watch officer aboard *U51*, *U46* and *U47* and first watch officer of *U48*, the most successful U-boat of the war. He already had the Knight's Cross by the time he became a commander and held the distinction of having shot more operational torpedoes than anyone else in the navy. (During surface attacks it was the IWO who aimed and fired torpedoes while the commander had overall control of the situation.) The half-moon above the Iron Cross on the edge of the man's pocket is a spanner, not a medal. Also notice the unofficial boat badges on the side of the hats.

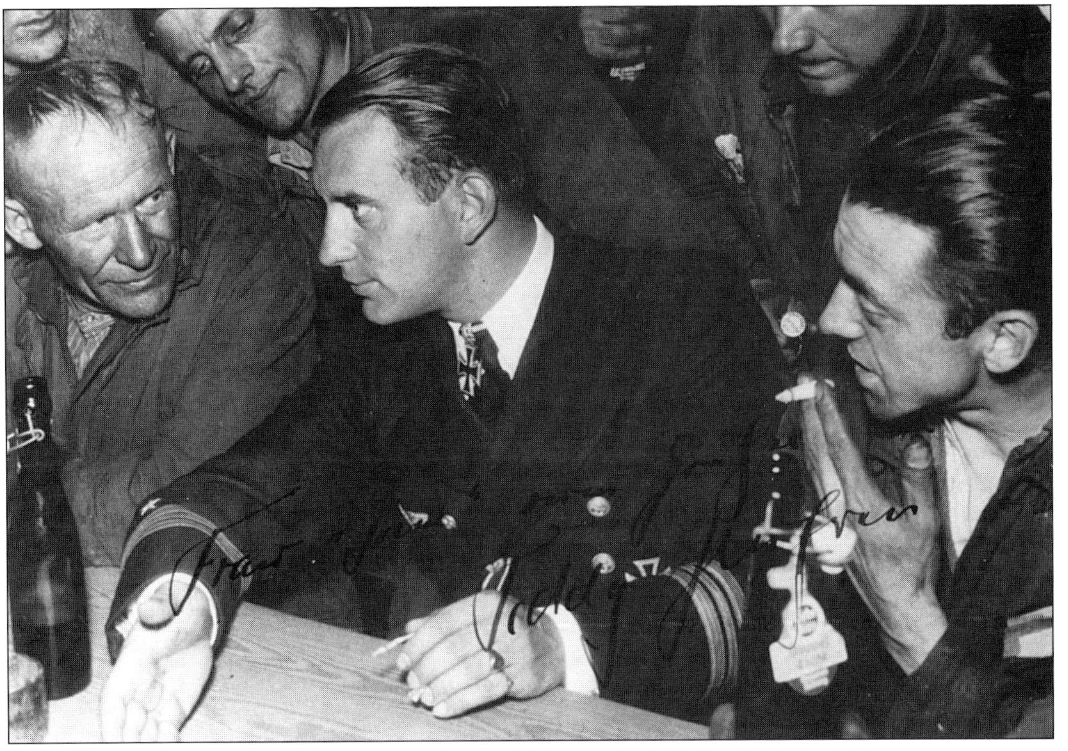

An obviously posed picture of 'Teddy' Suhren (*see* p. 110) talking to shipyard workers. The oak leaves above the Knight's Cross indicate that this photograph was taken after the end of 1941.

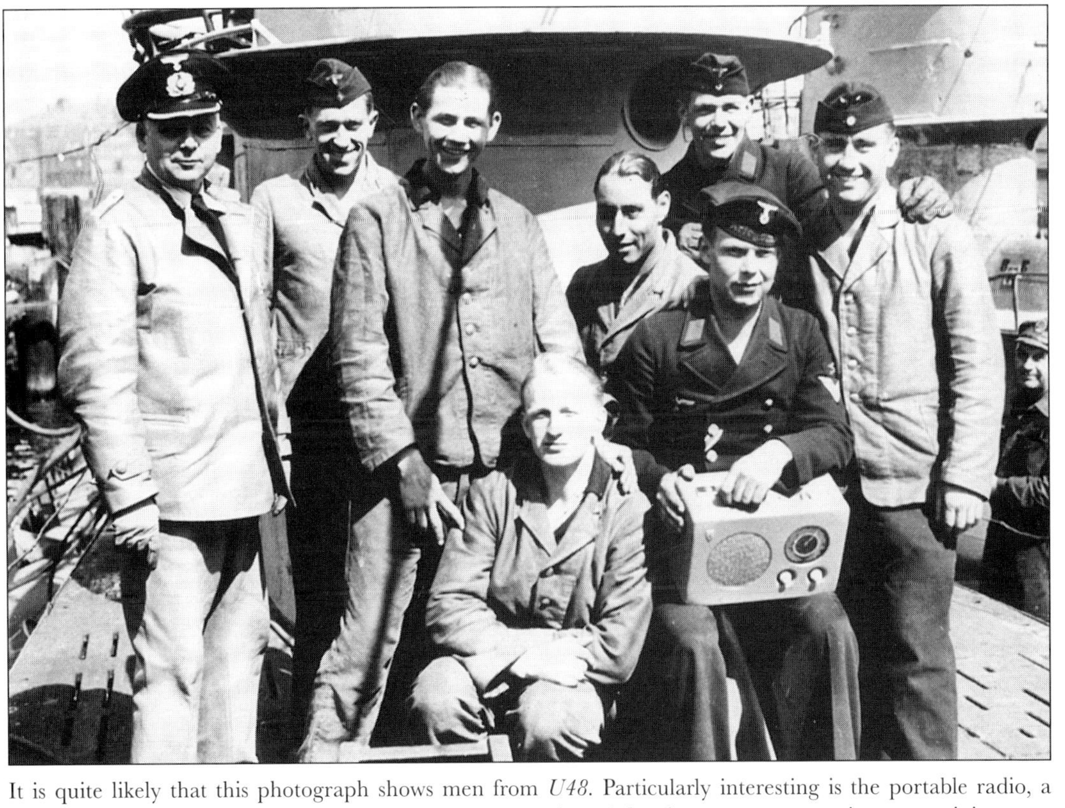

It is quite likely that this photograph shows men from *U48*. Particularly interesting is the portable radio, a valve-operated version of the modern ghetto-blaster and used for the same purpose, i.e. entertaining men while they were engaged in mundane activities.

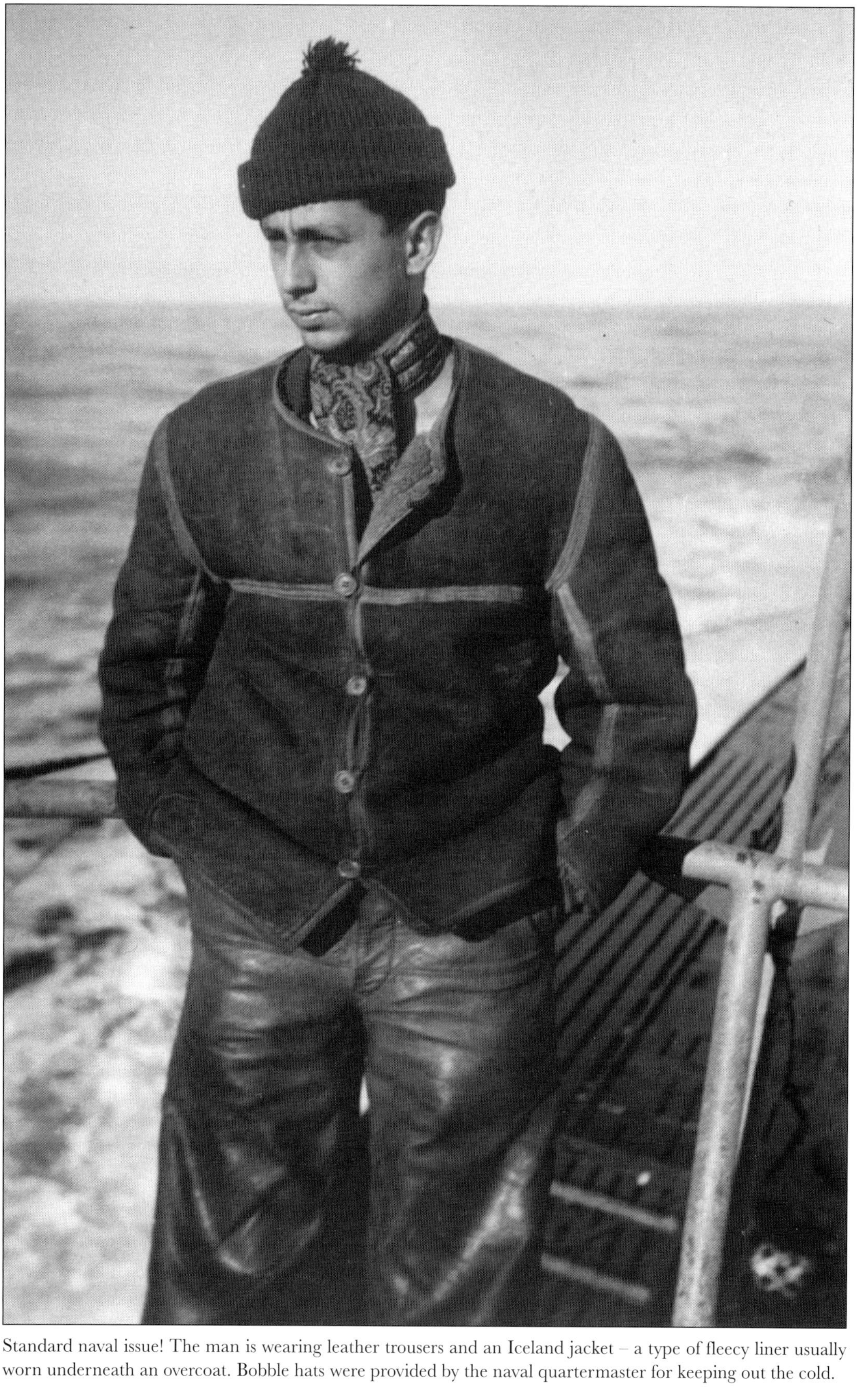

Standard naval issue! The man is wearing leather trousers and an Iceland jacket – a type of fleecy liner usually worn underneath an overcoat. Bobble hats were provided by the naval quartermaster for keeping out the cold.

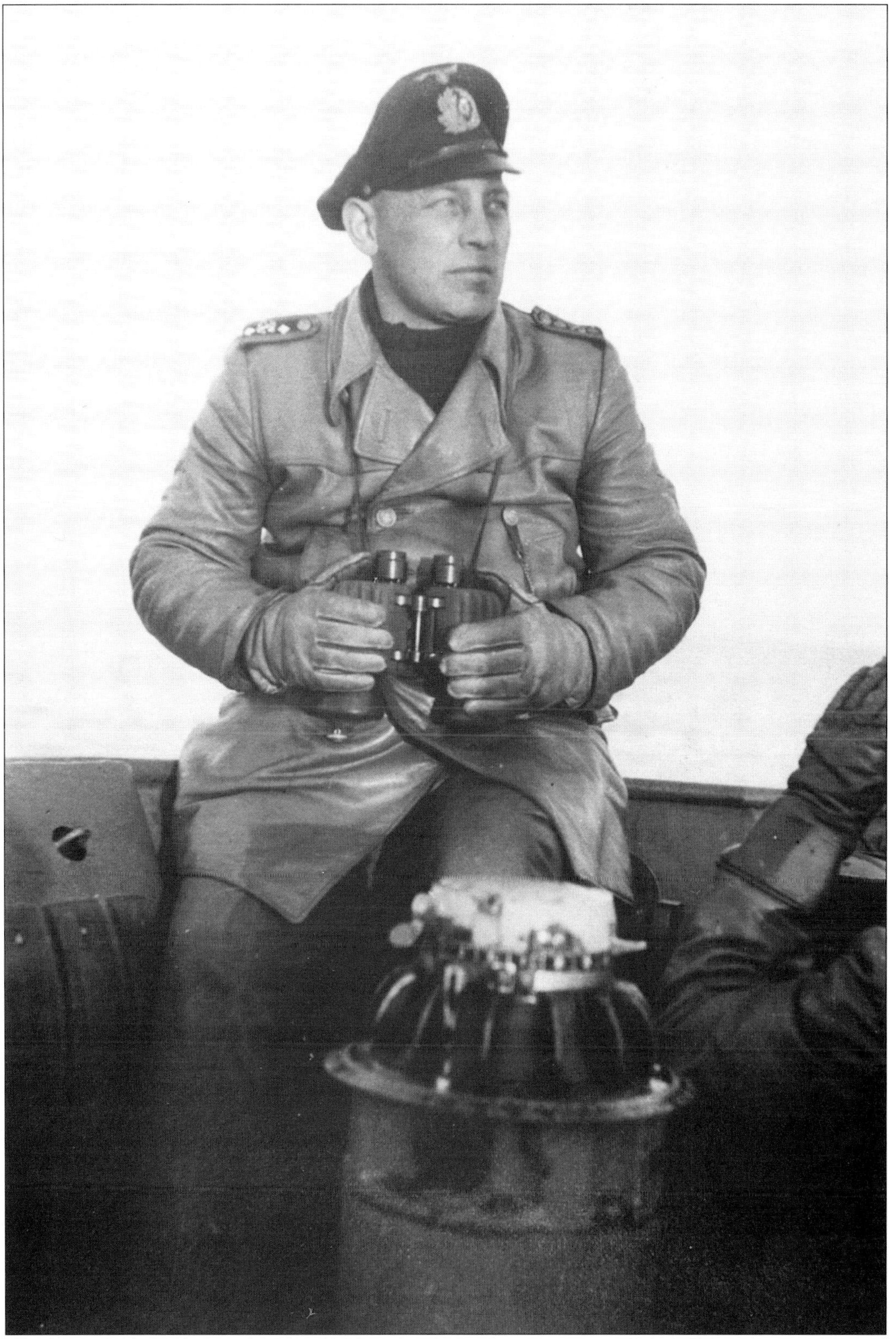

The IIIWO and Obersteuermann Gustav Brandt of *U215* wearing a leather coat with thick gloves. This kit was incredibly heavy, especially when compared with modern light-weight fibres. On the majority of U-boats the IIIWO and Obersteuermann position was filled by a warrant officer but often he would have had longer training and more experience than the commissioned officers above him.

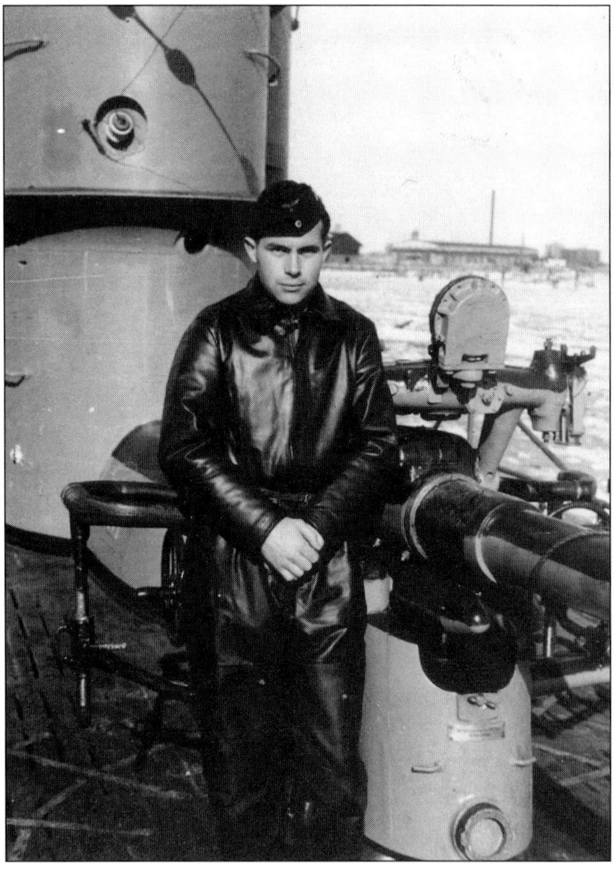

Maschinenmaat Hans Maier of *U125* wearing what looks like a one-piece leather garment. The abundance of ice in the background suggests it was pretty cold. Note the radio aerial intake on the front of the conning tower.

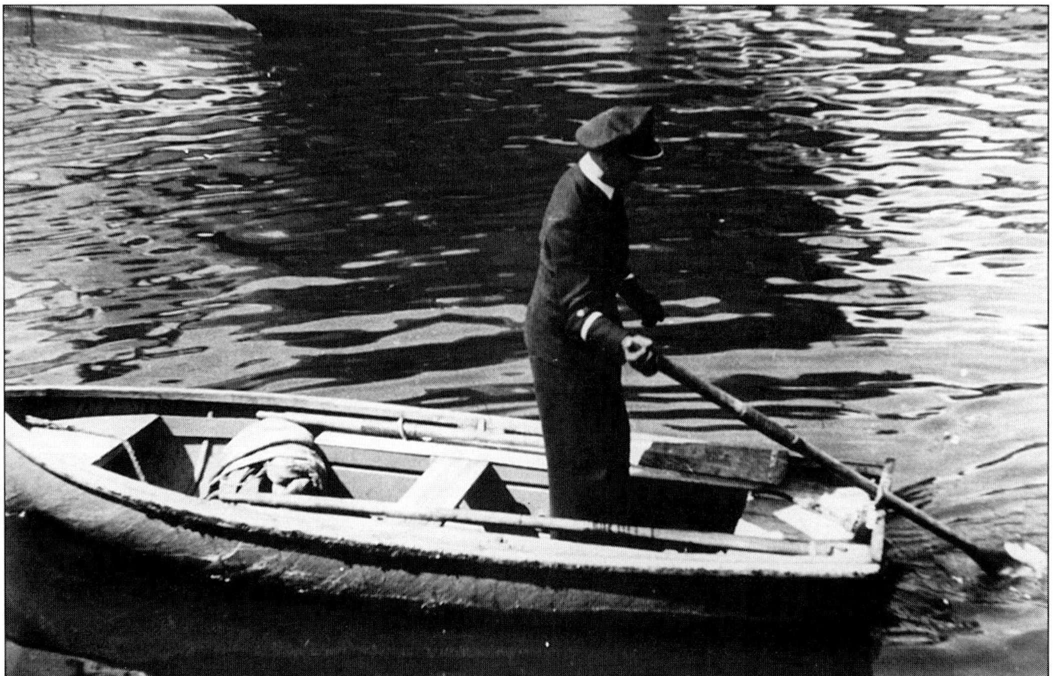

Lt Erdmann of *U72* trying his hand at sculling. This was a common way of moving small boats in North Germany and was most suitable in narrow waterways where the water was not wide enough for rowing. Practising rowing or sculling was always a good excuse for anyone who wanted to get away from the general bustle of ship life and many men devoted their spare time to cruising around harbours.

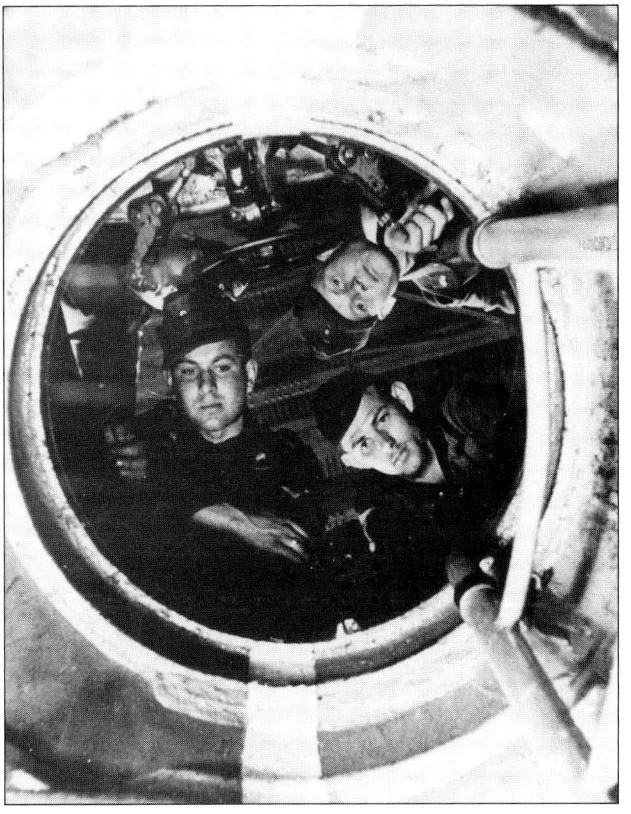

Maschinenobergefreiter Richard Klio of *U379* with two mountain fighters inspecting the boat in Norway. It seems highly likely that the men are outside of the boat on deck with the ceiling of a U-boat bunker above them.

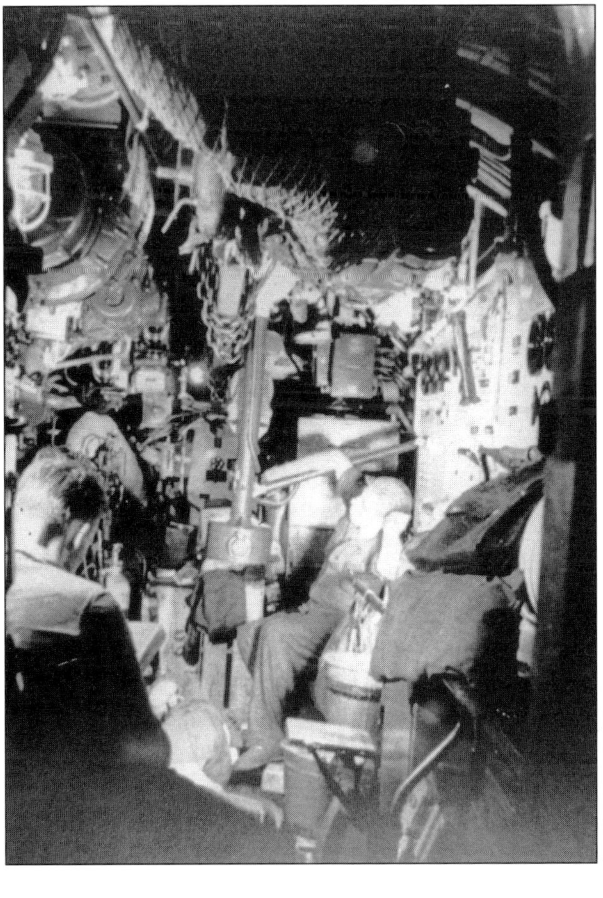

Anyone entering an operational U-boat for the first time was usually confused by the mass of stores covering essential machinery. This shows the cramped and claustrophobic interior of the rear torpedo compartment with controls for the electric motors on the right and a small hand-wheel on the larger disc like door of the torpedo tube in the background. This could be *U458* under command of KL Kurt Diggins, who became president of the Verband Deutscher U-Bootfahrer (German Submariners' Association) after the war.

Gericht
des Führers der Unterseeboote
Italien

Abschrift

O.Q.U., den 22.Dez. 1942

St. L. J Nr. 54/1942

An

Strafverfügung.

~~Sie werden beschuldigt, am~~ Der Mech.Maat
von der 29.U.-Flottille,
~~geb. am 4.3.1915 in Breslau, im Zivilberuf Dreher, ledig,~~
am 1.1.1937 in die Kriegsmarine eingetreten, von guter Führung, disziplinarisch nicht bestraft,
~~wird beschuldigt,~~
vorsätzlich einen Befehl in Dienstsachen nicht befolgt und dadurch fahrlässig eine Gefahr für die Schlagfertigkeit der Truppe herbeigeführt zu haben.

-Verbrechen nach § 92 MStGB.-

Sachverhalt: Am 18.10.42 verkehrte der Beschuldigte während seines Heimaturlaubs mit einem Mädchen geschlechtlich ohne, wie befohlen, ein Gummischutzmittel zu benutzen und sich anschließend sanieren zu lassen.

~~Übertretung — Vergehen — Verbrechen strafbar nach §~~

Beweismittel sind: Geständnis des Beschuldigten.

Strafverfügung nach § 48a K.St.V.O.

Wenden

Vordrucklager der Kriegsmarine: J. J. Augustin in Glückstadt. — (MG 16691) — 300. V. 41.

Din A 4

This punishment order is headed 'Court for the Flag Officer for U-boats in Italy' but there was a similar judicial system for the Higher Commander of the U-boat Arm's Education System. This order shows the severity of the rules and illustrates how much time was consumed by pen-pushing officials. The man in question was sentenced for having had sexual intercourse with a girl without a condom. The accusation states that the man endangered the readiness of the whole company by ignoring the standing order to wear rubber protection when making sexual contact with girls. In a way, this seems to be rather hard because the only evidence for the misdemeanour is a confession from the accused. Although this easily raises chuckles today, it does illustrate the serious problem of contagious diseases spreading through such close-knit communities where men could not avoid daily contact. It also illustrates the vulnerability of the massive steel war-machine and emphasises the importance of personal hygiene. Throughout the war, a number of boats were forced into quarantine due to an outbreak of a contagious disease. It has also been recorded that there were a large number of diseases and parasites – such as worms, ticks, fleas and bugs – prevalent throughout parts of the Continent towards the end of the war. One wonders how some of them originated in such incredible quantities while they were almost totally absent from the Allied side. Could this have been an attempt at deliberate biological warfare?

These two glances into the interior of the museum boat, *U995*, in Laboe, Kiel, show how confusing the interior was. Every available space was filled with something of importance and the crew not only had to know the function of all the switches, levers and wheels, but many of them also needed the ability to adjust the instruments in total darkness. Where two similar controls were positioned close together, they could be distinguished in the dark by different textured handles. This comparatively tidy layout in the museum boat would have looked considerably more cluttered during the war when provisions were stored in the spaces around the controls.

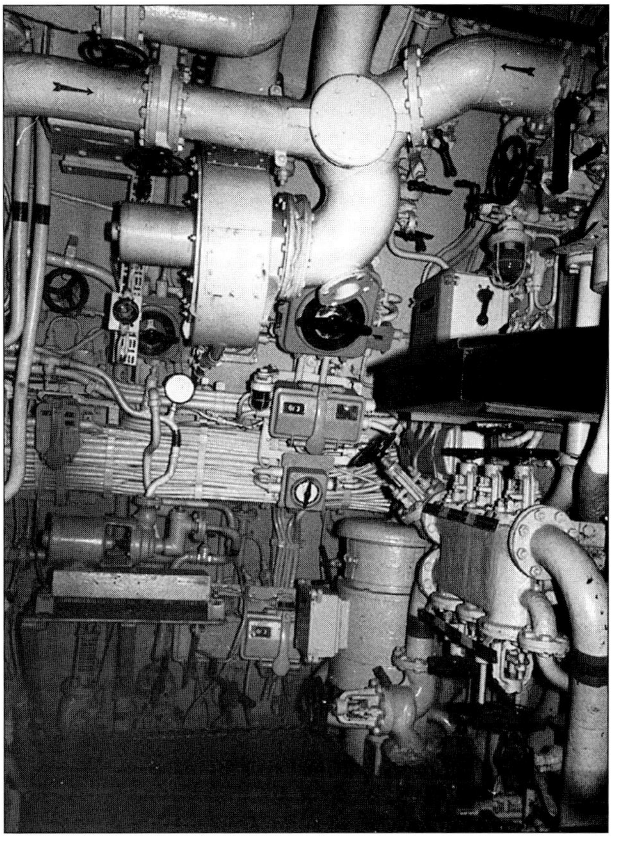

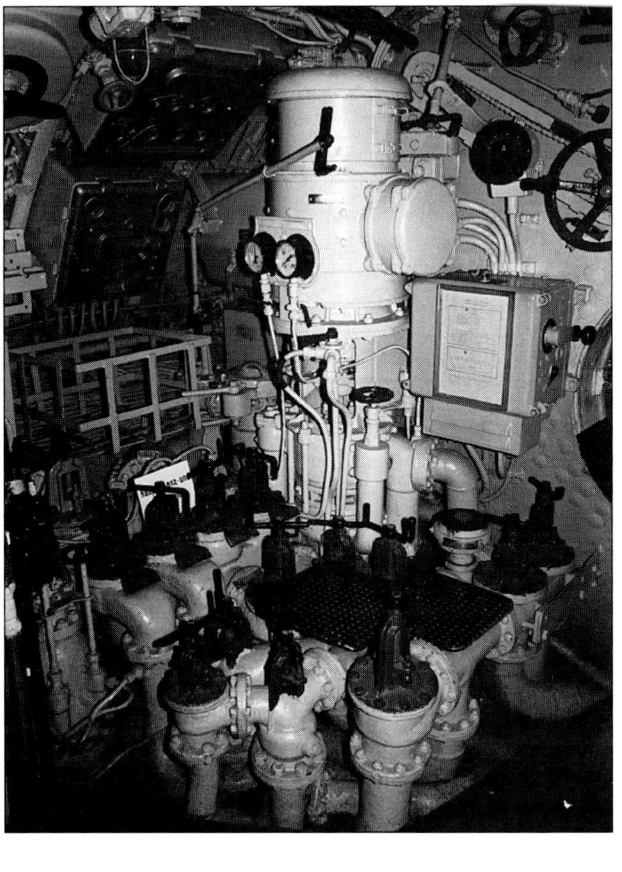

The main ballast pump was situated towards the rear of the central control room (left). The majority of pipes passed this point, making it possible to blow forward or aft tanks even when that part of the boat had been flooded. *U505*, the boat captured by American forces and now on display at the Science and Industry Museum in Chicago, was scuttled by removing the caps from the pipes to allow sea water into the interior. A quick-thinking American found the covers and replaced them to prevent the boat sinking. The large wheel towards the top right of the picture opens and closes the rear diving tank valves.

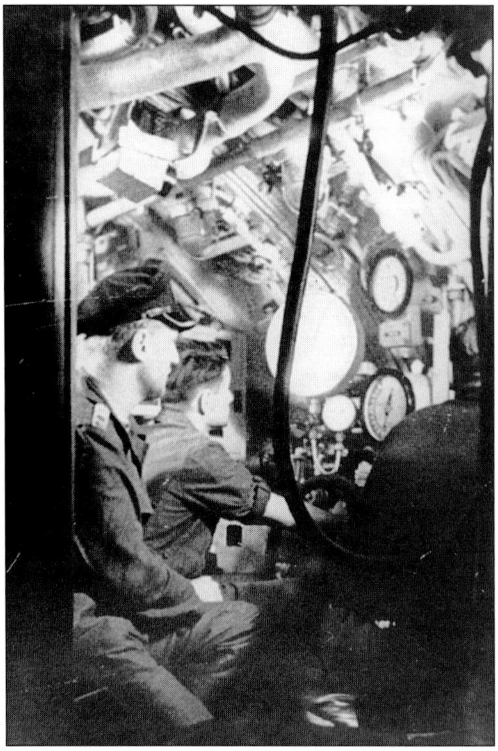

U458. The engineering officer casting a glance over the illuminated dials in the control room while two men control the hydroplanes. Automatic depth-keeping controls were not provided until the end of the war when such equipment was fitted to the electro boats of Type XXI. Other boats required two hydroplane operators and the engineering officer to issue the orders. The majority of men in a U-boat were capable of carrying out a variety of tasks and in an emergency the controls were operated by the man nearest to them. However, boats also had their action specialists and these would take over as soon as practical.

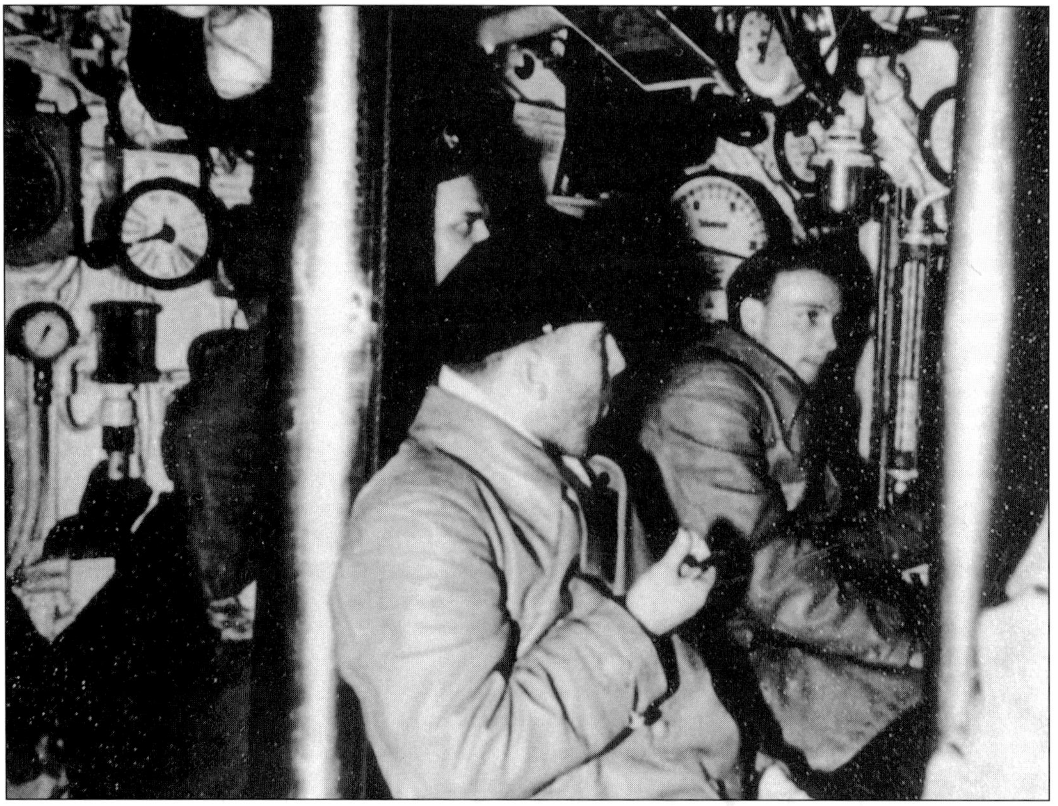

Another view of the main controls inside the central control room of *U203*. This view is slightly easier to understand because the hatch leading to the forward compartments can just be seen on the extreme left. The large depth gauge, between the men's heads, is reading about 22 m, suggesting that this photograph was taken inside a submerged boat.

U995. The controls and dials are in fact quite simple once one knows what to focus on. The big wheel around the electric control box with BBC (for Braun, Boveri & Co.) embossed on the front was used only in emergencies during power failures. The handle has been stolen, but the hydroplanes could originally have been adjusted by turning the wheel. The operator gripped the two black handles on the top of the box and pressed the electrical contact buttons under his wrists. The smaller dial immediately above the big wheel indicates the position of the hydroplane and the huge dial indicates depth up to 25 m. Above it is an engine revolution indicator and just above the floor are several bottles for compressed air. Towards the right of this picture is another dial for depths below 25 m.

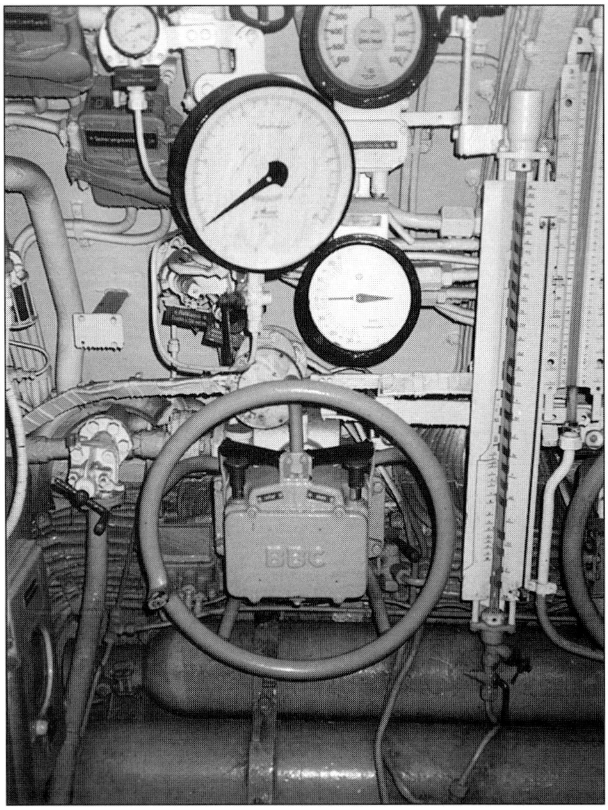

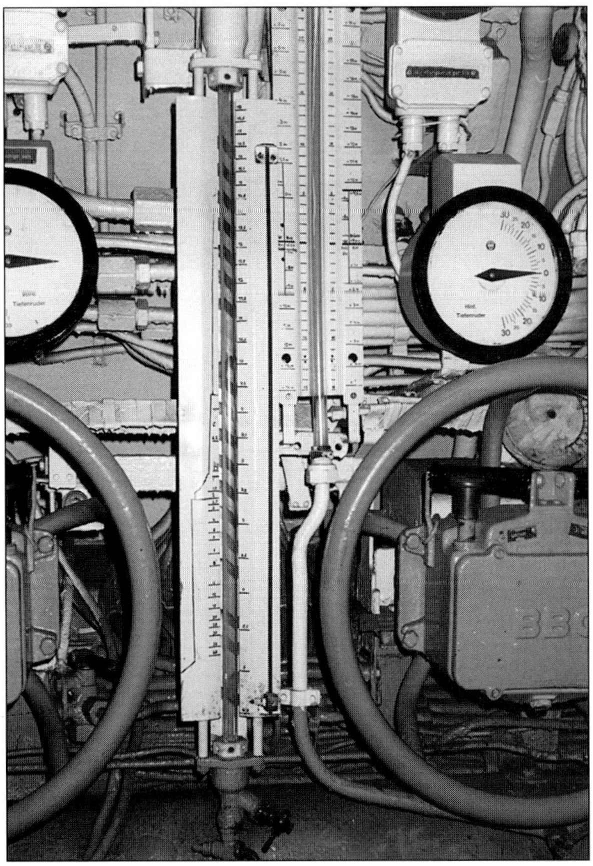

U995. Shallow or periscope depth was maintained by a simple manometer, seen here between the forward and aft hydroplane controls. There is a diagram of the conning tower with extended periscope and the indicator liquid in the glass tube shows the water level on the outside of the boat.

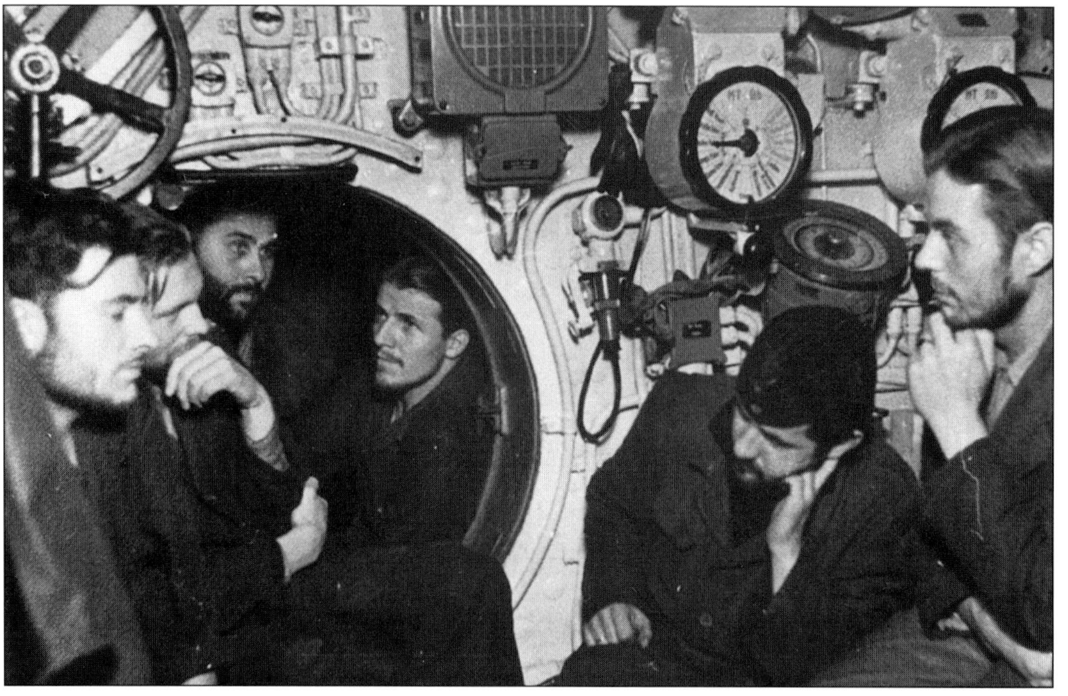

The hatch leading forward from the central control room. There is an engine telegraph to the right of the loudspeaker and below it is a repeater from the gyrocompass. The man on the right is sitting on the helmsman's seat; the latter faced forward when steering the boat. His controls consisted of an electric steering box similar to the hydroplane controls but without the wheel. There was an emergency steering wheel in the rear torpedo compartment for use during power failures. The wheel above the men's heads opened and closed the forward diving tank valves.

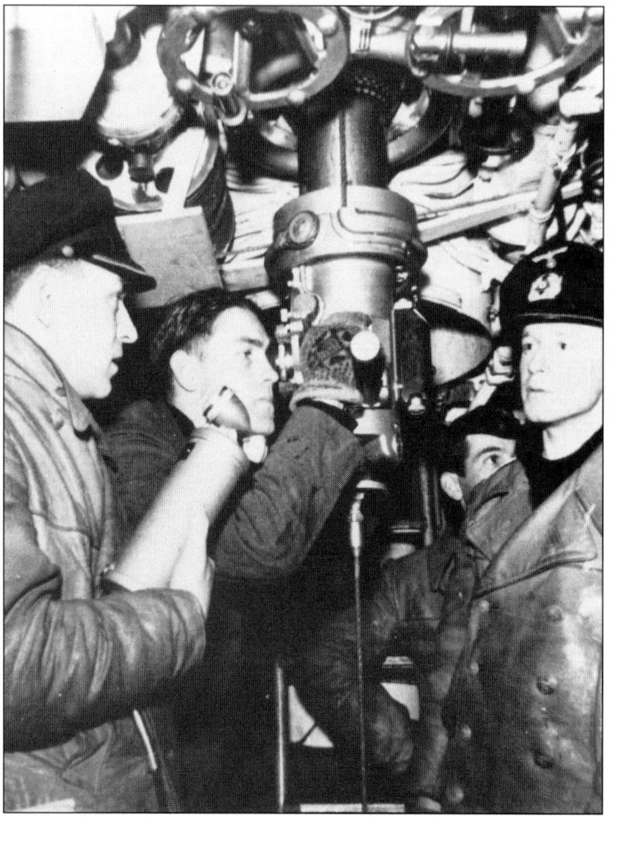

U121 central control room with periscope and a war correspondent holding a microphone to record the action.

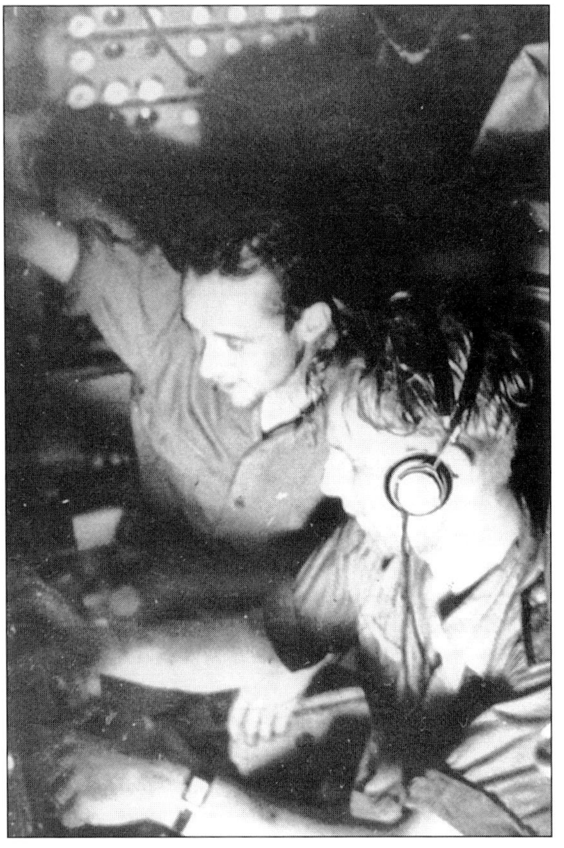

The radio operator of *U458*. Many radio operators considered themselves a cut above the rest of the crew and this image was perpetuated by the fact that they were exempt from the usual watch keeping duties. Their sensitive and highly essential Morse code fingers were usually considered too delicate for rough work.

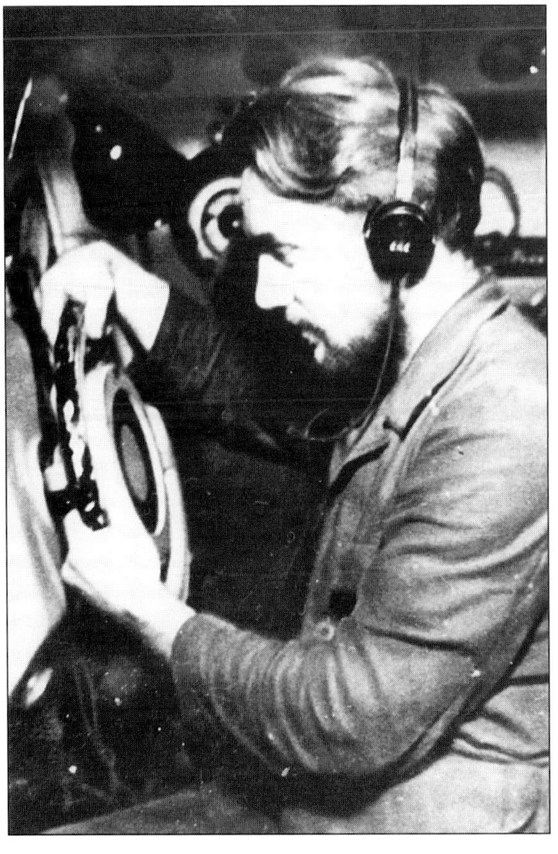

U458. Once the boat was submerged the radio operator would also control the underwater sound detection gear. There were various different versions of the equipment but they all functioned on the principle of having directional microphones inside a rotatable head. Therefore by turning the hand-wheel it was possible to determine the direction from which noises were coming. This gear was incredibly sensitive and could detect convoys too far away for lookouts to spot from the top of the conning tower. However, the gear did not function well on the surface because waves washing against the hull added too much background noise.

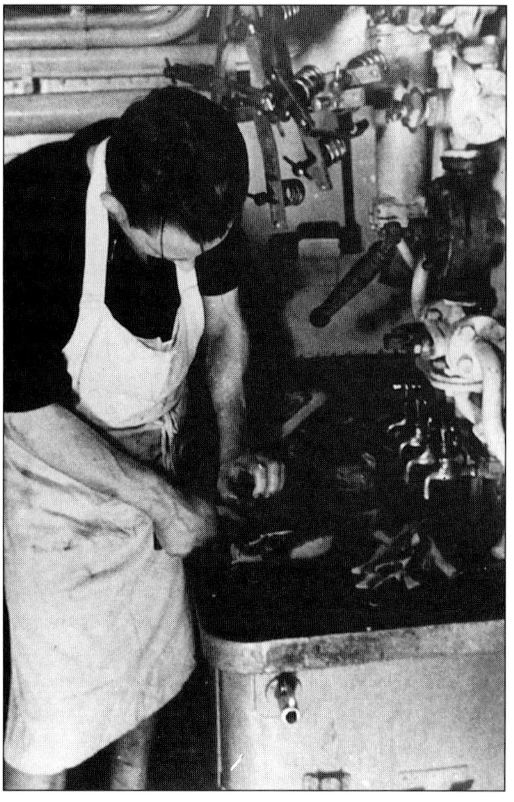

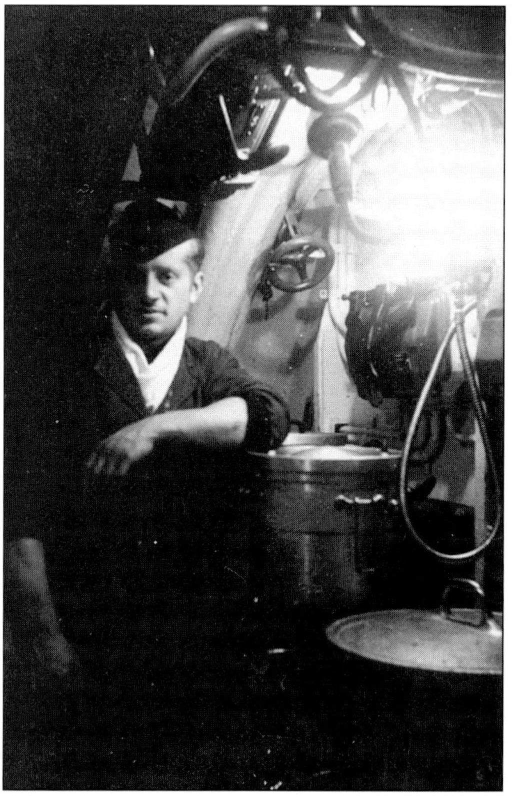

The galley of *U458*. The taps above the sink-cum-work-surface supplied washing water, filtered/distilled drinking water, warm saltwater and unfiltered water for cooking. There was also a hand pump for use during power failures. The cook's main duties were to prepare food for the boat's company, no matter what was going on outside, and for most days in the Atlantic that meant working on a constantly rocking surface. His only other duty was to report leaks from the hatch above his head. Work in the galley involved considerable strength to move heavy, hot pots in a confined space.

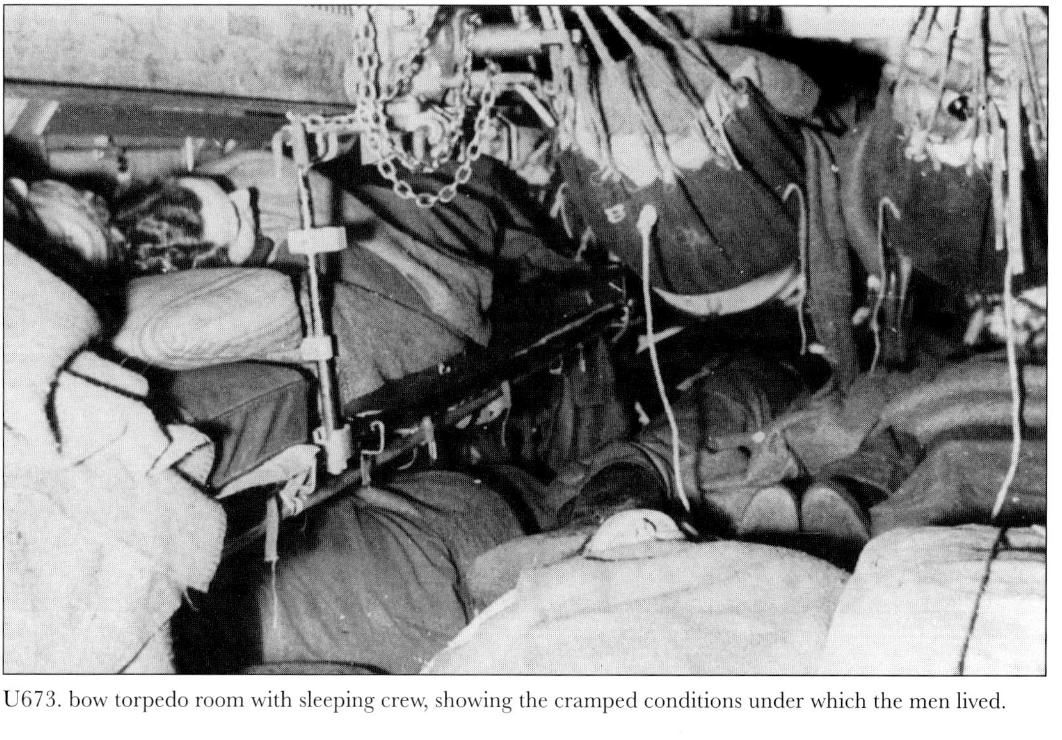

U673. bow torpedo room with sleeping crew, showing the cramped conditions under which the men lived.

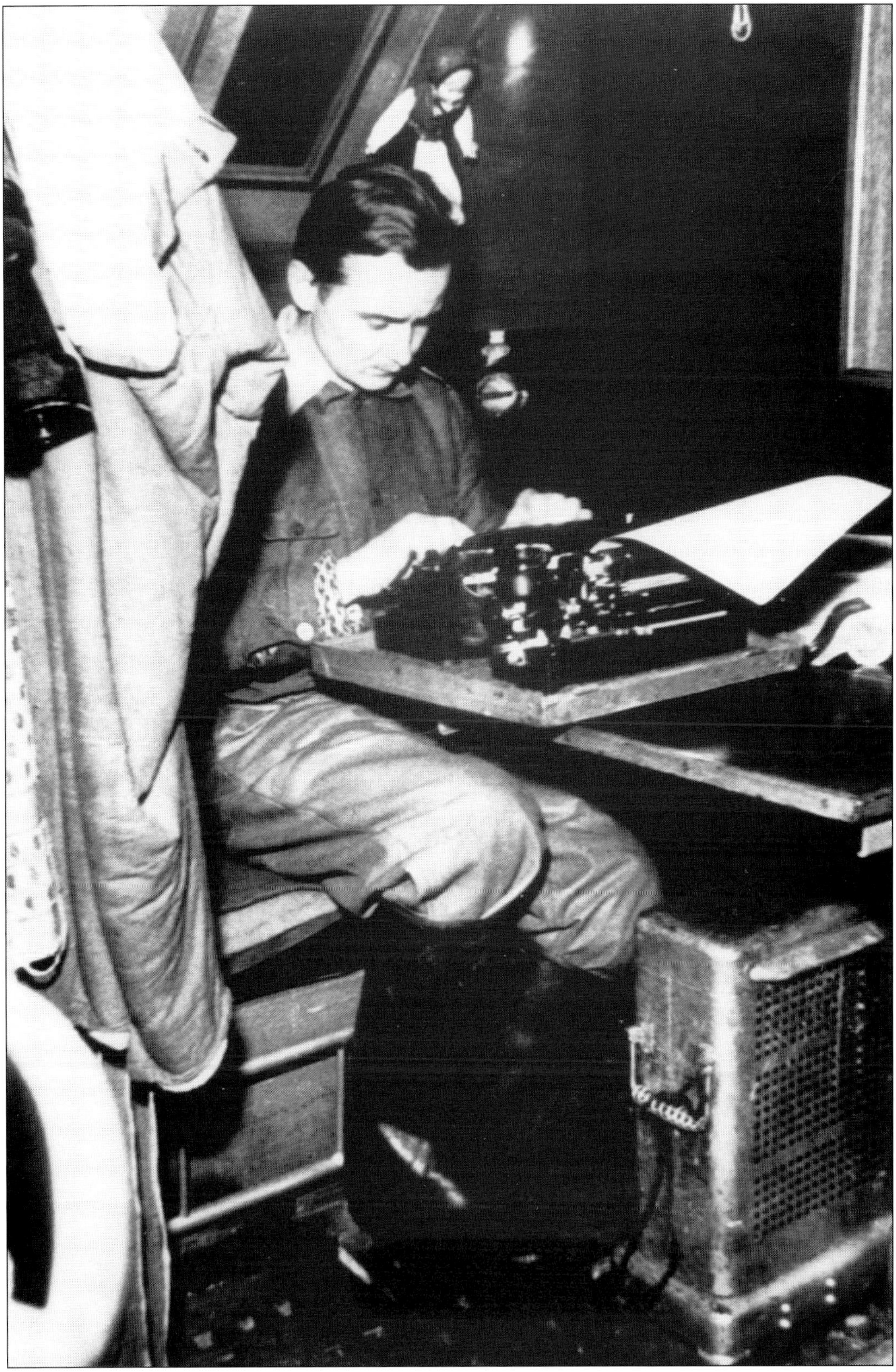

OL Wilhelm Gerlach, commander of *U490*; the commander naturally had the largest personal space of any of the men aboard a U-boat. The paper war was fought just as intensely as the action against the enemy and there were forms and reports for almost everything. Gerlach is sitting on his bunk and has a portable electric heater by his feet.

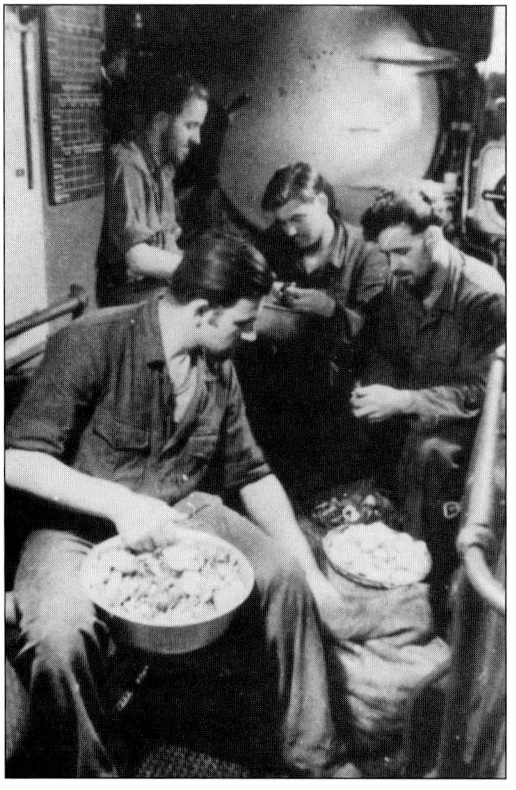

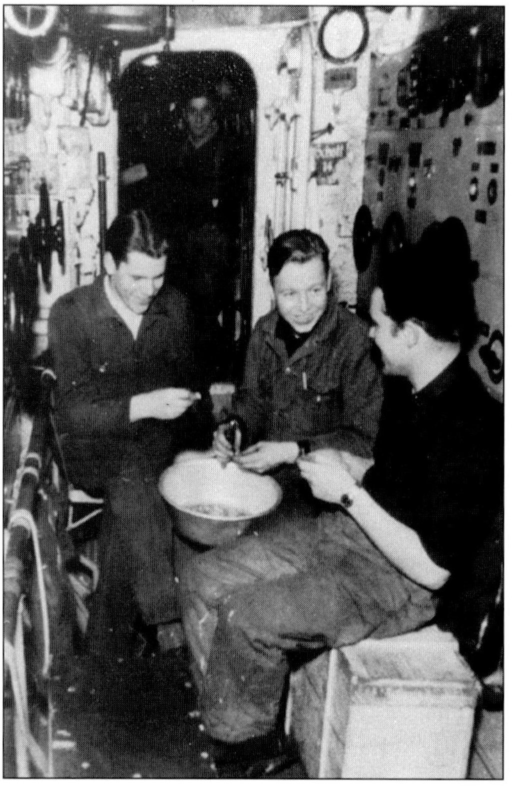

Left: *U178*. A team of 'volunteers' usually helped with the preparation of meals by peeling potatoes, cleaning vegetables and opening tins. Right: *U203*. Men peeling potatoes in the control room. The control panels for adjusting the electric motors can also be seen.

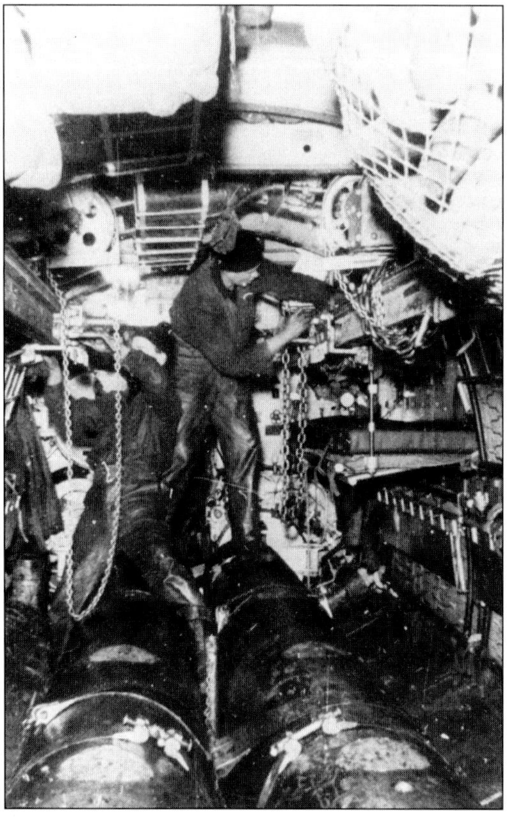

Bow torpedo compartment of *U673*. There was little room for crew members to manoeuvre.

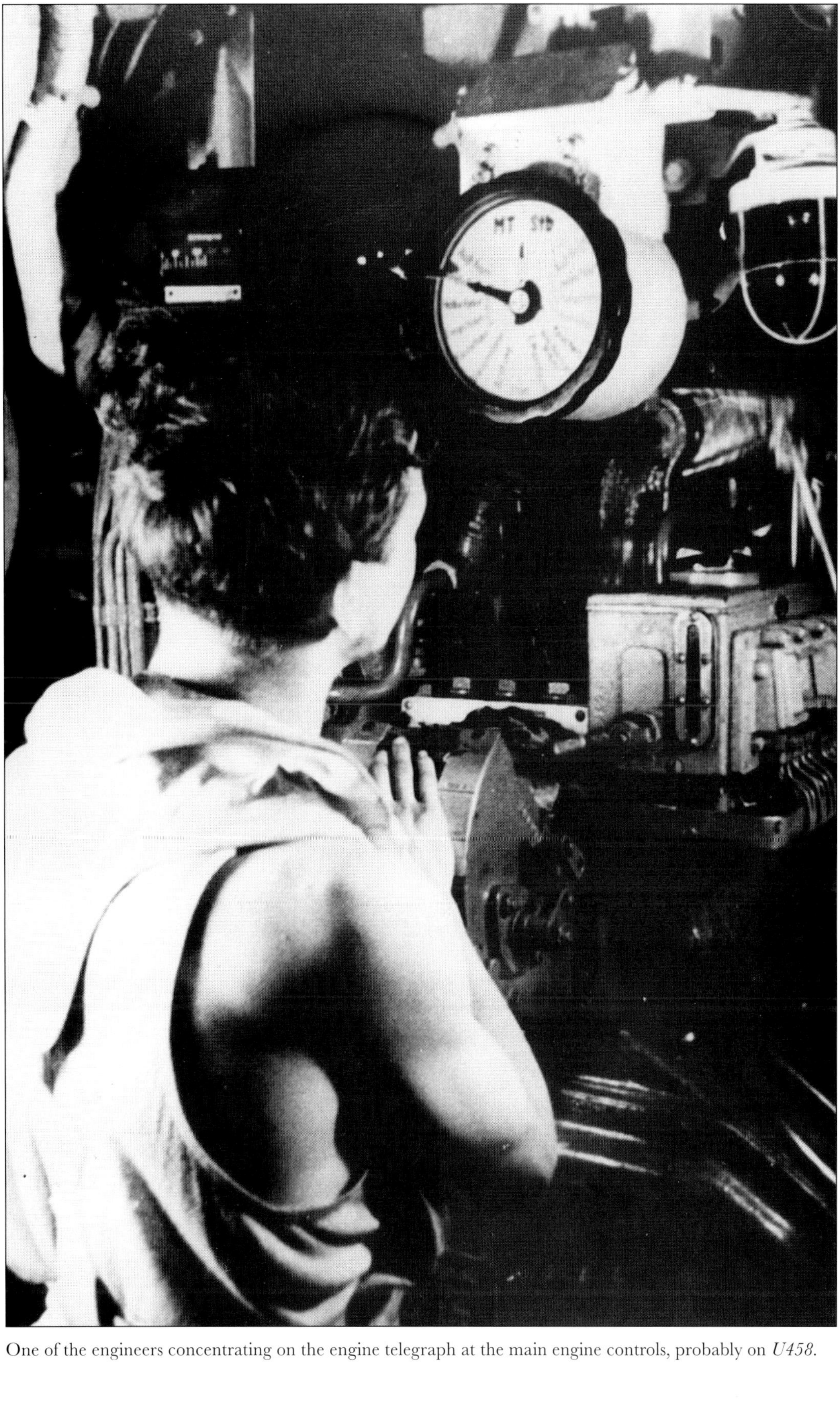

One of the engineers concentrating on the engine telegraph at the main engine controls, probably on *U458*.

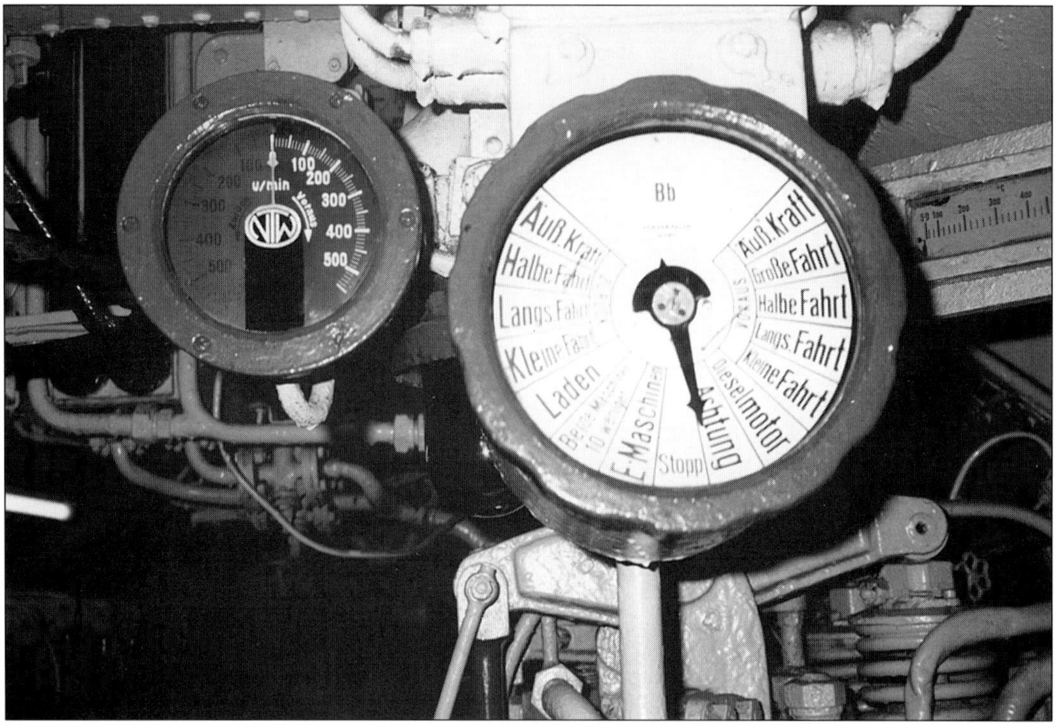

This is a close-up of what the engineer on the previous page was looking at. This is the engine telegraph for the port side. Bb stood for Backbord (port) and Sb stood for Steuerbord (starboard).

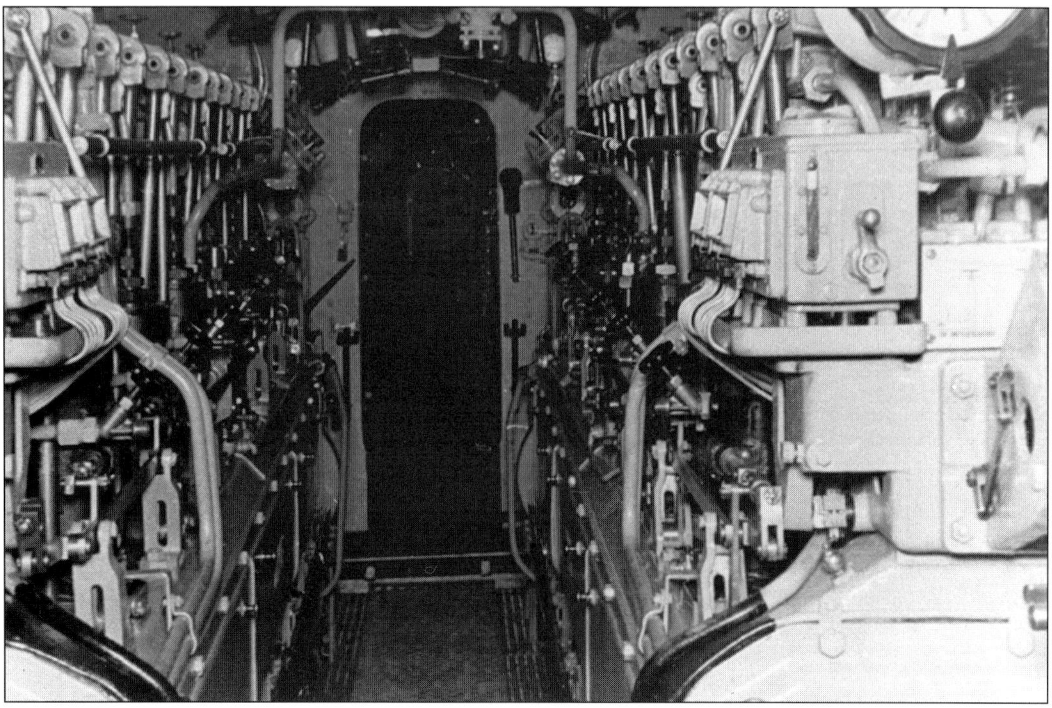

A diesel compartment looking aft. The doors at both ends were a means of shutting off the noise, although the engineers working in this confined space had to put up with the incredible din. While the boat was running, the rods moved up and down. For the diesel compartment crew, maintaining balance in rough weather was not easy and considerable skill was required to prevent injuries.

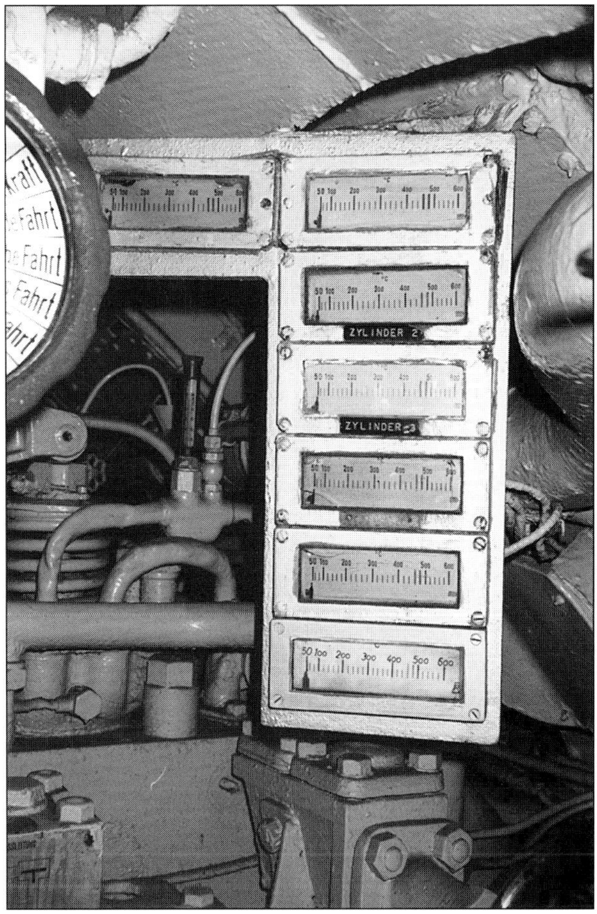

The engine temperature indicators beside the diesel controls.

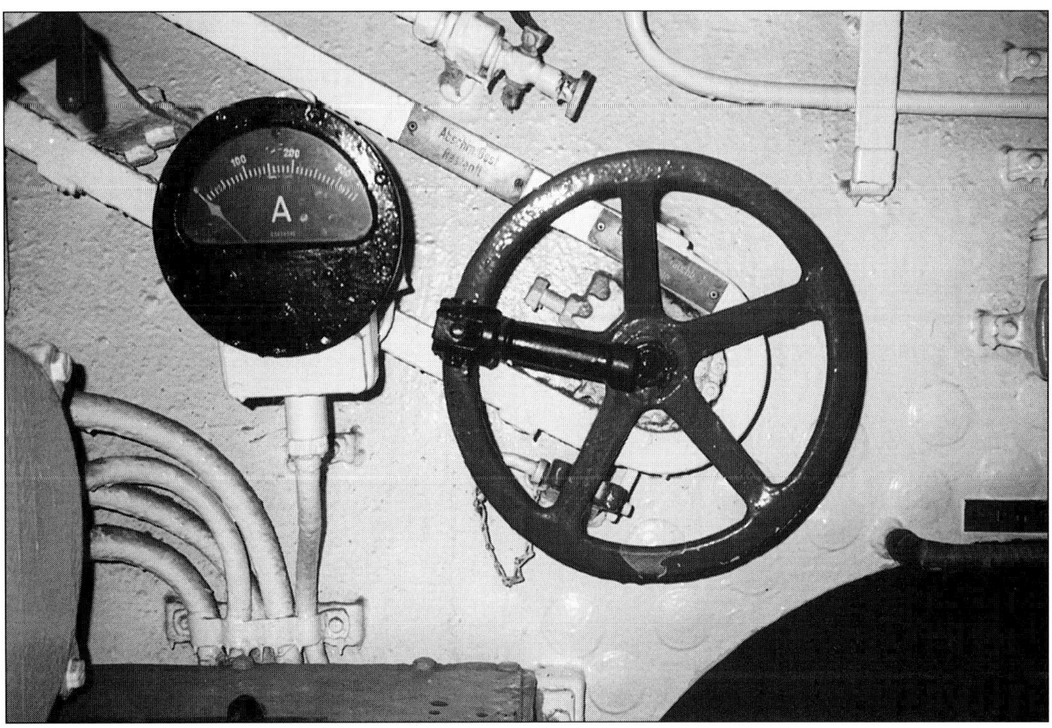

A hand-wheel for opening and closing vents.

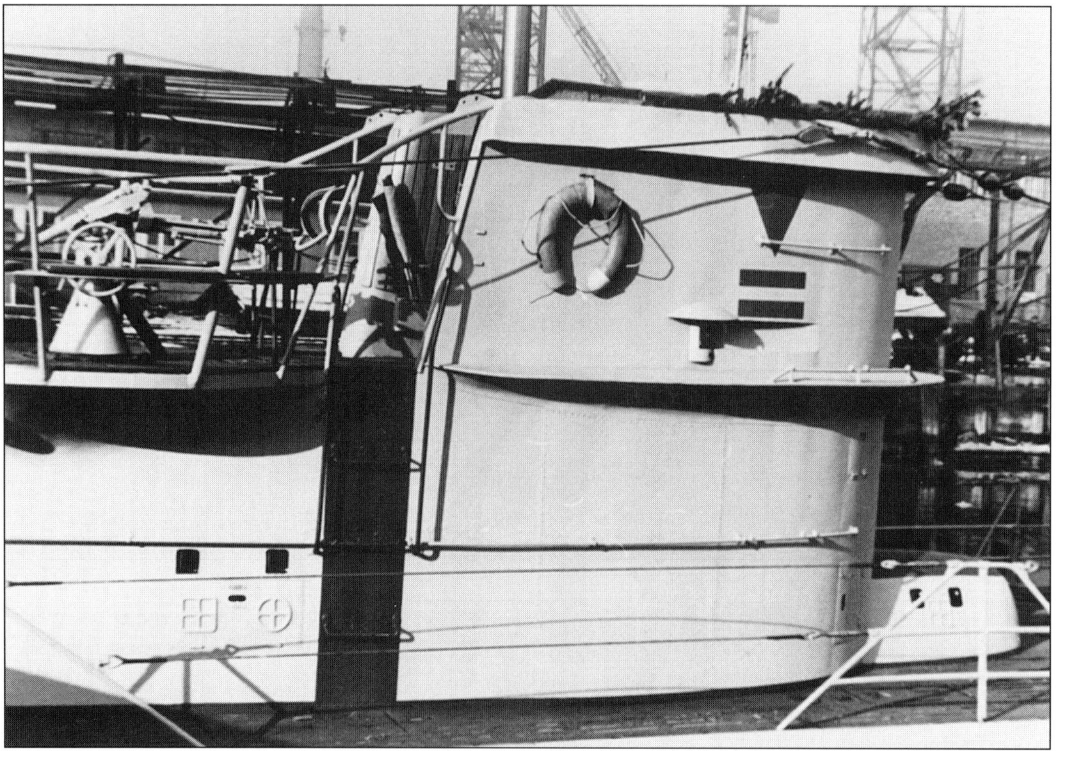

This symbol was painted on *U441*'s conning tower as a means of identifying the boat during training (*see* p. 21).

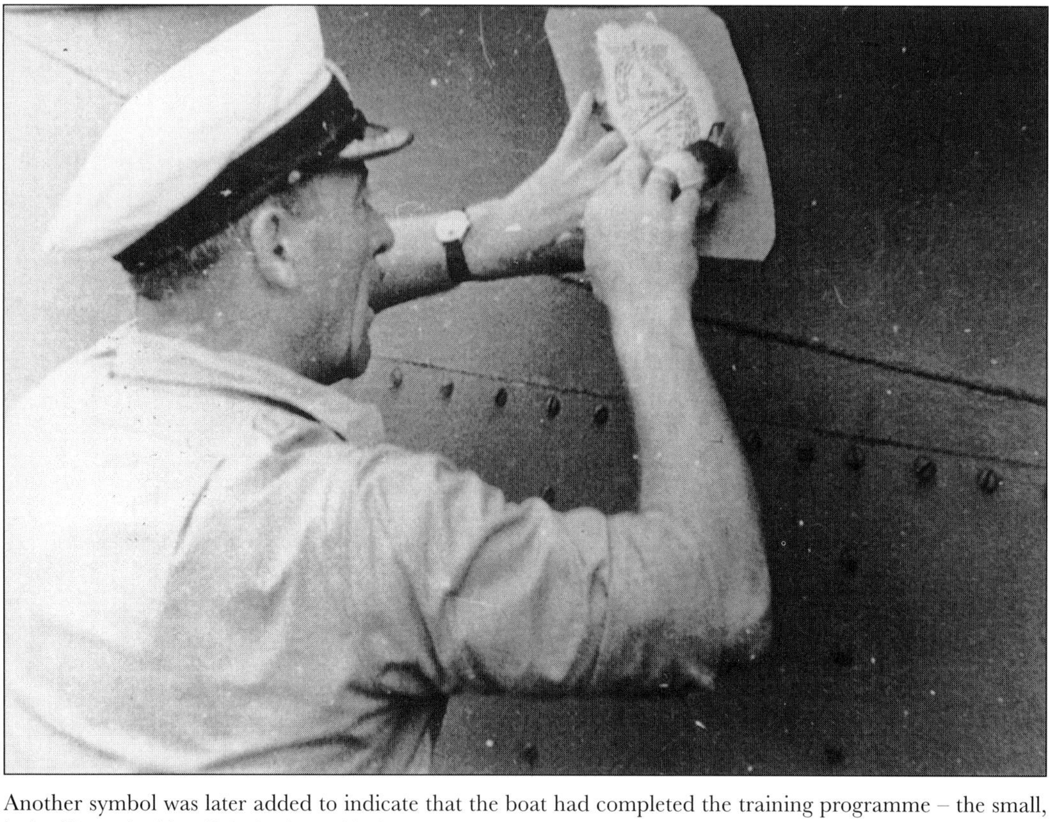

Another symbol was later added to indicate that the boat had completed the training programme – the small, insignificant-looking little badge said simply 'Frontreif' meaning 'Ready for the Front'. This is *U460* under KL Friedrich Schäfer.

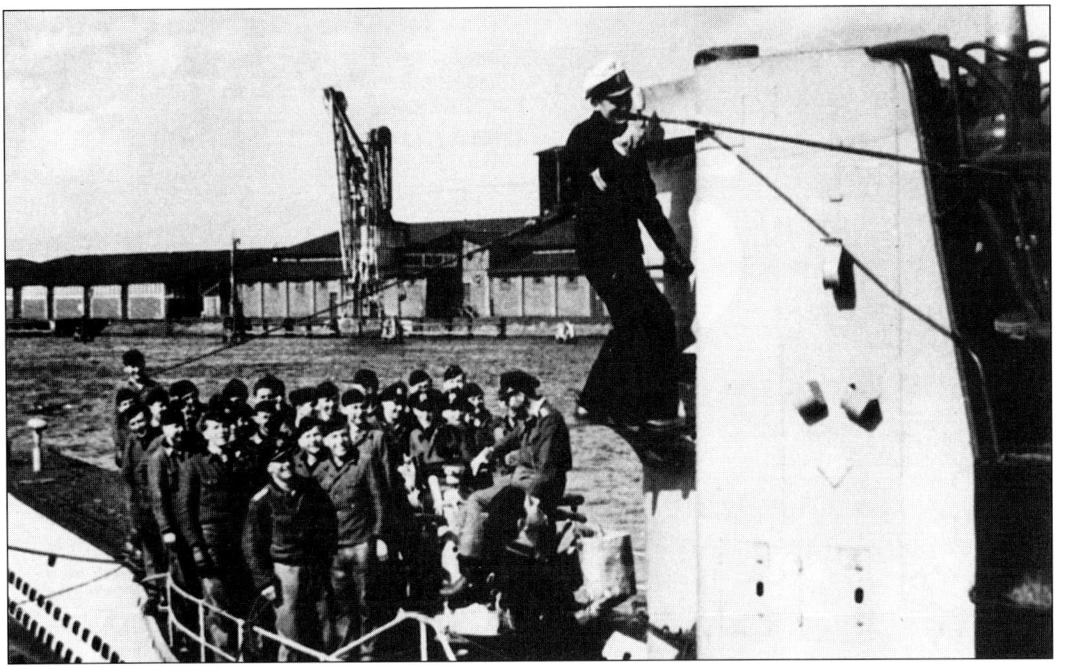

Although the acquisition of the Frontreif badge was a major landmark in the process of getting the boat out of the training grounds, many men disliked the presence of the tactical identification mark. In this case OL Götz Baur of *U660* has climbed up on the tower to remove the offending sign. It would hardly do to run into Kiel with the evidence that this was a fresh boat, which had never seen action. Baur, incidentally, was born in Shanghai in China, survived the sinking of his boat and became a prisoner of war.

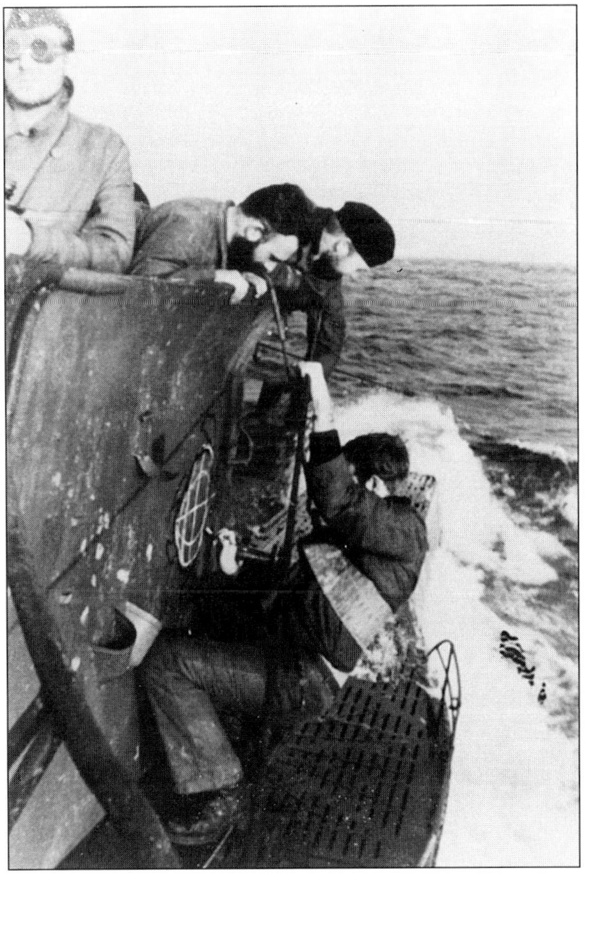

Some boats converted the tactical mark or the Frontreif badge into part of their emblem, others added their flotilla badges and many crews designed their own badges for display on the conning tower and for wearing on their hats. Some of the artwork involved considerable skill and discomfort.

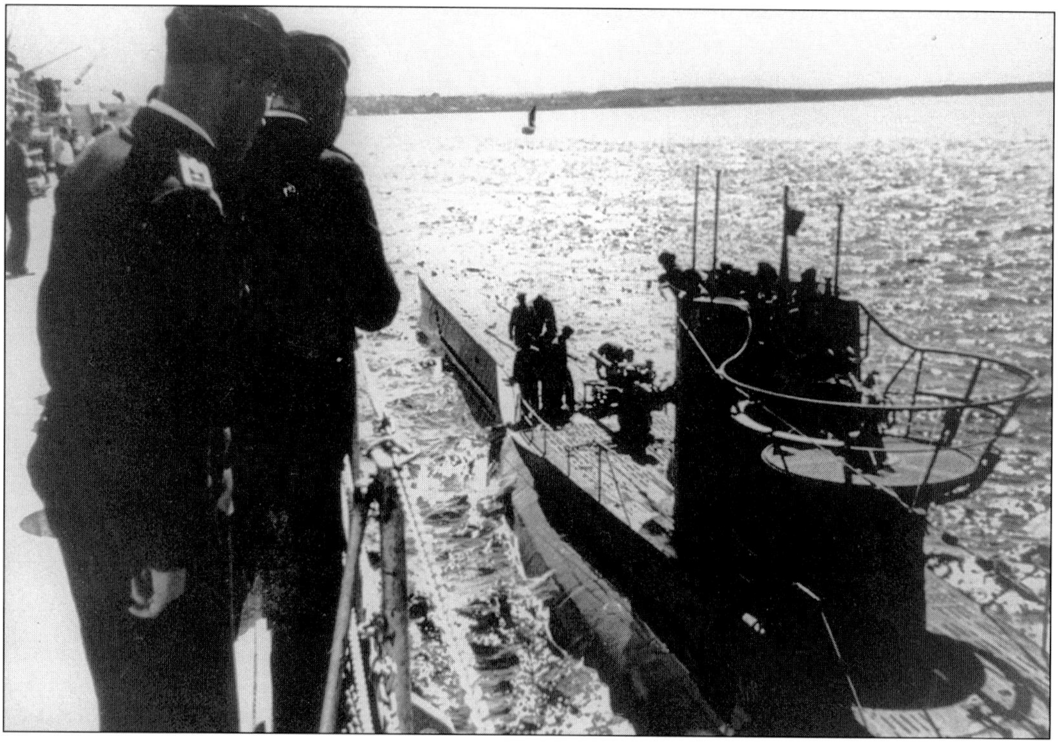

But the discomfort of adding an insignia to a conning tower was nothing compared to what followed. Being Frontreif meant the boat repeated the training performance – but this time it was for real.

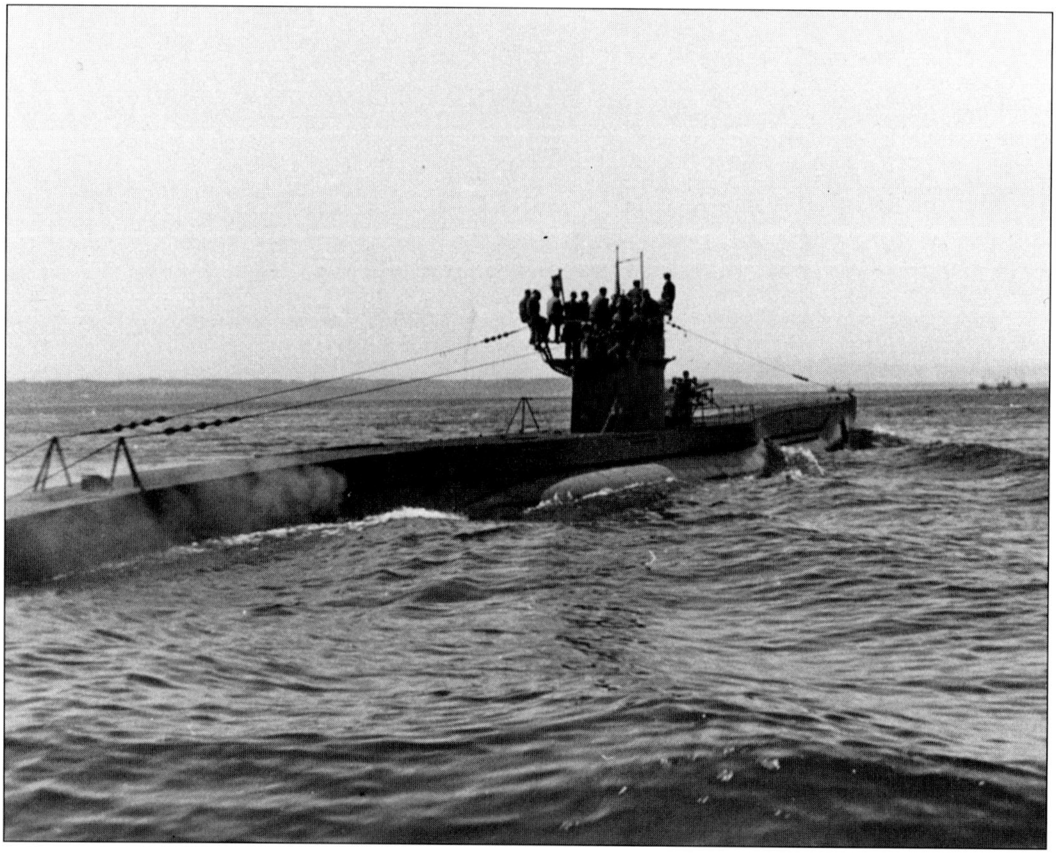

When all the training was completed the boat left for the cruel sea.

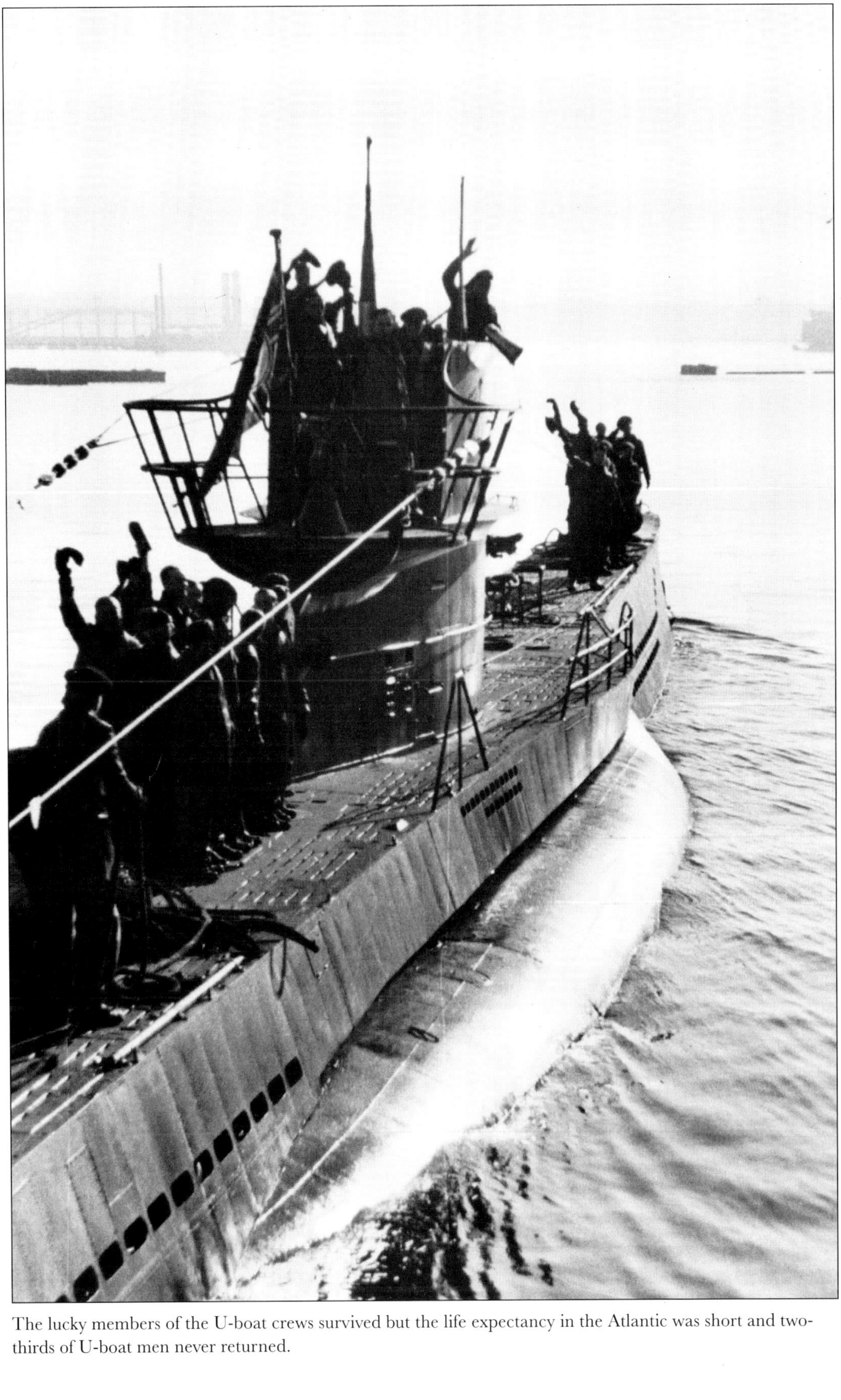

The lucky members of the U-boat crews survived but the life expectancy in the Atlantic was short and two-thirds of U-boat men never returned.

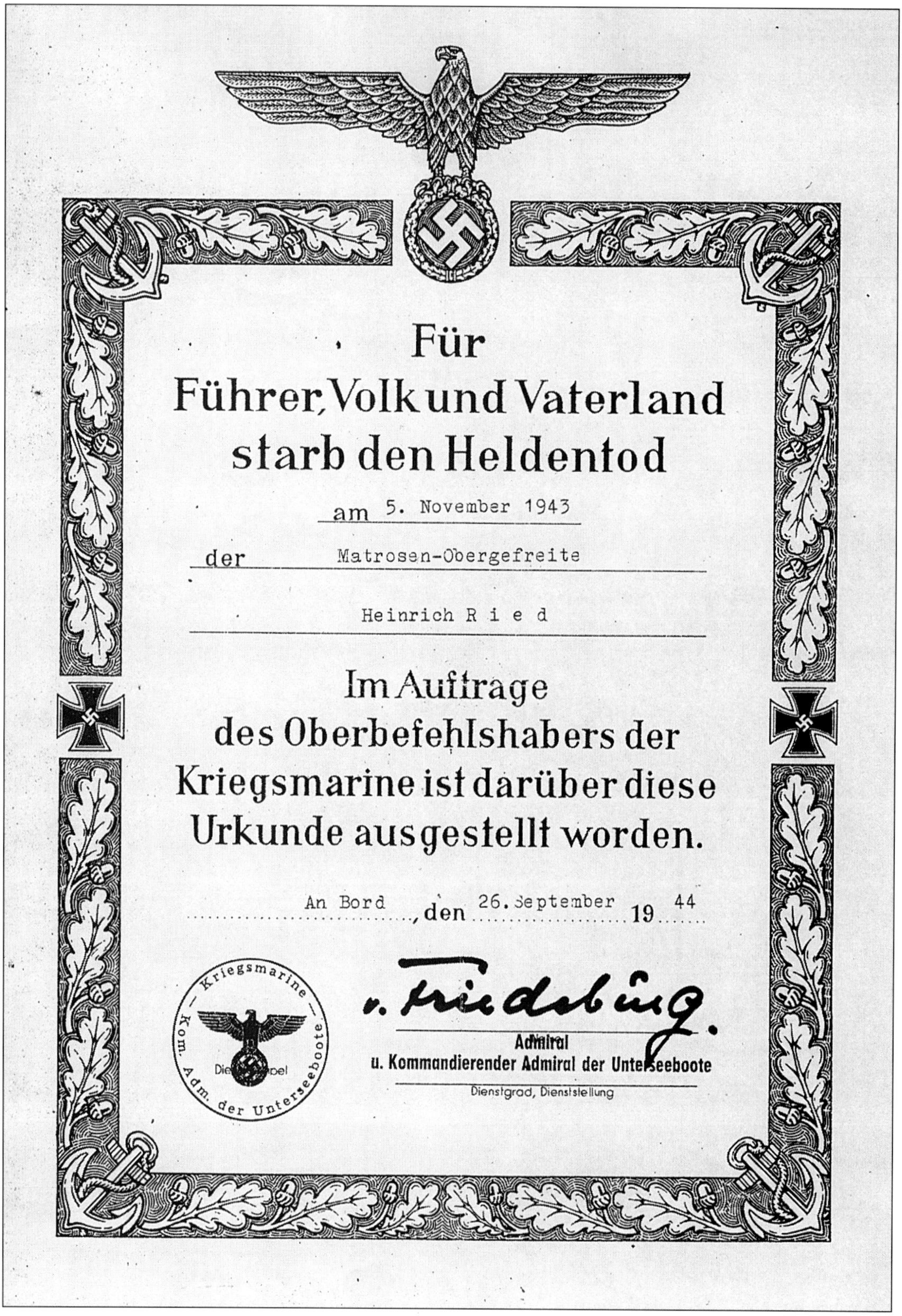

Für
Führer, Volk und Vaterland
starb den Heldentod

am 5. November 1943

der Matrosen-Obergefreite

Heinrich R i e d

Im Auftrage
des Oberbefehlshabers der
Kriegsmarine ist darüber diese
Urkunde ausgestellt worden.

An Bord, den 26. September 1944

Kriegsmarine — Kom. Adm. der Unterseeboote

v. Friedeburg

Admiral
u. Kommandierender Admiral der Unterseeboote

Dienstgrad, Dienststellung

'For Führer, People and Fatherland . . . has died a hero's death. The Supreme Commander-in-Chief of the Navy has ordered this certificate to be drawn up.'

Signed
Admiral Hans-Georg von Friedeburg

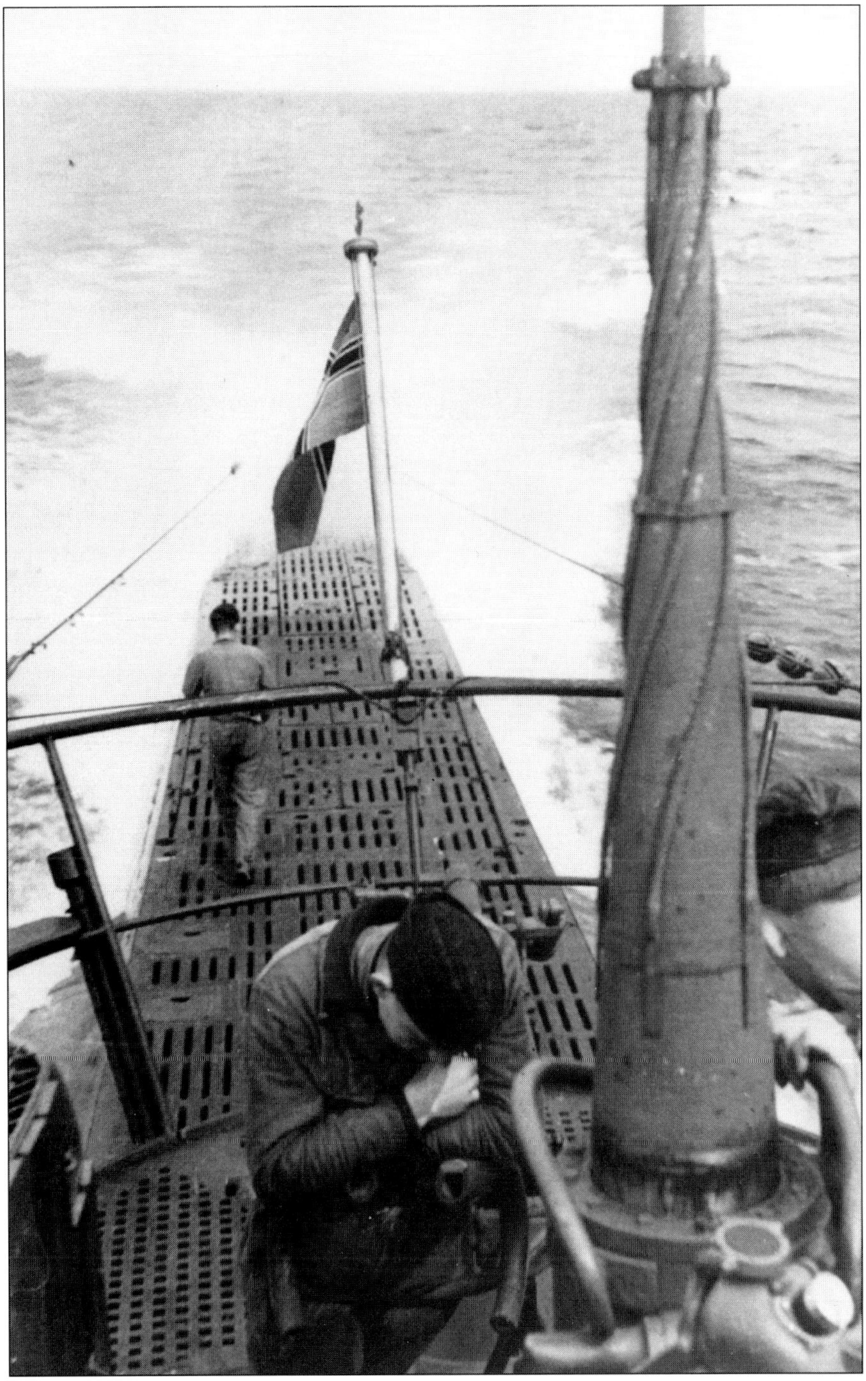

The men who survived the war very often left many years of service with a simple typed sheet of poor quality paper saying that they had been discharged from the armed forces. However, before this was issued, they filled out a lengthy questionnaire as part of the de-Nazification process. Only a few lucky men came out unscathed. Many had minor wounds and almost all had deep emotional scars. Many of those who received major physical wounds during the reign of the Third Reich were awarded special medals in a variety of grades. Men who died in action were commemorated with a rather impressive certificate (opposite), but these ornate pieces of paper were only small condolences. It is surprising how many flotilla chiefs found time to write heart-rending letters to the next of kin when men went missing or were known to have been killed.

Perhaps the saddest point of all the misery and suffering created by the Second World War is that the human race will never learn from its mistakes and that the making weapons of mass destruction is still a major industry in all of the so-called civilised nations. Will mankind ever learn?

INDEX

In this index the Roman numerals after the U-boat numbers indicate the type of submarine.